THE
INVASION
OF
JAPAN

VFW - Political Action Committee
Joseph H. Inglese
20 Tamarack Dr.
Hillsborough, CA 94010-6540

The Invasion of Japan
Alternative to the Bomb

John Ray Skates

University of South Carolina Press

© 1994 University of South Carolina

Published in Columbia, South Carolina, by the
University of South Carolina Press

Published 1994
First Paperback Edition 2000

Manufactured in the United States of America

04 03 02 01 00   5 4 3 2 1

The Library of Congress has cataloged the cloth edition as follows:

Skates, John Ray.
    The invasion of Japan : alternative to the bomb / by John Ray Skates.
        p.   cm.
    Includes bibliographical references and index.
    ISBN 0-87249-972-3 (alk. paper)
    1. World War, 1939–1945—Campaigns—Japan.   I. Title.
    D767.2.S56   1994
    940.54'25—dc20   93-34193

ISBN 1-57003-354-4 (pbk.)

Contents

Illustrations

Preface

I first became interested in the invasion of Japan from reading histories of the Pacific war. Without exception, the stories of the end of the war emphasized the bloody struggle for Okinawa and abruptly skipped over to the atomic bombings, the surrender, and the occupation. My original intent was to fill in the gap by writing a short monograph describing the invasion plans. Obviously, as this book testifies, the project grew. A narrative of the invasion plans proved woefully incomplete, for I soon found that some important and interesting historical questions either had never been addressed or had never been studied in the context of the plans to invade Japan. What was to be the role of the Soviets in the war against Japan? Why did the Joint Chiefs of Staff choose a strategy of invasion? What would have been the costs in casualties? Would Japanese homeland defenses have proved as formidable as those on Iwo Jima and Okinawa? What was the connection, if any, between the plans to invade and the decision to use the bomb? To what extent did the invasion plans depend on redeployment of forces from Europe? Finally, what were the invasion plans, and had they been carried out, what would have been the likely results?

Academic historians like their monographs to build toward a single thesis. But history seldom develops on one narrative line with a single clear message, and certainly the story of the last months of World War II in the Pacific cannot be told from a single viewpoint nor explained with a single neat thesis. The story of the invasion of Japan and the end of the Pacific war is filled with uncertainty, cross currents, misperceptions, and irrationality. The Japanese-American war in 1945 threatened to become a struggle without restraints. The German philosopher of war Carl von Clausewitz held that to win wars a state had not only to get at the enemy's means of making war but also to attack the "strength of his will." By any measure, the Allies had accomplished the former by 1945. The will of the Japanese leadership, however, seemed as strong as ever. In Clausewitzean terms, the will of the Japanese could only be broken by escalating the violence, which in turn further stirred the passions that drove the war into extremes of violence. In other words, the last months of the Pacific war were filled with passion, hatred, and frustration, moving almost beyond rational limits—hardly a subject for a tightly focused thesis.

Whatever faults this book may have, whether of accuracy, interpretation, or style, are of course mine alone. Whatever value it has, I must share with many others whose encouragement and counsel spurred me on when it would have been easier to quit. First among them is my wife, Craig, who not only pushed me when I flagged, but diagnosed the organizational ills of early versions of the manuscript and provided the cure which is embodied in the present organization. Neither would this book have been possible without the support and encouragement of Brigadier General (now Major General) William A. Stofft and the staff of the Center of Military History in the Department of the Army. In 1986 the center awarded me a two-year research professorship to gather materials and begin writing this study. The center supported my visits to archives in this country and sponsored a trip to Japan for me to visit the invasion beaches. In Japan I was the guest of the National Institute for Defense Studies, the senior service school for officers of the Japanese Self Defense Forces. While there I discussed World War II Japanese plans for homeland defense with the faculty, and, under the guidance of Professor Takahashi Hisashi, I visited the proposed invasion areas in southern Kyushu and in the Kanto Plain. This personal inspection of the invasion beaches and of existing Japanese cave defenses gave me a sense of the terrain and of Japanese defenses that I could have gained in no other way.

I thank the staff of the Air War College at Maxwell Air Force Base, Alabama, for allowing me time to finish the manuscript during my two-year visiting professorship there. I thank also many other scholars who have encouraged me along the way—especially Malcolm "Kip" Muir, Carl Boyd, and others who are regular attendees at the military history sessions of the Northern Great Plains History Conference. I am most indebted to Edward Drea of the Center of Military History and to Edward Miller of Stamford, Connecticut. Both of these scholars have written excellent books on the Pacific war, and their careful readings of the manuscript for this book saved me many embarrassments. Finally, I thank Dr. Glover Moore, Professor Emeritus of Mississippi State University, who many years ago undertook the task of training an unpromising former lieutenant to be a historian.

Abbreviations
and
Code Names

Abbreviations

ABDA	Australian-British-Dutch-American Command, 1942
AFPAC	U.S. Army Forces, Pacific (MacArthur's command after 3 April 1945)
CBI	China-Burma-India Theater
CCS	Combined British-American Chiefs of Staff
CINCPACFLT	Commander-in-Chief, Pacific Fleet (Nimitz)
CINCPOA	Commander-in-Chief, Pacific Ocean Areas (Nimitz)
FEAF	Far East Air Forces, MacArthur's SWPA-AFPAC air forces
JCS	U.S. Joint Chiefs of Staff
JPS	Joint Staff Planners
JWPC	Joint War Plans Committee
POA	Pacific Ocean Areas (Nimitz's area command)
SWPA	Southwest Pacific Area (MacArthur's area command)
VAC	V Amphibious Corps

Code Names

ARCADIA	U.S.-British Conference, Washington, DC, December 1941–January 1942
BLACKLIST	MacArthur's plan for the occupation of Japan
CAMPUS	Nimitz's plan for the occupation of Japan
CORONET	Plan for the invasion of the Tokyo (Kanto) Plain, 1 March 1946
DOWNFALL	Plan for the invasion of Japan that included Operations OLYMPIC and CORONET
ICEBERG	Invasion of Okinawa and the Ryukyu Islands
Ketsu-Go	Japanese plans for defense of the home islands
LONGTOM	Navy plans for an amphibious landing on the China coast at Ningpo south of Shanghai

MAGIC	U.S. ability to decipher Japanese diplomatic codes
OCTAGON	U.S.-British conference, Quebec, September 1944
OLYMPIC	Plan for the invasion of southern Kyushu, 1 November 1945
PASTEL	Deception plans for the invasion of Japan
QUADRANT	U.S.-British conference, Quebec, August 1943
SEXTANT	U.S.-British-Chinese conference, Cairo, November–December 1943
SPHINX	U.S. Army effort in 1945 to find better weapons and techniques to deal with Japanese cave defenses
TRIDENT	U.S.-British conference, Washington, May 1943
ULTRA	U.S.-British ability to decipher German and Japanese army, navy, and air force codes

THE
INVASION
OF
JAPAN

Introduction:
The Concept of DOWNFALL

After World War II had ended Admiral Ernest J. King, commander in chief of the U.S. Fleet, called amphibious operations "the most difficult of all operations in modern war."[1] Amphibious forces necessarily came from different services with different skills, different training, and different techniques of communications and supply. Air forces, naval gunfire support and carrier forces, and assault forces had to be brought together from widely separated bases to an objective they had never seen, and without rehearsal they had to blend smoothly into a single unit. They had to coordinate gunfire and air attacks, deliver assault forces onto beaches in the face of hostile fire from prepared defenses, and supply the landing forces with countless items in huge quantities over open beaches. A commander of an amphibious operation, wrote naval historian Samuel E. Morison, was like "a football coach required to form a team from different parts of the country, brief them with a manual of plays, and without even lining them up send them against a champion opponent."[2]

The countless Pacific landings from Guadalcanal in 1942 to Okinawa in 1945 raised amphibious doctrine and practice to a stylized art. The approach to the objective area, deployment, bombardment, and the climactic order to "land the landing force" became almost routine. The power and seeming ease, however, had been shaped and honed from tenuous beginnings in 1942 and 1943 at places like Guadalcanal and Tarawa. Problems in command, communications, logistics, gunfire support, and air support had plagued these early operations.

Squabbles at Guadalcanal between the amphibious force commander, Rear Admiral Richmond Kelly Turner, and the senior ground commander, Major General Alexander A. Vandegrift, led to the pattern of command used for amphibious operations throughout the remainder of the war in the Pacific. Command of the entire operation was vested in the amphibious force commander—a naval officer. As the landings occurred, he passed command successively up the chain of ground commanders as they were established ashore.

Naval gunfire was essential to support the landing forces until artillery could go ashore. At Tarawa in 1943, the naval preparatory fire was too light and too brief. In later operations naval gunfire support was immensely longer and heavier, sacrificing surprise for volume of fire. The

1

appearance of new large attack carriers in the fleet in 1943 and 1944 furnished mobile air bases for air support. Land-based planes were typically brought in soon after establishment of the beachhead to ensure air superiority and to free the carriers for other duties. General MacArthur, who seldom had carrier support as he bounded across the northern coast of New Guinea, usually measured his amphibious leaps by the range of his land-based fighter bombers.

New landing craft appeared in 1944. A landing ship tank (LST) was large enough to make the long voyage from staging area to objective, and it could land tanks and vehicles directly onto the beach. Similarly, a single landing craft infantry (LCI) could transport infantrymen from staging area directly to the beach. Amphibious tractors solved the problem of maneuvering across offshore reefs—a common concern in assaulting central Pacific atolls.

Ship-to-shore communications concerning naval gunfire support, air support, and logistics were strengthened by the creation of composite units made up of personnel who could deal directly with either gunfire control, air control, or shore parties. Teams from these units supported the landing force elements to speed up reaction time.

Logistical problems and beach congestion continued to plague amphibious operations until the end of the war. Yet problems encountered at Guadalcanal in 1942 were somewhat alleviated in later operations by loading equipment aboard ship in the staging area in precisely the order that it would be needed ashore, according to the tactical plan. Shore parties were created to eliminate beach congestion and confusion as supplies began to come in over the beaches. By 1945, the techniques and organization for amphibious operations were well-developed and proven in combat. With relatively short lead time, mammoth power could be brought to bear on a specific target.

In the fall of 1944 and the spring of 1945 the U.S. Joint Chiefs of Staff developed the basic concept and outline plans for an invasion of Japan. The plan called for the greatest amphibious operation of the war. The concept of operations for Japan's final defeat was presented to President Franklin D. Roosevelt and Prime Minister Winston Churchill at the Yalta Conference on 9 February 1945. The president and the prime minister were informed that the seizure in April of Okinawa, a Japanese island only three hundred miles from Kyushu, would be followed by further operations to "intensify the blockade and air bombardment of Japan." Finally, in the winter of 1945–46 U.S. forces would assault Kyushu "for the purpose of further reducing Japanese capabilities by containing and destroying major enemy forces and further intensifying the blockade and air bombardment" before "the decisive invasion of the industrial heart of Japan through the Tokyo Plain."[3]

Responsibility for detailed plans within the strategic framework would fall to General Douglas MacArthur's and Admiral Chester Nimitz's staffs. The overall plan, code named DOWNFALL, called for the invasion of Japan to be conducted in two distinct phases. Operation OLYMPIC, 1 November 1945, would secure the southern one-third of Kyushu, the southernmost of Japan's four main islands, and it would furnish air and naval bases to intensify the bombardment and blockade of the home islands. If OLYMPIC failed to produce unconditional surrender, then Operation CORONET, 1 March 1946, would furnish the knockout blow—a massive assault on the Kanto (Tokyo) Plain to occupy the industrial and political heart of Japan.

The directive to conduct OLYMPIC on 1 November went out from Washington on 25 May. Three days later, on 28 May, MacArthur issued "DOWNFALL, Strategic Plan for Operations in the Japanese Archipelago."[4] It was a general guide to help other headquarters prepare their more detailed and final plans. For such a massive undertaking, the DOWNFALL plan was brief, including short sections on directives from the Joint Chiefs, assumptions (both friendly and enemy), concepts of operations, forces and tasks, and logistics—all contained in only thirteen legal-sized pages.

The plan began with a synopsis of the recent command realignments. In preparation for the invasion, MacArthur had been named commander in chief, Army Forces, Pacific (CINCAFPAC), and given command of all army forces. Nimitz, as commander in chief, Pacific Fleet (CINCPAC), had received command of all navy forces. The 25 May OLYMPIC directive and the respective duties of these commanders were covered thoroughly.

The chief assumption about the enemy was that the Japanese would "continue the war to the utmost extent of their capabilities" and "defend the main islands of Japan with every means available to them." Planners believed that only three divisions would be located in southern Kyushu at the beginning of OLYMPIC and that this number could be increased to eight, nine, or ten divisions once OLYMPIC began. Presumably, only fourteen divisions would oppose CORONET. By exercising "rigid economy" and withdrawing planes to Asia to protect them from American bombardment, the enemy could amass two thousand to twenty-five hundred planes and could stage them through homeland fields to oppose OLYMPIC.

As for American forces, the planners assumed that all of MacArthur's and Nimitz's forces would be available for DOWNFALL, but that no major ground combat units could be redeployed from Europe before early 1946. Air superiority over southern Kyushu and sea domination in the waters east of the home islands and in the East China Sea south of Kyushu was assured.

OLYMPIC was designed to land the equivalent of fourteen divisions in three to four widely separated areas of southern Kyushu, after prolonged and heavy attacks by carrier-based planes and by land-based planes from Guam, Tinian, and Saipan in the Marianas and from Okinawa and other islands in the Ryukyus. After landing and establishing beachheads, invasion forces would advance northward to a diagonal line from the town of Tsuno on the east coast to Sendai on the west coast. That line marked the southernmost limits of the mountainous terrain of central Kyushu. Here American forces could block the passes and seal off the southern one-third of the island.

Southern Kyushu was to become a gigantic air and naval base and staging area for CORONET. Thus, the prized areas and prime military objectives were the great bays of Kagoshima and Ariake and the ports of Kagoshima and Shibushi. The Miyazaki Plain along the east coast, the Miyakonojo Basin on the north and the Ariake Plain on the west of Ariake Bay, and the Kushikino Plain on the west and Makurazaki Plain on the south of Kagoshima Bay all furnished good level ground for air bases. Forty air groups with three thousand airplanes would follow on the heels of the invasion forces. Naval bases and port facilities in Kyushu and the offshore islands would serve to tighten the blockade, breach the Tsushima Straits, and allow American naval forces to operate in the Sea of Japan.

Operation CORONET would land twenty-five divisions, "augmented by redeployment" and supported by "massed air and naval power in the Pacific," to destroy enemy forces in the Kanto Plain and seize the Tokyo-Yokohama area. Occupation of the Kanto Plain would be "followed by such operations . . . as may be necessary to terminate organized resistance in the Japanese Archipelago." As in OLYMPIC, air and naval power would follow directly on the heels of the invasion. Fifty air groups would be brought into the Tokyo Plain, and the Tokyo and Sagami bays would be transformed into a gigantic naval base.

MacArthur (CINCAFPAC) would command the land campaign and have responsibility for mounting the army landing forces and army service forces. He would also command land-based planes assigned to the Far East Air Forces. The Marianas-based B-29s of the Twentieth Air Force would remain under command of the Joint Chiefs. Nimitz (CINCPAC) would command all naval operations, strategic naval support (carriers), and the amphibious phases of DOWNFALL. He would also mount all naval and marine ground forces.

The numbers for DOWNFALL were huge—far beyond comparison with any previous operations of the war. The troop list for OLYMPIC called for fourteen divisions; CORONET called for twenty-five. The Allies assaulted the Normandy beaches with five divisions and dropped three airborne divisions behind the beaches to secure critical areas. OLYMPIC would be supported by 1,914 carrier-based planes from twenty-two American and ten British carriers. Another twenty-seven hundred land-based aircraft on Okinawa could reach southern Kyushu to support the landings. Within ninety days of the assault, forty air groups would be rushed into southern Kyushu.

OLYMPIC required the simultaneous lift of twelve divisions comprising 427,400 troops and 626,800 tons of supplies and equipment. This task would require 1,318 transports and landing craft. CORONET would require simultaneous lift for fourteen divisions with 462,000 troops and 609,000 tons of supplies and equipment. The initial DOWNFALL plan left unspecified additional hundreds of direct support ships—from minesweepers to gunfire support groups of battleships, cruisers, destroyers, and rocket ships.

Forces would be mounted in several distant locations—the Philippines, Ryukyus, and Marianas—and disembarked at their objectives. Soldiers setting out from the Philippines faced a voyage of twelve hundred miles, and those sailing from the Marianas were sixteen hundred miles from their objectives.

Perhaps the most worrisome problems facing the planners of DOWNFALL were logistical considerations: the great distances in the Pacific, the long turnaround time for ships, the scattered installations, the need to build facilities from air bases to ports to housing, and the demands of other theaters. There simply was not enough shipping nor enough service troops and engineers to go around. While these had been continuing problems in the Pacific, DOWNFALL intensified them. Plans were made to scour the rear areas of the Pacific for shipping equipment and service troops, and the rear of the Southwest Pacific Area forces (SWPA) was "rolled up" to bring shipping and bases further forward. OLYMPIC was to be done with combat forces already on hand in the Pacific, but CORONET required redeployment of some divisions from Europe. The first priority for redeployment went to service units. Yet, ironically, redeployment would add to the shipping shortage by absorbing needed transports to bring units from Europe.

Other concerns plagued the decision makers. What would the reaction be to the redeployment of troops from Europe to the Pacific? Would the public support it? Would morale suffer? Public concern already simmered over the casualties of Iwo Jima and Okinawa. What would the cost of

DOWNFALL be, and could Americans sustain it? Could any methods be used to minimize casualties? Despite these questions, the planners went forward. The scale, distances, and complexities embodied in DOWNFALL testified to the confidence, technological sophistication, technical ability, and devastating force achieved by amphibious operations in the Pacific.

Almost all books on World War II in the Pacific have something to say about the proposed invasion. The subject is usually covered in a single sentence squeezed between the story of the bomb and the beginning of the occupation. Certainly no invasion of Japan occurred, and historians prefer to deal in real events—is it history if it did not happen? Then too, historians may think that they have all the answers to the interesting questions that orbit the proposed invasion of Japan. The consensus is that the Japanese would have fought as fanatically as they had on Saipan, Peleliu, Luzon, Iwo Jima, and Okinawa; and they would have preferred death to surrender. Depending on the source, a quarter million, a half million, or a million American soldiers, sailors, and marines would have been sacrificed to the expected suicidal defense of the Japanese homeland. Even more Japanese would have died. Several thousand kamikazes would have incinerated American soldiers and sailors in their warships and troopships off the invasion beaches, and Japanese civilians, armed with sticks and stones, would have perished under the treads of American tanks. In the conventional view, this holocaust was prevented only by the decision to use the atomic bomb. Unfortunately, these facile assumptions have received little study; they have been accepted largely from repetition.

Though this massive Allied invasion of the Japanese home islands, scheduled to begin on 1 November 1945, never happened, it has nonetheless provided some of the major undergirdings for widely accepted interpretations about the end of the war against Japan. A number of assumptions about the invasion have supported an orthodoxy about Japan's final defeat, the use of the atomic bomb on Hiroshima and Nagasaki, and projected casualties (both Allied and Japanese). In the popular view, America had no alternative but to invade Japan because the Japanese military irrationally refused to face the reality of defeat—a suicidal blindness embodied in the bloody but hopeless defenses of Luzon, Iwo Jima, and Okinawa. That huge numbers of American soldiers, sailors, and marines would be sacrificed to Japanese fanaticism enraged Americans, who welcomed any cheaper means, no matter the cost in Japanese lives. The prospect of a massive attack on Japan's supposedly fanatical and suicidal population has even called into question the postwar survival of a Japanese nation. According to the orthodoxy, this tragic bloodbath was averted only by the decision to use atomic bombs against Hiroshima and Nagasaki, thereby shocking the Japanese into surrender.

Important as the DOWNFALL plans are in justifying the use of the atomic bombs, no complete study of the proposed invasion and the important questions that surround it has ever been written. Why did the U.S. Joint Chiefs choose a strategy of invasion over a strategy of naval blockade and air bombardment? What were the invasion plans, and how much combat power could the Allies bring to bear on Japanese defenses? How did U.S. planners hope to counter the same kind of stubborn cave defenses and kamikaze air attacks that had made Okinawa so costly? Conversely, how would the Japanese defend the home islands and how strong would their defenses be? What were the military casualty estimates for the invasion? What were the links between the invasion plans and the decision to use the atomic bomb? This study of DOWNFALL examines these questions by looking at the records, mostly from the vantage point of military history. These records point in some surprising directions.

NOTES

1. *The War Reports of General of the Army George C. Marshall, General of the Army H. H. Arnold, and Fleet Admiral Ernest J. King* (Philadelphia: J. B. Lippincott, 1947), 658.

2. Samuel Eliot Morison, *History of United States Naval Operations in World War II: Aleutians, Gilberts, and Marshalls, June 1942–April 1944,* vol. 7 (Boston: Little, Brown, 1964), 87–88.

3. *Foreign Relations of the United States, Conferences at Malta and Yalta, 1945* (Washington, DC: GPO, 1955), 395, 829–30. Hereafter cited as *FRUS.*

4. DOWNFALL, Strategic Plans for Operations in the Japanese Archipelago, RG 165, OPD 350.05, Sec. 1, Cases 1–45, National Archives and Records Administration, Washington, DC.

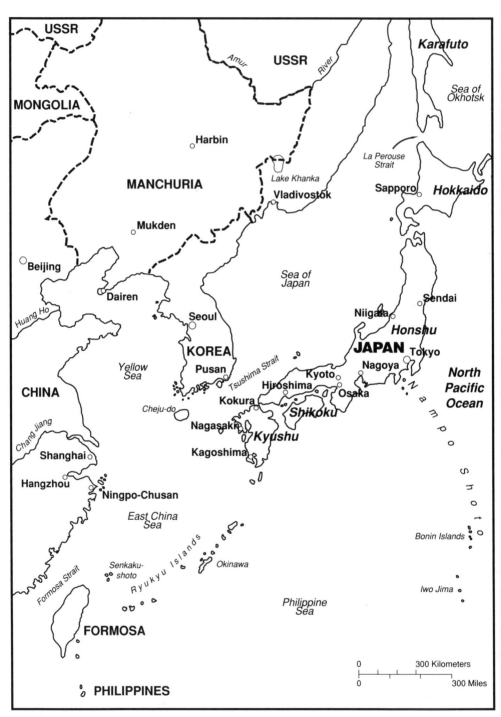

Japan and Northeast Asia

Chapter 1

Policies and Problems in the Pacific, 1940–43

War in Europe had begun in the first days of September 1939. Until mid-1940 American military leaders assumed that Britain and France would bear the brunt of the European war while the United States concentrated in the Pacific should war occur with Japan. Hitler's blitzkrieg of April–June 1940 changed everything. Suddenly and shockingly the Wehrmacht knocked France out of the war and drove the British from the continent. By July Hitler was poised to finish off the British. Preparing for the worst, American planners dusted off a prewar plan for defense of the western hemisphere without allies. The possibility that the French and British fleets would fall into Hitler's hands made the threat to the New World very real. To make the threat even more dire, American relations with Japan worsened daily. Japan's war against China and the probable expansion of the Japanese Empire into Southeast Asia threatened the Philippines and promised to draw America into a two-front war— defending against German expansion in the Atlantic and countering Japanese aggression in the Pacific.

In early November 1940 Chief of Naval Operations Harold R. Stark focused the issue precisely. He wrote a memorandum to Secretary of the Navy Frank Knox calling for strategic adherence to a modified version of prewar plan Rainbow 5, the plan that assumed an American-British-French alliance. He started from the premise that a war against Japan in east Asia and the southwest Pacific would add little to the defense of the western hemisphere. But, he argued, the survival of Britain was essential to the defense of the western hemisphere. Stark argued that American strategy ought to (1) ensure the survival of Britain, (2) concentrate American forces in the Atlantic, and (3) avoid war with Japan. If an American-Japanese war did break out, Stark advocated a defensive stand in the Pacific. Admiral Stark's memo brilliantly and succinctly pointed the strategic direction. The army staff concurred, President Roosevelt agreed, and, of course, the British were enthusiastic because Stark's memo clearly called for a Europe-first policy.

9

THE EUROPE-FIRST POLICY

Army and navy planners immediately began the work of translating Stark's memorandum into a plan of action. Until America became involved in the war, they reasoned, priority should go to hemispheric defense and security in both oceans. In case of a two-ocean war, the planners called for concentrating forces for an offensive in the Atlantic while avoiding war in the Pacific or conducting only defensive operations against Japan. So strongly did they feel the importance of the Atlantic that they advocated entering the European war immediately even if war with Japan occurred first. The plan was ratified by the chiefs of the army and navy on 21 December 1940. Within days, the secretary of war and the secretary of the navy approved the plan, and in mid-January President Roosevelt approved the strategy. By then, the army and navy staffs had already begun preparing position papers for upcoming meetings with their British counterparts.

In preparing for the meetings with the British, the staffs, with Roosevelt's approval, outlined the American position. First priority went to the defense of the western hemisphere. Next came aid to Britain. Finally, Japanese expansion was to be countered with diplomacy. If war with Japan came despite diplomatic action, the main effort would be placed in Europe to defeat Germany first.

Early in 1941 British military and political representatives arrived in Washington to meet with their American counterparts. Staff conferences continued from 29 January to 29 March 1941. The delegates met fourteen times and agreed that Germany was the most powerful enemy and priority should go to defeating it first. Thus, by mid-1941 a combined American-British strategy unequivocally mandated a Europe-first priority.

The conferees agreed less about how to defend against Japanese expansion. The British wanted all efforts to be directed toward the defense of Singapore. The Americans refused, and apart from the general agreement on a strategic defensive, no specific strategy was agreed on for the Far East. The U.S. Navy had studied strategy for a Pacific war with Japan for two decades, but after the ratification in late 1940 of Rainbow 5, the war plan that embodied the Europe-first strategy, navy planners lost interest in planning for a war in the Pacific. Army strategists had long been defensive-minded in the Pacific. Later, Admiral King would revive prewar naval plan Orange—a plan that would achieve victory with naval forces advancing across the central Pacific to defeat the Japanese fleet and gain control of the western Pacific.[1]

The 7 December 1941 Japanese attack on Pearl Harbor brought war between Japan and the United States. Within days, Britain also declared war on Japan. In support of his ally Japan, Hitler declared war on the United States, and congress reciprocated. A two-ocean war had been only a possibility when the chiefs met almost a year earlier. Prime Minister Churchill quickly brought his military chiefs to Washington to meet with their American counterparts while he met with Roosevelt. Now in the United States the bitterness of Pearl Harbor brought considerable public and political pressure to leave the European war to the British and concentrate American forces on Japan, and Churchill worried that the Americans would yield to the pressure. The meeting, known as the ARCADIA Conference, continued from 24 December 1941 to 14 January 1942. Roosevelt and his military chiefs refused to back away from the European war; the U.S. commitment to a Europe-first strategy remained firm. Despite some bitter disagreements with their British allies over how to prosecute the European war, the Americans would remain steadfast throughout the war.

For a year following Pearl Harbor, however, the American army and navy argued over priorities. With most of its ships and men deployed in the Pacific, the U.S. Navy seemed to place a higher priority on the Pacific war than its army colleagues or British allies preferred. Similarly, British reluctance in 1943 to commit to an early cross-channel invasion of Hitler's Europe brought threats from the Americans to take forces to the Pacific. Despite the stresses, the Europe-first policy held. It seemed coherent, consistent, and allowed, in the American mind at least, a straightforward military strategy.

The strategy, however, influenced all decisions concerning the Pacific and forced an opportunistic, ad hoc quality to efforts in the Pacific. Yet it soon became apparent that America would not need to stand entirely on the defensive in the Pacific, for early in the war the Japanese considered the Pacific secondary to their primary efforts in China and Southeast Asia. Consequently, using small amphibious forces, both army and navy forces were able to open limited offensives in New Guinea and the Solomons in late 1942. Despite the growing public interest in the Pacific, America concentrated its resources and strategic attention in Europe. Not until after the breakout from the Normandy beachhead in August 1944 could the end of the war in Europe be seen, and only then could attention be focused on the final defeat of Japan.

JURISDICTIONS AND RESPONSIBILITIES

Even though the Europe-first strategy relegated the Pacific to secondary status, those attending the ARCADIA Conference desperately tried to stem the Japanese onslaught into Southeast Asia and the East Indies by creating a combined command called ABDA (American, British, Dutch, Australian) "to maintain . . . the strategic defensive." The effort of this command collapsed as Japanese forces quickly overran the area.[2] By early March 1942 Allied resistance against the Japanese had ceased everywhere in the Pacific except in the Philippines.

The planning machinery of the old Joint Army-Navy Board, a weak advisory coordinating board formed in 1903, could not cope with the worsening crisis. The board had been devised only to provide high-level coordination between the army and the navy in a time when American military interests were limited primarily to the defense of the western hemisphere.

Carrying on coalition warfare with the British and presenting a unified American position on strategy called for closer interservice cooperation than had been provided by the board. The Joint Chiefs of Staff (JCS) was established early in 1942 during the ARCADIA Conference to mobilize, plan, and direct the American war effort. The members initially consisted of Chief of Naval Operations Admiral Stark; Commander in Chief, U.S. Fleet, Admiral Ernest J. King; Army Chief of Staff, General George C. Marshall; and Chief of the Army Air Corps, Lieutenant General Henry H. Arnold. In March 1942 President Roosevelt combined the offices of Chief of Naval Operations and Commander in Chief, U.S. Fleet, under Admiral King. Admiral Stark, the outgoing chief of naval operations was sent to London to command the U.S. Navy forces in Europe. His place on the Joint Chiefs was taken by Admiral William D. Leahy, former chief of naval operations, who had been recalled to active duty in 1942 as chief of staff to the president. Throughout the war the group operated as an ad hoc body without statutory authority. Sitting together, the U.S. Joint Chiefs and the British Chiefs of Staff formed the Combined Chiefs of Staff (CCS).

During the first half of March 1942 Roosevelt and Churchill exchanged messages discussing the division of the globe into strategic areas of responsibility. Simultaneously, the British and American military staffs studied the subject and quickly agreed that while the Combined Chiefs of Staff would keep direct responsibility for the allocation of resources to all theaters, the British chiefs would become primarily responsible for developing strategy for the Indian Ocean and Middle Eastern areas while the U.S. Joint Chiefs would develop strategy for the Pacific area. The two allies would share strategic responsibility in Europe and the Atlantic. The Joint Chiefs would direct the war against Japan. Their views and those of the principal Pacific commanders would determine strategy, command, and plans.[3]

The Joint Chiefs developed a number of committees to study and assist in developing strategy, to allocate resources, to gather intelligence, and to perform a number of other important functions. Directly responsible to the Joint Chiefs for strategic planning was the Joint Planners Staff (JPS) consisting of four members—two senior members each from the army and navy staff planning agencies. This group reviewed and passed to the Joint Chiefs war plans that had been developed by the Joint War Plans Committee, which in turn was assisted in technical matters by other special committees such as the Joint Intelligence Committee and the Joint Logistics Committee.[4]

Japanese offensives after Pearl Harbor succeeded beyond Japan's expectations. Within six months Japan had eliminated American, British, and Dutch naval forces from the western Pacific and had conquered Malaya, Singapore, the Dutch East Indies, and islands in the central and south Pacific. By mid-1942 the Allies feared a Japanese drive on Australia. Allied attempts to defend against this onslaught in the Dutch East Indies were weak and dilatory.

United States and Philippine forces, however, continued to hold out in the Philippines on the Bataan Peninsula and the island of Corregidor. Until May 1942 General Douglas MacArthur had commanded U.S. Army Forces Far East (USAFFE) since its creation in July 1941. After the dissolution of the ABDA Command, his command furnished the only resistance to the Japanese in the western Pacific and Southeast Asia. Shortly, with the fall of Bataan in April and the conquest of Corregidor in May 1942, the USAFFE Command, like the ABDA Command, ceased to exist. But in late February General MacArthur had been ordered by President Roosevelt to leave his besieged command and escape to Australia. The Joint Chiefs were still trying to contain Japanese expansion, and a glance at the map confirmed that Australia and its approaches must be held as a base for future offensives against the Japanese.

As MacArthur made his escape by PT-boat and bomber, the Joint Chiefs already had begun to debate a new command structure for the Pacific war. Because the Combined Chiefs of Staff had agreed that the United States would have primary strategic responsibility for Pacific strategy, the members of the Joint Chiefs were relieved from having to contend with allies in planning Pacific operations. The members were not, however, relieved from having to contend with each other. Although the benefits of a supreme commander for the Pacific were obvious and a prime candidate—General MacArthur—was already on hand, it was certain that the navy would never accept him. Prewar navy planners had given much attention to fighting a war in the Pacific, and the admirals had proprietary interests in the Pacific war.

Yet no admiral's reputation could match MacArthur's. Besides, Mac-Arthur was already in Australia, ready and eager to defend it as an allied base. Command organization in the Pacific reflected this interservice rivalry and suspicion. The Pacific was split into area commands. MacArthur was given command of the Southwest Pacific Area (CINCSWPA) consisting of Australia, New Guinea, the Solomon and Bismarck Islands, the Philippines, and eastern Malaysia. His orders were to defend Australia and its approaches and to prepare to take the offensive. Admiral Chester Nimitz, who had been named commander in chief, Pacific Fleet in the aftermath of Pearl Harbor, was also named commander in chief, Pacific Ocean Areas (CINCPOA). His orders were to hold the islands linking the United States with the Southwest Pacific Area and to prepare for amphibious operations against Japanese positions. Nimitz's Pacific Ocean Areas consisted of three subordinate area commands—North Pacific, Central Pacific, and South Pacific. Nimitz personally retained command of the Central Pacific. MacArthur and Nimitz each commanded their own integral air, naval, and ground forces, and each command functioned independently of the other. They received their orders from and reported directly to the Joint Chiefs.[5]

In May 1942 the Japanese received their first setback. In the Coral Sea the first great carrier battle of the war prevented the Japanese from gaining positions that they could use to dominate northern Australia and make communications with the United States more difficult. A month later the Battle of Midway turned the Pacific war in favor of the Americans.

UNCONDITIONAL SURRENDER

The members of the Joint Chiefs hardly had time in 1942 and 1943 to consider long-range strategic options for the Pacific. Their priorities were firmly fixed on the war in Europe, and at least until mid-1943 forces in the Pacific were too small for elaborate offensives against the Japanese. Furthermore, the existence of two major area commanders—one army and the other navy—discouraged any long-term strategy making. Well into 1944 the Joint Chiefs simply set short-term goals for the Pacific war. By mid-1944, however, events demanded a clear strategy for the final defeat of Japan. Getting agreement proved extraordinarily difficult, for an intractable problem complicated the issue. The military defeat of Japan was not enough; the Japanese had to surrender unconditionally.

If the Europe-first policy influenced Pacific strategy for the first two years of the war, the Allied policy of unconditional surrender dominated strategic planning for Japan's final defeat. President Roosevelt announced the policy at the 1943 Casablanca Conference with the British. On a bright January day, reporters gathered outside President Roosevelt's villa for a press conference. The president was joined by Churchill. The reporters, most of them in correspondent's uniforms, sat on the grass. It was the last day of the ten-day conference, where the two Allied leaders and their respective military staffs had met to consider operations after the end of the campaign in North Africa. Military strategy had dominated the meeting—whether to leap from Tunisia across the narrow straits to Sicily and Italy as desired by the British or to abandon ground operations in the Mediterranean and begin to prepare for the invasion of northwest Europe as the Americans wanted.

Obviously, the two Allied leaders could not discuss those matters with the reporters. President Roosevelt opened the press conference with some quotable generalizations, and then, in a seemingly off-hand way, he eased into a diplomatic question. Lately, said the president, he had been thinking of General Ulysses S. "Unconditional Surrender" Grant.[6] The president claimed that the Union general had gained the sobriquet by demanding nothing less than "unconditional surrender" of the defeated Confederates at Vicksburg. Then the president came to his point. "Peace can come to the world only by the total elimination of German and Japanese war power. The elimination of German, Japanese, and Italian war power means the unconditional surrender by Germany, Italy, and Japan. . . . It does not mean the destruction of the population of Germany, Italy, or Japan, but it does mean the destruction of the philosophies in those countries which are based on conquest and the subjugation of other peoples."[7]

The president later claimed that his remarks were spontaneous. Indeed, it was true that the statement had not received the exhaustive staffing given to most major policies, and the president's decision to make the announcement was a personal one. That it was spontaneous was untrue. In fact, a State Department committee headed by Norman H. Davis had recommended such a policy in May 1942, and Davis had apparently informed the president of the recommendation. Before Casablanca, Roosevelt had used similar language in speeches: "victory, final and complete," "absolutely and finally broken," "no compromise," and "total victory."[8] Roosevelt informed the members of the Joint Chiefs at a White House pre-conference meeting on 7 January 1943 that he planned to announce such a policy at Casablanca, but apparently, he did not seek their advice.[9]

Roosevelt presented the policy in such an off-hand and ingenuous manner that many thought the policy little more than a slogan—a rallying cry to inspire allies, troops, and citizenry. But there was much more to it than that. Roosevelt had obviously considered the diplomatic and political purposes of unconditional surrender and was immovably committed to the policy. But he seems to have given little attention to the *military* implications of his pronouncement. Aside from a 7 January 1943 meeting where he informed his military chiefs of his intentions, no consultation had taken place before the Casablanca announcement. On their side, the members of the Joint Chiefs apparently saw the policy as a diplomatic and political statement. They did not address the issue in formal discussions, nor did they offer opinions on its military implications.

Although they took no part in the formulation of the policy, apparently some informal discussion on the matter occurred among them at the Casablanca Conference. General Albert Wedemeyer accompanied General Marshall to Casablanca as his chief strategic adviser, and Wedemeyer recalled that Marshall brought up the subject of unconditional surrender "off the record" at a Joint Chiefs' meeting during the conference. In the course of the discussion Marshall asked for Wedemeyer's views on the subject. Wedemeyer, who had spent considerable time in Germany before the war, believed the policy would be counterproductive; it would "compel the Germans to fight to the very last," it would discourage anti-Nazi resistance inside Germany, and it would "weld all Germans together." Wedemeyer did not record the reaction of the Joint Chiefs to his remarks.[10]

Later in 1943 at the Cairo Conference, Roosevelt and Churchill met with Nationalist Chinese leader Chiang-Kai-Shek. The discussions focused wholly on the war against Japan. Out of that conference came a communique that spelled out more specifically the Allied war aims in the Far East and the Pacific. The Allied leaders pledged a fight to the finish and restated the doctrine of unconditional surrender. They also announced,

> The three great Allies are fighting this war to restrain and punish the aggression of Japan. They covet no gain for themselves and have no thought of territorial expansion. It is their purpose that Japan shall be stripped of all the islands in the Pacific which she has seized or occupied since the beginning of the First World War in 1914, and that all the territories Japan has stolen from the Chinese, such as Manchuria, For-

mosa, and the Pescadores, shall be restored to the Republic of China. Japan will also be expelled from all other territories which she has taken by violence and greed. The aforesaid three great powers, mindful of the enslavement of the people of Korea, are determined that in due course Korea shall become free and independent.[11]

Put simply, it was a pledge to dismantle the Japanese Empire.

In sum, then, the Allied war aims seemed straightforward. Unconditional surrender was the basis for the complete defeat of the Japanese government and military—for occupying Japan and eradicating its militarism, for liberalizing its political institutions, and for dismantling its empire. If these aims were politically and diplomatically desirable, their *military* accomplishment would soon pose a major problem for the Joint Chiefs.

NOTES

1. For the fascinating story of prewar planning by the navy for a Pacific war and how these plans influenced Pacific strategy in World War II, see Edward S. Miller, *War Plan Orange* (Annapolis: Naval Institute Press, 1991).

2. Grace P. Hayes, *The History of the Joint Chiefs of Staff in World War II: The War Against Japan* (Annapolis: Naval Institute Press, 1982), 50–51, 86–87.

3. Maurice Matloff and Edwin M. Snell, *Strategic Planning for Coalition Warfare, 1941–1942* (Washington, DC: GPO, 1953), 165–68.

4. Ray S. Cline, *Washington Command Post: The Operations Division* (Washington, DC: GPO, 1951), 103–4.

5. Hayes, 96–102.

6. Grant had earned the nickname at Ft. Donelson in 1862 when he informed the Confederate commander that his only terms were "unconditional surrender."

7. *FRUS, Conferences at Washington, 1941–1942, and Casablanca, 1943* (Washington, DC: GPO, 1968), 727.

8. Ibid., 506; Anne Armstrong, *Unconditional Surrender: The Impact of the Casablanca Policy upon World War II* (New Brunswick, NJ: Rutgers Univ. Press, 1961), 16–17.

9. Herbert Feis, *Churchill, Roosevelt, Stalin: The War They Fought and the Peace They Sought* (Princeton: Princeton Univ. Press, 1957), 109.

10. General Albert C. Wedemeyer, *Wedemeyer Reports* (New York: Henry Holt, 1958), 186–87.

11. *FRUS, Conferences at Cairo and Teheran, 1943* (Washington, DC: GPO, 1961), 448–49.

Chapter 2

The Pacific Strategists

Six men—all of them military officers who had shared the seclusion and relative obscurity of pre-World War II military society—directed, planned, and led the war against Japan. Four of them, King, Marshall, Leahy, and Arnold, were charged with strategic direction of the Pacific War. The other two, Nimitz and MacArthur, commanded the two major Pacific offensives. Born into the comfortable world of nineteenth-century small town America, all had grown up in a world of stability and certainty, and they had values to match. Arnold and MacArthur were West Point graduates. King, Leahy, and Nimitz were graduates of the Naval Academy. Marshall had graduated from the Virginia Military Institute, a school that prided itself on being more rigorous than the academies. As cadets, they had lived ascetic lives of spartan discipline, and instilled in them were the virtues of self-denial, integrity, persistence, and courage. Without the slightest cynicism, they believed in duty, honor, and country; in their ability to control events; and in their right to do so in time of war. They had served long and unappreciated apprenticeships in the almost invisible prewar army and navy. And after a brief taste of the drama and glory of history in World War I, they sank back into the obscurity of the interwar military to prepare themselves for the next crisis. When it arrived, they were ready.

KING

On the Joint Chiefs, Admiral Ernest J. King strongly supported the navy. From the time he entered the Naval Academy at Annapolis in 1897 until his death in 1956, he belonged to the navy. He had no other interests or diversions. Like a monk, his vows were for life—but he made a strange monk, for there was little humility in him.

King was handsome, arrogant, intelligent, stubborn, ambitious, and single-minded. He was also profane, petty, rude, disagreeable, and perhaps the most disliked allied leader of World War II. Only British general Bernard Montgomery may have had more enemies. Montgomery was a teetotaller and an ascetic; King loved parties and often drank to excess. Apparently, he reserved his charm for women; he had a weakness for the wives of fellow naval officers. On the job, he "seemed always to be angry

18

or annoyed."[1] Secretary of War Stimson "loathed" him, and his relationship with his own superior, Secretary of the Navy James Forrestal, was
one of "unconcealed hostility." The two men were reduced to communi-
cating through emissaries.[2] Though the story may be apocryphal, King
described his own rise to power in the gloomy days after Pearl Harbor
with the comment "when the going gets tough, they bring in the sons of
bitches."

But he was a fighting admiral, aggressive and willing to risk the fleet.
Confidence and daring were sorely needed in the post-Pearl Harbor navy.
King also had wide experience. He had served in submarines; he had
become a naval aviator at the age of forty-seven; he had commanded the
naval air forces; and he had commanded aircraft carriers. King had risen
wholly on his professional ability, hardly on his charm. At work he was
all business and, as one of his staff put it, "meaner than I can describe."[3]
Off the job he partied, drank, and gambled with his officers. Apparently,
King had a peculiar ability to separate a cold-blooded, serious, and
competent professional life from his private life, which he considered
nobody's business but his own. As a result, he had few friends in the
navy, and his relations with his superiors were often abrasive.

In peacetime, his personality and conflicts with his superiors would
almost certainly have kept him from becoming chief of naval operations
and commander in chief, U.S. Fleet. In fact, King had been passed over
in 1939 as Chief of Naval Operations in favor of Admiral Harold Stark.
Instead, King was assigned to the General Board, a billet for senior naval
officers nearing retirement. Only the prospect of war resurrected him.
Two qualities set him back on the road to greatness. He was dedicated to
shaking up the "business as usual" mentality of the peacetime navy, and
he refused to be discouraged by the navy's inadequate resources. "We
must," he said to his Atlantic Fleet, "do all we can with what we have."[4]
In the dark days of December 1941, King's personal qualities diminished
in importance. His aggressive confidence made him just the man to lead
the U.S. Navy back from Pearl Harbor.

Of all the members of the Joint Chiefs during the World War II, King
was the most Pacific-minded. Despite the Allied agreement that Germany
should be defeated first and that the Allies should stand on the strategic
defensive in the war against Japan, King consistently argued that more
resources be sent to the Pacific. Almost alone, he pushed for a limited
counteroffensive against the Japanese-held Solomons in 1942. The Guadalcanal campaign had to be done on a shoestring; there was hardly enough
of anything. And though it came close to failure, the operation succeeded.
The Solomons offensive of 1942 represented the end of strategic defense

in the Pacific and the beginning of a buildup hardly envisioned by the Europe-first strategists of two years before. That King would seek to open dangerous offensive operations in the Pacific so early stemmed from two considerations: (1) the best way to defeat Japan was to drive straight across the central Pacific, and (2) the offensive should be conducted by the U.S. Navy.

From the beginning of his tenure on the Joint Chiefs, King opposed creating unified commands. Unity of command—the idea that all forces, whatever their service, should be under a single supreme commander—ran counter to King's opinion that only admirals should command naval forces. In the aftermath of Pearl Harbor and the disasters that followed, the press placed much of the blame on lack of cooperation between the army and the navy. The idea of a unified command became popular. King objected. To him unity of command was not a panacea; it could conceivably create as many problems as it could solve. Also, the greatest figure in the Pacific, senior to all other generals and admirals and the hero of the Philippines, was General MacArthur. King had no intention of handing over to MacArthur the Pacific war, fleet and all.

There can be little doubt that the admirals, especially King, had little love for the army. "Army officers," said King, know "nothing about sea power." Pacific-minded though he was, King supported Marshall's obsessive desire for an early cross-channel invasion of Europe. Perhaps he expected that Marshall, in return, would relinquish the Pacific to the navy and support limited offensives there. But MacArthur was in the Pacific. King developed an almost paranoid antipathy toward MacArthur and believed that MacArthur was constantly scheming to be named supreme commander in the Pacific. Marshall, King believed, was intimidated by MacArthur.[5]

For years the navy had studied how to fight a war in the Pacific against Japan, while the army had devoted its thought to such things as the coast artillery and hemispheric defense. How to fight across the central Pacific and engage in a climactic fleet battle with the Japanese was the main problem for study at the Naval War College during the interwar years. Now that the war games had suddenly become real, King wanted no competition from the army. To him, the Pacific war was the navy's war.

Investigations of Pearl Harbor revealed a serious lack of army-navy cooperation before the Japanese attack. Even as the war went on, demands arose for postwar unification of the armed services. King certainly foresaw this postwar fight. The navy faced the prospect of losing its air power to a newly independent air force and its marines to the army. Perhaps King's jealous protection of the navy's role in the Pacific war stemmed, in part, from his desire to see the navy victorious in the defeat of Japan—so obviously and exclusively victorious that the politicians could not dare to weaken the navy through unification. In 1948 King testified before Congress against unification of the armed services. "Any step not good for the navy," he remarked, "is not good for the nation."[6]

British General Sir Hastings Ismay, Churchill's chief of staff, characterized King in spare and precise prose. According to Ismay, King was

> as tough as nails and carried himself as stiffly as a poker. He was blunt and stand-offish, almost to the point of rudeness. At the start, he was intolerant and suspicious of all things British, especially the Royal Navy; but he was almost equally intolerant and suspicious of the American Army. War against Japan was the problem to which he had devoted the study of a lifetime, and he resented the idea of American resources being used for any other purpose than to destroy Japanese. He mistrusted Churchill's powers of advocacy, and was apprehensive that he would wheedle President Roosevelt into neglecting the war in the Pacific.[7]

In mid-1944 as the question of the final defeat of Japan pressed in on the members of the Joint Chiefs, King's answer was predictable—amphibious forces should seize bases around the periphery of Japan, preferably on Formosa, the China coast, and Korea and tighten the naval blockade. Japan, King insisted, was particularly vulnerable to blockade, and there was no need for a costly amphibious assault on the home islands. King held to this argument into the spring of 1945 when he began to see some value in invading southern Kyushu, the objective for Operation OLYMPIC, the first phase of the invasion of Japan. First, he had been unable to convince Marshall and the army planners that a series of landings in China and Korea was feasible. Probably more important, King began to see the value of southern Kyushu as a better location for bases to tighten the blockade. However, even as he relented and supported OLYMPIC, King viewed invasion planning as only a contingency.

MARSHALL

If King was the most Pacific-minded member of the Joint Chiefs, then Army Chief of Staff General George C. Marshall was the foremost Europe-first advocate. Marshall's aim from the beginning of the war was to concentrate Anglo-American forces for an early invasion of northwest

Europe. Only by resisting the kinds of peripheral and scattered operations that had been historically so dear to British strategists could the Allies gather the necessary forces. Only by driving straight into the heart of Germany with massive force could they defeat Hitler.

Marshall took the oath as chief of staff of the army on 1 September 1939, the same day that the armored columns of Hitler's Wehrmacht smashed across the Polish border and began World War II. The picture that emerges of General Marshall is amazingly consistent. Hardly anyone who knew him disagrees about the values and ideals at the core of his character. He was cool, detached, and professional. Personal relationships counted for nothing; professional competence counted for everything. On the job were no friends, no enemies—only the able and the inept. In demeanor, he was formal and dignified; some even called him distant. President Roosevelt called him "George" on one occasion, and Marshall remembered that he never did it again. "I wasn't very enthusiastic over such a misrepresentation of our intimacy."[8]

His values were simple—honor, integrity, self-denial, discipline, and duty. He would listen to no special pleadings. When asked by a senator to promote a friend, Marshall replied, "Mr. Senator, the best service that you can do for your friend is to avoid any mention of his name to me."[9]

President Roosevelt liked to do business with subordinates informally over drinks or dinner, but Marshall refused to be drawn into the president's social orbit. "I found informal conversation with the President would get you into trouble," he explained. "He would talk over something informally at the dinner table and you had trouble disagreeing without creating embarrassment. So I never went. I was in Hyde Park for the first time at his funeral."[10]

But Marshall could not have worked through the war with political masters like Roosevelt and Churchill without some flexibility. Generally, Marshall argued the merits of his case. Then, whenever his superiors decided against him, Marshall would in good faith carry forward the decision.

Marshall's clear and unswerving vision of a direct invasion of northwestern Europe was in the American tradition of making war.[11] The plan would require concentrating immense forces in a single massive assault. Such a vision ran counter to two powerful lobbies against which Marshall had to contend—the British and the U.S. Navy. In wars with continental powers, the British historically favored a strategy that relied on naval blockade, peripheral raids, and reliance on continental allies. Remembering the butcher's bills of Ypres and the Somme in World War I, they were not eager to suffer similar casualties in a premature invasion of the continent. The navy planners could see little glory in an Atlantic war where the U.S. Navy shared the stage with the Royal Navy and where the chief duties would be countering the U-boat menace and escorting convoys. The U.S. Navy's war, they believed, should be in the Pacific.

In 1941 and early 1942 the rush of Japanese expansion in the Far East and the southwest Pacific and the collapse of allied defenses there forced Marshall to patch here and shore up there in a frantic effort to dam up the disaster. Despite his dedication to a Europe-first strategy, Marshall refused to write off MacArthur and his isolated garrison in the Philippines. Although MacArthur believed until his death that Washington had abandoned his forces in favor of a buildup in Europe, Marshall ordered scarce aircraft to the Pacific and even tried to charter Australian ships to carry supplies to the Philippines through the Japanese blockade.

Even as Marshall tried futilely to stamp out fires in the Pacific before the fall of Bataan, his planners designed a cross-channel invasion for 1943. Marshall flew to London in April 1942 hoping to get British approval for his plan. It called for holding a defensive line in the Pacific and undertaking no other operations in Europe. All efforts and resources would be devoted to a buildup in the British Isles (Bolero). A contingency invasion (Sledgehammer) was planned for 1942 if either the Germans or the Soviets appeared to be on the verge of collapse. A massive invasion (Roundup) would come in the spring of 1943. No other major operations would be undertaken; instead, all efforts and resources would be concentrated on the invasion of Europe.

Marshall left London convinced that the British had accepted his plan. Only weeks later, however, he found that they wished to open operations in North Africa in the fall of 1942 and that Roosevelt, his boss, had agreed with the British. Once again, in 1943, the British forestalled the cross-channel invasion by insisting on the invasions of Sicily and Italy.

Meanwhile, Admiral King opened an early counteroffensive against the Japanese in the southern Solomon Islands. The navy's assault on Guadalcanal in August 1942 was done with meager resources. Of the three essentials for amphibious operations—air superiority, control of the sea, and overwhelming combat power—they had none. Within days the Guadalcanal offensive was near failure. King asked for more forces, and by doing so, he threatened to derail the Europe-first strategy by incremental accretion of forces to the Pacific. Furthermore, King controlled the assets that could quickly make any strategy empty—the availability of landing craft and shipping.

Marshall was inclined to let King treat the Pacific as the navy's bailiwick, so long as King did not encroach on MacArthur's Southwest Pacific

Area nor undermine the cross-channel invasion by diverting too much to the Pacific. In short, from late 1942 to late 1944, Marshall gave little thought or attention to the Pacific war. He was absorbed by the war in Europe, although not as he had anticipated. Instead of planning and carrying out the invasion of northwestern Europe, he was planning and equipping the invasion of North Africa in 1942 and the invasion of Italy in 1943. Not until June 1944 did he get his cherished assault on northwestern Europe. Only afterwards, in late 1944 when it became apparent that Germany's collapse was imminent did Marshall and his planners turn their attention seriously to the Pacific. By then, the press of events had made attention imperative.

Like his views on the European war, Marshall's position on the final defeat of Japan emphasized direct assault and the concentration of forces under a unified command. He advocated planning a massive invasion of the Japanese home islands, while fearing that those who advocated the defeat of Japan through naval blockade and air bombardment would prolong the war and that after the defeat of Germany, the American people would soon lose patience with the Pacific war. Marshall became convinced that some strategy had to be found to force the defeat of Japan within no more than a year after the defeat of Germany.

LEAHY

Despite advanced age and long service, Admiral William D. Leahy was the last member to take his place on the Joint Chiefs. He was born in 1875 when President Grant was in his second term. Leahy graduated from the Naval Academy in 1897. He had served on the battleship *Oregon* and participated in the destruction of the Spanish fleet off Santiago in the Spanish-American War. As a young ensign he had been at anchor in the harbor at Shanghai during the Boxer Rebellion.

The original membership of the Joint Chiefs had included Chief of Naval Operations Admiral Stark; but in March 1942 when he was relieved and sent to London to head U.S. Navy forces in Europe, King became the only naval representative, outnumbered by two army colleagues.

At that time Leahy was retired from naval service and was serving as U.S. ambassador to the Vichy government of France. Previously, he had served as chief of naval operations from 1937 to 1939 and as governor of Puerto Rico from 1939 to 1940. He was recalled from Vichy in May 1942. Simultaneously, General Marshall was concerned that the continuing imbalance in army and navy membership on the Joint Chiefs might prejudice its decisions. He urged Roosevelt to appoint Leahy as chief of staff to the president. Thus, Leahy could fulfill several roles. On the Joint Chiefs he could serve as ex officio chairman; he could bring an additional navy voice; and he could furnish liaison with the president. Roosevelt recalled Leahy to duty in July 1942.

Leahy was navy, and he shared the navy's aims, fears, and prejudices. Unlike many of his colleagues, he did not, however, share their sense of insularity and their overriding concern for technical ability. He claimed to be a simple sailor yet was urbane and politically sophisticated. While he admired King's professionalism, he thought his fellow admiral "explosive" and "undiplomatic." Also, Leahy did not share King's intense naval parochialism. In turn, King thought of Leahy as a "fixer."[12]

Nonetheless, Leahy's background as a "battleship" admiral ensured his suspicion of airpower and its proponents' sometimes extravagant claims. His specialty in the navy had been ordnance and gunnery. He hated to fly, preferring to travel by ship or train. He held the uncommon position throughout World War II that strategic bombing was immoral; that warriors did not make war on women and children. He thought that using atomic bombs against the Japanese would put the United States on "an ethical standard common to the barbarians of the dark ages." Later, he thought the bombing unnecessary; naval blockade alone would force them to unconditional surrender. "These new concepts of 'total war,' " he observed, are "distasteful to the soldier and sailor of my generation." The new weapons of "uncivilized warfare represent a . . . barbarism not worthy of Christian man."[13]

Although Leahy was chairman of the Joint Chiefs and senior in service to any of the other members, the circumstances of his job prevented his direct involvement in the details of planning and decision-making. He seldom took direct part in the sometimes heated debates. Despite his rank and his clout with Roosevelt, Leahy commanded neither troops nor ships nor bombers; he had no domain to protect. On the Joint Chiefs he acted as presiding officer, peacekeeper, and arbitrator. Even though he had distinct opinions on strategic matters, membership was only part of Leahy's job. As the war went on, Leahy and the ubiquitous Harry Hopkins became the president's principal advisers. While no division of responsibility between the two was ever made, Hopkins came to be the president's alter ego in diplomatic matters, and Leahy specialized in military advice. Such duties left little time for detailed participation in debates and decision-making.

As the war in the Pacific neared its end, Leahy held firmly to several opinions concerning the final defeat of Japan. He believed that invasion was unnecessary. It would be far too costly in lives, and naval blockade alone could defeat Japan. Avoiding the ongoing struggle between army and navy over turf and supreme command, Leahy at times tended to favor MacArthur as supreme commander. Similarly, in the great 1944 strategic debate between army and navy over whether to bypass the Philippines and proceed directly to Formosa, Leahy sided with the army planners in favor of conducting operations against the Philippines.

ARNOLD

Although each member of the Joint Chiefs was equal to the others, Henry H. (Hap) Arnold found himself in an unusual position. As chief of Army Air Forces, Arnold served as Marshall's subordinate. Yet, while the air force was technically a part of the army, its special missions, unique organization, and dependence on technology made it quasi-independent. Despite Arnold's belief that the air force would someday be an independent service, he was content throughout the war to report to General Marshall. Arnold's respect for Marshall was profound. They shared an intense professionalism and dedication to duty, and both were somewhat suspicious of the motives of the U.S. Navy and of Admiral King.

Arnold, who had received his pilot training from Orville and Wilbur Wright, held Army Aviation Certificate number 2 (fellow officer Lieutenant Tommy Milling had soloed a few days earlier than Arnold). Thus, Arnold's career spanned military aviation from its tentative infancy when the Aviation Service of the U.S. Army Signal Corps had a total of three airplanes (the second and third were built by the Wright brothers for their students Arnold and Milling) to its decisive role in World War II when, as chief of the Army Air Forces, Arnold commanded 2.4 million airmen equipped with seventy-two thousand airplanes.

Arnold earned his nickname "Hap" as a relaxed, happy-go-lucky, practical-joking cadet at West Point. In those days his dream was to become a dashing cavalry officer. Instead, his commission into the infantry disillusioned and embittered him. Largely to escape the infantry, he transferred to the signal corps and accepted pilot training.

Sometime during World War I ambition set in. Arnold spent the war as a Washington staff officer and never made it to France. Nonetheless, before the war ended, he had become at age thirty-one the youngest colonel in the army. He also became a thoroughgoing disciple of Billy Mitchell, a zealous and controversial advocate of air power who, after his court-martial in 1925, became somewhat of a martyr to younger air officers. After World War I, Arnold excoriated the enemies of air power as relentlessly as Mitchell. Like Mitchell, he believed that air power in the next war would be decisive—so decisive that fleets of heavy bombers would make armies and navies unnecessary and obsolete. Two decades later as chief of Army Air Forces, Arnold gave form to these early beliefs in the American strategic bombing campaigns against Germany and Japan.

With Arnold's ambition came both a driving impatience that frequently intimidated subordinates and an intense advocacy of airpower that often offended traditionalists. In 1940 Roosevelt threatened to remove Arnold to Guam because of some undiplomatic testimony before a congressional committee. Arnold had been critical of administration policy that allocated U.S. airplane production to Britain when Arnold believed that it was desperately needed to build up U.S. air forces.

Arnold's strategic view of the war was an airman's counterpart to the strategy of George Marshall—concentration of forces followed by massive assault. Like Marshall, Arnold was dedicated to the defeat of Germany first. His belief in strategic bombing was unshakable, and the key weapon was at hand—the B-17 "Flying Fortress," a heavily armed four-engine bomber that could carry two tons of bombs to targets a thousand miles from its base. Massed formations of B-17s in daylight raids against German strategic targets might win the war, and nothing should be allowed to interfere with the rapid concentration of a fleet of strategic bombers in the United Kingdom and the air assault against Germany.

Also like Marshall, Arnold was unable to turn seriously to the Pacific war until 1944. The B-17s and B-24s used in Europe could not reach Japan from bases in China or the Pacific. To provide a very-long-range bomber for use against Japan, Arnold nurtured the problem-plagued B-29, an advanced very heavy bomber that could carry 7.5 tons of bombs to targets sixteen hundred miles away. Planning for the new bomber had begun before the war, but the distances in the Pacific war added urgency to B-29 development. The bomber first flew in 1942. Yet technical problems proved so numerous and so stubborn that not until 1944 did the plane become reliable enough and plentiful enough to be effective. Early in 1944 Arnold hoped that bases in China could be the launching points for B-29 raids against Japan, but logistical problems doomed that effort. In mid-1944 Arnold found the answer when the Marianas, only fifteen hundred miles from Tokyo, fell to Admiral Chester Nimitz's forces. Bases there were within range of all Japanese cities from Tokyo south, and the bombers could be plentifully supplied.

In late 1944 Arnold turned his bomber offensive against the Japanese. In November 1944 the first raids against Tokyo were launched from Saipan. By the beginning of 1945 more than two hundred B-29s were operating with the Twentieth Air Force from Saipan, Guam, and Tinian. To ensure that the B-29s would remain concentrated and would not be turned to tactical use by Nimitz or MacArthur, Arnold convinced his colleagues on the Joint Chiefs to retain the bombers under their control and to make him the commander of the Twentieth Air Force.

Arnold believed that the B-29s could defeat Japan and make invasion unnecessary. He believed that "a total drop of 1,051,000 tons of bombs in 1945 . . . would make possible the complete destruction of interior Japan."[14] If such a campaign failed to force Japan's surrender, Arnold promised, it would, at least, make the invasion much easier and less costly.

NIMITZ

Of all the major commanders of World War II, Admiral Chester W. Nimitz may have been the most affable and self-effacing. These character traits served him well, for he was buffeted by the stresses of fighting the war in the Pacific, by the frequently bullying and arbitrary views of his immediate superior, Admiral King, and by the imperial ego of General MacArthur with whom he shared the Pacific. Under Nimitz, commander in chief, Pacific Fleet-commander in chief, Pacific Ocean Areas (CINC-PAC-CINCPOA) was a happy headquarters. Nimitz gave his staff considerable independence, he usually took their advice; when necessary, he protected them and his commanders from higher headquarters. He pitched horseshoes; he had an enormous stock of stories that he delighted in telling over drinks; he loved children; he kept a dog throughout the war; he disliked protocol and personal publicity; and with subordinates he was patient and tolerant.

In 1941 Nimitz had thirty-six years of naval service. He had been reared in the German settlements of the hill country of central Texas before going to the Naval Academy in 1901. During years when promotions were notoriously slow, Nimitz made rapid progress. He was a captain after twenty-two years, and he was selected for rear admiral in 1938 at age fifty-three. Nimitz had pioneered diesel engines in U.S. naval vessels and had very early experience in submarines. Despite his Texas country background, his fund of rustic stories, and his folksy ways, Nimitz was something of a sophisticate. One of his great joys was classical music, especially Brahms. He enjoyed good food and good drink and was a free thinker on religious matters.

When the Japanese attacked Pearl Harbor, Nimitz held one of the three most important jobs in the navy—chief of the Bureau of Navigation—a powerful agency that handled all the navy's personnel matters. He was, therefore, in a strategic position when Admiral Husband E. Kimmel, commander in chief, Pacific Fleet, was relieved of command in the aftermath of Pearl Harbor. President Roosevelt and Secretary of the Navy Frank Knox settled on Nimitz as his successor.

Like King, Nimitz was old navy. He had turned down lucrative offers from industry to stay in the navy. Yet Nimitz was not obsessive in his attachment. While King's first instinct was to examine a matter for its effect on the navy, Nimitz was broader and more cosmopolitan. Like Leahy, Nimitz was never completely comfortable with techniques and weapons of twentieth-century warfare. He had moral doubts about the Twentieth Air Force's campaign to firebomb Japanese cities. After the war he had mixed feelings about America's having used the atomic bomb. Repelled by the idea of destroying a city in a single blast, he reluctantly justified the bomb's necessity because of the fanatical and suicidal Japanese defense of the islands of the Pacific. In fact, he really believed that dropping the atomic bomb had not defeated Japan. The Japanese, he maintained, were already defeated by blockade because Japan was "a maritime nation, dependent on food and materials from overseas" and had been "stripped of her sea power."[15]

Nimitz's urbanity carried over into his military views. While he sometimes became irritated with the interservice bickering that plagued the Pacific effort, unlike King, he believed in unity of command. Unlike some other Pacific commanders, Nimitz was not paranoid or suspicious about motives. Pragmatism and flexibility guided his strategic views. At first he sided with King in the argument over bypassing the Philippines in favor of assaulting Formosa (King favored it). Later, Nimitz changed his view and, with MacArthur, advocated taking Luzon. On the question of invading the Japanese home islands to force unconditional surrender, Nimitz was ambivalent. His superior, King, argued that invasion was unnecessary and ordered Nimitz to prepare plans for landings on the China coast to seize bases for blockade. Nimitz dutifully did so. He hoped, and perhaps believed, that invasion would prove unnecessary. Yet Nimitz was the first major naval leader to come over to Marshall's and MacArthur's view that the invasion of Kyushu in the fall of 1945 was the best of a number of unpleasant alternatives.

MACARTHUR

General Douglas MacArthur seldom went to conferences, pleading that he could not be away from his headquarters and preferring instead to be

represented by a member of his staff. Nonetheless, the supreme commander's presence was felt at every major conference and in every major
decision of the Pacific war. Despite his high-sounding title—commander
in chief, Southwest Pacific Area (SWPA)—MacArthur's command was
comparatively small, his resources limited, and his location geographically
off in left field. Yet his influence on the direction of the war in the Pacific
was large.

World War II gave MacArthur the chance for a second career. He had
already fulfilled his early promise. He had served with great valor and
initiative in the Philippines and in the intervention at Vera Cruz. He had
come home from World War I as a very young and highly decorated
brigadier general, having earned both his rank and decorations in combat.
After the war, still not yet forty years old, he went back to his alma mater
at West Point, where, against bitter opposition from some conservative
and traditionalist faculty members, he led a campaign to modernize the
academy's training and curriculum. From 1928–30 he headed the Philippine Department. He was appointed chief of staff of the Army in 1930 by
President Herbert Hoover and served until 1935 when he again went to
the Philippines to guide the formation of a national army in preparation
for Philippine independence. In 1937 MacArthur retired but stayed on as
military adviser to the newly formed Philippine army. He had served on
active duty for thirty-four years, nineteen of those years as a general
officer. In 1937 MacArthur was fifty-seven years old. In 1941, as war
loomed with Japan, he was recalled to active duty as commander, U.S.
Army Forces, Far East.

MacArthur's actions, purposes, and character have defied simplifica-
tion. Like his contemporary Roosevelt, he was a tangle of complexities
and contradictions. He was capable of playing different roles. Many
biographers and observers have tried to find the core of his character.
Some see only ambition. Some see only right-wing ideology. Some fall
back on epithets and cliches—vainglorious, fascist, Dugout Doug, bril-
liant, gifted, Caesar. According to his best biographer, D. Clayton James,
the truth may be simpler. MacArthur, James admits, was a consummate
role player who projected whatever demeanor suited his purposes. At his
core, however, MacArthur was a patrician, conscious of his aristocratic
heritage and motivated by nineteenth-century ideals—honor, courage,
noblesse oblige. Like antebellum southern aristocrats, MacArthur had a
touchy sense of pride. Conduct that men of more modern values considered petty or self-serving may have stemmed from an acute antique sense
of a gentleman's personal honor.[16]

MacArthur also displayed a streak of paranoia; somebody or some clique was always striving to subvert his appointment with destiny. During World War I and the 1920s his nemesis was Pershing's staff at the American Expeditionary Force Headquarters at Chaumont. During World War II, in MacArthur's mind, Washington abandoned the Philippines as prey to the Japanese. As the war progressed, MacArthur became convinced with some evidence that the navy was conspiring to freeze him out of "their" Pacific war or at best to relegate his Southwest Pacific Area to a supporting role for the principal thrust by naval forces across the central Pacific. MacArthur's strategic views were almost wholly dominated by a single consideration—to redeem the Philippines. He saw Philippine liberation as a moral responsibility for the United States and as a personal mission. He had even considered disobeying President Roosevelt's order that he leave the beleaguered islands in March 1942. His promise "I shall return" was more than a melodramatic war cry; it was a demand for personal atonement.

In The Philippines disasters of 1941–42 also lie the origins of MacArthur's considerable bitterness and suspicion toward the navy. He believed until his death that the navy had abandoned the Philippines—that the navy could have reopened lines of supply to the islands but refused, preferring instead to husband their few remaining resources following Pearl Harbor.[17]

Before 1944 MacArthur was absorbed in building up his forces in the southwest Pacific and in the New Guinea campaign. Like his superiors on the Joint Chiefs, he could not see far enough into the future to consider an overall strategy for the Pacific war. If he had any strategic aim, it was simple—to liberate the Philippines. By early 1944, however, both MacArthur's and Nimitz's drives were gathering speed. The members of the Joint Chiefs faced a decision—to find the best staging area for the final air, naval, and, if necessary, ground assault on Japan. Admiral King favored Formosa. MacArthur argued for Luzon in the Philippines. In July 1944 Admiral King returned home from a visit to the Pacific thinking that he had prevailed on his subordinate Nimitz to support the Formosa option. A few days later, at a conference in Hawaii between Roosevelt, MacArthur, and Nimitz, Nimitz supported the invasion of Luzon. Marshall and Leahy also came to favor Luzon over Formosa. Roosevelt, who earlier had favored Formosa, acquiesced. MacArthur would, indeed, return.

In the last great strategic argument of the war—whether or not to invade the Japanese home islands—MacArthur was unequivocal; he favored invasion. Air bombardment alone could not force Japan into surrender any more than it had forced Germany into submission. Seizing bases on the China coast to tighten the naval blockade would divert forces from the main axis of advance into an area of little strategic importance. So, for MacArthur, only the alternative of invasion remained. And he wanted to command it.

NOTES

1. Robert W. Love, Jr., ed., *The Chiefs of Naval Operations* (Annapolis: Naval Institute Press, 1980), 140.

2. Leonard Mosley, *Marshall: Hero for Our Times* (New York: Hearst Books, 1982), 225; Love, 140.

3. Love, 161.

4. Thomas B. Buell, *Master of Sea Power: A Biography of Admiral Ernest J. King* (Boston: Little, Brown and Company, 1980), 136–37.

5. Ibid., 215–17.

6. Love, 170.

7. General Lord Ismay, *The Memoirs of General Lord Ismay* (New York: Viking Press, 1960), 253.

8. Forrest C. Pogue, *George C. Marshall: Education of a General* (New York: Viking Press, 1963), 323.

9. Ismay, 251.

10. Pogue, 324.

11. See Russell F. Weigley, *The American Way of War: A History of United States Strategy and Policy* (Bloomington: Indiana Univ. Press, 1977).

12. William D. Leahy, *I Was There* (New York: McGraw-Hill, 1950), 104; Henry H. Adams, *Witness to Power: The Life of Fleet Admiral William D. Leahy* (Annapolis: Naval Institute Press, 1985), 223.

13. Ibid., 441–42.

14. Henry H. Arnold, *Global Mission* (New York: Harper & Brothers, 1949), 596.

15. E. B. Potter, *Nimitz* (Annapolis: Naval Institute Press, 1976), 400.

16. D. Clayton James, *The Years of MacArthur*, vol. 1, *1880–1941* (Boston: Houghton Mifflin, 1972), 572–73.

17. D. Clayton James, *The Years of MacArthur*, vol. 2, *1941–1945* (Boston: Houghton Mifflin, 1975), 22.

Chapter 3

Hard Strategic Decisions, 1943–44

Military strategy at the beginning of the war in the Pacific was a hodgepodge of indecision, irresolution, and conflicting goals. Navy planners had already decided that the Philippines were not defensible, and Admiral Thomas C. Hart, commander, Asiatic Fleet, had already been advised that he could withdraw his surface fleet when he thought it necessary. The army, lacking forces to defend the Philippines, nonetheless could not abandon them, and the War Department, encouraged by MacArthur, decided to mount a vigorous defense of the islands.[1] In the months before Pearl Harbor, political leaders encouraged a strategy of forward defense upon the army and the navy but refused to furnish the troops and weapons that were needed to do the job. Even this fragmented and disconnected strategy disappeared in the aftermath of Pearl Harbor.

For the next six months the United States operated in the Pacific without a coherent strategy. Indeed, even after the battles of the Coral Sea and Midway stopped the Japanese onslaught, no overall strategy was developed. All that guided the planners were some vague and general assumptions—that Chiang-Kai-Shek's Nationalist Chinese would bear the brunt of the land war against Japan; that the principal American strategic objective would be a huge ill-defined "strategic triangle" with its apex at Luzon and its base formed by a line from Hong Kong to Formosa; and that Japan would eventually be squeezed into capitulation by naval blockade and devastated by air bombardment. Even the offensives that had begun in late 1942 in the southern Solomons at Guadalcanal and in Papua were not dictated by any overall strategy; they were undertaken (with insufficient resources) only to counter immediate Japanese threats. After the successful campaigns for Guadalcanal and for Papua ended in early 1943, forces had built up in two remote and hitherto unknown areas of the south Pacific. Thus, circumstances, not strategic goals, dictated the next moves.

In the summer of 1943 the attention of the members of the Joint Chiefs was clearly on Europe—clearing North Africa, preparing for operations against Sicily and Italy, and perhaps most difficult of all, trying to hold Churchill and the British to their cross-channel invasion commitment. Yet despite the primacy of the war in Europe, operations in the Pacific proceeded. Offensive pressure was needed to keep the Japanese from strengthening their defenses; momentum had to be maintained. The Joint Chiefs wanted forces in position to end the war against Japan quickly once Germany was defeated. For all those reasons, they concluded that despite the Europe-first strategy, offensive actions were necessary in the Pacific.

The campaigns in the Solomons and in New Guinea arose from expediency. As a result, at the beginning of 1943 the major U.S. forces were deployed in a far corner of the Pacific, an area that seemed to offer little opportunity for a direct thrust against Japan. Furthermore, beyond defending the Philippines, the army had never given much thought to Pacific strategy. In contrast, almost all interwar naval officers had studied Pacific strategy at the Naval War College. How to defeat the Japanese navy in the far Pacific was their problem. The "school solution" was Plan Orange—a naval advance through the islands of the central Pacific climaxed by a general fleet engagement in the Philippine Sea. In mid 1943, when no other Pacific strategy was offered, Admiral King resurrected the school solution.

A STRATEGY OF OPPORTUNISM

Since no overall plan for the defeat of Japan existed, opportunism ruled. On a playing field without boundaries, interservice rivalries thrived—not entirely from personal interest or parochialism, but from the natural tendencies of service leaders to see the war from the perspectives of their own services. King saw the central Pacific as decisive; this vast ocean dotted with thousands of atolls suited the great mobility and power of the fast carriers. Conversely, MacArthur and other army planners favored the New Guinea-Philippines route, in part because the larger land masses there suited the power inherent in ground and land-based air forces.

In mid-1943 Admiral Nimitz was informed that by October he could expect to have ten attack carriers, seven escort carriers, twelve battleships, sixty-six destroyers, and thirty-six transports.[2] To allow this fast and powerful force to stand idle would be inexcusable. MacArthur's campaigns in his Southwest Pacific Area (SWPA) could rely on long-range and heavily armed land-based airpower. Besides, the restricted waters in which MacArthur's forces operated made carriers vulnerable to Japanese land-based planes. An offensive in the open waters of the central Pacific would put the new carriers to good use, would further spread and disperse Japanese defenses, and would complete the encirclement of the Japanese Empire.

The army staff reacted to King's plan to use amphibious forces and carrier air power in a drive across the islands of the central Pacific with tentative assent mixed with caution. General Marshall wanted assurances that a new central Pacific offensive would not siphon resources from the already established operations in the Solomons and the southwest Pacific. Army planners tended to see the new front as a supporting drive on MacArthur's flank. MacArthur, however, saw it for what it was—the beginning of an independent and competing offensive that the navy would inevitably push as the primary drive against Japan. He wasted no time in cabling Marshall a list of criticisms. First, he doubted that carrier-based airpower could cope with Japanese land-based planes in the Marshall Islands. In addition, the drive would reach no strategic objective until it arrived in the Philippines, and, MacArthur promised, he could get there sooner.[3]

King proposed opening the new drive with an assault on the Marshall Islands on 1 November. Army planners began to sense that the elephant's trunk was already in the tent. They argued that so great an undertaking as a direct assault on the Marshalls would inevitably divert ground forces from SWPA and the Solomons. They also feared that land-based planes would be diverted from Europe to provide air cover over the Marshalls once the carriers withdrew. It would be better, they argued, to assault the Gilbert Islands first. These islands were more lightly defended than the Marshalls and were closer to the ongoing operations in the Solomons. Once taken, the Gilberts could provide bases for a later assault on the Marshalls.

King conceded this wisdom and thus sealed the bargain between the army and navy that set in motion the second arm of twin offensives aimed at the western Pacific. According to one official historian, the new offensive "built about the mobility of the new fast carriers" changed the character of the war. "The overland and island-hopping advances hitherto characteristic of the Pacific war," he continued, "were now to be gradually supplanted through swifter, bolder strikes by large naval forces knifing behind the Japanese lines of defense and cutting off their forward defense positions."[4]

Yet despite Nimitz's successful assault on the Gilberts in November 1943, continuing progress in the Solomons, and MacArthur's accelerating progress in eastern New Guinea, these operations from mid-1942 to the end of 1943 were expedient and opportunistic. The Joint Chiefs refused to examine long-term strategic goals well into 1944; nonetheless, that year produced great leaps along both axes. By the spring of 1944 Nimitz's drive was poised for a leap to the Marianas, and MacArthur expected to return to Leyte in the central Philippines by the end of the year. The Joint Chiefs gave both Nimitz and MacArthur considerable latitude and set flexible and rather short-term schedules for operations. The policy was producing rich dividends. Gathering momentum in the Pacific offensives and events in Europe soon forced some hard decisions upon the Joint Chiefs—decisions that could no longer be dodged.

CONFERENCES AND PLANS

In the fall of 1944 the end of the war in Europe could now be seen with some clarity. The time had come to consider a strategy for the final defeat of Japan: to address difficult and complex questions. What were the strategic objectives? What forces would have to be redeployed from Europe? Would invasion be necessary, or could Japan be forced to surrender unconditionally through naval blockade and air bombardment? What would be the roles of China and the USSR? Would British forces be needed or desired? How quickly could Japan be defeated?

In fact, as early as May 1942 chief army planner Brigadier General Thomas T. Handy had tried to spur a long-range study on the defeat of Japan. Should the war be limited to blockade and air bombardment or would it be necessary to invade the home islands, he asked. Clearly, May 1942 was far too early to formulate even tentative answers. Indeed, the Allies were at that moment struggling over the entire globe to stem a hitherto uninterrupted string of Axis victories. But Handy had asked the most fundamental question of the Pacific war. It would take nearly three more years to provide a definitive answer.[5]

Over the course of the next year, however, the axis onslaught was stemmed, and initiative in all theaters passed to the Allies. With a sense that the worst was over, the Joint Chiefs met with the British in Washington at the TRIDENT Conference in May 1943. The British had indicated four months earlier at the Casablanca Conference that they held a strict view of the Europe-first agreement—that is, they believed that American forces should stand strictly on the defensive in the Pacific, lest that theater become a sponge gradually soaking up resources from Europe. At the TRIDENT Conference, King, interested in opening his new front in the central Pacific, again pressed the issue of a new offensive there. The British chiefs of staff once more expressed misgivings about opening new offensives in the Pacific. The U.S. Joint Chiefs, however, pressed their case for a new offensive in the central Pacific and proposed an interim strategy to be pursued until events allowed a more definitive strategy for the final defeat of Japan. While the primary effort went on in Europe, the Allies would "maintain and extend unremitting pressure" to weaken Japan's military forces and to get "positions from which her ultimate unconditional surrender can be forced." The plan was flawed, depending heavily on British and Chinese forces to recover Burma and Hong Kong and to reopen the Straits of Malacca. Meanwhile, American forces would recover the Philippines. Once supply routes were thus reopened to China, the Chinese could seize sites in eastern China "from which to launch an overwhelming bombing offensive against Japan." Finally, American forces, assisted by British and Chinese forces, would "invade Japan." On the last point the planners explicitly said that the invasion could occur only after Japan was considerably weakened "by a sustained, systematic, and large-scale air offensive." The British agreed to accept the study "as a basis for a combined study and elaboration for future plans." Whereupon, the planners went back to work.[6]

By the time of the QUADRANT Conference at Quebec in August 1943, a combined team of American and British planners had worked through June and July in Washington and London to construct the "Appreciation and Plan for the Defeat of Japan." This plan called for multiple offensives against the Japanese Empire—through the central and the southwest Pacific, and, perhaps, through the northwest Pacific (the Aleutians and Kuriles) by American forces. British forces would clear Burma to open a supply route to Chiang's Nationalist Chinese forces and to open the Strait of Malacca.[7]

Considerable disagreement emerged between the Americans and the British. The British argued that Nationalist China could not play a major role in the final defeat of Japan. They had little faith in Chinese abilities or their will to fight, so the British saw no urgency in an early conquest of Burma to open lines of supply to China. Disagreement also erupted over the relative importance of the central Pacific and southwest Pacific routes of advance. The British wanted to give clear priority to the central Pacific. The Americans, with Marshall as spokesman, argued against relegating MacArthur to a subsidiary role.[8]

But the most disturbing part of the plan was its timetable. Offensives against the southern Philippines and northern Burma were not scheduled until late 1944 or early 1945, and they would continue into mid-1946. Offensives against Luzon, Formosa, Hong Kong, and perhaps the Ryukyus would come in the latter half of 1946. The last phase of the war against Japan, "Serial 8," included two tersely described operations to be carried out "from 1947 onwards"—Bomb Japan and Invade Japan.[9]

The U.S. Joint Chiefs objected strenuously to such an extended schedule for the defeat of Japan. Fearing war weariness among the troops and the American people, they insisted that the war had to end within twelve months after the defeat of Germany even though the British feared that such a timetable might trigger a premature redeployment of U.S. forces from Europe. On this issue the American view prevailed, and the lengthy timetable was disapproved. The planners were sent back to work on a scheme that would defeat Japan within twelve months, not two or three years, after VE-Day.[10]

By the time of the SEXTANT Conference at Cairo in December 1943, it was clear that the British had been right; Chiang's Nationalist Chinese forces could not be counted upon to bear the brunt of the ground war against Japan. The members of the Combined Chiefs of Staff tacitly recognized that reality when they approved an "Overall Plan for the Defeat of Japan." In a single sentence, "The main effort in the war against Japan should be made in the Pacific," the planners recognized the growing potency of the twin drives in the Pacific and the innate weakness of basing the strategy for Japan's final defeat on Chinese and British offensives. The plan called for invasion of the Japanese home islands only if air bombardment and sea blockade failed to bring the Japanese leaders to unconditional surrender.[11]

The "Overall Plan for the Defeat of Japan" approved at the SEXTANT Conference became the basic strategic plan for the remainder of the Pacific war. By recognizing that the main effort would come in the Pacific, the combined chiefs could put aside some plaguing problems—building up Chiang, encouraging the British to undertake early operations in Burma, and finding the shipping resources for these tasks.

While the decision to recognize the Pacific as the main drive against Japan clarified and simplified many problems, the Sextant plan left other major strategic decisions unresolved. Would the invasion of Japan be necessary? What intermediate objectives should be seized? Should Nimitz's central Pacific drive or MacArthur's southwest Pacific operations receive strategic priority? Who would command the final operations against Japan? Resolving these issues required another eighteen months.

By the beginning of 1944, time and events pressed in on the Joint Chiefs. Nimitz's central Pacific drive was poised to assault the Marshall Islands while MacArthur's forces drove along the northern coast of New Guinea. The twin drives promised to gather even more speed and momentum in the first half of 1944. No longer could the Joint Chiefs pursue a strategy of opportunism; the time had come to make hard strategic choices for the final defeat of Japan.

The need for bases to blockade and bombard the Japanese home islands and to furnish staging areas for invasion forces had concerned the members of the Joint Chiefs from the time they first began to plan for Japan's final defeat. Vague and indefinite plans involved the strategic triangle of

Luzon, Formosa, and the east China coast to provide bases and staging areas. Just as vague and indefinite was the assumption that the twin drives of MacArthur and Nimitz would converge in that strategic triangle. In January 1944 an intertheater staff conference met at Pearl Harbor and reendorsed two assumptions: bases on the China coast were required, and the route to the China coast led through the Philippines.

King, however, had another objective in mind. Supported by most of his navy planners, he proposed to bypass the Philippines entirely and strike out directly for the more strategically located island of Formosa. In the late spring and early summer of 1944, King's plan appealed to some influential army planners; even Marshall and Arnold were attracted to the Formosa proposal. The Japanese had not yet heavily fortified the island, and a bold, quick strike might pay immediate dividends. The island could provide bases for B-29 raids against Japan. It could serve as a base from which to seize a port on the China coast to supply Chiang's forces and American airbases inside China. Naval and air forces based on Formosa could more easily sever the Japanese lines of communication with Southeast Asia than could forces based on Luzon. Finally, bypassing Luzon would immensely speed up the final defeat of Japan.

MacArthur unfairly saw King's proposal as a navy plot. Even Nimitz and the usually aggressive and daring Admiral William F. "Bull" Halsey conceded the necessity of seizing air bases in the Philippines before assaulting Formosa. MacArthur argued that the United States had a binding moral obligation to liberate the Philippines and pointed out the very large troop requirements needed to move directly on Formosa— requirements of combat and service troops that were beyond the capability of the Joint Chiefs to provide without redeployment from Europe. Finally, such huge forces would be required for the Formosa operation that all other offensive operations in the Pacific would come to a standstill.

In September 1944, as often happens, events, not arguments, began to decide the issue. MacArthur's instructions called for him to assault the southernmost island of Mindanao in the Philippines on 15 November and to take Leyte beginning 20 December. Halsey's carrier planes raided Leyte in early September, and Halsey reported that Leyte was lightly defended. The Joint Chiefs immediately ordered MacArthur to bypass Mindanao and to strike Leyte two months early. MacArthur's Leyte landings on 20 October enabled him to speed up his timetable for the assault on Luzon. The assault on the Philippines also lured the remainder of the Japanese fleet to destruction in the great naval battle of Leyte Gulf.

Meanwhile, Japanese offensives in China recaptured the airbases from which the Fourteenth Air Force was to support the Formosa landings and later conduct strategic bombing raids against Japan. With the bases lost, a port no longer had to be seized on the China coast. Suddenly, Formosa operations appeared less desirable. Moreover, Nimitz's seizure of the Marianas made the need for B-29 bases in China and Formosa less pressing.

Military events brought the balance down on the side of taking Luzon. Freed from the necessity of the Formosa operation, Nimitz could now move against Iwo Jima and Okinawa. In fact, he had already proposed going to Iwo in late January and to Okinawa on 1 March 1945. On 3 October 1944 the Joint Chiefs issued orders to MacArthur to assault Luzon on 20 December and ordered Nimitz to take Iwo Jima and Okinawa. With the order of 3 October, the question of intermediate objectives was settled. The questions of command and invasion were still outstanding.[12]

As the members of the Joint Chiefs began to think systematically about the final defeat of Japan, they ran head-on into the policy of unconditional surrender. The policy put them into a strategic box. Unconditional surrender had grown into an intimidating policy that military leaders could hardly question or challenge. Yet now the military implications of unconditional surrender could no longer be ignored. First, the members believed that the defeat of Japan had to come no later than twelve months after the defeat of Germany because of war weariness and resistance to the redeployment of troops from Europe to the Pacific. Such a timetable made defeat by blockade and air bombardment uncertain. On Luzon and Okinawa, Japanese commanders adopted a strategy of attrition. They withdrew into prepared defenses in key places and forced the Americans to root them out. High American casualty rates in both campaigns attested to the effectiveness of the enemy's new strategy. Invading the home islands promised to be as costly. That Japan could eventually be defeated was militarily certain; that the Japanese could be forced to accept unconditional surrender, a term they understood to mean national extinction, was problematic. Perhaps even invasion would fail to produce unconditional surrender. Thus, the military leaders began to have second thoughts about the wisdom of a policy that might sacrifice thousands of lives on the altar of semantics. Out of this realization came a lively three-way confrontation between the military leaders, the State Department, and the presidency over the possibility of ameliorating and explaining the policy of unconditional surrender.[13]

In truth, some highly placed people had reservations about the rigidity of the policy almost from the day it was announced. On the eve of D-Day, studies by the Joint Chiefs indicated that the German leaders were having considerable success stiffening the nation's will to fight by using the Allied demand for unconditional surrender. The Joint Chiefs sought to convince Roosevelt that it would make military sense to explain that unconditional surrender should be aimed solely at the Nazi leadership. Roosevelt flatly refused, stating firmly, "I am not willing at this time to say that we do not intend to destroy the German nation."[14]

In the spring of 1945, the necessity of making strategic decisions for the final defeat of Japan brought the issue of unconditional surrender to the front once more. Furthermore, the death of Roosevelt on 12 April removed the doctrine's most ardent defender. To be sure, President Truman inherited a commitment to the policy, but he had not participated in its formulation and presumably could examine the issue with a fresh eye. Secretary of War Stimson, long a doubter of the wisdom of the policy, was not averse to reopening the issue. He had a powerful ally in Under Secretary of State Joseph C. Grew, former ambassador to Japan. Grew's influence was critical, for most of the resistance to any softening of the policy came from the State Department.

In December 1944 General George Strong, a member of the Joint Postwar Committee, sent draft proposals of Japanese surrender documents over to the State Department. The Joint Postwar Committee was established by the Joint Chiefs in June 1944. The committee was charged with studying all "post-war military problems of interest to the Joint Chiefs of Staff."[15] The committee's proposals would allow the Japanese to retain the emperor and some civil government after the war but subordinated them to the occupying forces. At the insistence of the State Department, the proposals were modified to include absolute adherence to the doctrine of unconditional surrender.

As this attack on the policy was being thwarted, another desertion from the orthodoxy occurred. At Yalta, Churchill suggested some "mitigation" of the policy if it would bring the defeat of Japan sooner and at less cost.[16] With Churchill's opening and Secretary of War Stimson's tacit agreement, General Marshall delayed approving the harsh surrender policy forged by the State Department.[17] Yet unconditional surrender remained the chief Allied policy regarding the defeat of Japan, and the Joint Chiefs had to construct a military strategy that fulfilled the policy.

NOTES

1. Edward S. Miller, *War Plan Orange* (Annapolis: Naval Institute Press, 1991), 60–61.

2. Samuel Eliot Morison, *History of United States Naval Operations in World War II*, vol. 7, *Aleutians, Gilberts, and Marshalls, June 1942–April 1944* (Boston: Little, Brown, 1964), 85.

3. Maurice Matloff, *Strategic Planning for Coalition Warfare, 1943–44* (Washington, DC: GPO, 1959), 188.

4. Ibid., 193.

5. Henry G. Morgan, Jr. "Planning the Defeat of Japan: A Study of Total War Strategy" (Manuscript, U.S. Army Center of Military History, 1961), 98–99.

6. Grace P. Hayes, *The History of the Joint Chiefs of Staff in World War II: The War against Japan* (Annapolis: Naval Institute Press, 1982), 283; *FRUS: Conferences at Washington and Quebec, 1943* (Washington, DC: GPO, 1970), 93–94, 289–93, 289n.

7. *FRUS: Conferences at Washington and Quebec*, 987–88.

8. Hayes, 463; *FRUS: Conferences at Washington and Quebec*, 978.

9. *FRUS, Conferences at Washington and Quebec*, 976–77, 987–88.

10. Hayes, 466–67, 492.

11. *FRUS: Conferences at Cairo and Teheran* (Washington, DC: GPO,1961), 766.

12. For the best treatment of the Luzon-Formosa debate, see Robert Ross Smith, "Luzon versus Formosa," in *Command Decisions* (Washington, DC: GPO, 1960), 461–77.

13. The story of this conflict is told in great detail in Brian L. Villa, "The U.S. Army, Unconditional Surrender, and the Potsdam Proclamation," *Journal of American History* 63 (June 1976): 66–92.

14. Matloff, 430–31.

15. Ray S. Cline, *Washington Command Post: The Operations Division* (Washington, DC: GPO, 1951), 323–24.

16. *FRUS: Conferences at Malta and Yalta* (Washington, DC: GPO, 1955), 826.

17. Villa, 79–80.

Chapter 4

Blockade, Bombing, and Invasion

In the years between the world wars, planners had assumed that any future war against Japan in the Pacific would be almost wholly a naval war. The only role for the army would be static defense—to hold island bases in the Philippines and in the Western Pacific from which naval forces could operate. The war would be decided by grand battles between the warships of the two fleets. Once the Japanese Navy was destroyed or forced to retire and American naval supremacy was established in the waters around Japan, the enemy would be choked into submission by a naval blockade.

Such a scenario was sensible, for Japan was almost an Asian counterpart of Great Britain—industrialized but largely devoid of critical resources like oil and steel. Like Britain, Japan was an island nation with a growing empire tied together by long seaborne lines of communications over which came food and critical raw materials. These circumstances made Japan especially vulnerable to naval blockade, and during the first two years of the war, American strategists believed that Japan could be defeated by a combination of naval blockade and bombing. In fact, the various prewar versions of the navy's War Plan Orange had presumed the defeat of Japan through a strategy of blockade and bombing.[1] Certainly, in 1942 few could see far enough ahead to advocate an invasion of the home islands. After all, the great bulk of Japan's ground forces were deployed in the empire—in China, Southeast Asia, Korea, Formosa, and the South Pacific.

At the Casablanca Conference in January 1943, in their discussions of Pacific strategy, the combined chiefs had declared that the Allies could defeat Japan "by measures which greatly resemble those which would be effective against the British Isles—blockade . . . bombing . . . and assault." The last, they hoped, would prove unnecessary.[2]

Prewar planners believed that Japan could be defeated with naval blockade and air bombardment. But before this "Siege of Japan" could be undertaken, the Japanese fleet would have to be destroyed and a stepladder of bases seized leading to Japan. Only after the seizure of bases from which the U.S. Fleet could cut Japan's communications with the continent across the Sea of Japan could the siege be made complete. Navy strategists feared that naval blockade alone might prove indecisive, and beginning in the 1920s their plans for defeating Japan also included an intense campaign of strategic bombing. Even then, they admitted, such a strategy could take two or more years and might yield only a limited victory over Japan.[3]

Nonetheless, invasion as a means of defeating Japan was considered out of the question. Prewar army and navy planners alike pointed to the ferocity of the Japanese Army, the rugged terrain, the poor roads, the heavily defended ports, and the scarcity of good landing beaches as factors that should make invasion a strategy of last resort. If, however, invasion proved to be necessary, the planners saw southern Kyushu and Tokyo Bay as the most likely invasion sites.[4]

STRATEGY OF BLOCKADE AND BOMBARDMENT

In early 1944 one of the reasons King and others urged the invasion of Formosa was that Formosa's strategic geographic position would better support a strategy of blockade than would Luzon.[5] During the argument about a Formosan invasion, King had maintained that a blockade supplemented with air bombardment could force the Japanese to surrender and prevent the necessity for invasion. Leahy, chairman of the Joint Chiefs, admitted that the "strangulation of Japan by an effective sea and air blockade" would require more time, but he argued that such a course would be less costly in lives and material.[6]

Nevertheless, when the combined chiefs met in Quebec at the OCTAGON Conference in September 1944, they expanded the strategic goal in the war against Japan to include "invading and seizing objectives in the industrial heart of Japan." Two months later the U.S. Joint Chiefs tentatively approved a plan for the invasion of Kyushu with a target date of September 1945.[7]

Even while acquiescing in these decisions, neither King nor Leahy was agreeing that the invasion of Japan was inevitable. In fact, they argued almost to the end of the war in favor of securing more bases on the China coast, in Korea, and on islands near Japan to complete the blockade. Even at the end of the war, however, the blockade was not impenetrable. B-29s had strewn the harbors of western Japan with mines, and some submarines sneaked into the Sea of Japan through the Straits of Tsushima. Yet neither the Straits of Tsushima in the south nor the La Perouse Straits in the north had been breached by surface vessels.

By late 1944 several developments had brought into question ending the war by blockade. First, the Allies had not only to defeat Japan but also to force unconditional surrender. Could blockade alone produce that result? Second, at the QUADRANT Conference at Quebec in 1943, the combined chiefs had set the goal of defeating Japan within twelve months of the surrender of Germany. Blockade alone almost certainly would fail to meet that timetable. Third, large ground forces had built up in the Pacific in concert with naval and air power—forces that by 1944 had developed large-scale amphibious operations to a high art. Despite fanatical Japanese resistance, MacArthur's and Nimitz's amphibious force seemed invincible. To allow such a force to stand idle while the navy and the air force carried out protracted blockade and bombardment might have suited the soldiers and marines but could hardly be justified to the politicians and the people back home.

King agreed that planning the invasion was necessary, but he saw it only as contingency planning. Plans did not mean invasion. In fact, King was convinced that naval blockade and air bombardment would defeat Japan before an invasion could be launched. Even if Kyushu were invaded, King saw the assault as necessary only to gain more naval and air bases to tighten the blockade and intensify the bombing.

Japanese leaders feared a slow strangulation by blockade and bombing. Lieutenant Colonel Michinori Ureshino served as shipping staff officer at Imperial General Headquarters from August 1943 to the end of the war. Like many of his American enemies, he saw naval and air power as decisive in the defeat of Japan. By mid-1945 Colonel Ureshino feared that Japan was nearing complete paralysis of its seaborne shipping. The volume of tonnage transported declined from 1,180,000 tons in April 1945 to 800,000 tons in June. He estimated that tonnage would fall to two hundred thousand by September, and "by autumn Japan's shipping would be rendered immobile."[8]

Like the officers of the U.S. Navy, the airmen of the U.S. Army Air Corps (previously the Air Service and later the Army Air Forces) carried considerable doctrinal baggage as they entered World War II. Between the wars they had developed rather rigid and passionate ideas about the proper organization and use of airpower in future wars. Young officers of the Air Service emerged from World War I convinced that the future of warfare lay in the air, and their wartime leader, Brigadier General William Mitchell, set forth on a crusade for airpower so zealously and fervently that it cost him his career. Three causes, all set forth by Mitchell, determined and dominated air doctrine in the interwar years. Above all, air officers sought independence for air power and parity with the army and the navy. They chafed at the ground support mission, and they wanted recognition for an independent, war-winning role for airpower—strategic bombing. Finally, they wanted to develop a long-range heavy bomber to carry out that mission.[9]

The demands interlocked to form a doctrinal mosaic. Air power advocates were convinced that the ground support role was an incomplete use (if not a misuse) of airpower. If they could gain recognition for the war-winning potential of strategic bombing and develop a heavy bomber to carry such a strategy into effect, then they would have a role equal in importance to the army's mission of land war and the navy's role of sea war. They could then argue for parity with the two older services so that the nation's defense should rest on three equal forces—land power, sea power, and air power.[10]

But the Air Service was a part of the U.S. Army, and the new air doctrines ran head-on into an infantry-dominated army. Army staff officers looked on airmen as loosely disciplined upstarts whose performances in World War I had failed to live up to promises, whose sense of self importance was unwarranted, and whose claims for their weapons in future wars were vastly overrated.[11]

While Mitchell's views on air power changed during the 1920s, he came ultimately to advocate strategic bombing as the chief role for air power. He saw bombardment as so effective that it would subordinate, if not eliminate, the traditional roles of armies and navies. To ensure the best use of this devastating new weapon, airmen developed a number of principles. They advocated that the command of the strategic air force should be absolutely independent and that only air officers should command air units. Behind these demands were three beliefs. First, nonairmen would fail to understand the purposes and techniques of strategic airpower and would thus subordinate strategic air power to the ground support role. Second, to achieve maximum effect, strategic air power must be concentrated. Scattering airplanes over a wide area to perform a multitude of missions would diffuse the impact. Finally, in selecting strategic targets, the airmen must have absolute autonomy. Implicit in all these articles of faith was fear that the ground support role would subsume the strategic role of airpower—the role upon which the rationale for service independence rested.

Airmen, of course, failed to gain independence from the U.S. Army before World War II. Yet they had achieved considerable autonomy, and before the war ended, American air power in World War II, indeed, had become a mammoth force. Of the 8,248,780 soldiers in the U.S Army in May 1945, 2,316,059 (28 percent) were airmen. Army Ground Forces numbered 3,190,169. The remainder served in Army Service Forces.[12]

The desire to carry out a campaign of strategic bombing against the Japanese homeland drove much of Pacific strategy. The acrimony in China dividing General Joseph Stillwell from Chiang-Kai-Shek and Major

General Claire Chennault stemmed at least in part from their differing views over the role of strategic bombing. Chennault had convinced Chiang that the best use of the extremely limited supply lines into China would be to bring in fuel and bombs to supply strategic bombers operating against southern Japan from forward bases in China. Stillwell wanted to bring in materiel to equip Chinese ground forces. Chennault won the struggle when Stillwell was relieved, and by mid-1944 new B-29s under the Twentieth Bomber Command operated from bases in the Chengtu area of China. Yet the supply requirements so overwhelmed the carrying capacity that even this limited effort soon had to be abandoned.

When Admiral Nimitz argued in favor of moving in 1944 against the Marianas, he found ready allies among the proponents of strategic bombing who coveted Guam, Saipan, and Tinian for B-29 bases. For the same reason airmen had long favored giving priority in the Pacific to Nimitz's central Pacific drive over MacArthur's southwest Pacific drive. From the Marianas the new bombers could reach Tokyo and all of Japan's major industrial cities. The costly campaign for Iwo Jima in February 1945 came at the behest of the airmen. That small island lay halfway between the bases in the Marianas and Tokyo. Iwo Jima could provide the airmen with an advanced escort fighter base and an auxiliary field for crippled B-29s. Also, the Japanese would be denied an outpost that gave them early warning of oncoming raids.

While the origins of the strategic bombing campaign against Japan lay in China, its culmination came from bases in the Marianas. On 12 April 1944 the Joint Chiefs established the Twentieth Air Force. The new unit's mission was to carry forward the strategic bombardment of Japan with B-29s. To ensure absolute autonomy for this strategic air force, the Joint Chiefs retained direct control and named General Arnold commander. The Twentieth Air Force consisted of the XX and XXI Bomber Commands. The former, based in China, carried out its first mission against southern Japan on 15 June 1944. The latter, organized in Kansas in the spring of 1944, was ordered to the Marianas to begin operations in November. The XXI Bomber Command conducted the first B-29 raid against Tokyo on 24 November 1944.

By the beginning of 1945 it was obvious that the efforts of the XX Bomber Command from China were ineffective. China remained closed to Allied shipping because the Japanese controlled all ports in southeast Asia and eastern China. Moreover, the high Himalayas, called "the Hump" by U.S. transport pilots, lay between U.S. supply bases in India and the B-29 bases in western China. Bombs, fuel, and parts had to be flown in over the Hump; that effort absorbed more than 80 percent of the command's energy. Distances were too great to reach any but the south-ernmost Japanese cities, and the Chinese failed to keep the forward bases secure. In March 1945 the XX Bomber Command was dissolved and its bombers were ordered to the Marianas to join the XXI.

Meanwhile, the XXI faced formidable problems as well. Cloudy weather over Japan hampered operations. Although still not free of technical bugs, the B-29s were forced to bomb at the extreme end of their fifteen-hundred-mile range. Most disappointing of all, the techniques of precision daylight bombing proved to be very difficult, and bombing results came under criticism from the air staff in Washington. The pressure on the commander of the XXI, Brigadier General Haywood "Possum" Hansell, became intense. A pioneer advocate of precision bombing, Hansell either did not take the hints to change his bombing tactics or chose to ignore the pressure. In January 1945 Hansell was relieved and replaced by Brigadier General Curtis LeMay, who soon turned the B-29s to low-level incendiary attacks on Japanese cities at night. The initial 10 March 1945 raid on Tokyo burned out 15.8 square miles and killed almost eighty-five thousand people.[13] By mid-June major por-tions of Japan's six largest cities had been reduced to cinders; then the attackers turned on smaller cities. First priority went to cities with high "congestion and inflammability." In all, perhaps 174 square miles in 66 cities were burned out, and an estimated 330,000 Japanese were inciner-ated.[14]

The abandonment of precision daylight bombing after only three months of trial in favor of area incendiary attacks has been justified in several ways—Japanese industry was less concentrated than that in Ger-many; constant cloud cover made precision bombing difficult; the extreme range of Japan from the bases in the Marianas made high altitude daylight raids only marginally effective. Yet the factor of time may have been the most important consideration of all. If the strategic bombers hoped to prove the war-winning effect of their strategy, they had to do it quickly. The Joint Chiefs had set the target date for the defeat of Japan at twelve months after the defeat of Germany, and by January 1945 the collapse of Germany was clearly imminent. The invasion of Kyushu was tentatively targeted for the fall of 1945, and some enthusiastic airmen had promised that invasion would be unnecessary.

Meanwhile, over the protests of many senior airmen, the Twentieth Air Force reluctantly undertook a campaign of aerial mining that tightened the blockade of the home islands. To the bombers the mining campaign "looked like another diversion by a surface commander."[15] But to others, to the Japanese especially, it looked as threatening as the incendiary attacks.

The impetus for sowing mines in the strategic harbors and straits of Japan came from the navy. But that service lacked the necessary long-range aircraft. Neither General Hansell, then commander of the XXI Bomber Command, nor the Army Air Force staff back in Washington viewed aerial mining with much excitement. Bombing enthusiasts had just perfected the very-long-range B-29s and had just acquired the bases necessary to carry forward their long-held and single-minded devotion to winning the war against Japan with bombs. An untested strategy pressed by another service hardly excited them.

Yet the navy pressed its case to the air force, and General Arnold finally endorsed a scaled-down version of the navy's plan. Even then, as the official air force history notes, his chief motive may have been to prevent the navy from developing long-range planes of its own. Whatever Arnold's motives, orders went out; the bomber command in the Marianas should plan a mining campaign with the navy to begin in mid-March under the code name Starvation.[16]

General LeMay, who had recently succeeded General Hansell, directed the 313th Bombardment Wing to mine the Shimonoseki Straits, a narrow channel between Kyushu and Honshu that linked the Inland Sea with the Sea of Japan. By the beginning of 1945, Japan's shipping routes from the Pacific ports were broken. Most of the shipping had to enter ports on the Sea of Japan and the Inland Sea through the Tsushima and Shimonoseki straits. Thus, these narrow straits and the many harbors of western Japan became ripe and vulnerable targets.

The mining campaign, though begun on a small and tentative scale, surprised the Japanese and paid immediate dividends by immobilizing shipping in the mined channels and harbors. This modest, yet successful beginning in late March had to be curtailed when the bombers of the Twentieth Air Force were ordered to support the assault on Okinawa in April. But in May the mining effort was renewed and enlarged. During that month mines for the first time sank more Japanese shipping than did submarines.[17]

The campaign continued through June and July. Despite Japanese efforts to clear channels, by the beginning of August Japan's "shipping situation was hopeless," with ports abandoned and ships paralyzed. American planes, now based in Okinawa, could reach southern Korea, and in the final weeks of the war mining was also begun there.[18]

During the last months of the war, mines were the most destructive of all weapons against Japanese shipping. In less than five months B-29s flew

1,528 mining sorties and planted 12,053 mines. Of the shipping tonnage lost by the Japanese during this period, one-half was lost to mines. The remainder fell victim to submarines and land-based and carrier planes. Japanese ships that remained afloat were effectively immobilized. Japan faced imminent starvation for its industry and people.[19]

Arnold and other air force leaders denied that they advocated a discrete strategy of victory over Japan through strategic bombardment or that a plan ever existed to do so. Their simple mission, according to Arnold, was to destroy targets and wear down Japan's ability to continue the war. Neither was there overt cooperation between the air force and the navy, Arnold and King, to press for a strategy of blockade and bombing without invasion. Certainly the Joint Chiefs made no clear demarcations between strategies of blockade, bombing, and invasion, but instead saw each as part of a single overall strategy of progressive force. Blockade and bombing would be pressed until the end. The members of the Joint Chiefs hoped that Japan would surrender unconditionally before OLYMPIC. If not, the invasion of southern Kyushu would go forward. Kyushu would provide naval bases to further tighten the blockade and air bases to intensify the bombing. If Japan still resisted, then CORONET, the invasion of the Kanto Plain, would go forward.[20]

The official air force historians of World War II state that the air staff made its targeting criteria on the assumption that an invasion of the home islands would be necessary: "The lessons of the combined bomber offensive in Europe had had a sobering effect, and no person of authority in the AAF urged the probability of a victory by air power alone."[21] Nonetheless, the pressure on Arnold to prove the decisive nature of strategic bombing was intense, not only as a prerequisite for independence but also to justify the immense effort expended in manpower and money. Despite their hesitancy to publicly predict victory over Japan through strategic bombing, Arnold and his doctrinaire disciples hoped for time to prove their theories of precision bombing. The efforts of the strategic air forces in Europe had proved less than decisive, and Arnold, impatient and hard driving by nature, understood that the last chance to prove the devastating effect of strategic bombing would come in the air campaign against Japan.[22]

STRATEGY OF INVASION

As the debate over how best to defeat Japan gathered momentum, Admiral King and his navy planners pushed a Pacific strategy of bombardment and peripheral, encircling operations not unlike Churchill's European strategy of nibbling at the edges of Hitler's empire. General Marshall and his army planners, on the other hand, favored a direct thrust into the Japanese homeland.

In mid-1944 the Allies still operated with an overall strategic concept for the defeat of Japan that was more than a year old and that sanctioned invasion of the home islands only as a remote contingency—a last resort to be pursued only if blockade and bombardment failed to bring Japan to unconditional surrender. Marshall pressed for a more explicit strategic concept—one that met the question of invasion more forthrightly. The Joint Chiefs in July 1944 adopted the following statement:

> The overall objective in the war against Japan, to be brought about at the earliest possible date is:
> —Lowering Japanese ability and will to resist by establishing sea and air blockades, conducting intensive air bombardments, and destroying Japanese air and naval strength.
> —Invading and seizing objectives in the industrial heart of Japan.[23]

But the adoption of this statement hardly made an invasion inevitable. Assaulting the home islands still was only a contingency to be pursued if blockade and bombardment failed to convince the Japanese to surrender unconditionally.

As the fight for Okinawa opened on 1 April 1945, the members of the Joint Chiefs could dodge the question of invasion no longer. Before the struggle for the Japanese homeland could take place, a contest between army and navy—between Marshall and King—had to be decided in Washington. The conflict occurred in April and May 1945 and hinged on two questions—should the invasion of southern Kyushu be ordered for 1 November 1945, and, if so, who would command it?

On 3 April 1945 the Joint Chiefs forwarded a directive to Pacific commanders MacArthur and Nimitz ordering them to begin planning for OLYMPIC. But in their agreement to issue the planning directive, King and his navy strategists did not preclude the probability of further interim operations between Okinawa and southern Kyushu.[24]

Marshall favored a direct, massive invasion of southern Kyushu to be launched as soon as possible after securing Okinawa. Like Churchill in Europe, King favored the eventual invasion of Japan if necessary, but only after securing more bases from which to tighten the blockade and intensify the air bombardment. King favored a "round-the-Yellow-Sea" approach to Japan.

The first step in King's strategy of encirclement was to be Operation LONGTOM, the seizure of a lodgment on the Chusan-Ningpo archipelago near Shanghai. Next would come lodgments on the Shantung peninsula, Korea, and Quelpart and Tsushima Islands. These areas would furnish air and naval bases for further blockade and bombing. LONGTOM was not entirely a new plan, for planners in 1943 had mentioned the necessity of seizing bases near Japan before any invasion could take place. Nimitz, who was charged with planning LONGTOM, was finished with the plan by 18 April. Like King, Nimitz believed that a hasty invasion of Japan would produce unacceptable casualties and that Okinawa was too far from Kyushu to provide good fighter cover. Thus, he concluded, more encircling operations should be ordered—beginning with LONGTOM.[25]

On 28 March 1945 Deputy Chief of Staff General Thomas Handy wrote a lengthy memo to Marshall outlining his understanding of the navy's desires. The navy talked, he reported, of a "series of encircling operations including Ningpo-Chusan, Shantung Peninsula, possibly Korea, Quelpart Island and Tsushima Island." The navy contended, Handy noted, that further operations "beyond the Ryukyus" were necessary "to cut off Japan from the mainland." But Handy's main object was not merely to alert Marshall that the navy advocated further peripheral operations before undertaking OLYMPIC. His principal purpose was to furnish Marshall with ammunition to counter King's argument. Handy emphasized that the proposed "round-the-Yellow-Sea" approach would require as many forces as OLYMPIC and would cost as much, leaving the invasion of Japan still to be done. Furthermore, Handy argued, the areas under consideration (Ningpo-Chusan, Quelpart, Tsushima) were unsuitable for large naval and air bases.[26]

On 12 April Marshall radioed a message to MacArthur outlining the essentials of the debate. Marshall's summary of the issues was wonderfully lucid. "One school of thought," wrote Marshall, believed that "more preparation is necessary." Then he came to the heart of the "round-the-Yellow-Sea" strategy: "Hence, a campaign of air-sea blockade and bombardment should be adopted which involves a Chosan [operation] and perhaps others such as a lodgment on Shantung or Korea or the islands in the Tsushima [Strait] area." The arguments for such a strategy, Marshall reported to MacArthur, were "the high casualties incident to landings on Japan proper, the necessity for further beating down Japanese airpower, the cutting off of Japan from reinforcements moving from the mainland of Asia, and the possibility of bringing about surrender without a major landing on Japan proper."

The other view, Marshall continued, was to drive "straight into Japan proper as soon as the forces can be mounted from the Philippines and land-based air established in the Ryukyus." The pro-invasion group argued that Japanese air and sea power would be weak enough by the end of 1945 to allow invasion. Similarly, they argued that the Japanese would be unable to bring enough troops from the mainland of Asia to affect materially the balance of combat power. Besides, Marshall noted, "Russian entry into the war would be a prerequisite to a landing on the Japanese homeland by [December 1945]." Finally, those who favored invasion contended that a series of peripheral lodgments around the Yellow Sea would likely require as many troops and produce more casualties than would direct invasion. Marshall requested MacArthur's "thoughts on this problem for use within the next few days in possible discussions."[27]

MacArthur's reply read like the solution to a Command and General Staff College problem. He began by outlining three possible courses of action:

1. Encirclement of Japan to the west followed by invasion as suggested by the Navy.
2. Encirclement of Japan to the west followed by blockade and bombardment without invasion.
3. Attack Kyushu [Operation OLYMPIC] and install air forces to cover a decisive assault on Honshu [Operation CORONET].

Then he proceeded to analyze each. Encirclement followed by invasion would bring to bear more air power, cut off Japanese communications with the mainland, and allow Kyushu to be bypassed in favor of a direct assault on Honshu. But, MacArthur noted, a strategy of encirclement would "deploy our resources off the main axis of advance" without giving any better "short range air coverage" than was already available from Okinawa. Peripheral operations would tie up a great part of American resources in the Pacific so that Japan could be invaded only after redeployment from Europe. Lodgments on the China coast carried the danger of drawing American forces into "heavy involvement" on the Asian mainland and perhaps of postponing the invasion of Japan into 1947. Finally, MacArthur warned, a series of peripheral operations "prior to the delivery of the main attack would result in greater loss of life."

Bombing and blockade without invasion MacArthur found to be the least acceptable alternative. Such a strategy would "prolong the war indefinitely," and it assumed that the Japanese could be subdued by air power alone "in spite of its demonstrated failure in Europe."

Not surprisingly, MacArthur concluded that the invasion of Kyushu before the end of 1945 was the preferred course of action. It would "permit application of full power of our combined resources, ground, naval, and air, on the decisive objective." The longer the invasion was delayed, he warned, the more time the enemy had to strengthen defenses. Finally, combined assault might convince the Japanese to surrender earlier than anticipated.[28]

Although Marshall had not specifically requested Nimitz's thoughts on the matter, Nimitz, who had received an information copy of Marshall's message to MacArthur, volunteered his views. Nimitz, too, favored an invasion of Kyushu "at the earliest date" but warned that shipping, supplies, and bases were the most critical factors. "Until we are able to invade Japan with assurance of success," he advised, "we should continue to encircle and isolate by occupying positions which will cut off Japan from China and Korea and from which bombings of Japan can be intensified." Furthermore, Nimitz noted, a lodgment on the China coast would ensure Russia's entry into the war and open an all-season sea route to Russia.[29]

Meanwhile, the Joint Intelligence Staff weighed in with a paper entitled "Defeat of Japan by Blockade and Bombardment." The intelligence experts acknowledged that blockade and bombing would make the Japanese navy "impotent," would "virtually neutralize" Japan's air forces, would reduce its army's combat ability to "only a few months," and would break the will of the Japanese people to continue the war. But the nub of the question was—when? The intelligence staff observed, "Probably all will agree that such operations if kept up long enough would inevitably produce at some future date unconditional surrender of whatever might remain of Japan's economy and the Japanese people, but estimates with regard to the time element vary from a few months to a great many years." While the Japanese might accept "a rationalized version of unconditional surrender" before the end of 1945, in the absence of Allied clarification of the doctrine of unconditional surrender there was little likelihood "that unconditional surrender could be . . . forced upon the Japanese before the middle or latter part of 1946, if then, as a result of air-sea blockade and air attacks alone."[30]

Even as Marshall pressed for direct invasion of Japan, he was working with Stimson and Grew to find some means of ameliorating the policy of unconditional surrender and averting a costly assault on the Japanese homeland. Marshall ordered detailed studies by committees of the Joint Chiefs specifically addressing the *military* implications of unconditional surrender on the defeat of Japan.[31] The conclusions of the studies clearly supported backing away from an uncompromising adherence to the doctrine. The Joint Intelligence Staff (JIS) report began on a positive note—perhaps Japan would admit defeat as early as the fall of 1945. However, the Japanese almost certainly would not accept unconditional surrender; they could not even comprehend the term. Three major conclusions emerged from this report. First, the doctrine should be explained to the Japanese as meaning simply complete defeat, not national extinction. Second, the Japanese military and the people of Japan would accept only a surrender "with the authority and sanction of the emperor." Third, political stability in any occupation of Japan following surrender could be assured only if a Japanese government "was supported by the emperor as well as by Allied authority." Simultaneously, the JIS analyzed the defeat of Japan through naval blockade and air bombardment. Their conclusions were sobering. With rigid adherence to the policy of unconditional surrender, such a strategy could cause the war to last "a great many years." A "clarification" of unconditional surrender could produce surrender by late 1945 or early 1946. Yet the State Department continued to oppose any softening of the policy, and the Joint Chiefs were left with no practical alternatives to a strategy of invasion.[32]

As the "round-the-Yellow-Sea" and direct invasion advocates pressed their respective positions, another related argument surfaced—designating a commander for the invasion of Japan. From the earliest days of the Pacific war, the two services had been unable to agree on a supreme commander for the Pacific. Neither the navy nor the army would accept a supreme commander from the other service. Thus, the Joint Chiefs created a system of area commands. The two largest and most important were MacArthur's Southwest Pacific Area and Nimitz's Pacific Ocean Area. Each contained its own air, naval, and ground forces. As Nimitz's advance through the central Pacific and MacArthur's drive through New Guinea and the Philippines neared Japan, these area commands made less and less sense. Moreover, a combined assault on Japan would require much closer coordination and unity of command than had hitherto been necessary in the two far-flung operations.

On 3 April 1945 at the same time that the Joint Chiefs ordered the Pacific commanders to begin planning for the invasion, they issued a command directive ordering a major realignment of forces in preparation for the invasion. The Joint Chiefs retained the two major area commands, Southwest Pacific Area and Pacific Ocean Area, but they gave MacArthur the added title commander in chief, Army Forces Pacific (CINCAFPAC). Nimitz already held the counterpart navy title of commander in chief, Pacific Fleet (CINCPACFLT). The intent of the Joint Chiefs was to realign all army forces under MacArthur and all navy forces under Nimitz in preparation for the invasion. In fact, this realignment was achieved after considerable struggle. Following the previous pattern of establishing separate area commands in the Pacific, the navy wished to create still another area command for the invasion and designate a commander in chief, Japan (CINCJAPA). But Admiral King relented on this issue so that the planning directive for OLYMPIC would not be delayed. The command directive, designed to simplify, only gave rise to a new round of army-navy squabbling over prerogatives and turf.[33]

The new controversy over command produced a direct confrontation between Marshall and King. Before the conflict was finally compromised, memos filled the in-out boxes in the offices of the Joint Chiefs, staff officers debated how the word "coordinate" differed from "correlate," and, like two sovereigns, MacArthur and Nimitz met in Manila and produced agreements as detailed as treaties.

At issue was the precise wording for the missions to be assigned to Nimitz and MacArthur in the proposed OLYMPIC directive. Admiral King threw down the gauntlet in early April when he proposed a directive that would ensure a primary role for the navy in the invasion. King's draft emphasized blockade and bombardment followed by limited invasion. King's conception called for MacArthur's ground forces to secure naval and air bases and to deliver a coup de grace on the Tokyo plain if necessary. Nimitz was to "plan and prepare for the occupation of Southern Kyushu by amphibious operation, target date late 1945," while MacArthur was to "plan and prepare for the occupation of such positions in Kyushu as are necessary to the establishing of naval and air blockade of the Japanese homeland." Nimitz's other tasks were to seize a naval base in northwestern Kyushu, force open the Straits of Tsushima, and gain a beachhead on the Tokyo Plain. Meanwhile, MacArthur would be ordered to defend the naval and air bases established by Nimitz's forces and exploit the beachheads established by Nimitz.[34]

Not surprisingly, Marshall and MacArthur objected. Army planners preferred a directive that gave MacArthur primary responsibility for the Japanese campaign "including control of the amphibious assault through the appropriate naval commander." Army strategists called for Nimitz to make an amphibious plan "in conformity" with MacArthur's overall campaign plan. The navy, objecting to the subordination of Nimitz to MacArthur, offered the alternative phrase that Nimitz would "coordinate his plans" with MacArthur's. Navy strategists saw OLYMPIC in two distinct phases—the amphibious assault and the land campaign that would follow. Nimitz, they said, should plan and command the amphibious phase. The land campaign would be controlled by MacArthur. Army thinkers could see no such clear division. They conceived of OLYMPIC as one continuous operation; therefore, a single commander should plan and execute the entire operation.[35]

When King and Marshall reached an impasse in Washington, they presented the problem to the two Pacific commanders. When Nimitz and MacArthur met at Manila in mid-May, they had generally agreed on matters of tactics and strategy, and their draft plans for OLYMPIC proved to be very similar. Although they too failed to agree on command, they did agree to continue the development of two plans—one for naval and amphibious operations and another for the land campaign. "After very considerable frank discussion," Nimitz reported to King, "it was agreed that I will prepare and issue my plans as directed by JCS clearing with [MacArthur] the parts which affect his forces and that he will do likewise." Then he added revealingly, "The drafting of an overall campaign plan by MacArthur would prove tedious in the extreme and be mechanically difficult to keep up to date. It would further carry with it the *implication* of unity of command."[36]

Meanwhile, back in Washington, King, Marshall, and their staffs continued to search for a way to word the invasion directive that would satisfy the desires of both army and navy but not be so vague as to cause chaos in command. Marshall was adamant: the overriding purpose of OLYMPIC was the land campaign in Japan; therefore, the ground forces commander should have primary responsibility for the entire campaign. King agreed that the land campaign was paramount, but he viewed the naval and amphibious phases as almost separate operations that had to be commanded by an admiral.[37]

On 16 May King wrote a memo to Marshall indicating his concern that the "protracted discussions . . . regarding the wording of the directive" might delay the operation past the good weather of the fall season, and he suggested that the Joint Chiefs ignore any mention of command and simply order the invasion with a target date of 1 November 1945. Marshall refused to yield, and on 22 May he indicated in a memo to King that he considered the two of them in "complete disagreement" and suggested that the matter be brought before the Joint Chiefs "without further delay."[38]

At that point King yielded to new wording. MacArthur was to have "primary responsibility . . . including control, *in case of exigencies*, of the actual amphibious assault through the appropriate naval commander." Nimitz was charged with "the responsibility for the conduct of the naval and amphibious phases," and would "*correlate* his plans" with Mac-Arthur's. Furthermore, the directive noted that "the land campaign and requirements therefor are primary in the OLYMPIC operation. Account of this will be taken in the preparation, coordination, and execution of plans." The directive was approved and forwarded to the Pacific commanders on 25 May. Marshall's victory became complete on 27 May when the Joint Chiefs ordered Operation LONGTOM, the navy's lodgment on the China coast, indefinitely deferred.[39]

Even with these seemingly decisive developments, the issue was not completely settled. In June President Truman requested that the Joint Chiefs meet with him to review the plans for the invasion. In their meeting with the president at the White House on June 18, they presented a united front. Both King and Marshall argued for OLYMPIC as the only alternative. Even Leahy, who was most opposed to invasion, raised no objections in front of the president. The conference concluded when Truman told the Joint Chiefs to proceed with OLYMPIC. The president added only one proviso—that he be given another review before the operation began.[40]

Even then, all hoped that somehow the war could be ended short of invasion. Though the order had gone out and the president had approved it, the invasion still had an air of contingency about it. As General John E. Hull, Chief of the Operations Division, noted years afterwards, "History will show that we decided to invade Japan. As a matter of fact, there was no change in the basic philosophy of invading Japan *if necessary*."[41]

NOTES

1. Edward S. Miller, *War Plan Orange* (Annapolis: Naval Institute Press, 1991), 150.

2. Grace P. Hayes, *The History of the Joint Chiefs of Staff in World War II: The War against Japan* (Annapolis: Naval Institute Press, 1982), 299.

3. Ibid., 162–65.

4. Ibid., 165–66.

5. Ibid., 603–4.

6. Ibid., 603–4, 618–19.

7. Ibid., 627–28, 657.

8. Statements of Japanese Officials, document number 53013, "Statement Describing the Critical State of Japan's Sea Transportation around June 1945," 4:444. Compiled and translated by U.S. General Headquarters Far East Command, Military Intelligence Section, Historical Division. U.S. Army Military History Institute, Carlisle Barracks, PA.

9. Wesley F. Craven and James L. Cate, eds., *The Army Air Forces in World War II*, vol. 1, *Plans and Early Operations, January 1939 to August 1942* (Chicago: Univ. of Chicago Press, 1948), 17.

10. Ibid., 33.

11. Ibid., 21.

12. Strength Reports of the Army, 1 May 1945, copy in Center of Military History Library.

13. Wesley F. Craven and James L. Cate, eds., *The Pacific: Matterhorn to Nagasaki*, vol. 5, *June 1944 to August 1945* (Univ. of Chicago Press, 1953), 617.

14. Michael S. Sherry, *The Rise of American Air Power: The Creation of Armageddon* (New Haven: Yale Univ. Press, 1987), 258; Haywood S. Hansell, Jr., *Strategic Air War Against Japan* (Washington, DC: GPO, 1980), 72.

15. Hansell, Jr., 42.

16. Craven and Cate, *The Pacific*, 663–64.

17. Ibid., 668–70.

18. Ibid., 672.

19. Ibid., 674. 20. Sherry, 236–39.

21. Craven and Cate, *The Pacific*, 552.

22. Sherry, 258–60.

23. Strategic Plan for Operation DOWNFALL, RG 165, OPD 350.05, Sec. 1, Cases 1–45, NARA.

24. JCS 1259/4, "Command and Operational Directives for the Pacific," 3 April 1945, RG 165, ABC 381 Pacific Ocean Area (1–29–43), sec. 3, NARS.

25. Various messages in Nimitz Command Summary, Book 6 (1 January–1 July 1945), Navy Historical Center, Washington, DC.

26. Memorandum for the Chief of Staff, Sub: Ningpo-Chusan Operations, 28 March 1945, RG 165, OPD 381 TS, NARA.

27. Message, Marshall to MacArthur, Sub: Strategy in the Western Pacific, 12 April 1945, Historical Record Index Cards, GHQ SWPA, Washington National Records Center, Suitland, MD.

28. Message, MacArthur to Marshall, 20 April 1945, Historical Record Index Cards, GHQ SWPA, WNRC.

29. Message, Nimitz to MacArthur, 28 April 1945, Historical Record Index Cards, GHQ SWPA, WNRC.

30. Japan (6 April 1945) and JIS 141/3 (14 April 1945), RG 218, CCS 381, NARA.

31. Brian L. Villa, "The U.S. Army, Unconditional Surrender, and the Postsdam Proclamation," *Journal of American History* 63 (June 1976): 79–80.

32. Ibid., 81–83.

33. Memo, Lincoln to Hull, Sub: Report on Progress in Pacific, 12 March 1945, and JCS 1259/4, Command and Operational Directives for the Pacific, 3 April 1945, RG 165, ABC 381 Pacific Ocean Area (1–29–43), Sec. 3, NARA.

34. Draft Directive for Occupation of Southern Kyushu (11 April 1945), NHC.

35. Messages, Marshall to MacArthur, 19 May 1945; MacArthur to Marshall, 21 May 1945, RG 165, ABC 384, Kyushu (4 July 1944), Sec. 1-B, NARA.

36. Message, Nimitz to King, 17 May 1945, Box 166, 0–17, Operations in Southern Kyushu 6/45–10/45, NHC.

37. Various memos, 1–19 May 1945, RG 165, OPD 381 TS, NARA; Hayes, 704–6.

38. Memos, King to Marshall, 16 May 1945; Marshall to King, 17 May 1945 and 22 May 1945, RG 165, OPD 381 TS, NARA; Hayes, 704–6.

39. Olympic Directive, Kyushu, Sec. 1-B (4 July 1944), RG 165, ABC 384, NARA; Nimitz Command Summary, Book 6, 1 Jan–1 Jul 1945, NHC.

40. Minutes of JCS Meeting with President Truman on 18 July 1945, RG 218, CCS 334 (JCS Meetings 106–94), NARA.

41. John E. Hull Papers, U.S. Army Military History Institute Research Collection, Carlisle Barracks, PA.

Chapter 5

U.S. Redeployment to the Pacific

Four days after D-Day Army Chief of Staff George Marshall stood on the beach at Normandy talking with First Army Commander Omar Bradley. The subject of redeployment arose when Bradley asked Marshall for a job in the Pacific once the European war had ended. A few days later George Patton made a similar request; he would accept any command in the Pacific down to a division for a chance to fight the Japanese.[1] These were the sentiments of the generals, not of the average soldier. For them, the joy of finishing the war in Europe would be haunted by the fear of redeployment to the Pacific.

The task of redeploying one million troops from Europe to the Pacific was immense and complex, and some highly emotional nonmilitary considerations had to be carefully balanced with urgent military needs for finishing the war. How could veterans be selected for demobilization with equity and fairness? How could troop unit cohesion and efficiency be maintained if the most experienced veterans were discharged? How should units be selected for redeployment, and how could morale be maintained in those units? How could the occupation needs for Europe be balanced with the need for a strategic reserve in the United States and the requirements of the Pacific war? Which units would be redeployed directly from Europe to the Pacific; which would be redeployed through the United States? How would units selected for redeployment be re-trained and reequipped? Where could planners find shipping to carry out this redeployment, history's largest military movement in so short a time, while simultaneously preparing for the greatest amphibious invasion in history?

The need for a massive redeployment of forces from Europe to the Pacific after the defeat of Germany had been generally considered from the time large American forces were committed to the European war. But a number of critical unknowns plagued the members of the Joint Chiefs. The unpredictable date of VE-Day, the status of the war in the Pacific at the time of German surrender, the kinds of units likely to be needed in the Pacific, and the role of Britain in the Pacific war were all unknown. Shipping shortages, meager port and rail facilities on the West Coast, and insufficient service troops to build new bases for the redeployed units added to the concerns.

Redeployment of forces from Europe to the Pacific following the defeat of Germany had to be delicately balanced with the beginnings of demobilization in the Pacific. Even before the defeat of Germany, military planners knew they would face heavy public and political pressure to "bring the boys home." The Joint Chiefs had implicitly recognized the impatience and increasing war weariness of the American people when they insisted that the Pacific war had to end no later than twelve months after VE-Day. The determination to conduct a mini-demobilization of long-service veterans immediately following the surrender of Germany complicated and confused the planning for redeployment more than any other single consideration.

A number of factors, some old and some new, pointed toward the possibility of major logistical problems in the final assault on Japan. Immense distances, scattered operations, and lack of established base and port facilities had plagued Pacific operations since the first American offensives and had placed a high premium on construction and supply units.

By late 1944 both Nimitz and MacArthur had run far ahead of their bases and depots in Hawaii, the Marshalls, the Gilberts, New Guinea, and Australia. Both Nimitz's and MacArthur's commands needed desperately to "roll-up" their rear areas and establish bases, ports, and depots further forward. Such a policy would have obviated the continuing necessity for adding to already overstretched lines of communications and would have positioned staging areas and depots in the Philippines and Marianas for the final assault on Japan.[2]

The effort proved disappointing. Rolling up the rear areas was difficult and proceeded slowly. The plan called for closing out rear bases and bringing stocks and personnel forward while simultaneously building new bases, ports, and staging areas in the Philippines, the Marianas, and the Ryukyus. To add to the problem, the campaigns for Luzon and Okinawa still raged. The plan proved to be too ambitious, and the roll-up was still not completed at the end of the war. Philippine port capacities and staging areas also remained uncompleted. Consequently, plans for OLYMPIC, the invasion of southern Kyushu, called for some divisions to be mounted in Hawaii and for troops ashore to be supplied from ships loaded far to the rear and sent forward to the beaches as needed—almost five hundred floating depots.[3]

The problems of the roll-up emphasized the need for early redeployment of service forces from Europe, and the point was underlined by the anticipated direct and immediate redeployment from Europe of almost all the air groups based there. Heavy bombardment groups were scheduled to arrive by air soon after the German surrender, and fighter groups would come on ships with their planes lashed to the decks. Bases did not yet exist. In the redeployment of air and service forces, time was dear. Thus, only those air and service forces that needed retraining and reequipping would be redeployed through the United States All others would go directly from Europe to the Pacific.

Though the need for service troops, especially engineers, was immense, all of the fighting divisions scheduled for OLYMPIC were already on hand in the Pacific. Redeployed combat units would not be needed until CORONET, the invasion of the Tokyo Plain, in March 1946. All ground combat forces scheduled for redeployment would travel to the United States for leave, retraining, and reequipping before proceeding to the Pacific. The decision to redeploy ground combat units through the United States was justified by shipping and retraining considerations, yet the implications on morale and public opinion were extremely important to the decision makers. Army Service Forces Commander General Brehon B. Somervell opposed redeploying units through the United States because of the added burdens on an already overloaded logistical system. He pointed out especially the duplication of shipping requirements in the Atlantic and the Pacific, the overburdening of American railroads, and the likely congestion of West Coast ports. He was overruled by Marshall and Secretary of War Stimson, who were convinced that considerations of morale overrode the additional logistical strain.[4]

The initial War Department plan for demobilization was presented to the public on 6 September 1944, and it contained a fundamental decision that was destined to dominate redeployment and demobilization. The rapid and largely unplanned demobilization after World War I had been accomplished very quickly by deactivating entire units. World War II planners rejected that precedent. Following the defeat of Germany, the planners would not face a general demobilization of the troops—only the discharge of about two million soldiers who would not be needed in the war against Japan. "The simplest plan of demobilization," noted the planners, "would have been to return . . . surplus units to this country and discharge their personnel intact." But unit demobilization, the planners observed, would prove vastly inequitable. In combat-weary units selected for demobilization, recent replacements would be mustered out alongside old veterans. Conversely, men with long records in combat could be retained merely because they happened to be in units not selected for demobilization. To ensure fairness, they instead chose a plan of individual demobilization based on a point system that was designed to favor soldiers with long overseas service in combat.[5]

On 10 May 1945 Stimson, assisted by the chief War Department demobilization planner, Major General William F. Tompkins, held a press conference to announce the point system and to explain how these would be calculated. One point was given for every month of service, and an additional point was awarded for each month of overseas service. Each battle star or decoration earned five points, and twelve points were given for every child in the soldier's immediate family, to a maximum of three. Point values were calculated immediately after VE-Day. Not only would high-point men from Europe be released from service, but veterans of the Pacific war would be brought home for demobilization as soon as replacements arrived in that theater. Of the two million soldiers to be demobilized in the twelve months following VE-Day, 50 percent were in Europe, 33 percent in the Pacific, and 17 percent were veterans who had already been returned to the United States but had not yet been released from service.[6]

The accumulation of high points, however, furnished no absolute guarantee of release. Those with essential skills and those in units that would be redeployed immediately to the Pacific would not be discharged. General Tompkins made a critical point. "Because of the requirements of the war against Japan," he said, "the initial rate of release will be more rapid among ground troops than among those assigned to Air Forces or Service Forces."[7]

Shortly before VE-Day, General Marshall asked General Dwight D. Eisenhower, supreme Allied commander in Europe, to plan for the immediate return of high-point veterans to the United States following Germany's surrender. Unless the demobilization of veteran combat soldiers was handled properly and quickly, Marshall warned, adverse public opinion and low troop morale might force "measures that will interfere with redeployment and result in the prolongation of the Japanese war." He went on to suggest that the "first . . . men to be demobilized should be drawn from combat troops . . . deepest in Germany," and, if necessary to speed up the process, they should be flown to ports of embarkation. Eisenhower agreed with this point. "The soldier must be convinced that the system is fair and impartial," he noted. Perceptions of slowness or favoritism would inevitably lower morale. Eisenhower's staff planned briefings to all soldiers on the continuing necessity for defeating Japan, and radio, motion pictures, and military newspapers were used to combat rumors.[8]

Efforts to combat rumors and to prepare troop morale for redeployment began in 1944. General Marshall and General Tompkins asked famed film director Frank Capra, then a colonel in the Signal Corps, to justify redeployment in a film to be called "Two Down and One to Go." Stimson, Marshall, and Arnold all appeared in the film and explained that while two of the Axis powers had been defeated, the war was not yet over—for Japan still fought on. The film's tone was businesslike and unemotional, simply conveying the message that while much tough fighting remained, Allied victory was certain. The sooner the job was finished, the sooner the soldiers would go home. Marshall ordered that the film be shown to all troops immediately following VE-Day, and he wrote a personal letter to all major commanders explaining its importance. He even ordered special planes to get prints quickly to isolated garrisons. Within four weeks after Germany's surrender, 83 percent of all soldiers had seen it; more than nine out of ten were favorably impressed.[9]

War Department demobilization and redeployment plans called for sorting all units in the army into four categories:

Category I   units to be retained in their current commands
Category II   units to be redeployed
Category III units to be reorganized, retrained, or redesignated before being placed in categories I or II
Category IV   units to be inactivated

The War Department supplied major commanders with the number and types of units required in each category. The task of placing specific units within the categories fell upon the theater or other major commanders. Eisenhower, from whose command most of the category II and IV units would come, adopted a simple formula: those units with the highest percentage of low-point soldiers went into category II for redeployment; units with the greatest percentage of high-point veterans became category IV and were scheduled for inactivation; units with the highest percentage of personnel in the middle range went into categories I or III. Some air and service units, however, had to be shipped out to the Pacific before scores could be compiled. Those units were selected by the simple criterion of length of overseas service.[10]

How to readjust personnel in units was perhaps the most critical and confusing of all the redeployment policies. At the end of the fighting in Europe, combat units were mixtures of old veterans and young replacements. The fundamental aim was to move all soldiers who were ineligible for discharge into categories I, II, and III units, and all who were eligible for separation into category IV units. The point system had been announced before VE-Day, but point values were only announced afterwards. On 12 May, declared "R-Day," every soldier totaled his points on an Adjusted Service Rating (ASR) card. Soldiers had to amass eighty-five points to be eligible for separation. Those with fewer points were automatically classified as essentials and were ineligible for discharge.

Then began the great exchange. "Personnel readjustment" was the swapping among units of high-point and low-point soldiers. Units scheduled for redeployment gave high-point veterans to units scheduled for deactivation. Low-point soldiers in units scheduled for deactivation were reassigned to units that had been selected for redeployment. The numbers were hardly insignificant. The 28th Infantry Division was selected for redeployment, and its enlisted men had a 20 percent turnover in a single week. The turnover among officers in the same division was 46 percent in forty days. When the 5th Infantry, a division that had fought from Normandy into Germany and suffered heavy casualties, was selected for redeployment, six thousand high-point veterans were stripped from the division overnight; two thousand were returned home for discharge, and the remainder went to the 103d Infantry, a division scheduled for early deactivation.[11]

This readjustment of personnel from the European and Mediterranean theaters proved to be perhaps the most difficult and problem-filled phase of redeployment. It almost guaranteed that unit cohesion, efficiency, and esprit would break down. The administrative problems involved in making these gigantic personnel shifts in such a short time were all but overwhelming. The plans allotted thirty days for readjustment. Almost all readjustment was supposed to be done within major commands before the units moved toward assembly areas and ports of embarkation; only a few individual cases would remain to be handled in the assembly areas or in the United States.[12]

The process never worked that neatly. Units often received movement orders before completing readjustment, or a unit's battle credits might be readjusted, thus changing point totals for unit members. The 2d Infantry Division, selected for redeployment, had just succeeded in replacing all men who were eligible for separation. Just before embarking from Europe the division was awarded two additional campaign credits, making twenty-seven hundred more men eligible.[13]

Powerhouse and marine engineers, translators and interpreters (Asiatic languages), orthopedic and radar mechanics, and a number of other critical specialists were retained regardless of their points. Rumors circulated that the critical score of eighty-five points would soon be lowered by the War Department. Eisenhower's headquarters credited these rumors enough to operate for a time on a working critical score of seventy-five points. In short, the shuffling of personnel among units became a continuous process occurring all through the transportation pipeline—from unit location to assembly area to port of embarkation and even to the United States. Readjustment became a great ragged-running administrative engine that kept redeploying units in a constant state of personnel change and administrative turmoil.[14]

No redeployed divisions would be used in OLYMPIC, and the Army Forces Pacific staff study for CORONET, published on the last day of the war, listed fifteen redeployed divisions, two armored and thirteen infantry, for that operation. They were the 13th and 20th Armored Divisions and the 2d, 4th, 5th, 8th, 28th, 35th, 44th, 86th, 87th, 91st, 95th, 97th, and 104th Infantry Divisions. Except for the 91st Infantry Division, which had fought in Italy in the Mediterranean, all had been in the European theater.

No redeployed divisions were to be in the assault phase for CORONET. All U.S. armored divisions had been deployed in North Africa, the Mediterranean, and Europe; because of the amphibious island-hopping in the Pacific War, no armored divisions were assigned there. The two redeployed armored divisions, the 13th and the 20th, were formed into the XIII Corps to be committed on Y-Day-plus-ten. The 97th Infantry Division would serve as a floating reserve on Y-Day. Six of the redeployed infantry divisions would be grouped into two corps—one corps to reinforce each field army on Y-Day-plus-thirty. The 4th, 8th, and 87th divisions would reinforce the Eighth Army, and the 5th, 44th, and 86th would reinforce the First Army. Another corps formed of the 2d, 28th, and 35th infantry divisions would make up the AFPAC reserve. The 91st, 95th, and 104th would form a strategic reserve in the Philippine Islands. Two of the infantry divisions, the 86th and the 97th, had originally been scheduled for the Pacific theater when the Battle of the Bulge forced their diversion to Europe. They were the only divisions to actually be redeployed. The 86th arrived in the Philippines on 7 September 1945, and the 97th arrived in Japan on 24 September 1945.

The turmoil of readjustment had produced divisions filled with green troops who had never worked as a team. Also, the character of fighting in the Pacific differed from that in Europe. Fighting the Germans had been open and fluid, with great emphasis on armored, mechanized tactics; fighting the Japanese, particularly in the last campaigns of the war, required close work by small teams of infantrymen to reduce caves and bunkers that were impervious to artillery and manned by suicidal defenders. Consequently, retraining was essential.

Divisions selected for redeployment were supposed to begin training for the Pacific even before leaving Europe. Army Ground Forces developed a training program, which Eisenhower's headquarters had approved in May 1945. It included eight weeks of training after readjustment and before the move to the United States. But readjustment became a continuing process—occupation duties interfered, schedules to the United States were speeded up, training facilities were scarce, and poor coordination plagued the relations between Army Ground Forces in Washington and Eisenhower's headquarters. Thus, little training was accomplished in Europe.[15]

All redeploying divisions were supposed to undergo a formal eight-week cycle of training in the United States. They would bring with them from Europe only "minimum essential equipment." Full allocations of combat-ready equipment would be placed at the training sites so that when the members of the units reassembled from their thirty-day furloughs, they could immediately begin training. Training would emphasize the destruction of log and earth fortifications by small teams working with flame throwers and tank dozers. Soldiers would also learn about Japanese tactics and equipment, chemical warfare, and small unit tactics.[16]

But, training fell far short of expectations. Schedule changes and continuing personnel readjustments played havoc with plans. Units arrived in the United States before their equipment could be placed at the training sites. The 13th and 20th Armored Divisions were scheduled to train at Camp Polk, Louisiana, and Fort Benning, Georgia. Procedures were begun to place equipment for an armored division at each site. Suddenly, both divisions were rerouted to Camp Cooke, California, where they received amphibious training. In addition, schedules for shipment to the Pacific were accelerated. The first two infantry divisions to return to the United States, the 86th and the 97th, were due in the Pacific so early that they would have had no time for training in the United States The 13th Armored would have been sent to the Pacific with only nine days of training; the 20th Armored would have had only twenty days of training. The Army Ground Forces historian who studied redeployment training remarked, "The course of events during the months before August 1945 had been such as to make the prospects of redeployment training unfavorable in the extreme."[17]

The first to arrive in the United States was the 86th Infantry Division on 26 June 1945. The men were given the mandatory thirty-day leave and ordered to report to Camp Gruber, Oklahoma, on 22 July for eight weeks of training for the Pacific. Two weeks later, on 7 August, the division received orders to move to the West Coast; along with the 97th Infantry Division, they would be deployed to the Pacific immediately. By then, according to the division historian, morale had dropped "immeasurably low." The division received the news of Japan's surrender while at sea on the way to Luzon.[18]

The 95th Infantry Division came home on 29 June 1945. They had arrived in France on 15 September 1944 and entered combat in October. The division had credit for all European campaigns except Normandy, but casualties, compared to those of some other divisions, were moderate. The division was scheduled to train at Camp Shelby, Mississippi, before going to the Philippines to become part of the AFPAC strategic reserve for CORONET. "After the Division's arrival in the U.S.," wrote Major General Harry L. Twaddle, the division commander, "there was a continuing and growing opposition to being ordered to the Pacific. A very disturbing situation arose approaching open sedition and mutiny." Some veterans in the division took the position that they had done their fighting in Europe; they should be discharged, and the Pacific fighting should be done by those who had not yet been overseas. In General Twaddle's opinion, the situation was "attributable directly to the system of demobilization by individuals."[19]

Redeployment presented no great problems for the U.S. Navy. The vast majority of the fleet was in the Pacific already. Throughout the war, except for the efforts to eliminate the U-boat threat, the British Royal Navy had borne the burden of the naval effort in the Atlantic and the Mediterranean. Nonetheless, naval headquarters in Europe and the Mediterranean began shutting down immediately after VE-Day.

For the Army Air Forces, redeployment posed greater problems than for the Army Ground Forces. Unlike Army Ground Forces and Army Service Forces, early planning in the Army Air Forces called for no demobilization of personnel or inactivation of units following the defeat of Germany. Except for a few groups that would remain in Europe with the occupation forces, all other air units in the European and Mediterranean theaters would be redeployed directly to the Pacific.[20]

The War Department plan calling for the early discharge of high-point personnel forced the air forces to abandon their early position that demobilization of personnel could come only after the defeat of Japan. Even though the plan was applied to enlisted personnel, the air leaders fought efforts to apply the same criteria for discharge to officers. They preferred instead to separate officers on the criteria of efficiency and effectiveness—to keep the good officers and to weed out those with low efficiency ratings. The War Department overruled the air staff and ordered that high points for officers be used along with effectiveness and military necessity.[21]

In fact, Army Air Forces (AAF) Commanding General "Hap" Arnold and his air staff had already foreseen a disastrous decline in morale once it became clear that unlike Army Ground Forces personnel, airmen would not be redeployed through the United States Arnold proposed, therefore, to discharge airmen in the same proportions as the Army Ground Forces and Army Service Forces. He would get replacements from new inductees and from Army Ground Forces and Army Service Forces soldiers who were not eligible for separation but whose units were being inactivated. He hoped that promises of early rotation from the Pacific and early discharge would arrest any decline in morale.[22]

Redeployment in the AAF, according to one unit historian, was characterized by "utter confusion, pervading all echelons of command." He blamed the War Department, the air staff, and the AAF headquarters "from theaters and air forces on down." Like their compatriots in the ground forces, the airmen were forced to yield to fears of low morale and adverse public opinion. Original plans had called for direct redeployment of air units from Europe and the Mediterranean. In late 1944 plans were changed to allow most units to redeploy through the United States and to receive leave en route. Originally the air forces had hoped to maintain unit integrity by keeping separations to a minimum and by keeping down the number of personnel "readjustments." In early 1945 the AAF abandoned those goals and moved instead toward the same kind of massive high- and low-point personnel exchanges that would soon hamper the Army Ground Forces.[23]

Like the planners in the Army Ground Forces, the AAF planners had laid out a logical and effective scheme for redeployment. They even created a new command to direct it—the Continental Air Forces. Again, redeployment of the air forces, like that of the ground forces, broke down in the execution. Most personnel readjustments were supposed to take place in the local commands overseas. Once these personnel shifts of high- and low-point people were done, according to the plan, the units would proceed to the United States They would be received at an initial processing station, and within forty-eight hours would be on trains going home for leave. At the end of thirty days, the units would reassemble at central assembly stations where they would complete their personnel readjustments, be given refresher training, and start toward the Pacific.[24]

Readjustment of personnel and redeployment by the AAF proved to be as chaotic as that of the ground forces and for some of the same reasons. Most units failed to complete readjustment before leaving their overseas bases. After arriving in the United States, the troops immediately went on leave, and they later faced massive turnovers in personnel once the unit reassembled for training. Readjustments continued in training. Often replacements had no training in the slots they were supposed to fill. Unit commanders who had been told months earlier to prepare to retrain for a specific mission were suddenly directed to retrain for an entirely different mission. Processing dragged on. Uncertainty was compounded by changing and conflicting directives from higher headquarters.

The members of the 489th Heavy Bombardment Group arrived at Bradley Field, Connecticut, after their leave and prepared to receive some refresher training and fly away in new B-24s. They found, instead, that they would be retrained in B-29s and that training would take an additional five months. The 319th Medium Bombardment Group was based on Corsica when its commander received three days notice to be at a port of embarkation in Italy. After home leave, the unit members reported to Columbia, South Carolina, Army Air Base. The unit had been in combat from November 1942 to December 1944. Morale sagged after members were informed that the unit would be redeployed to the Pacific. The commander had anticipated a 20 percent turnover in personnel from readjustment. In fact, the turnover rate was 76 percent. Many of the airmen had to be replaced when it was found that they were unqualified for their jobs. Because of incomplete personnel records, some unit members who were two-year veterans in the Mediterranean were forced to undergo basic training.[25]

The demobilization of high-point veterans after VE-Day produced chaos in the European and Mediterranean units. Trained, experienced veterans were replaced overnight with green soldiers. The turnover produced by readjustment continued until the end of the war—while morale plummeted. Redeployed units filled with large numbers of fresh replacements arrived in the Pacific without the intensive training that produces unit efficiency, morale, and esprit. Far more service units than combat units were scheduled for OLYMPIC, and all of the redeployed combat units scheduled for CORONET were put in follow-up echelons. Yet old Pacific units were also adversely affected by readjustment. The demobilization of high-point men gutted European units of veteran NCOs and officers; it had a similar effect on units in the Pacific. As the Sixth Army prepared for the invasion of Japan, it was threatened with the loss of twenty-three thousand veteran enlisted men and twenty-one thousand officers. This exodus would come with many Sixth Army units already understrength with combat officers in chronic short supply. So bad was the situation that MacArthur considered deactivating a division and using its members as replacements. The situation improved somewhat, however, as the European war wound down and more replacements began to reach the Pacific.[26]

After VJ-Day a key staff officer in the G-3 section of Headquarters, Army Ground forces remarked, "The capitulation of Hirohito saved our necks. . . . It would have been absolutely impossible for us to have sent well-trained teams to the Pacific for participation in the scheduled invasion of Japan."[27]

Japanese leaders planned to defend the homeland mainly with green, newly raised ground forces. In the invasion of Japan they would have faced American assault forces almost equally untested.

NOTES

1. Message, Marshall to MacArthur, 6 April 1945, RG 4, USAFPAC correspondence, folder 3, MacArthur Archives, Norfolk, VA.

2. Robert W. Coakley and Richard M. Leighton, *Global Logistics and Strategy, 1943–1945* (Washington, DC: GPO, 1968), 565, 568–69.

3. Ibid., 617–20.

4. John D. Millett, *The Organization and Role of the Army Service Forces* (Washington, DC: GPO, 1954), 89.

5. "War Department Demobilization Plan after the Defeat of Germany," in John C. Sparrow, *History of Personnel Demobilization in the United States Army*, DA Pamphlet 20–210 (Department of the Army, July 1952), 302–5.

6. Ibid., 308, 312–13.

7. Ibid., 313–14.

8. Mildred V. Hester, "Redeployment," Occupation Forces in Europe Series, 1945–1946 (Manuscript, Office of the Chief Historian, European Command, U.S. Army Center of Military History), 36–37.

9. Sparrow, 121.

10. Hester, 11, 22–23, 41–42.

11. Sparrow, 312–14; Hester, 11, 40–41.

12. Robert R. Palmer, Bell I. Wiley, and William R. Keast, *The Procurement and Training of Ground Combat Troops* (Washington, DC: GPO, 1948), 638; *The Fifth Infantry Division in the ETO*, 1945, Center of Military History Library.

13. Hester, 42–45

14. Palmer, Wiley, and Keast, 638–39.

15. Hester, 50–52.

16. Palmer, Wiley, and Keast, 641–43.

17. Ibid., 626–27, 644; Bell I. Wiley, *Redeployment Training*, Army Ground Forces Study No. 38, 1946, 2–3, Center of Military History Library.

18. Palmer, Wiley, and Keast, 644, 646–47.

19. Richard A. Briggs, *Black Hawks over the Danube: The History of the 86th Infantry Division in World War II* (West Point, KY: Richard A. Briggs, 1953), 102–4.

20. Sparrow, 138n.

21. Chauncey E. Saunders, "Redeployment and Demobilization," USAF Historical Study No. 77, USAF Historical Division, 1953, 6, Air Force Historical Center, Bolling Air Force Base, Washington, DC.

22. Ibid., 15.

23. Ibid., 16.

24. Ibid., 22, 24–25.

25. Ibid., 27–28.

26. Ibid., 31, 34–37. 27.

27. *Reports of General MacArthur*, vol. 1, *The Campaigns of MacArthur in the Pacific* (Washington, DC: GPO, 1966), 393–94.

28. Wiley, 10.

Chapter 6

Casualties

Since 1943 Japanese aircraft and pilots had been outclassed by the Americans, and U.S. submarines and aircraft dominated the shipping lanes. Japan had lost air superiority and the ability to supply or reinforce overseas Japanese armies. Almost all of Japan's remaining naval strength was destroyed in October 1944 at the Battle of Leyte Gulf. Yet despite Japan's military weakness and overpowering U.S. strength, the last and largest campaigns of Luzon and Okinawa proved to be the most costly of the Pacific War.

General Yamashita Tomoyuki organized a new Japanese strategy for the defense of Luzon. He expected that the invasion was coming, and he knew that the Americans would land at Lingayen Gulf and proceed down the great central valley of Luzon toward Manila. Even so, he had to construct a strategy based on weakness. Short of food and equipment, with little mobility and no air or naval strength, Yamashita had to defend a large land area against an American enemy superior in every way. He could count on no help once the invasion began. He had to fight with whatever troops, supplies, and equipment he had on hand.

He chose a strategy of attrition. He placed his troops in prepared defenses on the high ground on either side of the central valley that formed a natural avenue from Lingayen southeastward toward Manila. He planned to dominate strategic spots—airfields, roads, key terrain—that he knew the Americans had to have. From fortified places, he would neutralize the enemy's superior mobility and air power and force the Americans into a slow, slogging, and costly battle of attrition.

This new defensive strategy, when combined with suicide air attacks against the invasion fleet, produced a new and very costly kind of warfare. The Japanese had first used kamikazes at Leyte. The tactic proved effective, and before the invasion of Luzon, the Japanese prepared to use the new "special attack" units on a grander scale. They devoted more aircraft to the effort, and they improved pilot skills and tactics. The destructive result became apparent on 3 January 1945 as the advance elements of minesweepers, escort carriers, and gunfire support ships began to move toward Lingayen Gulf. On 4 January a kamikaze sank an escort carrier, the *Ommaney Bay*. On 5 January the attacks intensified and produced more damage. Two escort carriers, two cruisers, two destroyers,

74

and four smaller vessels were hit and heavily damaged. In only two days kamikazes accounted for 160 dead and 190 wounded. The damage on 6 January was still worse. Kamikazes hit two battleships, four cruisers, seven destroyers, and several smaller vessels. An additional 170 men were killed and 500 wounded.

The Japanese had transformed a desperate tactic into a devastating weapon. By flying at very low levels and maneuvering violently, kamikaze pilots avoided radar detection and neutralized American advantages in gunfire and pursuit. The kamikazes proved so effective and so destructive that Admiral Jesse B. Oldendorf, commanding the gunfire support group, considered retiring from Lingayen Gulf. From 13 December 1944 to 13 January 1945, the Japanese sank twenty-four ships and damaged sixty-seven. They killed 1,230 men and wounded 1,800.[1]

Less than three months after General MacArthur's SWPA forces assaulted Luzon, forces from Admiral Nimitz's Central Pacific Area were set to assault Okinawa on the southern doorstep of the Japanese home islands. The Japanese commander on Okinawa, like his counterpart on Luzon, did not intend to have his forces annihilated on the beaches. Instead, Lieutenant General Ushijima Mitsuru planned to withdraw the bulk of his forces into the southern hills, prepare defenses, and force the American ground forces to come to him. Ushijima's strategy, so similar to Yamashita's on Luzon and coupled with an even heavier reliance on kamikaze attacks, promised to bleed the Americans into some political settlement short of unconditional surrender.

Again, the Japanese strategy of attrition paid rich dividends in American casualties. Assault troops went ashore without opposition and wondered, "Where are the Japanese?" Ten days were spent in establishing a beachhead in the center of the island. On 6 April, five days into that initial task, four hundred Japanese planes attacked the ships supporting the landings. Twenty-two kamikazes struck home and sank six ships. Throughout April the attacks continued. By the end of that month, the Japanese had sunk fourteen ships and damaged ninety. They had killed 956 sailors, wounded 2,650, and an astonishing 897 were missing.

Meanwhile, as the ground forces turned north and south from their central beachhead, the infantrymen and marines found the Japanese holed up in the rugged ridges that ran from coast to coast just north of Naha. The area was small, only ten miles by ten miles, but it contained 120,000 Japanese soldiers and sailors, led by a determined commander, resolved to die fighting. It took the Tenth Army almost three months to reduce the defenses, and battle casualties among the soldiers and marines were high—almost forty thousand. The entire campaign for Okinawa cost fifty thousand casualties, more than twelve thousand of whom were killed or missing. Almost five thousand of the dead were sailors, a grim testimony to the increasing effectiveness of kamikaze air attacks. The navy lost 26 ships and had 168 damaged by these suicide attacks. An estimated 110,000 Japanese died. Among the dead were the two opposing commanding generals. General Simon Bolivar Buckner was killed by Japanese artillery on 18 June. Four days later, General Ushijima disemboweled himself in a ritual ceremony as American soldiers hurled grenades at the mouth of his command-post cave.[2]

Luzon and Okinawa sobered the planners. The same effective and fanatical resistance, transferred to the larger land masses of the home islands and multiplied twenty-fold in troop strength, promised to make the invasion of Kyushu, only four months away, a bloodbath of unparalleled scale. Reports by ship commanders acknowledged that attacks on the fleet at Luzon were carried out by inferior pilots in obsolescent planes diving in single-plane attacks. However, one commander noted that if these attacks were continued and perfected, in later campaigns they might become *"quite a serious menace to our ships."* More frightening still, wrote Commander of Amphibious Forces, Pacific Fleet, Admiral Richard K. Turner, was the possibility that the Japanese would attack in large groups, a tactic that would "almost certainly produce a very high percentage of hits." Navy reports contained a tone of frustration and fear for future operations, while the commanders, in sound military fashion, searched for measures to counter the threat—blinding the pilots with searchlights, improving radar, destroying Japanese planes on the ground, and pursuing the kamikazes more effectively. As they sought solutions, however, all agreed that the kamikaze threat would grow and that the best defense was more accurate gunfire in greater volume. The reports noted particularly the special vulnerability of the lightly armed escort carriers.[3]

As the prospect of invading Japan grew nearer, no doubt all of the planners and decision makers and participants from the president to the lowliest infantryman were uneasy about the possibility of extremely high casualties. Iwo Jima had proved the deadliness of suicidal cave and bunker defenses. Okinawa had shown that last-ditch ground defenses coupled with land-based kamikazes flying from bases in the homeland could raise the casualty stakes high enough to shake the nerves of generals and admirals and foster public criticism in the United States.

At various times after the war Truman justified the use of the atomic bombs by claiming that his decision precluded a bloody invasion that would have cost one million casualties. The numbers varied with the occasion—sometimes two hundred and fifty thousand, sometimes five hundred thousand, sometimes one million; sometimes the numbers described deaths, sometimes total casualties, sometimes only Americans, or sometimes Japanese and Americans. In his memoirs Truman claims that "the Chiefs of Staff were grim in their estimates of the cost we would have to pay to invade the Japanese mainland" and that "our military experts had estimated that an invasion of Japan would cost at least five hundred thousand American casualties." Later in the same volume, Truman writes, "General Marshall told me that it might cost half a million American lives to force the enemy's surrender on his home grounds." In the notes for his memoirs, Truman claimed that the invasion would cost the United States about two hundred and fifty thousand casualties. Long after the war Truman told INS correspondent Robert Nixon that the decision to use the atomic bomb was made to preclude a bloody invasion and to save one million American lives.[4] After the war Stimson justified the use of the atomic bombs against Japan, claiming that the invasion "might be expected to cost over a million casualties to American forces alone."[5] Churchill claimed after the war that the invasion could be expected to cost one million American and five hundred thousand British lives.

The source of the large numbers used after the war by Truman, Stimson, and Churchill to justify the use of the atomic bomb has yet to be discovered. Nor is there any record that Truman, Stimson, or Churchill used such large casualty estimates in the weeks before or following the use of the bombs against Japan. The large estimates first appeared in their postwar memoirs. No evidence has been produced that such large estimates came from the staff of the Joint Chiefs. After the war Truman told the official historians of the air force that Marshall had informed him at Potsdam that if both OLYMPIC and CORONET had to occur, American casualties could range from two hundred and fifty thousand to one million. Yet there is no substantiation beyond Truman's own memory. Such a casual and informal estimate would have been out of character for Marshall, whose statements were always careful and measured. The numbers were far beyond the conservative casualty estimates given by Marshall for OLYMPIC at a conference with Truman on 18 June. Furthermore, Marshall's own planner, George Lincoln, believed that the Kyushu operation would produce about thirty-one thousand battle casualties, seven to eight thousand of which would be deaths.[6]

If Truman received such high casualty estimates for the invasion of Japan, they may have come informally from Secretary of War Stimson. In June 1945 Stimson circulated a memo from former President Herbert Hoover through the army staff stating that the invasion of Japan would cost five hundred thousand to one million American lives. Marshall's deputy, General Handy, commented that the figure was too high. Such a high number of deaths would presume total casualties of two to five million, since experience showed that only 20 to 25 percent of total casualties were deaths.[7]

In fact, during the spring and summer of 1945 Stimson had good reason to exaggerate casualties and to encourage a belief in the extreme bloodiness of any invasion of Japan. Along with Joseph Grew in the State Department, Stimson was actively seeking to ameliorate the doctrine of unconditional surrender. He had become convinced that the war could end quickly if the Allies gave assurances that the Japanese emperor's position would be protected. To exaggerate the possible cost of an invasion would further that campaign.[8]

Wherever Truman and Stimson got their large numbers, similar estimates did not emerge in the 1945 Joint Chiefs' debates about the invasion, nor did the planners ever cite such high numbers. Such prophecies of extremely high casualties only came to be widely accepted after the war to rationalize the use of the atomic bombs. The Joint Chiefs were, nonetheless, concerned about casualties. They took note of the outcry against the heavy casualties suffered at Iwo Jima, and they called Elmer Davis, the Office of War Information chief, to a Joint Chiefs' meeting. His office, the Joint Chiefs warned, should begin preparing the American public for heavy losses to be incurred in the invasion of Japan.[9]

The costs of the 1945 campaigns in Luzon, Iwo Jima, and Okinawa were the heaviest of the Pacific war. In the Luzon campaign the Japanese inflicted 37,870 casualties on American ground forces. Of those, 8,310 were killed. Clearing the entire Philippine archipelago from Leyte through Luzon cost 60,717 battle casualties—13,160 were killed in action and 2,934 died of wounds. Okinawa cost the lives of 12,281 soldiers, sailors, and marines. The battle for Iwo Jima left 5,931 marines dead and 17,372 wounded. Some battalions suffered more than 90 percent casualties in this brutal fight for an island of less than twelve square miles. For a military that relied on firepower rather than manpower in subduing the enemy, these were high costs. They did not, however, justify the high casualty figures cited after the war for the invasion of Japan by Truman and Stimson. The numbers cited by Truman and Stimson would have far exceeded the total casualties suffered in all the previous campaigns of the Pacific war and would have approached the number of American casualties for the entire war.[10]

Independent casualty estimates for OLYMPIC were made by three different groups of staff planners. The most conservative came from the joint planners; they adopted an optimistic stance, but refused to project absolute numbers. MacArthur's operations from 1 March 1944 to 1 May 1945, noted the planners, had produced a favorable kill ratio of twenty-two to one—310,165 Japanese to 13,742 Americans dead. For the same period total American casualties in the Pacific—killed, wounded, and missing—showed a ratio of five to one. The planners also noted that "the nature of the objective area in Kyushu gives maneuver room for land and sea operations," an opportunity that had been lacking on many of the small islands and atolls of the central Pacific. They approvingly cited Mac-Arthur's judgment that "the [OLYMPIC] operation is the most economical in effort and lives that is possible." MacArthur argued that in the long run a decisive strike at Kyushu would be far less wasteful in lives than would a series of indecisive, peripheral operations. According to the planners, casualties for the first thirty days of OLYMPIC should not exceed those for Luzon. Navy casualties would compare with those suffered at Okinawa. As for CORONET, the planners noted that the open character of the terrain on the Tokyo Plain favored American "superiority in maneuver and equipment," while it simultaneously handicapped the concentrated, fixed defenses of the Japanese.[11]

MacArthur's staff predicted casualty numbers with great precision. They also looked to Luzon for a model. In size and terrain, that island resembled Kyushu. Operations on Luzon absorbed a field army roughly paralleling the troop requirements for OLYMPIC. MacArthur's planners forecast the following battle casualties for OLYMPIC:

X-Day-plus-15	9,727
X-Day-plus-30	22,576
X-Day-plus-60	55,906
X-Day-plus-120	124,935[12]

Assuming, as experience indicated, that battle deaths typically were about 25 percent of total battle casualties, then about fourteen thousand soldiers and airmen would die in the first sixty days of OLYMPIC, and approximately thirty-one thousand could die if the operation persisted until 1 March 1946. Such a loss rate would have been roughly equivalent to the losses sustained at Okinawa and in the Normandy campaign. During the first forty-eight days following D-Day, General Omar Bradley's First U.S. Army had suffered 63,360 casualties of whom 16,129 had been killed.

Nimitz's staff planners also made casualty predictions for OLYMPIC. Whether their projections were for total casualties or battle casualties was left unclear. The relatively small numbers would indicate the latter. In any case, Nimitz's planners predicted forty-nine thousand casualties in the first thirty days—five thousand sailors, twelve thousand marines, and thirty-two thousand soldiers. Among the sailors, 43 percent (2,150) were expected to be killed, while 20 percent (8,800) of the marines and soldiers would be killed or would die of wounds. These estimates were slightly under the actual casualties suffered at Okinawa.[13]

On 18 June 1945 President Truman called the Joint Chiefs to the White House for a discussion of their plans to invade Japan. Also present were Stimson, Secretary of the Navy James Forrestal, and Assistant Secretary of War John J. McCloy. Truman specifically asked that the Joint Chiefs be prepared to discuss casualties. Two days before the meeting, General John E. Hull, Chief of Army Staff's Operations Division (OPD), informed General Lincoln, the chief army planner, that "the President is very much perturbed over the losses on Okinawa." Hull recommended that Lincoln prepare Marshall's briefing notes for the upcoming meeting so that they not only include casualty data on Okinawa, Iwo Jima, Leyte, and Luzon but also "overall figures on MacArthur's operations to date," for the casualty rate in MacArthur's command was far lower than in Nimitz's central Pacific area.[14]

In order to answer the president's questions about casualties, Marshall requested MacArthur's estimates for "battle casualties in OLYMPIC up to D+90." MacArthur replied promptly, furnishing "estimated total battle casualties from which estimated return to duty numbers are deducted." For unknown reasons, the estimates in MacArthur's reply differed from the earlier estimates for the first thirty days. But the total numbers for OLYMPIC were not far different from the earlier numbers put together by MacArthur's planners,

D-Day to D-Day-plus-30:	50,800
D-Day-plus-30 to D-Day-plus-60:	27,150
D-Day-plus-60 to D-Day-plus-90:	27,100

MacArthur estimated another forty-two hundred nonbattle casualties for each thirty-day period.[15]

Marshall was apparently disturbed by the large number of casualties predicted for the first thirty days of OLYMPIC, for he immediately asked MacArthur to clarify the figure. Was the number "based on plans for medical installations," he asked, or was it "your best estimate of the casualties you anticipate from the operational viewpoint." Marshall explained that President Truman was "very much concerned" about the casualties to be received from the OLYMPIC operation. MacArthur lost no time in rationalizing the figure. The estimate, he explained, "had not come to my prior attention," was "purely academic and routine," and was made "for planning alone." The estimate had been calculated from experiences at Normandy and Okinawa, the highest casualty rates experienced by Americans in any campaigns of the war. He did not expect such high casualty rates, MacArthur informed Marshall, and he concluded with a strong argument in favor of OLYMPIC.

> I believe the operation presents less hazards of excessive loss than any other that has been suggested and that its decisive effect will eventually save lives by eliminating wasteful operations of a nondecisive character. I regard the operation as the most economical one in effort and lives that is possible. In this respect it must be remembered that the several preceding months will involve practically no losses in ground troops and that sooner or later a decisive ground attack must be made. The hazard and loss will be greatly lessened if an attack is launched from Siberia [by the Soviets] sufficiently ahead of our target date to commit the enemy to major combat. I most earnestly recommend no change in OLYMPIC. Additional subsidiary attacks will simply build up our final total casualties.[16]

At their 18 June meeting with the president, the Joint Chiefs addressed the casualty question, but they refused to estimate precise numbers. "Our experience in the Pacific war is so diverse," they informed the president, "that it is considered wrong to give any estimate in numbers." They noted, however, that "General MacArthur has not yet accepted responsibility for going ashore where there would be disproportionate casualties." Then they cited casualty rates from Leyte, Luzon, Iwo Jima, Okinawa, and Normandy. "There is reason to believe that the first thirty days in Kyushu should not exceed the price we have paid for Luzon," they ended. Truman seemed satisfied, for he did not raise the question of casualties with the Joint Chiefs again, and he approved the decision to go ahead with OLYMPIC with the proviso that the Joint Chiefs consult him again before the operation began.[17]

Immediately following the meeting, Marshall sent his thanks to MacArthur "for the promptness of your reply . . . to my query regarding OLYMPIC and casualty estimates." MacArthur's last message, Marshall noted, had "arrived with 30 minutes to spare and had a determining influence in obtaining formal presidential approval for OLYMPIC."[18]

The record does not support the postwar claims of huge Allied casualties to be suffered in the invasion of Japan. On the contrary, much evidence exists that casualty estimates for the invasion were realistic and based on past experience. These estimates were furnished to both Truman and Stimson. While there is little evidence except assertion and repetition to support the huge numbers used by Truman and Stimson after the war, the U.S. leaders, both civilian and military, were extremely conscious of the costs of Okinawa and reluctant to repeat those losses. The thought that OLYMPIC might cost no more than Normandy or Okinawa was small comfort. The earlier fanatical and suicidal, yet hopeless Japanese defenses created a psychology that the normal conventions of war did not apply against a nation of potential kamikazes. That psychology may be seen at work in the special weapons considered for use against the Japanese homeland.

NOTES

1. Casualty and loss figures are from Robert Ross Smith, *United States Army in World War II: The War in the Pacific: Triumph in the Philippines* (Washington, DC: GPO, 1963), 60–67.

2. Casualty and loss figures are from Roy E. Appleman, James M. Burns, Russell A. Gugeler, and John Stevens, *Okinawa: The Last Battle* (Washington DC: GPO, 1948), 489–90.

3. Reports from naval commanders compiled and published by Headquarters, United States Fleet, entitled "Amphibious Operations: Invasion of the Philippines, October 1944 to January 1945," COMINICH P–008, 30 April 1945, 3–6, 3–9.

4. Harry Truman, *Memoirs*, vol. 1, *Year of Decision* (Garden City, NY: Doubleday, 1955), 265, 315, 417; Oral History Interview No. 265, 315–17, Truman Library; Memoirs, foreign policy folder, Atomic Bomb, Truman Library.

5. Henry L. Stimson, "The Decision to Use the Atomic Bomb," *Harper's*, 194 (February 1947): 102.

6. Michael S. Sherry, *The Rise of American Air Power: The Creation of Armageddon* (New Haven: Yale Univ. Press, 1987), 335–6; Rufus E. Miles, Jr., "Hiroshima: The Strange Myth of Half a Million American Lives Saved," *International Security* 10 (Fall 1985): 121, 137; Wesley F. Craven and James L. Cate, eds., *The Pacific: Matterhorn to Nagasaki*, vol. 5, *June 1944 to August 1945* (Chicago: Univ. of Chicago Press, 1953), 712–13.

7. Sherry, 335; Memorandum of Comments on "Ending the Japanese War," RG 165, OPD 387.4TS, 14 June 1945, NARA.

8. Stimson, 102.

9. Minutes, JCS meeting, 27 February 1945, RG 218, CCS 334, NARA.

10. Casualty figures for Luzon are in Smith, 692; for Okinawa in Appleman, Burns, Gugeler, and Stevens, 487; those for Iwo Jima are from Whitman S.

Bartley, *Iwo Jima: Amphibious Epic* (Washington, GPO, 1954), 218–21; all other casualty data are in *Army Battle Casualties and Nonbattle Deaths in World War II, Final Report* (Department of the Army, 1953).

11. JCS 1388/4, Details of the Campaign Against Japan, 11 July 1945, RG 218, CCS 381, Japan (6–14–45), Sec. 1, NARA.

12. "From Olympic to Blacklist," (Manuscript, U.S. Army Center of Military History, n.d.), 18. "X-Day" was the day of the landings. Planners were not always consistent in the designation they used for the day of the landings. Frequently they used "D-Day" but most common was X-Day. The numbers given are cumulative.

13. OLYMPIC, Naval and Amphibious Phases, 18 June 1945, U.S. Pacific Fleet, RG 218, NARA.

14. Memo, Hull to Lincoln, 16 June 1945, OPD 704, Verifax copy #3073, Marshall Library, Lexington, VA.

15. Messages, Marshall to MacArthur, 16 June 1945 and MacArthur to Marshall, 17 June 1945, RG 4, USAFPAC Correspondence WD, folder 4, MacArthur Archives, Norfolk, VA. The figures given in this table are not cumulative but are for each thirty-day period.

16. Messages, Marshall to MacArthur, 19 June 1945, and MacArthur to Marshall, 19 June 1945, RG 4, USAFPAC Correspondence WD, folder 4, MA. The dates cited are Manila time.

17. Minutes of meeting held at the White House on 18 June 1945 at 1530 hours, CCS 334, Joint Chiefs of Staff Meetings 106 through 194 (2–2–45), RG 218. NARA.

18. Message, Marshall to MacArthur, 19 June 1945, RG 4, USAFPAC Correspondence WD, folder 4, MacArthur Archives, Norfolk, VA.

Chapter 7

Special Weapons

The high casualties and the tenacious, suicidal Japanese defenses in the last campaigns of the Pacific war sent scientists, technical experts, and staff planners on a search for new weapons that could save American lives and break the Japanese will to resist. Some ideas were simply new adaptations of old weapons and techniques. Others were wholly new, and two proposals, seriously considered for use if the Japanese continued their hopeless defiance, skirted the edges of chemical and biological warfare.

Allied policy since 1942 had foresworn the use of gas except in retaliation, and Roosevelt had publicly pledged that the United States would not initiate chemical warfare. But the military would be prepared to retaliate should Germany or Japan use gas. The president did not specifically mention biological agents, but presumably his remarks covered germ warfare as well.[1]

But readiness to retaliate required research, and by 1943 the United States had already created a Special Projects Division within the Chemical Warfare Service. This division was located at Camp Detrick, Maryland, with smaller field testing areas at Horn Island off the Mississippi Gulf Coast; at Granite Peak, Utah (part of the Chemical Warfare Service's Dugway Proving Ground); and at the Vigo manufacturing facility near Terre Haute, Indiana. Special Projects directed the development and mass production of biological warfare agents and the testing and construction of weapons to deliver them. The project's scientists studied such deadly diseases as anthrax, glanders, brucellosis, tularemia, botulism, plague, and various plant diseases. The project manufactured a number of anthrax bombs (none were ever filled with anthrax) and at the Horn Island facility conducted at least twenty-three field tests of a bomb to deliver botulism toxin. These deadly agents were developed strictly as contingency weapons—retaliatory devices only to be used in case Germany or Japan introduced them first.

In fact, long before the Special Projects Division was ever formed, the Japanese had already used crude biological warfare in China. Beyond doubt, the Japanese had conducted extensive research in biological warfare, especially of anthrax, botulism, plague, and cholera, at a large, well-supported research center at Harbin, Manchuria. Directed by Lieutenant General Ishii Shiro, this organization experimented with human subjects and may have dropped some crude bombs loaded with infected feathers and plague-infected fleas on Chinese cities.[2]

By early 1945 the American Special Projects Division had developed "LN" plant-killing chemicals, and the production of these herbicides forced army leaders toward hard choices that edged toward the introduction of chemical and biological warfare. On 8 March 1945 George W. Merck, chairman of the War Department's Biological Warfare Committee and a special consultant to Stimson, wrote a memorandum to General Marshall explaining the nature and possible military uses of LN chemicals. These agents, he informed Marshall, could "kill certain food crops or reduce their yield." They could be mixed with water or oil and sprayed on crops or soil, and, furthermore, Merck noted, the chemicals were not poisonous to humans or animals. When he wrote Marshall, Merck had already sought a legal opinion from the Judge Advocate General of the army (JAG) on the legality of using the new chemicals. The JAG, Major General Myron C. Cramer, advised that unless the chemicals produced "poisonous effects upon enemy personnel, either from direct contact, or indirectly from ingestion of plants and vegetables," he could find no legal reason for prohibiting the military use of the agents. Merck suggested that the new chemicals "might be employed to destroy or to reduce the yield of crops being raised by the Japanese on 'by-passed' Pacific islands."[3]

About 375,000 Japanese soldiers and sailors had been by-passed and isolated in 1943 and 1944 as Nimitz's and MacArthur's amphibious, island-hopping offensives leaped across the central and southwest Pacific. The by-passed garrisons fed themselves by cultivating gardens in jungle clearings. These isolated Japanese posed no offensive threat; they were without regular supplies or communications with higher headquarters. Using combat forces to root them out would produce casualties far out of proportion to the benefits gained. General George Kenney, chief of MacArthur's Far East Air Forces, had sprayed some gardens with oil in 1944, but the results were disappointing. He asked the Chemical Warfare Service to work on some other method for destroying these gardens.[4]

Major General John E. Hull, chief of OPD, advised Marshall to take no immediate action on Merck's memo but, instead, to wait for additional information that was due on the chemicals in four to six weeks. He also recommended that Marshall request further study to determine with absolute certainty that the chemicals were not poisonous to humans. Hull feared that the Japanese could accuse the United States of initiating chemical warfare and could retaliate. Marshall took Hull's advice.[5]

On 30 March 1945 Major General William N. Porter, chief of the Chemical Warfare Service, sent one of his regular weekly reports to his superiors in Headquarters, Army Service Forces. He advised that new symbols had been adopted for the various forms of the LN chemicals: VKA (Vegetable Killer Acid) was the pure chemical; VKS (Vegetable Killer Salt) was the chemical in ammonium salt form; VKL (Vegetable Killer Liquid) was a 30-percent solution of the acid in tributyl phosphate. Porter also reported that the chemicals had proved effective when sprayed from low-flying planes. At Bushnell Army Air Field in Florida two A-26 planes, each equipped with two 30-gallon tanks filled with a 3-percent solution of VKL in diesel fuel, had sprayed seventy acres. "Toxic effects on broadleaf plants were visible in less than one hour," Porter reported, "and death of tender species . . . occurred in 24 hours." Dow Chemical Company, Porter advised, was already producing VKA "of quality superior to specification." Dow could produce forty thousand pounds of VKA and ten thousand pounds of VKS by 10 June.[6]

Until the end of March, planners thought of using the new chemicals to destroy only the gardens of isolated Japanese garrisons on by-passed islands in the Pacific. Then, Major General Walter A. Wood, Jr., chief of Plans and Operations in the Army Service Forces, raised the possibility of using the chemicals to destroy the Japanese rice crop in the home islands. General Porter replied that complete destruction of the Japanese rice crop was "an objective impossible of accomplishment with facilities it would seem reasonable to provide." But, he added, total destruction was unnecessary. Rice made up 60 percent of the Japanese diet, and the home islands were only marginally self-sufficient in food production. He reasoned that the destruction of 30 percent of the crop would produce "serious consequences" for the Japanese. Neither were the requirements for destruction unreasonable—3.5 million pounds of VKA and fifteen hundred spray-equipped airplanes flying twenty-six sorties each. In fact, he concluded, the requirements might be further reduced by "intensification of experimentation on rice disease organisms" that could be spread from airplanes.[7]

On 14 April General Brehon Somervell, commander of Army Service Forces, wrote Hull to indicate that sufficient VKA for use against the gardens of by-passed Japanese garrisons was already on order. However, he cautioned, if a decision were made to use the chemical against the rice crop in the home islands, Dow Chemical would need six months to begin production, and ordering the necessary chemicals would require an expenditure of $4,375,000. "Prior to implementing any further action," General Somervell concluded, he needed "a statement of War Department policy with regard to the use of this agent on agricultural areas of Japan proper" and on the "practicability of the proposal covering the . . . use of 1500 airplanes for dissemination."[8]

Hull sent Somervell's request forward to General Marshall. The project, Hull told Marshall, had "passed the stage of experimental development," and a policy was needed. The ultimate decision on whether or not to use the chemical plant killer, he admitted, might have to be made by the president or "ultimately on the combined level." Nevertheless, Hull advised, the military implications of the use of VKA should be considered by the Joint Chiefs. The beginning, he suggested, was to order a study by the joint planners and to seek advice from MacArthur and Nimitz.[9]

While the joint planners wrestled with the study, General Porter of the Chemical Warfare Service noted that time and logistical limitations made it impossible to plan for the destruction of more than 10 percent of the Japanese rice crop in 1945, and he listed some complicated technical and logistical problems that would have to be overcome even to meet that modest goal. Nonetheless, he requested permission to proceed. Within days, on 9 May, a meeting was convened for Porter to meet with representatives from Marshall's staff and Somervell's Army Service Forces Staff. The conferees decided that lack of time had already doomed any attempt to spray Japanese rice crops in 1945 and that those tentative plans would have to be abandoned.[10]

The joint planners had been handed their task on 30 April. Three weeks later, on 21 May, they presented their report to the secretary of the Joint Chiefs. The report was brief, and it indicated division in the seven-member committee. All agreed, however, on several conclusions: that food was a "legitimate military target"; that VKA "if used in a long war emphasizing attrition and blockade would be of substantial military value"; that logistical problems doomed any 1945 program against crops in Japan; and that local use against by-passed Japanese troops was possible and would be effective. On the other hand, the planners pointed out, any 1946 spraying of the Japanese rice crop could create grave problems for the Allies. The effects of crop destruction would become acute in late 1946, just at the time when the war was supposed to end, and millions of starving Japanese would have to be fed by Allied occupation forces. Finally, the planners pointed out the obvious: the Japanese might interpret the campaign as America's first use of chemical warfare and retaliate.

While the committee was united on these conclusions, the seven members divided four to three on their recommendations. The minority report recommended the use of VKA "only in the event that the strategy of the war develops into one emphasizing attrition and blockade." Even the report of the majority was hardly a ringing endorsement for a 1946 campaign to destroy Japanese crops. It recommended that the Joint Chiefs approve the use of VKA if "quantities used to bring about crop destruction" were not judged to be toxic to people or animals. The report recommended that before undertaking any spraying campaign in 1946, the Joint Chiefs should restudy the proposal in January and, in the meantime, seek advice from MacArthur and Nimitz.[11]

No firm policy was ever decided on; the proposals for widespread spraying of the Japanese rice crop were never approved, and no spraying was ever done. Yet, at the war's end, the option was still open. Spraying would probably have depended on the success of OLYMPIC.[12]

For the combat infantryman, perhaps the toughest feature of fighting the Japanese in the Pacific was to attack dug-in positions where the defenders were determined to die in their caves and bunkers. By the last campaigns of the war, the Japanese had become masters of field fortification and camouflage. They dug gun positions, reinforced the walls with several thicknesses of upright coconut logs, and covered the roofs with several layers of twelve-inch logs. Over the top they piled coral or sand and a layer of dirt and camouflaged the entire bunker with living trees and bushes. A bunker so constructed could withstand direct hits from all but the largest shells and bombs, and frequently, advancing infantrymen failed to see the bunkers from fifty feet.

At Biak, Saipan, Guam, Peleliu, Luzon, Iwo Jima, and Okinawa, the Japanese used fortified natural caves, or they dug caves in hills that overlooked strategic spots. Central living and command rooms were sometimes sixty feet inside the hills. Lateral tunnels led out to hillside openings and gun positions. Gun crews could pull their weapons inside in case their positions were detected and opposing fire became too heavy. On Peleliu, a single cave had nine levels of living quarters and could house two hundred men. On Iwo Jima, one hundred caves were discovered in an area four hundred by five hundred yards. Cave defenses on Okinawa slowed the campaign to a crawl and almost created a stalemate.

Such fortifications were all but impervious to artillery, naval gunfire, and aerial bombing; and they presented formidable problems for infantrymen. Cave defenses were organized for all-around, mutually supporting, interlocking fire. Hence, they were protected on all sides from enemy attack. Riflemen in foxholes protected the cave openings from which machine guns or heavy artillery fired. The Japanese also fortified the reverse slopes of hills. Even when the attackers took the forward slopes and the hilltops, they often had to fight down the backsides of the hills. Mortars and artillery were sited in defilade positions to fire concentrations on the attackers. Soldiers had to get close enough to use flame throwers or hand grenades or satchel charges—at best an extremely hazardous business. The effect of explosives was often reduced by "grenade" walls or sharp angles just inside the tunnel entrances. The fortifications negated the American policy of using overwhelming firepower to keep casualties low. The result was close, small-group combat that produced high casualties. That the terrain on Kyushu was ideal for cave and bunker defenses worried the planners.

To search for better ways of attacking Japanese caves and bunkers, the SPHINX project, under a specially formed army staff agency called the New Developments Division, was established in the early summer of 1945. The artillery tested various guns and fuzes against cave entrances; engineers tested explosives; and ordnance looked for new weapons. In the end, however, no dramatic new weapons or techniques came from the project. The best solutions to the problems presented by cave defenses were refinements and the greater use of weapons that had proved effective in earlier campaigns.

Flame-throwing tanks were improved and ordered in greater numbers. The early portable flame throwers of short range and questionable reliability were being replaced by 1945 with newer, longer-range portable models and by very-long-range tank-mounted flame throwers. Lengths of rubber fuel hose could serve as extensions to give even greater range. Fired into the mouths of caves, these weapons could nullify turns in the tunnels and could blast through the small firing ports of bunkers and pillboxes incinerating the defenders or driving them into the open where they could be killed by rifle fire. OLYMPIC plans called for more than double the number of flame-throwing tanks used at Okinawa. Planners wanted even more, but the quantity could not be produced in time. At war's end, the Chemical Warfare Service was working on a "super flame thrower."

While caves and bunkers were very resistant to ordinary artillery and mortar fire, they were vulnerable to large caliber gunfire directed straight into the gunports or entrances. Artillerists conducted tests at Fort Sill and proved the effectiveness of self-propelled 8-inch and 155mm howitzers against caves and bunkers. Direct fire from smaller high-velocity 90mm and 75mm guns also proved effective. To give more protection to individual infantrymen who attacked caves, the army began shipping body armor to the Pacific in preparation for OLYMPIC.[13]

On 11 August 1945 the War Department published a 32-page training circular dealing with the destruction of Japanese cave fortifications. "Japanese talent for tenacity, exploitation of terrain, and camouflage," the circular warned, "has resulted in the evolution of cave warfare from a last-ditch stand by fanatics into a formidable defensive doctrine. . . . The probability of its use as the ultimate defensive doctrine in the Japanese homeland must be considered."

The planners offered few new ideas and suggested only more effective use of existing techniques and weapons: better intelligence and reconnaissance; closer cooperation between infantry, armor, artillery, and air; and, most important of all, more reliance on specially trained infantry teams supported by direct cannon fire and mechanized flame throwers. Defoliation was considered particularly important in uncovering cave entrances for direct artillery fire. The preferred methods were air-dropped napalm or, for smaller areas, mechanized flame throwers.[14]

Despite the Army Air Forces' almost complete strategic supremacy in the skies over Japan, some airmen continued to look for new weapons and techniques for battering the Japanese home islands. Newly developed aimable bombs, an American version of the German V-1 "buzz bomb," and even captured German V-1 and V-2 rockets were considered for use if the war lasted into 1946.

The Joint Committee on New Weapons and Equipment recommended using Azon, Razon, and Bat bombs against Japanese targets. The Azon bomb, a thousand-pound general-purpose bomb, could be directed laterally by a radio receiver in the tail and steered onto the target by the bombardier. The Azon bomb had produced excellent results against bridges in Burma in 1944. The Razon bomb was similar but could be controlled in both range and azimuth. The Bat was a radio-controlled winged glide bomb. These last two weapons were still experimental, however, and would not be available in sufficient numbers for employment until 1946.[15]

Perhaps the air force project that received the most serious attention and promised to pay the greatest dividends for the invasion was Project APHRODITE, or WEARY-WILLIE. In 1944 both in Europe and at the Eglin, Florida, Army Air Forces Proving Ground, experimenters began to work on radio-guided "war weary" B-17s loaded with twenty thousand pounds of TNT or napalm. These "robot" bombers could be launched against targets that were invulnerable to conventional bombs. In August 1944 six missions including eleven war wearies were launched against V-1 launching sites in northwest Germany. The raids were unsuccessful, but the technique seemed promising. By early 1945 the Joint Chiefs were suggesting the use of war-wearies against Japan. The program had been given high priority in October 1944, but it was plagued by problems and never produced appreciable results. Crews had to fly the planes into the air and then bail out. Controlling the planes from a "mother" ship had proved erratic, ground control was hard to perfect, and war-weary aircraft were often so worn and patched that they were hardly flyable. No war-wearies were used against Japan.[16]

Following the defeat of Germany, Major General Clayton Bissell, intelligence chief for the army staff, raised the possibility of using captured German V-2 rockets against Japan. Marshall drafted and circulated for his staff's comments a proposed message to Eisenhower suggesting that V-1s (buzz bombs) and V-2s (ballistic missiles) might be "manufactured in Germany for operations in the Pacific." He proposed that Eisenhower appoint a "general officer assisted by necessary personnel . . . to study and report upon [the] practicability of manufacturing quantities of V-1s and V-2s . . . utilizing German facilities," and training U.S personnel to fire them against the Japanese.[17]

For a variety of reasons neither the proposal to use captured V-2s nor the possibility of manufacturing them in Germany was well received. Brigadier General William A. Borden of the New Developments Division opposed both ideas. The complications and burdens of training personnel, manufacturing the rockets, and shipping them to the Pacific far outweighed any benefits that could be gained from the use of the V-2s against Japan. "Better results," Borden noted, "could be obtained by . . . approximately 40 B-29 airplanes on one sortie each." As for using captured V-2s, "One hundred . . . are needed urgently in this country for research and development." Diverting any V-2s to the Pacific could "seriously handicap our whole guided missile program."[18]

Arnold also vigorously opposed the proposal. He pointed out that the Army Air Forces already had industrial plants geared up to produce an improved American version of the German V-1. Arnold argued that the United States ought to concentrate on developing its own capacity for building rockets. Instead of considering the building of V-1s and V-2s in Germany, he suggested, the army should bring all the German scientists, information, and equipment to the United States. Furthermore, he cautioned, manufacturing rockets in Germany clearly would violate the Yalta agreements and "give support to those groups who are already challenging the Army as being advocates of a soft peace."[19]

On 14 July 1945 the proposal was declared dead. In a memo to General Somervell of Army Service Forces, Major General Howard A. Craig, acting chief of Operations Division, noted that neither the volume nor the accuracy of American bombing could be improved by deploying V-2s. Indeed, doing so would only add more burdens to an already overstrained logistical system. The war would probably be over before the V-2s could be deployed. "There are no present plans for their use against Japan," he concluded.[20]

As the V-1 and V-2 proposal was dying, the Army Air Forces staff began pushing for approval to use its own "buzz bomb," the JB-2, in CORONET. The JB-2 was essentially a copy of the German V-1. In fact, the prototype was built at Wright Field, Ohio, in a period of three weeks during August 1944 using parts salvaged from crashed V-1s. In October Arnold asked for enough production to launch a thousand JB-2s per month. Tests continued at Eglin, and 1,391 had been produced by war's end. According to Brigadier General Reuben C. Hood, Jr., deputy chief of Air Staff, one Special Weapons Unit of 1,066 men could be deployed in the CORONET beachhead by D-Day-plus-14 and on D-Day-plus-24 could start launching forty-eight missiles per day for a period of sixty days. Only seven liberty ships, fuel tankers, troop transports, and an assigned area within the beachhead would be required. The JB-2s, Hood promised, would supplement conventional aircraft in times of bad weather.[21]

Operations Division Chief Craig said no to this plan. CORONET, Craig replied, was "planned on so vast a scale" that no more requirements could be added. Shipping and beachhead space would be especially critical. Moreover, he noted, all lucrative targets within range of the JB-2s would have already been destroyed by conventional bombing, and ample tactical air support would be available from carrier- and land-based planes.[22]

Allied policy on gas warfare was a policy of retaliation only, and early in the war real fears existed that the Germans or the Japanese would initiate the use of gas. Chiang-Kai-Shek's Nationalists insisted that the Japanese had used gas attacks in the China war. Roosevelt had apparently believed the accusation, for in mid-1942 he made a clear policy statement on the use of poison gas. Should the Japanese continue their gas attacks on China or use gas against "any other of the United Nations," he had warned, they could expect swift and overwhelming retaliation. In late 1942 the U.S. and British chiefs of staff approved an Anglo-American agreement which specified that neither party could initiate gas warfare except with the approval of both governments.[23]

Officers in the Chemical Warfare Service during World War II were acutely conscious that a policy of retaliation and "no first use" by the United States placed their service in a contingency role away from the center of the war. Driven by desires to carve out other, more active functions, the Chemical Warfare Service formed chemical mortar battalions, operated smoke generators, developed incendiary devices and flame throwers, and on occasion, called for the use of gas. For an immediate retaliation, stocks of lethal gases, including mustard and phosgene, were distributed to the active theaters of war.

The tenacious nature of Japanese cave and bunker defenses at Luzon and Okinawa and the resulting high American casualties raised the question of using poison gas. By June 1945 OLYMPIC was only six months in the future. Because of the terrain in southern Kyushu, it was all but certain the Japanese would adopt cave defenses. The campaign for Kyushu was likely to be a grander version of the costly campaign for Okinawa. Moreover, Roosevelt, the most stubborn and powerful opponent of initiating gas warfare, was now dead. The Joint Chiefs had already worked out plans for the retaliatory use of gas. For a number of reasons—climate, predictable winds, and equipment—the Japanese were considered especially vulnerable. Predictably, the question of using gas in the invasion of Japan was seriously debated.[24]

In June, July, and August 1945 military pressures mounted to abandon the policy restricting the use of poisonous gas to retaliation only and to employ gas offensively in Operation OLYMPIC. On 5 June General Porter, chief of the Chemical Warfare Service, learned of a staff study for the Joint Chiefs outlining the gas munitions requirements should gas warfare begin on 1 November, the target date of OLYMPIC. He quickly warned Marshall's staff that if such use was anticipated, actions to produce and procure bomb and shell casings, protective clothing, and masks, and to train personnel should begin immediately. In fact, the joint planners were studying the offensive use of poison gas against Japanese caves and bunkers, but the Joint Chiefs had not approved the study.[25]

Both Joseph W. Stillwell, commanding general of the Army Ground Forces and Brigadier General William A. Borden, director of the War Department's New Developments Division, favored the use of gas. That Marshall advocated the use of lethal gas in the invasion of Japan against dug-in Japanese is also clear. On 29 May 1945 he met with Stimson to discuss "methods of concluding the war with minimum casualties." A memorandum of the conversation, which Marshall later read and approved, was prepared by Assistant Secretary of War John J. McCloy. After a discussion of the atomic bomb (Marshall favored warning the Japanese to evacuate several cities before hitting one of them), the chief of staff brought up the subject of using gas. He saw gas as no more inhumane than phosphorous and flame throwers, and he saw no reason to use gas against "dense populations or civilians—merely against these last pockets of resistance which had to be wiped out but had no other military significance." It might even be possible, he suggested, to "saturate an area, possibly with mustard, and just stand off," thus avoiding the attrition caused by "such fanatical but hopeless defense methods" of "suicidal Japanese."[26]

Just as in the policy of unconditional surrender, the death of Roosevelt gave top military planners an opportunity to reopen the question of offensive gas warfare. In June the Strategy and Policy Group of Operations Division circulated a study prepared at the request of Marshall. The Joint Chiefs had not yet approved the use of gas against the Japanese, but an effort to gain approval was in motion. Marshall forwarded the study to Admiral King, suggesting, "If you agree with the proposed action, I believe we should discuss the subject informally with General Arnold and Admiral Leahy." "Gas," the study began, "is the one single weapon hitherto unused which we can have readily available and which assuredly can greatly decrease the cost in American lives and should materially shorten the war." The enemy "resists fanatically down to the last individual, burrowing into the ground and forcing our troops to engage in costly, time consuming . . . diversionary operations." Gas, suggested the study, would neutralize these enemy positions allowing mobile forces "to move rapidly forward, as we have done in Europe." According to the study, neither the United States nor Japan had signed the 1925 Geneva Protocol prohibiting the use of gas, and approval would be needed from Britain, China, and Russia. Nonetheless, "we can be prepared to use gas at the same time that we start Operation OLYMPIC, which is militarily the sound time to initiate this action." Yet, concluded the study, "In order to meet this target date, instructions must be issued to start necessary production of the agents."[27]

Within the SPHINX project, the Chemical Warfare Service conducted extensive tests of gas against caves and bunkers at Dugway Proving Ground in Utah. On 13 July General Porter reported the results to Borden. "For attack on caves and underground fortifications," Porter reported, "gas is superior to all other weapons tested." All of the gases tested were lethal. In caves, agents H (mustard), CK (cyanogen chloride), and CG (phosgene) were deemed the most effective. The thick, cold vapors of CK and CG "pour into a cave almost like water." As the gas warmed and expanded in the caves, it produced concentrations five to ten times as high as could be obtained outside—enough to overwhelm gasmasks and kill even masked Japanese. Mustard, on the other hand, was a liquid; evaporation carried the vapor into the caves by normal air circulation. This characteristic reduced the concentrations inside the caves. Nonetheless, mustard gas could be absorbed through the skin; even in small doses against masked defenders, it was highly effective.

Bombs or artillery could thrust gas into caves. Gas-filled bombs or droppable tanks could cover entire hillsides, making defoliation or identi-fication of cave openings unnecessary. Or, if a cave opening were visible, "a few rounds of H- or CK-filled howitzer shell in the mouth of a cave will reduce it without question." Better still, Porter noted, barriers and turns in caves and tunnels would not stop the flow of gas.[28]

The logistical apparatus also began to turn in the summer of 1945 so that if the decision to use gas against Japanese cave defenses was made, the proper supplies would be ready. On 6 July MacArthur reported to Marshall's staff on the readiness of his command for either the offensive or defensive use of gas. First, he reported, stocks of chemical munitions presently stored in Australia and New Guinea were being brought forward to Luzon; they included almost seven thousand chemical bombs, almost two hundred thousand chemical-filled artillery and mortar rounds, and more than three thousand tons of bulk. However, he stressed an urgent need for ten-pound cluster bomb casings to be filled with mustard gas and for gas grenades. Training of chemical officers and NCOs "in the tactical employment of chemical agents" was being intensified.[29]

On 13 August Marshall prepared a memorandum for the Joint Chiefs declaring that enough stocks of "non-persistent" gas bombs (phosgene and cyanogen chloride) would be available by 1 November. But since persist-ent agents (mustard gas) required the same ten-pound bomb casing used in incendiary bombs and since the entire supply of those casings was going to the incendiary attacks on Japan's cities, no further supply of mustard gas bombs could be obtained without curtailing these incendiary attacks.[30]

Preparations for the use of gas were built into the OLYMPIC plans. In early June letters went out to commanders in Europe and the Mediterra-nean to ship excess gas masks to the United States. The Quartermaster General was ordered to provide enough protective clothing for all troops engaged in the invasion. Two shiploads of toxic chemicals were to be available for use by the air forces between X-Day-plus-5 and X-Day-plus-45 and another two shiploads for X-Day-plus-45 to X-Day-plus-90. Simi-larly, one shipload of eighty-five hundred tons of artillery ammunition was to be available in floating reserve for ground forces on the same schedule. Troops in the OLYMPIC assault were to carry protective under-wear, socks, and gloves; units were to carry a complete protective suit for each soldier; and extra suits were to be ready for resupply on X-Day.[31]

Other factors besides the stubborn problem of caves and bunkers no doubt encouraged the effort to abandon the policy of using gas only for retaliation. As long as Germany remained undefeated, using gas against the Japanese could give the Germans an excuse to use gas against the

Allies in Europe. But the defeat of Germany removed that threat. Following Roosevelt's death, the planners doubtless considered that Truman would prove less rigidly opposed to using gas. Finally, however, the anticipated cost of defeating Japanese cave, bunker, and pillbox defenses opened once again on the eve of DOWNFALL, a hitherto closed subject.

The military schemes that were offered to speed the defeat of Japan ranged from the improbable and unnecessary to serious and potentially effective proposals. The number and variety of proposals emphasized the frustration felt by the military—that the Japanese were defeated yet still determined to bleed U.S. forces for no rational purpose. The suicidal defenders of Iwo Jima and Okinawa, and especially the kamikazes, seemed to justify the use of weapons that would otherwise have seemed cruel and unnecessary. Thus, Marshall, a man of icy objectivity, could make a perfectly rational defense for the tactical use of gas, and Stimson, who abhorred the firebombing of Japanese cities, could become the architect for the atomic bombings of Hiroshima and Nagasaki.

No doubt some of the schemes were put forward by patrons with special interests who wanted their pet projects to be tried before the war ended. The benefits of other proposals, like the use of JB-2 unpiloted bombs were properly judged to be of insufficient value to justify the resources needed for their deployment. Still other proposals were premature. Further field tests in June 1945 indicated that VKA crop-killing chemicals were highly effective against broadleaf plants like beans and sweet potatoes but largely ineffective against rice and other cereal crops.[32]

Of all the proposals to employ special weapons in the war against Japan, the use of lethal gas was the most probable. It was hardly coincidental that invasion advocates raised the question of initiating gas warfare in early June just as the costly campaign for Okinawa was coming to an end. All the studies done in 1945 by the Chemical Warfare Service and the Special Projects Division of the War Department were predicated on a planning date for the initiation of gas warfare of 1 November 1945—the projected date of OLYMPIC. Marshall favored the tactical use of gas. Roosevelt, the chief opponent of gas warfare, was dead, and the inexperienced Truman, who was particularly concerned about casualties, would no doubt have proved more sympathetic. Nor is it credible that the British, or the Soviets, or the Chinese would have withheld approval. Marshall met his only resistance from Admiral Leahy who objected on moral grounds, but he also opposed the incendiary bombing campaign and the use of the atomic bombs on the same grounds.

The studies of the use of gas that were done in Project SPHINX were based only on the tactical use of gas against last-ditch, suicidal Japanese in caves and bunkers that could not be bypassed. The massive strategic use of gas was not seriously studied, nor proposed by any major leader. The U.S. Army Air Forces, the service most dedicated to strategic warfare, was unenthusiastic about the strategic use of gas.[33]

Fear of Japanese retaliation lessened because by the end of the war Japan's ability to deliver gas by air or by long-range guns had all but disappeared. In 1944 ULTRA revealed that the Japanese doubted their ability to retaliate against U.S. use of gas. On 15 July 1944 Japanese commanders were ordered to cease using any munitions such as smoke shells that might be mistaken for gas. "Every precaution must be taken not to give the enemy cause for a pretext to use gas," the commanders were warned. So fearful were Japanese leaders that they planned to ignore isolated tactical use of gas in the home islands by U.S. forces because they feared escalation.[34]

Finally, while the supply of chemical munitions in the western Pacific was short, and production of mustard gas bombs was particularly restricted, enough munitions were on hand for selected tactical use of gas against caves and bunkers. Had Japanese resistance persisted and had their cave and bunker defenses in southern Kyushu proved as formidable as those on Okinawa, the tactical use of gas against dug-in defenders would have been a difficult option to reject.

NOTES

1. Frederic J. Brown, *Chemical Warfare: A Study in Restraints* (Princeton: Princeton Univ. Press, 1968), 262–65; see also Barton J. Bernstein, "The Birth of the U.S. Biological Warfare Program," *Scientific American* 256 (June 1987): 119.

2. John W. Powell, "A Hidden Chapter in History," *The Bulletin of Atomic Scientists* 37 (October 1981): 44–53.

3. Memo, George W. Merck to Marshall, 8 March 1945, Sub: Destruction of Crops by "LN" Chemicals, RG 165, ABC 475.92 (2 February 1944), Sec. 1-B, NARA.

4. Rexmond C. Cochrane, "History of the Chemical Warfare Service in the United States" (Manuscript, Office of the Chief, Chemical Corps, 1947), 433.

5. Memo, Hull to Marshall, 9 March 1945, Sub: Destruction of Crops by "LN" Chemicals, RG 165, ABC 475.92 (2 February 1944), Sec. 1-B, NARA.

6. Memo, Porter to Commanding General, Army Service Forces, 30 March 1945, Sub: Weekly Progress Report on LN8 Agent, Ibid.

7. Memo, Porter to Commanding General, Army Service Forces, 31 March 1945, Sub: Military Requirement for Crop Destruction in Japan, Ibid.

8. Memo, Somervell to Hull, 14 April 1945, Sub: Military Requirements for Crop Destruction in Japan, Ibid.

9. Memo, Hull to Marshall, 22 April 1945, Sub: Policy on Use of Chemical Agent for Destruction of Japanese Crops, Ibid.

10. Memo, Porter to Commanding General, Army Service Forces, 2 May 1945, Sub: Military Requirements for Crop Destruction in Japan in 1945, and Memo from MG Wood to OPD, WDGS, 11 May 1945, Sub: Military Requirement for Crop Destruction in Japan, Ibid.

11. Report by the Joint Staff Planners and the Joint Logistics Committee on Policy on Use of Chemical Agents for the Destruction of Japanese Food Crops, 21 May 1945, Ibid.

12. Almost certainly the crop-killing chemicals were never used on the gardens of by-passed garrisons. Dale Birdsell, author of *The Chemical Warfare Service: Chemicals in Combat* (Washington, DC: GPO, 1966), believes that no spraying was ever done except in tests. Colonel (Ret.) Augustin M. Prentiss, USAF, who was a chemical air officer on General George Kenney's Far East Air Forces staff, remembers no chemical spraying ever being done in SWPA.

13. Memo, BG William A. Borden, Director, New Developments Division, to Marshall, 19 June 1945, Sub: Equipment for Use against Japan, RG 165, OPD 400 PTO, NARA.

14. War Department Training Circular No. 34, 11 August 1945.

15. Joint Committee on New Weapons (4 May 42), RG 165, ABC 334.8, Sec. 1, NARA; Wesley F. Craven and James L. Cate, eds., *Men and Planes*, vol. 6 (Chicago: Univ. of Chicago Press, 1951), 259–60.

16. Wesley F. Craven and James L. Cate, eds., vol. 3, *Europe, Argument to V-E Day, January 1944 to May 1945* (Chicago: Univ. of Chicago Press, 1951), 531, 727; Minutes of 8 February 1945 meeting, RG 218, CCS 334, NARA; Craven and Cate, *Men and Planes*, 254–55.

17. Draft message, Marshall to Eisenhower, n.d., RG 165, ABC 471.6 (7 October 43), Sec. 1-A, NARA.

18. Memo, New Developments Division to OPD, 31 May 1945, Sub: Use of V-2 Bombs against Japan, RG 165, ABC 471.6 (7 October 43), Sec. 1-A, NARA.

19. Memo, Arnold to Marshall, n.d., Sub: Manufacture of V-1 and V-2 Missiles in Germany, RG 165, ABC 471.6 (7 October 43), Sec. 1-A, NARA.

20. Memo, Craig to Commanding General, ASF, 14 July 1945, Sub: German V-2 Rockets, RG 165, ABC 471.6 (7 October 43), Sec. 2, NARA.

21. Memo, Hood to OPD, 14 July 1945, Sub: Employment of JB-2 (Buzz Bomb) in Operation "Coronet," Ibid.; Craven and Cate, *Men and Planes*, 256–57.

22. Memo, Craig to Commanding General, AAF, 23 July 1945, Sub: Employment of JB-2 (Buzz Bomb) in Operation CORONET, RG 165, ABC 471.6 (7 October 43), sec. 2, NARA.

23. Leo R. Brophy and George J. B. Fisher, *The Chemical Warfare Service: Organizing for War* (Washington, DC: GPO, 1959), 62–65, 88.

24. RG 165, ABC 475.92 (25 February 44), Sec. 1-B, NARA.

25. "Preparation for a Decision to Conduct Gas Warfare," 5 June 45, OPD 385TS, RG 165, NARA.

26. Brophy and Fisher, 87–88; Memo of conversation between Marshall, Stimson, and McCloy, Sub: Objectives towards Japan and Methods of Concluding War with Minimum Casualties, 29 May 1945, Records of the Secretary of War, RG 107, S–1 folder, NARA.

27. "U.S. Chemical Warfare Policy," 14 June 45, OPD 385 TS, RG165, NARA.

28. Memo, Porter to Borden, 13 July 1945, Sub: The Use of Gas Against Caves, RG 165, OPD 385 CWP, NARA.

29. Letter, USAFPAC to TAG, 6 July, 1945, File No. AG 381 TS, RG 165, OPD 385 TS, Sec. 1, Cases 5–14, 17 February 45–13 August 45, NARA.

30. Memo for Secretary, Joint Chiefs of Staff, 13 August 45, in "Availability and Production of Chemical Munitions," 9 August 45, OPD 385 TS, RG 165, NARA.

31. "Preparation for a Decision to Conduct Gas Warfare," 5 June 45; AFPAC Staff Study OLYMPIC.

32. Report of Army Air Forces Board, "Developments and Techniques for Dissemination of Chemicals from Aircraft for Crop Destruction," Project No. 4675A373.1, 26 June 1945, Documents Division, Air Univ. Library, Maxwell Air Force Base, AL.

33. Stephen L. McFarland, "Preparing for What Never Came: Chemical and Biological Warfare in World War II," *Defense Analysis* 2 (1986): 112.

34. Warren F. Kimball, ed., *Churchill and Roosevelt: The Complete Correspondence*, vol. 3 (Princeton: Princeton Univ. Press, 1984), 256; McFarland, 115.

Chapter 8

Ketsu-Go: Defense of the Homeland

The Japanese Imperial General Staff gave little attention to the defense of the home islands before mid-1944. Up to then, the threat of invasion seemed negligible. War leaders perceived only minor threats from possible small-scale American air raids carried out to weaken Japanese morale, to strengthen American morale, or to divert Japanese attention away from planned offensives. Thus, the early emphasis in homeland defense was almost wholly on air power, and even that effort was hampered by poor training and inadequate equipment. The few available anti-aircraft guns and defensive aircraft were obsolescent, and the air warning system depended heavily on visual observation and picket boats stationed off-shore.[1]

On 18 April 1942 Lieutenant Colonel James H. Doolittle led sixteen bombers from the carrier *Hornet* in an air raid against Tokyo. The Doolittle raid pointed up the inadequacies of the Japanese system of air defense, and the Imperial General Headquarters ordered modern fighters, bigger guns, and better radar. Defensive air forces were removed from the control of ground commanders, organized into an air army, and placed directly under the commander in chief of defense. Yet an invasion of the homeland was still considered virtually impossible, and air defense continued to receive the primary emphasis. Indeed, the entire homeland defense effort received little attention from the Imperial General Staff, whose generals and admirals concerned themselves with more pressing problems in overseas theaters.[2]

For the Japanese, the months of mid-1944 brought the war to a dangerous new phase. On 15 June Nimitz's central Pacific forces had landed on Saipan only fifteen hundred miles from Tokyo, and Mac-Arthur's forces in the southwest Pacific were poised to assault the Philippines. That same day, for the first time in the war, China-based B-29s struck industrial targets on Kyushu. A month earlier the Imperial General Staff had ordered the commander in chief of homeland defense to submit a new comprehensive plan; he was specifically ordered to include coastal defense measures to protect strategically important areas, especially the Tokyo-Yokohama, Nagoya, and southern Kyushu areas.[3]

Japan's terrific naval losses in the Battle of the Philippine Sea and the subsequent fall of Saipan forced upon Imperial General Headquarters a complete reevaluation of Pacific strategy. Invasion of the home islands now ceased to be a possibility and became a probability. Japanese strategists concluded that the United States would seek air and naval bases closer to Japan in the Philippines, in Formosa, and on the China coast before launching the final assault. In assessing possible approaches to Japan, they now concluded that a northern approach through the Aleutians and Kuriles was unlikely. The fall of the Marianas and the anticipated loss of the Philippines increased the threat from the south and east.[4]

In July, as a result of the grave new threats, Imperial General Headquarters issued a new comprehensive operational plan for the Pacific called "Sho-Go" (victory operation). The strategic underpinnings for Sho-Go were defense, delay, and attrition in the Philippines, Formosa, and the Ryukyus. The aim was twofold—first, to inflict such losses and delays on U.S. forces that Allied leaders would have to accept a negotiated peace and second, if that failed, to buy time for organizing homeland defenses. Parts 1 and 2 of the Sho-Go plan covered the defense of the Philippines, Formosa, and the Ryukyus; part 3 covered Hokkaido, and part 4 dealt with defense of the homeland in Honshu, Shikoku, and Kyushu.[5]

Some basic policies for defense of the homeland that appeared in Sho-Go would be carried over into the final 1945 homeland defense plan, Ketsu-Go (decisive operation). Sho-Go emphasized defense on the beaches and energetic counterattacks against landing forces before they could establish beachheads; it called for self-sufficient battalion-sized fighting positions and gun emplacements. The decision was also made not to withdraw large overseas forces to the homeland, but instead, to conduct the defense with standing homeland divisions, garrison troops, and newly raised forces, leavened with some veterans from the Kwantung Army in Manchuria.[6]

Construction of coastal defenses began in the fall of 1944. Some construction was planned for northern Honshu around Sendai, but by early 1945 little had been accomplished. The weight of the construction effort fell in three regions: Tokyo Bay, Ise Bay (Nagoya) and Shikoku, and southern Kyushu. Construction on the offshore Izu Islands near the mouth of Tokyo Bay and in southern Kyushu progressed more rapidly than elsewhere, but the entire construction program lagged behind goals. Japanese officers, long trained to think exclusively of offensive warfare, found it difficult to plan a defensive campaign. Steel and cement, two materials critical to building fortifications, were in short supply. The effort had to be hidden from the enemy and, for fear of spreading defeatism, from the Japanese people as well.[7]

By mid-April 1945 events were fast making the Sho-Go plan obsolete.

The plan had called for protracted defenses in the Philippines and Okinawa. The fight for the Philippines was almost over, and with that loss went the destruction of an entire Japanese area army—General Yamashita Tomoyuki's Fourteenth Area Army. The fight for Okinawa had just begun and would go on for another ten weeks. The futility of Japan's position was embodied not only in the frantic kamikaze attacks on the Okinawa invasion fleet but perhaps more dramatically in the futile and desperate fate of the mammoth battleship *Yamato*. Accompanied by a light cruiser and several destroyers, the world's largest warship sortied from the Inland Sea on 6 April to attack the U.S. fleet at Okinawa. The next day the *Yamato* and five escort vessels were sunk by U.S. carrier planes. The loss destroyed the Japanese navy's last desperate hope of maintaining communications with Lieutenant General Ushijima Mitsuru's 32d Army defending Okinawa. Even though the fight for Okinawa was just beginning, the outcome had to be known even to the most diehard Japanese. On 8 April, the day following the death of the *Yamato*, Imperial General Headquarters issued Ketsu-Go, the final plans that outlined mobilization, command structure, and strategic guidance for the defense of the home islands against Allied invasion.

PREDICTIONS AND ESTIMATES

In the spring of 1945 Japanese estimates of American intentions were very accurate. Even while the Joint Chiefs still debated the necessity for invading the home islands, Japanese intelligence analysts in the Imperial General Headquarters had already concluded that an invasion of the home islands was inevitable. They were less certain when it would come and what intermediate operations might precede it. As the battle for Okinawa raged, most Japanese military leaders predicted that the next step would be an American assault on the island of Kyushu. They even assessed correctly the outlines of the American scheme—a limited invasion of southern Kyushu to gain naval and air bases for a later knockout blow to the Tokyo-Yokohama area. Some feared that U.S. forces would strike at lightly defended Shikoku; others believed that northern Kyushu could also become a target. If no invasion had taken place in southern Kyushu by 1 November or if preliminary assaults were made against Cheju (Quelpart) and the Tsushima islands, then the threat to northern Kyushu would be upgraded. Perhaps the greatest fear was that the Americans would assault Kyushu with ten divisions in the spring or early summer when the fortifications would be only half complete.

Throughout the spring and early summer as the battle for Okinawa moved relentlessly to its inevitable conclusion, the central question for Japanese planners remained: would the United States seize more bases on the China coast, in southwest Korea, and, perhaps, on Oshima during the summer before invading Kyushu in the fall, or would U.S. forces drive straight into Kyushu without any further intermediate operations? Army analysts were inclined to believe the former and navy analysts predicted the latter.[8]

The collapse of Germany in early May forced the Japanese to refine their estimates. Now that Germany was defeated, the Japanese reasoned, public opinion in America would not stand for a long and costly campaign against Japan, and the American people would put tremendous pressure on the military to finish off Japan quickly and with relatively few American losses. Japanese analysts, however, overestimated the speed and efficiency of redeployment of U.S. forces from Europe. They expected thirty divisions to arrive in the Pacific from Europe—ten to be in the Philippines by the end of July and another twenty to come by the end of August. Their assessments led the Japanese to conclude that the American strategists would abandon any further peripheral operations and instead would launch a direct invasion of the home islands. By June Imperial Headquarters had concluded that the next American operation would be an invasion of southern Kyushu.[9]

Having ruled out further intermediate, peripheral operations, Japanese military leaders now predicted that U.S. forces would conduct an assault against southern Kyushu with a force of ten to twelve divisions (an estimate later revised upwards) sometime after 1 October. The Kyushu landings would gain bases to cover a massive thirty-division invasion of the Kanto Plain about three months after the Kyushu operation.[10]

Terrain assessments of southern Kyushu and studies of previous American landings pointed the Japanese defenders toward the same conclusions already reached by American planners. The main objectives would be the large airfields at Kanoya and Miyakonojo and the harbor and port facilities on southern Kyushu's two great bays, Kagoshima Bay and Ariake (Shibushi) Bay. The Japanese foresaw possible American landings to secure these prizes on three separate beaches—Ariake, Miyazaki, and Kushikino. At first, the Japanese were inclined to believe that the main American effort would come at Miyazaki, but by August the Japanese analysts had concluded that the U.S. commanders had sufficient forces to carry out simultaneous landings on all three beaches without making any one the primary effort. They now correctly believed that the total U.S. invasion force for the assault on Kyushu would comprise about fifteen divisions.[11]

The Japanese also correctly predicted that the Kyushu landings would be preceded by landings on the offshore island of Tanega to secure bases for small naval vessels and for patrol aircraft. Then, simultaneously or in quick succession, would come landings by five or six divisions at the head of Ariake Bay, by four divisions near Miyazaki, and by two divisions near Kushikino. A two-division force would land on southern Shikoku, and one or two airborne divisions would be dropped to secure inland airfields. While the Japanese estimate was generally accurate about American objectives, force levels, and timing, their concern about airborne assaults and landings on Shikoku were off the mark. American planners would play on these fears in the deception plan PASTEL by encouraging the Japanese to believe that large airborne operations were being prepared and by using the OLYMPIC floating reserve force in a feint against Shikoku.[12]

Even though they had correctly estimated American intentions, the Japanese faced a fundamental dilemma. Like all defenders against amphibious assault, they had to decide whether to meet the invaders at the beach and drive them back into the sea or to hold a mobile reserve in the interior, away from the enemy's naval guns and air power and attempt to destroy the enemy beachhead with a well-timed and violent counterattack. Both strategies held dangers. Staking everything on beach defense meant guessing correctly about enemy landing sites and strength. Even then, if the enemy broke through the hard crust of beach defenses, the battle would be over. Holding mobile reserves in the interior would give the defenders more freedom to see the enemy plan develop, but it would necessitate consolidating scattered forces, moving them over some distance, and bringing them together in a coordinated attack. As the Germans discovered the previous year at Normandy, Allied air power could seriously disrupt the movement of large units by road or by rail.

The Japanese planners forthrightly addressed the question of beach defense and provided clear and unequivocal instructions. All commanders were ordered to prepare fortifications and to deploy their troops for a defense "at the water's edge." American assault forces must not be allowed to establish a beachhead. Static, coastal defense divisions were organized to man the fixed fortifications at the beaches. These units would stop the landing forces and contain them on the beaches. Held behind the beaches, mobile assault divisions could move to the battle within ten days to strike the landing forces in violent and incessant counterattacks aimed at stopping the establishment of a beachhead. In addition, by engaging in a close, confused, face-to-face melee on the beaches, the Japanese could neutralize the greater U.S. advantages of naval gunfire support and air power. The American guns would be unable to fire, and air strikes would be canceled for fear of hitting friendly troops.[13]

FORCES, WEAPONS, AND TACTICS

American military leaders feared almost to the end of the war that the crack Kwantung Army would be withdrawn from Manchuria to defend the homeland. Beyond bringing home a few units, the Japanese never had any such plans. The best Kwantung units had already been withdrawn to defend islands in the Pacific, and in training, equipment, and overall quality, the Kwantung Army had declined considerably. But the Japanese had other reasons as well. Japanese leaders tended to view the resources of Manchuria and Korea as indispensable to the survival of the home islands. Also, they feared a Soviet attack on Manchuria.

Japanese military leaders planned to defend the home islands with a newly mobilized army consisting of recruits bolstered by garrison troops and a few units from the Kwantung Army. The Japanese leaders planned to raise a new homeland army of forty fresh divisions, twenty independent brigades, and attendant support units—more than two million men. These new units would be of two types—static coastal defense divisions and better trained and armed maneuver divisions to serve as counterattack forces. The former had more heavy artillery but less mobility than the latter. So that their logistical resources would not be overwhelmed, they would conduct three separate mobilizations spread over the months from March through July. Because of fears that the Americans would come early, the mobilizations were carried out more quickly than originally planned. Consequently, the fragile Japanese logistical system strained under the load. Transportation bottlenecks developed, and because all the new units were to be equipped from current production, serious scarcities appeared in weapons and ammunition. Some units reported to their commands without weapons or adequate training. To compound the problems, shortages of experienced commanders, staff officers, and specialists handicapped the creation of headquarters for the new units.[14]

The first mobilization, carried out in March, was dedicated to building eighteen new coastal defense divisions; thirteen of them were allocated to the defenses of Honshu, Shikoku, and Kyushu. They were given little training and put to work building fortifications. The second mobilization, carried out during May, brought into being eight new maneuver-attack divisions, six tank brigades, and five tank regiments. Simultaneously, four veteran divisions arrived from Manchuria. The third mobilization came in June and created sixteen new divisions—nine destined for coastal defense and seven designated for maneuver-attack. Army leaders also organized fourteen independent brigades, five infantry regiments, and large numbers of artillery regiments and battalions in this last mobilization.[15]

Miraculously, the Japanese seemed to raise large new forces quickly. Looked upon from afar, the new homeland forces appeared formidable, yet in reality there were grave problems in equipping, supplying, and transporting the new army. A staff officer described the logistical system: "Some 400,000 men . . . were to be equipped with approximately 12,000 motorized vehicles, 470,000 horses and 70,000 transport carts." The motorized vehicles would be requisitioned from the twenty-four thousand civilian cars that were still "in operating condition." The horses represented "one-seventh of all horses in the country," and "the army could furnish . . . 20,000 transport carts, but the additional 50,000 carts would have to be built or requisitioned by troops in their responsible areas."[16] Clearly, the Japanese logistical plans were based on thin substance and wishful thinking; they could not have sustained a prolonged defense.

The Japanese military leaders certainly recognized the untried nature and questionable quality of the troops called up in the three 1945 mobilizations. After the war a Japanese staff officer remembered that the third mobilization "exhausted practically all the reserve manpower of Japan, and the majority of those called up were either untrained or old. If Japan had been attacked at this time [June 1945] it would have been impossible to conduct an adequate defense."[17]

With the fall of the Philippines, Japan's supply lines with southeastern Asia were severed; with the invasion of Okinawa, the East China Sea was effectively closed to Japanese shipping. All overseas armies "were instructed . . . to become self supporting and to live off the land over which they were fighting." Even inside the homeland "hazards of land and sea transportation" caused an order for each area army "to establish a system of self sufficiency whereby it could conduct operations without assistance from outside agencies," particularly in "food supply, repair of equipment and production of fuel, weapons and other implements of war." Japan was so "pitiably short of requirements" that the defense of the homeland depended upon the production available during the months of the mobilizations. Resources were routed to Kyushu, the most immediately threatened area; other areas could wait for later production.[18]

Ketsu-Go divided the homeland, including Korea, into seven geographic areas. Each area was organized as a military district, and the defensive forces for each district were organized into an "area army." A Japanese area army consisted of two or more armies; in turn, each army consisted of two or more divisions. A Japanese army was equivalent in size and combat power to a U.S. corps, and an area army was equivalent to a U.S. field army.

Ketsu-Go contained a section for each of the area armies. Ketsu-Go 1 applied to the Fifth Area Army in Hokkaido, the Kuriles, and southern Sakhalin (Karafuto); Ketsu-Go 2 dealt with the Eleventh Area Army in northern Honshu; Ketsu-Go 4 and 5 dealt respectively with the Thirteenth and Fifteenth Area Armies in south-central and southern Honshu. Ketsu-Go 7 provided for the defense of Korea by the Seventeenth Area Army. From the birth of the plan, Ketsu-Go 3 and 6 provided for the defense of the two most important and immediately threatened areas in the homeland. Ketsu-Go 3 was the plan for the defense of central Honshu by the Twelfth Area Army. In this area was the Kanto Plain, the industrial and political heart of the empire. Ketsu-Go 6 provided for the defense by the Sixteenth Area Army of Kyushu, the most immediately threatened of the home islands. The Fifth (Hokkaido) and Seventeenth (Korea) Area Armies reported directly to Imperial General Headquarters. Two general armies were created to command the others. The Eleventh, Twelfth, and Thirteenth Area Armies reported to the First General Army in Tokyo, and the Fifteenth and Sixteenth Area Armies reported to the Second General Army in Hiroshima.[19] From the beginning of preparations, because they defended the most threatened areas in Japan, the Twelfth Area Army in the Kanto Plain and the Sixteenth Area Army in Kyushu had priority over the others. They received the greatest share of supplies and could get the materials and labor they needed for building fortifications. The overwhelming weight of combat power—combat units, heavy guns and artillery, ammunition, airplanes, and anti-aircraft defenses— were allocated to these armies.[20]

Imperial General Headquarters reorganized the structure of Army Air Force command in preparation for Ketsu-Go. Previously, army air units had been commanded by local area commanders. Now all army air units were placed under the command of a homeland "Air General Army" commanded by General Kawabe Mazakazu. The Kanto Plain (1st Air Army) and Kyushu (6th Air Army) received the lions' share of resources. The 2d Air Army in Manchuria and the 5th Air Army in Korea were ordered to aid the homeland air units in case of invasion.[21]

The navy high command was also reorganized. With the surface fleet sunk, aside from shore units that would pass to the army in case of invasion, the navy's most important asset was its now land-based air force. Hence, the old Headquarters, Combined Fleet was abolished, and in its place the new "Navy General Command" was activated under Admiral Toyoda Soemu. Chief subordinate commands were the 3d Air Fleet (Kanto), the 5th Air Fleet (Kyushu), and the 10th Air Fleet (training and overall homeland defense). Although navy and army air were ordered to cooperate and to make joint plans for homeland defense, the two air forces were never integrated.[22]

Interservice rivalry between the Japanese army and navy resembled the jealousies and divisions that sometimes complicated U.S. operations in the Pacific. Yet just as Nimitz and MacArthur were forced to cooperate in planning the American invasion, Ketsu-Go emphasized joint service cooperation in the defense of Japan. Army air forces would cooperate with submarines, suicide boats, and naval air units in attacking the invasion forces that were still at sea. In case Allied forces established a beachhead, naval ground forces would be commanded by the army ground commander. Ketsu-Go also stressed to commanders that they must be mutually supporting; commanders were ordered to prepare plans for shifting units among the area armies as the situation developed and American intentions became clearer.[23]

In fact, Japanese naval planes, both conventional and kamikaze, outnumbered those of the army. Naval air power, along with submarines, human torpedoes, and suicide boats, formed the navy's commitment to Ketsu-Go. Surface power was negligible. Except for the nineteen operational destroyers at anchor in the Inland Sea waiting to make suicidal sorties, Japan's surface fleet was at the bottom of the sea, damaged, or immobilized by lack of fuel. Only four damaged battleships, five damaged aircraft carriers, and two cruisers remained. They were designated floating anti-aircraft batteries to protect the naval bases where they were anchored.[24]

By far the most deadly weapon in the Japanese defensive arsenal was the massive use of kamikaze air attacks. Ketsu-Go relied heavily on kamikaze attacks, or, as the Japanese preferred to call them, "Tokko" or "To-Go" forces, a contraction of the Japanese expression "Tokubetsu Kogeki Tai" (special attack units).[25] Suicide planes had proved their destructiveness at Leyte, Luzon, and Okinawa. At those places the attacks had been desperation attempts by the navy to make use of its now almost carrierless air fleet. In those battles the Japanese leaders had selected enemy warships, especially the carriers, as the highest priority targets.

For the final defense of the homeland, suicide tactics would be used on an unprecedented scale. In fact, reliance on suicide units to attack and destroy the enemy invasion fleet at sea was viewed as the first and most decisive phase of Ketsu-Go. Instead of launching their attacks piecemeal as was often done in the earlier campaigns, the air force and naval air units planned to cooperate in incessant mass suicide attacks as soon as the invasion force came within range. Priority targets would no longer be enemy warships, but the transports carrying the assault forces. Japanese planners estimated that they could have ten thousand planes available at the time of the invasion, and they planned to expend five thousand of them during the first ten days of the battle for Kyushu. Simultaneously, two thousand small, fast suicide boats would dart from the many hidden harbors and bays to attack the convoys at night. Midget submarines and manned torpedoes would attack, and nineteen destroyers, the last remnants of Japan's once formidable surface fleet, would sortie to do battle. The most optimistic Japanese planners predicted that such tactics would destroy 50 percent of the invasion force before a single American soldier hit the beach. More realistic and dispassionate analysts put the figure at 34 percent or the equivalent of five divisions. Remembering that only one in six kamikazes had hit any target at Luzon and only one in nine at Okinawa, conservative planners predicted the destruction of 15 to 20 percent of the invasion force before any landings were made.[26]

Undoubtedly, the kamikaze threat to the invasion forces was dire. It is difficult, however, to calculate exactly the number of suicide planes the Japanese would have had ready for the invasion. Uncertainties cloud any precise estimate. The number of planes available varied over time, and the numbers cited by the Japanese may have been actual inventories or predictions of the numbers they expected to have at the time of OLYMPIC. The figures given by the Japanese after the war exceeded those in American sources.

Yet the numbers are roughly consistent. At the end of the war the Japanese navy had about twenty-seven hundred planes ready for use as kamikazes, and the army had another twenty-one hundred. The army projected another five hundred to a thousand kamikazes to be available by October. The Japanese navy, even judging by the lowest estimates, would have more than two thousand reconnaissance and attack aircraft by the time of OLYMPIC, while the army would have another eleven hundred. Some estimates for reconnaissance and attack planes number more than five thousand.[27]

Some questions remain. The discrepancies among sources is not so great for special attack planes as it is for reconnaissance and attack aircraft. Whether conventional aircraft equipped for orthodox reconnaissance and attack would eventually have been used as kamikazes is another uncertainty. Moreover, the Japanese leaders never made a firm decision on allocating kamikaze units between Kyushu and the Kanto Plain, although most evidence indicates that they intended to use them all in defense of Kyushu.

Whatever the precise numbers, beyond question the Japanese planned to use kamikazes on a massive and unprecedented scale. The sources may not agree on precise numbers, but all the estimates are large. Probably, the Japanese would have had at least five thousand kamikazes ready to meet OLYMPIC, but whether they could have been saved from destruction on the ground by U.S. planes is questionable.

Behind these impressive numbers lay some glaring weaknesses. The aircraft designs that had proved so superior to U.S. planes early in the war, by 1945 had been far surpassed and outclassed by new U.S. planes. In the last months of the war the Japanese refused almost all air combat, trying to hide and hoard their planes for the coming invasion. Yet conceding air supremacy to the Americans made their planes highly vulnerable to destruction on the ground. Compounding obsolescence were the twin problems of low fuel supplies and inexperienced pilots. By early 1945 U.S. submarines and surface attacks had cut off Japan's oil supplies from Southeast Asia. To accumulate a stockpile for Ketsu-Go, the Japanese had to curtail pilot training programs drastically. They could not afford to burn scarce gasoline to train new pilots, but their young pilots who replaced the veterans lost in the air battles of 1944 had desperately needed more training hours in the air.[28]

Early kamikaze volunteers in the Philippines had come from among the most highly trained and dedicated veteran pilots. In the early days Japanese commanders claimed that the kamikaze spirit arose spontaneously and that all suicide pilots were volunteers. In the defense of the homeland the role of kamikazes became a coldly rational military policy. Experienced pilots were reserved for orthodox air attacks while entire units of pilot trainees were designated special attack units. Not all were volunteers. Generally, in both the army and the navy, the least trained were selected for suicide duty.[29]

The great majority of the planes selected for use as kamikazes were old trainers that required modifications. First, a bomb rack had to be installed under the fuselage. The trainers could carry only light bombs, which often failed to penetrate the decks of heavily armored ships. Japanese technicians believed that greater penetrating power could be achieved if the pilot released his bomb moments before striking his target. Thus, bomb release mechanisms had to be added. Also, to increase the spread of fires, additional fuel tanks were installed.[30]

The Japanese even developed and produced a special suicide rocket plane. The oka (or as the Americans called it, "baka," Japanese for "stupid") was a rocket-propelled, twenty-foot long, piloted bomb, which could be carried near its target by a bomber. The oka could then glide the last miles into the target. Using a small rocket motor, the pilot could accelerate his final dive to speeds over six hundred miles per hour. The

2,645-pound warhead had devastating effect. One model, the oka 43, was a manned version of the German V-1. With its jet engine, it could be launched from a ramp to a range of 130 miles.[31]

Most Japanese military leaders believed that kamikazes, the centerpiece of homeland defense, could deal the invaders a devastating blow. Both Japanese and Americans agreed that the kamikazes promised to be Japan's most potent weapon.

Special attack units were organized by the navy for surface attacks. The naval counterpart of the oka manned rocket plane was the kaiten. This fifty-four-foot-long, eight-ton manned torpedo carried a thousand-pound warhead and could travel up to twenty miles at twelve knots. At its top speed of twenty-eight knots, the kaiten could travel eight miles. These manned torpedoes could be launched from caves and tunnels on shore, from large submarines, or from destroyers. At war's end the Japanese had 177 kaiten.[32]

The navy also produced large numbers of suicide boats (shinyo) and planned to deploy almost all of them in defense of Kyushu. The navy estimated that by the time the invasion took place, it could have as many as two thousand of these small, fast craft, designed to speed out at night from their hiding places in bays and inlets to attack the American invasion fleet in its anchorages. Two types of these boats were produced; they differed in size and speed but not in method of employment. The smaller shinyo was approximately seventeen feet in length with a narrow 5.5-foot beam. Its six-cylinder Toyoda truck engine gave the craft a speed of twenty-six knots and a range of 250 miles. When the single crew member drove his boat headlong into an enemy ship, an explosive charge protruding from the bow had the blast of a torpedo. The larger and faster type of shinyo had a length of twenty-two feet and a speed of thirty knots; it was manned by a two-man crew. Approximately thirteen hundred crewmen were selected by the navy and trained to man these boats.[33]

In addition, the navy allocated a large number of small submarines for the defense of Kyushu. The koryu was eighty-six feet in length and slightly under seven feet in the beam. This seventy-ton boat, operated by a crew of five, carried two eighteen-inch torpedoes. The kairyu was smaller—with a length of only fifty-five feet and a beam of slightly more than four feet and with a displacement of twenty tons. Armed with two twenty-one-inch torpedoes, this small craft could be produced quickly and in great numbers. The Japanese surrendered 393 small submarines when the war ended.[34]

Japanese defensive plans were a mirror image of the U.S. invasion plans. United States' planners had designed DOWNFALL with two clearly defined phases—a naval and amphibious phase followed by a ground combat phase. Japanese planners did likewise. Great emphasis was placed on delivering crushing blows to the invasion force while it was still at sea or in its invasion anchorages. If the Americans managed to land despite these violent offshore attacks, a furious defense on the beaches would keep the invaders from establishing a beachhead.[35]

Submarines and reconnaissance aircraft would patrol out to sea two hundred to three hundred miles to discover the invasion fleet as far offshore as possible. The Japanese planners hoped to gain at least a twenty-four-hour advantage before the invasion fleet reached the objective. Once contact was made, the Japanese were prepared to launch their entire remaining army and navy air strength in furious and incessant attacks. Two thousand fighters would contest U.S. planes for control of the air. Meanwhile, mass suicide attacks would be launched as soon as the invasion fleet was within range. Priority targets were to be the troop transports.[36]

As the invasion convoys reached their offshore anchorages and prepared to land the assault forces, the Japanese would intensify and broaden their attacks. Large submarines would close in behind the invasion force and attempt to cut off the lines of communications. After the time and location of the invasion became obvious, one hundred transport planes would take off carrying twelve hundred airborne troops to assault and disrupt the air bases on Okinawa, which furnished air cover for the invasion.[37]

In the invasion anchorages, the invasion fleet would be set upon by thousands of navy and air force planes, the majority kamikazes. The Japanese were prepared to keep up these attacks incessantly, night and day, for up to ten days or until all their planes were expended. Japanese commanders were cautioned not to waste planes in piecemeal attacks and to make certain before attacking that the invasion was the real thing. Although the primary kamikaze targets were the transports carrying the assault forces and their equipment, more than three hundred first line navy combat planes were equipped for suicide missions and ordered to attack the carriers and fire support warships. The Japanese hoped to distract these ships from their primary mission of supporting the landings.[38]

The Japanese aimed to saturate and overwhelm the American air defenses with waves of three to four hundred planes at one-hour intervals. While conventional attack planes tied up the naval anti-aircraft guns and the U.S. fighters, the kamikazes would aim for the transports. But therein lay a problem. Because of U.S. air power, the Japanese had been forced to disperse their planes over 125 air fields and air strips on Honshu, Shikoku, and Kyushu. If this multitude of small, scattered bases made it difficult for U.S. airmen to locate them, equally difficult would be the Japanese task of concentrating their scattered forces for mass attacks.[39] A severe shortage of radios further hampered the prospects of coordinating both kamikaze and ground attacks.

Nineteen destroyers, all the effective fighting ships left in the Japanese surface fleet, would await the invasion by hiding behind islands and under promontories in the western Inland Sea. Their orders were to attack only at night in unison with air attacks. Each was armed with conventional torpedoes and with two kaitens. However, low fuel supplies handicapped all Japanese preparations. The battleship *Nagato* was immobilized in Yokosuka by lack of fuel, and total naval fuel supplies would allow only a single major battle.

Small submarines would be held in the Inland Sea and used to attack transports. Because of their immense destructive effects, the kaitens would be used chiefly against large warships supporting the landings. The shinyos would be employed in night attacks against enemy transports in the invasion anchorages.[40]

The Japanese navy estimated that two thousand transports would be required to carry the American invasion force to the objectives in Kyushu. The navy planners expected to destroy 480 of the transports at sea or in the anchorages. They estimated that air attacks would destroy 210; small submarines and kaitens, 180; and shinyo, 90. Such losses would have cost the Americans the equivalent of two divisions.[41]

The heart of the Japanese army was the infantry division. Although larger than its American counterpart (eighteen thousand men to fifteen thousand men), the Japanese infantry division was more lightly armed. Division artillery contained fewer guns of lighter caliber than did the equivalent American division. The base of firepower in a Japanese infantry division came from its small arms, 9,500 rifles and 585 machine guns. Japanese tanks were few in number, light, and decidedly inferior to U.S. models. Japanese commanders realized that their tanks would be of little use in opposing U.S. armor; they planned to dig them in and use them to supplement their artillery.

The Japanese decision to deploy static divisions to hold the beaches until the arrival of the counterattack forces spawned a new coastal defense divisional organization to meet the superior firepower of the Americans. Once in position, the division was not expected to move. It was also expected to have in place enough food and ammunition for the final battle. Little need therefore existed for normal logistical and support troops. The strength of the division rested in four infantry regiments (as opposed to the normal three). Three of the regiments had strengths from thirty-five hundred to thirty-eight hundred whereas the fourth regiment (division reserve) was smaller with a strength of twenty-five hundred to thirty-two hundred men. Divisional anti-tank, artillery, and rocket units accounted for another seventeen hundred men. Total divisional strength numbered approximately 17,500; of these only one thousand men were devoted to logistical activities—principally transportation, signal, and medical. The division was designed to hold a coastline of twelve thousand yards with three regiments forward and one in reserve.[42]

If Japanese tanks could provide no defense against American armor, neither could their anti-tank guns. The 37mm light gun was completely ineffective against the M-4 U.S. Sherman tank; the slightly heavier 47mm gun could penetrate the M-4's armor only in vulnerable spots at very close range. Worse still, a shortage of tungsten steel forced the Japanese to use less effective carbon steel in their armor-piercing ammunition. Late in the war a shortage of fuzes forced them to rely on nonexploding solid shot. Although Japanese researchers had produced some bazooka-type rocket launchers, recoilless rifles, and high velocity anti-tank weapons, none had reached the ranks of the army.[43]

Weakness in the air had already led the Japanese to rely on kamikazes; similarly, weakness against U.S. tanks also led to the suicide tactic—one life, one tank. As an American intelligence officer put it, "The enemy's answer, for anti-tank defense, has been the development of simple economical close-combat weapons of intense firepower and demolition capabilities . . . [and] by liberal injection of the suicide factor." The same analyst went on to describe the "lunge mine," an armor-piercing explosive charge attached to one end of a long pole that could be thrust against the side of a tank and detonated; a suction mine that could be attached to the side of a tank by an infantryman; and "human mines," explosives tied to the backs of infantrymen who could throw themselves under advancing tanks.[44]

Japanese planners recognized the immense superiority of American air, sea, and ground combat power; they had seen the weight of that power overwhelm the most dedicated and the fiercest defenses that could be mustered to defend Luzon, Iwo Jima, and Okinawa. They had little hope that they could completely defeat an American invasion. However, they did believe that they could stop the first wave on the beaches. Perhaps if the cost of invasion escalated high enough, the Americans could be forced to abandon their invasion strategy. The Japanese also realized from many unfortunate past experiences that if the Americans were allowed to establish a secure beachhead, the weight of American resources would inevitably doom the defenders. The object, then, was to prevent the establishment of a beachhead; the Japanese would stake everything on a ferocious defense of the landing beaches.

Commanders of coastal defense divisions were ordered to build battalion-size positions with machine guns and direct fire guns located for interlocking fire. Care would be taken to camouflage these strong points from air observation. Underground tunnels would connect firing positions with central underground shelters for command posts, communication and medical facilities, and supplies. Water, rations, and ammunition would be accumulated for an extended defense. Commanders were cautioned to select the positions with care. The strong points were both to dominate the beaches and to block exits from the beaches into the interior. Raids and local counterattacks could be launched from any strong point. Special care would be taken to provide enough overhead cover to stop direct hits from naval gunfire. Extensive construction of anti-tank obstacles and anti-tank gun positions was ordered, and special anti-tank teams were trained. Construction and clever concealment of defenses on the rear slopes of hills would allow the defenders to attack the enemy even if the main positions were overrun. All positions were to be constructed in depth. The job of these coastal defense units was to stop the invaders on the beaches and hold them there for up to ten days.[45]

Meanwhile, the maneuver-attack divisions would be moving to the battle from 100 to 120 kilometers inland. Even though these divisions were more mobile than their coastal defense counterparts, they would move to the battle area on foot with their equipment pulled by horses. At a rate of twenty kilometers per day they could reach the battle area in five to six days. There they would move into fortified holding positions seven to thirteen kilometers behind the beaches and prepare to counterattack the invading forces. The counterattacks would come seven to ten days after the landings. Together with the remnants of the coastal defense divisions, they would force a close, direct fire-range melee on the beaches—a battle so crowded and chaotic and co-mingled that the great American advantages of naval gunfire and air power would be useless.[46]

NOTES

1. Japanese Monograph No. 17, 4–8. All Japanese Monographs and Statements of Japanese Officials cited in this chapter are housed at Department of Army, Center of Military History, Washington, DC.
2. Ibid., 9–13.

3. Ibid., 18–20.

4. Ibid., 22–23.

5. Ibid., 24–31.

6. Ibid.

7. Ibid., 26–28, 32–35.

8. Ibid., 75, 101–2; Japanese Estimate of Situation, Spring 1946, IGHQ, Army Department, 1 July 1945, and Estimate of Situation, Naval General Staff Headquarters, 1 June 1945, in vol. 12 of *War in Asia and the Pacific, 1937–1949,* eds. Donald S. Detwiler and Charles B. Burdick (New York: Garland Publishing, 1980).

9. Japanese Estimate of Situation, Spring 1945, IGHQ, Army Department, 11 July 1945, GHQ, FEC, USAMHI; Japanese Monograph No. 85, 6–7; Statements of Japanese Officials, Ohmae Toshikazu, Chief, Operations Sections, IGHQ.

10. Japanese Monograph No. 17, 82. The accuracy of Japanese estimates has led to the widespread belief that Japanese spies had penetrated MacArthur's Manila headquarters. No evidence for this belief has ever been found. See Alvin D. Coox, "Japanese Military Intelligence in the Pacific Theater: Its Non-Revolutionary Nature," *The Intelligence Revolution: A Historical Perspective* (Washington, DC: Office of Air Force History, 1991).

11. Statements of Japanese Officials: Hashimoto Masakatsu, operations staff officer, Second General Army; Haba Yasunobu, operations officer, Sixteenth Area Army; Tabata Ryoichi, operations staff officer, 57th Army; and Fuchida Mitsuo, air operations staff officer, General Naval Command.

12. Ibid.

13. Matsumoto Keisuke, Japanese Ground Self Defense Staff College, "Japanese Preparations to Conduct a Decisive Battle in Kyushu," Paper, U.S. Army-JGSDF Military History Exchange, Carlisle Barracks, PA, 26 October 1987; Statements of Japanese Officials, Miyazaki Shuichi, Chief of Operations Bureau, Army Section, IGHQ.

14. Japanese Monograph No. 17, 77–78, 80, 117.

15. Japanese Monograph No. 45, 247–48, 295–96.

16. Ibid., 249–50.

17. Japanese Monograph No. 17, 79–80.

18. Japanese Monograph No. 45, 265, 289, 296–97.

19. Japanese Monograph No. 17, 62–66, 203.

20. Ibid., 64–65, 203.

21. Japanese Monograph No. 23, 11, 20, 77–81.

22. Ibid., 28–29.

23. Japanese Monograph No. 17, 66–67.

24. Japanese Monograph No. 85, 16.

25. Japanese Monograph No. 157, 13, 15.

26. K. Jack Bauer and Alan C. [Alvin D.] Coox, "Olympic *vs.* Ketsu-Go," *Marine Corps Gazette* 49 (August 1965): 40; *Reports of General MacArthur*, vol. 1, 419–20; Matsumoto Keisuke, "Japanese Preparations . . . in Kyushu."

27. For precise estimates see Japanese Monographs No. 23 and No. 85 and the U.S. Strategic Bombing Survey.

28. Statements of Japanese Officials, Tanaka Koji, staff officer, IGHQ.

29. *United States Strategic Bombing Survey: Pacific War*, no. 62, "Japanese Air Power" (Washington, DC: Military Analysis Division, 1947), 61, 71. Hereafter cited as *USSBS*.

30. Ibid., 68, 72.

31. Japanese Intelligence, Military Research Bulletin, OPD 350.05, JAPAN, 9 May 1945, RG 65, NARA; *USSBS*, no. 63, "Japanese Air Weapons and Tactics," 22.

32. *USSBS*, no. 63, 22.

33. Report on Operation Olympic and Japanese Countermeasures by British Combined Operations Observers (Pacific), 4 April 1946, CAB 106, No. 97, PRO, Kew, London.

34. Ibid.

35. Japanese Monograph No. 85, 17–18.

36. Ibid., 18–20.

37. Ibid.

38. Ibid., 19–20.

39. *USSBS*, no. 62, 71.

40. Japanese Monograph No. 85, 22–24, 26.

41. Ibid., 28.

42. Report by the British Combined Operations Observers.

43. Statements of Japanese Officials, Yoshinaga Oshitake, Technical Department, Army Ordnance Administration Headquarters.

44. Ibid.; SWPA Intelligence Summary No. 1214, WNRC.

45. Matsumoto Keisuke, "Japanese Preparations . . . in Kyushu"; Japanese Monograph No. 17, 161–73.

46. Japanese Monograph No. 17, 161–73.

Chapter 9

Defense of Kyushu and the Kanto Plain

The Japanese military leaders faced a crucial dilemma: would the decisive battle be fought in Kyushu or on the Kanto Plain? Was Kyushu so important that all available resources should be poured into that island, leaving nothing to defend the Kanto? Or should resources be held back to defend the Kanto even at the risk of losing Kyushu? Perhaps both areas would be declared decisive, thereby weakening the defenses of both. These questions were further complicated by the possibility that the American planners might bypass Kyushu and strike directly at the Kanto Plain. Any large forces in Kyushu would therefore be removed from the battle by a massive end run. On the other hand, if the Kanto defenses were strengthened at the expense of Kyushu and if the United States quickly and easily established air and naval bases there, would not the defense of the Kanto Plain be automatically doomed? The Japanese needed to guess correctly, for Allied air power, poor transportation, and the geography of the islands would make large troop movements impossible once the battle began.

On this strategic question the Japanese never really made a formal and unequivocal choice. According to the Ketsu-Go plan, the Kanto Plain held priority over Kyushu for ground and air defense resources. Yet by July the Japanese had adopted a de facto position that the decisive battle would be fought in Kyushu. Events strengthened that choice. Although it was possible that U.S. forces would bypass Kyushu and go straight into the Kanto Plain, the Japanese believed that this was improbable. Many times during July and August, planes, suicide boats, combat units, and supplies were routed to Kyushu instead of Kanto with the assurance that production after October would replace the Kanto deficit. As the war ended, officers in the Imperial Headquarters were involved in heated debate over transferring the formidable 36th Army (six infantry and two tank divisions) from the Kanto Plain to Kyushu.[1]

DEFENSE OF KYUSHU

Ground defense of Kyushu was in the hands of the Sixteenth Area Army, one of the area armies that had been activated in April 1945 to prepare for Ketsu-Go. The army air force units deployed in Kyushu were commanded by the 6th Air Army. Navy units—air, sea, and ground— were under the commanders of Sasebo Naval Base and Kure Naval Base. The former commanded units in southern Kyushu and the latter commanded those in the north, though Japanese naval air was supposed to "cooperate" with army air forces. Once the ground battle was joined, naval ground force units were supposed to pass to the command of the army.

As if the overwhelming power of the Americans were not enough, geography added complications to the problems faced by the commander and staff of the Sixteenth Area Army. The central mountains, which divided northern Kyushu from the south, made it difficult to look at the island as a single defensive problem. In fact, the mountains separated Kyushu into two almost self-contained defensive areas. Both north and south were strategically important—the north for its industrial base around Yawata (the most extensive outside the Kanto Plain) and its geographic proximity to both the Shimonoseki and Tsushima straits, while the south was attractive to the Americans for its air bases, harbors, landing beaches, and proximity to Okinawa.

Early in 1945 the Japanese had only six divisions on Kyushu—three in the northern part of the island and three in the south. By August 1945 they had fourteen divisions and seven independent mixed brigades in Kyushu, and these were primarily concentrated in the south to resist the most immediate invasion threat.

In May and June 1945, after they recognized that Okinawa was lost, intelligence analysts at Japanese headquarters reasoned correctly that the next U.S. assault would come not on the China coast as previously expected, but directly against Kyushu—probably southern Kyushu. In July and August the Japanese began to pour new forces into southern Kyushu on a huge scale. In April, when the Sixteenth Area Army was activated, the defense of southern Kyushu was solely in the hands of the 57th Army. The forces available were meager—three divisions (one each disposed at Miyazaki, Ariake, and Kushikino beaches), one independent mixed brigade, and one independent infantry regiment. Another division, two tank brigades, and various field artillery units were assigned but had not yet been activated or transferred.[2]

In early June another army was assigned to southern Kyushu. The 40th Army Headquarters was redeployed from Formosa. Commanding General Nakazawa Mitsuo and his staff flew into Kyushu on 10 June and activated their command five days later. Henceforth, the defense of southern Kyushu would be divided between the 57th and the 40th Armies.

The 57th Army was responsible for southeastern Kyushu, including Miyazaki and Ariake beaches and the Osumi Peninsula. The 40th Army was assigned southwestern Kyushu including Kushikino and the Satsuma Peninsula. By August, thirteen divisions, three mixed brigades, five tank brigades, and various field artillery units were available to defend southern Kyushu. The 57th Army comprised five divisions, one mixed brigade, and two tank brigades. The 40th Army included four divisions and one mixed brigade. Sixteenth Area Army held a mobile counterattack force made up of four divisions and three tank brigades in the center of the island ready to move to the decisive battle area.[3]

The Japanese had so accurately predicted the beaches in the American assault plans that any surprise would be extremely unlikely. They anticipated landings in Kushikino, Ariake Bay, and Miyazaki, and considered landings on the southern beaches of the Satsuma Peninsula to the west of Lake Ikeda likely. Consequently, they disposed their defense forces to cover these areas.

The 40th Army deployed three of its four divisions in a coastal defense role. The 303d Division was deployed to hold the southwestern coast from Akune southward to Kushikino. It was to guard the Koshiki Straits and be prepared on short notice to move southward to reinforce the 206th Division. The 206th Division was the 40th Army's principal coastal defense force and guarded the most vulnerable coast in southwestern Kyushu—the beach from Kushikino to Tojimbara. The 146th Division defended the southern coast of the Satsuma Peninsula. The 77th Division was held at the head of Kagoshima Bay ready to counterattack in support of the 206th Division.[4]

The Japanese especially feared an American attempt to break through the minefields at the entrance of Kagoshima Bay or to capture the guns covering the mouth of the bay by first taking the Lake Ikeda area. Consequently, the 125th Independent Brigade, under the command of the 146th Division, was to guard the southern tip of the Satsuma Peninsula. Reinforcements could come from the 77th Division, centrally positioned at the head of Kagoshima Bay, and from the 216th Division, under the command of the Sixteenth Area Army and located north of the mountains in Kumamoto. In case of decisive battles at Miyazaki or Ariake beaches, the 77th Division would be transferred to the command of the 57th Army. The possibility also existed that the 206th Division would be sent to support the 57th Army. The commanding general of the 40th Army knew that if the 206th and 77th Divisions had to fight in the Miyazaki area, he could not defeat the Americans on the beaches and would be forced to retreat to prepared positions in the hills.[5]

The ground defense of southeastern Kyushu was the responsibility of the 57th Army, under the command of the Sixteenth Area Army. Three of the 57th's divisions—the 212th, the 154th, and the 156th—were located on the coastline of Miyazaki. The 154th on the central coast and the 156th in the south were coastal defense units and were supposed to remain in place. The 212th in the north could be moved to support either of the other two divisions within forty-eight hours of a landing or move even further south to Ariake if a landing took place there.[6]

Another division of the 57th Army, the 25th Division, had a central location in the area of the Kobayashi Plain and could move wherever necessary, probably to the Miyazaki Plain. Under the 25th Division was the 5th Tank Brigade, which would throw its force of fifty-six medium tanks, twenty-six light tanks, six self-propelled guns (150mm), and twenty-four self-propelled guns (75mm) into a strong counterattack in concert with the 25th Division within four to seven days of the landing. The brigade would use its medium and light tanks as mobile units to battle other tanks—it had no heavy tanks. The self-propelled guns would be used as anti-tank weapons from already prepared positions. The 150mm guns could also be used as normal supporting artillery. During the Leyte campaign, the Japanese mobile reserve had not moved quickly enough. Now the principle of speed and strong counterattack was insisted upon.[7]

The plan for the defense of the Miyazaki coast by the 57th Army was similar to the one for the coast of Kushikino by the 40th Army— annihilation of the enemy and no retreat. Deployment within each division was also similar: three regiments would defend the coast while one would be held in close reserve.[8]

Upon arrival the invaders would not encounter underwater obstacles. Neither would they likely find land mines on the beaches because the Japanese had been unable to produce them in quantity. The invaders would first encounter infantry in foxholes, trenches, and tunnels built into the dunes. These defenders were expected to relay information to troops behind the lines and then to fight to the death. A second defense line behind the dunes would provide stronger resistance. Behind this line would be the main defenses of battalion-strength strongpoints in prepared positions on high ground. Each battalion strongpoint would be organized for all-around defense with approximately a thousand rifles, two 70mm guns, twelve heavy machine guns, thirty-one light machine guns, two 75mm guns, four 37mm anti-tank guns, and a number of mortars.[9]

Although the Japanese had never perfected central control and massed fire of their artillery, the artillery guarding this coast could both fire on the beaches and cover the areas between the fighting units. The Japanese did not emphasize the use of coastal guns to defend against the invasion. Instead, they used the guns primarily to protect critical industrial areas and to guard the sea approaches to these areas. The Japanese expected more damage to the American ships from suicide attacks than from coastal guns.[10]

To protect crucial posts such as command posts and communication centers, commanders instructed that they be dug in seventeen meters deep. Widespread use of concrete was impossible because of lack of materials.[11]

In the area of Miyakonojo, the Japanese had positioned a special tank unit to meet the threat of American airborne troops. The unit's twenty-seven light tanks were ordered to move any place troops landed. Also, the Japanese erected poles and dug large plane traps to frustrate glider and plane landings.[12]

In addition to artillery units and other supporting arms, the army commanders could use special sea attack companies equipped with shinyo suicide craft. In the 40th Army plans, one of the companies would move to the Sendai River or to Kagoshima Bay by road. There were no definite objectives for these craft, but they probably would make night attacks against U.S. transports. Without any coordination with the navy's suicide craft, the 40th Army commander would have used the craft to benefit his own units. The commanding general of the 57th Army commanded the 31st and 32nd Special Sea Attack companies with 150 suicide craft. Major General Nishihara Kansi, commander of the 57th, said after the war that he had good coordination with the navy. The army boats would attack close inshore at night in small units. Craft manned by the navy would attack further offshore. Both army and navy craft would primarily attack transports and the LSTs.[13]

Coordination, which existed to some extent between the army and navy, was almost totally lacking with the air force. The channels of command were so complicated that any communication would have been improbable. Requests for air support would be routed through the Sixteenth Area Army at Fukuoka to the 6th Air Army headquarters and then down the air force chain of command. The 57th Army could not request aid directly from the air units located in its own area. In any case, the air force was hardly interested in air support to the ground forces—its sole effort was to attack enemy convoys.[14]

With the three possible major landing areas of Miyazaki, Ariake, and Kushikino to protect, the Japanese faced a grim problem in estimating when and where the enemy's main landings would occur. If their defensive scheme were to work, it was a critical decision. On it depended the precise positioning of their coastal defense divisions. More importantly, if the Japanese commanders deliberated and vacillated, they could throw off the timing of the counterattack by their maneuver-attack force.

Of the three major landing beaches, the Japanese planners always considered Miyazaki and Ariake the two most dangerous. In April and May they were inclined to believe that the main landings would come at Miyazaki with supporting landings at Ariake. They discounted almost completely the possibility of landings on the beaches of Kushikino.[15]

When July came and the Americans had not yet shown signs of invasion, the Japanese began to rethink their estimates. First, they reasoned, the coming typhoon season would postpone any landings until October. Meanwhile, the Americans could accumulate larger forces. Second, the Japanese had considered the airfields near Miyazaki and Ariake as the objectives most desired by the Americans. Now they began to see the great importance of Kagoshima as a naval base. Miyazaki furnished the best landing beaches, but in comparison to Ariake and Kushikino, that beach was relatively isolated from the airfields around Kanoya and from Kagoshima. Ariake would place the Americans near the airfields and only a short distance from the head of Kagoshima Bay. Landings at Kushikino would place the Americans directly across the narrow Satsuma Peninsula from Kagoshima. Thus, the Japanese were forced to consider the possibility of three simultaneous landings, each of which could be considered decisive.[16]

Of the three possible landing sites, the Japanese realized correctly that the greatest immediate danger would come from landings at Ariake Bay. Space would not allow as large an assault force at Ariake Bay as at the other two beaches, yet success at Ariake would place the Americans in command of the Kanoya airfields, the road to Kagoshima, and the back door to the Miyazaki Plain. Thus, if it proved impossible to discern the main attack quickly, Japanese commanders decided that Ariake Bay would automatically be designated the decisive battle area.[17]

In the Kanto Plain, a single army, the 36th, was designated to command, concentrate, and deliver the decisive counterattack to the invading forces that had been held on the beaches by the coastal defense divisions. A third army was planned for southern Kyushu to fulfill a similar role, but it was never formed. At the end of the war, the transfer of the 36th from the Kanto to southern Kyushu was still being debated. Thus, the counterattack force for Kyushu would have to be put together from elements in the 56th Army in northern Kyushu and units of the 40th and 57th. Units from less threatened areas would be withdrawn and consolidated into an attack force. The mobile counterattack divisions would be the 77th (40th Army), 25th (57th Army), and the 57th and 216th divisions from northern Kyushu. The 5th and 6th tank brigades from the 57th Army would give the counterattack force armored thrust.[18]

Japanese planners mandated that the counterattack must come within seven days or the Americans would be successful in establishing a beachhead. The attack units were to march twenty kilometers per day for five to six days to concentrate for the attack. Another three to four days were needed to organize and deploy. This was considered too long. Consequently, Japanese commanders eliminated the organization and deployment phase—the attacking units would be committed as they arrived in the battle area.[19]

DEFENSE OF THE KANTO PLAIN

Defense of central Honshu, including Tokyo and the Kanto Plain was the duty of the Twelfth Area Army. Its responsibilities included all of central Honshu from the Pacific shore across to the Sea of Japan. Yet, from the beginning of Ketsu-Go, all agreed that the ultimate aim of the Americans was to conquer the 75-by-100 mile flat lands that fan out from the head of Tokyo Bay. The Kanto was the heartland of the new Japan. From Kyushu had come the samurai who led the Meiji restoration in 1868, and Kyoto was the nation's spiritual center, but the Kanto Plain formed the political, industrial, and emotional center of modern Japan. And Tokyo and Yokohama embodied and symbolized its ambitions.

Together with the Sixteenth Area Army in Kyushu, the Twelfth Area Army received the great majority of the defensive troops and weapons that had been raised for Ketsu-Go. Yet, in June and July 1945, the danger to Kyushu became clear and imminent. Resources went to bolster against the most immediate threat, and, while the Kanto still ranked officially ahead of Kyushu in order of priority, the Twelfth Area Army leaders were told that the needs of Kyushu would be met first and that their needs would have to await future production.

Although Imperial General Headquarters never officially chose between Kyushu and the Kanto as the decisive battleground, it became clear by July that all kamikaze forces and air and naval forces would be expended in defense of Kyushu. None would be left for Kanto. The shift of emphasis away from the Kanto Plain toward Kyushu began in May and gathered momentum in June and July 1945. When the Americans failed immediately to followup their Okinawa victory with landings on the China coast, the Japanese revised their estimates and accurately concluded that Kyushu would be the next target and that the assault would come in September or October after the end of the typhoon season. That realization was embodied in new policies. Emergency shipments of munitions were stockpiled in Kyushu; the 57th Division from Manchuria, originally ordered to strengthen the 36th Army in the Kanto, was diverted to Kyushu; artillery and engineer units in Kyushu received priority for supplies and reinforcements over those in the Kanto; and Kyushu received priority in forming and equipping new units. Finally, a bitter debate erupted in Imperial Headquarters over the transfer to Kyushu of the 36th Army, the main striking force in the Kanto Plain of the Twelfth Area Army. This debate was still going on when the war ended, but according to one Imperial Headquarters staff officer, the transfer of the 36th Army to Kyushu would have occurred by the end of August. As Lieutenant General Miyazaki, chief army planner, noted after the war, Japanese military leaders decided to concentrate their strength "entirely in the area where American forces would make their first landing, thereby forcing the enemy to abandon their intention of attempting a second landing or else seriously delay this move."[20]

What were the prospects of defending the Kanto after an unsuccessful defense of Kyushu? By pouring forces into Kyushu, the Japanese admittedly weakened the Kanto defenses. After the war, most high-ranking army leaders were optimistic that great losses could have been inflicted on the enemy at Kyushu. They also admitted that they had little hope of mounting a planned and coordinated defense of the Kanto Plain should Kyushu be lost. Lieutenant General Kawabe Torashiro, deputy chief of the General Staff, did not think that a "systematic, organized decisive battle" could have been fought in Kanto. The only plan the Japanese could have followed, he despairingly noted, "was to scrape together [Japan's] remaining strength . . . and offer the best resistance possible." An all-out decisive battle would have developed in Kyushu and all air and sea suicide forces and "maximum available strength of ground forces" would have been committed there, believed chief planner Major General Amano. He was "absolutely sure" of victory in Kyushu. Yet if defeat occurred there, Amano believed that any later defense of the Kanto would necessarily have to be ad hoc. For the Kanto, Ketsu-Go would have to be abandoned and operations would be conducted "in accordance with the situation at the time."[21]

In the Kanto, just as in Kyushu, the Japanese had guessed with some precision the American landing beaches, and they had deployed their forces accordingly. Three armies—the 51st, 52d, and 53d—formed the heart of the coastal defenses. The 51st Army, consisting of three coastal defense divisions, two independent brigades, and one tank brigade, guarded the Kashima beaches north of Choshi. Although Kashima was threatened, the Japanese planners considered that area the least likely to attract an American landing. The most likely American invasion target was the crescent-shaped thirty-mile-long Kujukuri Beach below Choshi. Here the Japanese placed the strongest of their coastal forces—the 52d Army, made up of four divisions and one tank brigade. Just behind Kujukuri in priority came the Sagami Beach at the top of Sagami Bay. Landings there would provide the Americans with the shortest and most direct route to Yokohama-Tokyo. Here the Japanese deployed the 53d Army with three divisions, one independent brigade, and one tank brigade.[22]

To prevent the U.S. Navy from entering Tokyo Bay, fixed defenses were placed at the mouth of the bay. One army division and a single brigade manned fortifications at the tip of the Boso Peninsula, while naval forces at Yokosuka Navy Base, supplemented by an army brigade, manned the defenses across the mouth of the bay on the Miura Peninsula.[23]

A special, elite Tokyo Defense Army was established to defend Tokyo, the imperial palace, and the Izu Islands off the mouth of Tokyo Bay. A division and two brigades guarded the strategic off-shore islands. The First Guards Division, an anti-aircraft division, and three guards brigades held the mission of defending Tokyo. The First Guards Division was charged with the special mission of defending the imperial palace. The commander of the Tokyo Defense Army, Lieutenant General Iimura Jo explained that the defense of Tokyo "was mainly based on spiritual demands rather than its strategic necessity." The main defenses were disposed in the western part of the city because of fear that U.S. forces landing at Sagami Bay would rush to the western part of the city while major Japanese forces were countering landings far to the east at Kujukuri Beach. The final defense was to be made around the imperial palace.[24]

The 36th Army formed the mobile counterattack force that would move to the decisive area to destroy the landing forces that had been held on the beaches by the coastal defense forces. The 36th consisted of six maneuver-attack divisions and two tank divisions. The headquarters of the 36th Army was placed at Urawa, north of Tokyo. Subordinate divisions were disposed in the surrounding area so that they could move within two to three days to the decisive battle area.[25]

Defending units were initially responsible for constructing fortifications in their own areas. This practice, however, proved to be less than satisfactory. Inexperienced officers failed to take advantage of key terrain features; green units were placed in key places; weapons were not properly sited; and construction of fortifications interfered with training of newly mobilized units. The First General Army stepped in and took over the direction of fortifications. Heavy, fixed gun emplacements received top priority. By June these were relatively complete at key points on Kashima, Kujukuri, and Sagami beaches. Fortifications had existed at the mouth of Tokyo Bay since before the war. Beach positions for the troops of the coastal defense divisions were slower to be completed. As on Kyushu, most field fortifications were constructed of earth and logs.[26]

Defense of the Kanto Plain posed problems that were not present in the defense of Kyushu. By August it was clear that all air power and almost all remaining naval power would be expended in defense of Kyushu. Thus, the kamikazes would not be available to strike the invaders before they reached the Kanto beaches. In Kyushu, escarpments rose steeply immediately inland from the beaches placing the defenders on dominant terrain; in the Kanto the terrain was flat and open favoring the mobility and speed of the Americans. In Kyushu the pockets and corridors of flat land channelized attacking forces into readily apparent avenues—the open terrain of the Kanto meant that the defenders must be strong everywhere.

With three inviting and long beaches to protect, each leading to vital objectives, and with the Americans capable of landing superior forces on all of them simultaneously, the Japanese were in a constant quandary about the disposition of their forces. They believed the Americans could land a thirty-division force on the Kanto Plain. If they waited too long to determine the main attack, they could be overwhelmed before getting their mobile attack divisions in motion for a counterattack.

Japanese leaders realized that delay in committing all ground units to battle could be disastrous. As Colonel Fuwa, the operations staff officer of the Twelfth Area Army, said, "Judging the enemy's main landing area was extremely difficult, and if our decisive battle area were to be selected according to such an estimate, there would be great possibility of miscalculating the opportune time for battle." Consequently, "Our plan was to select the decisive battle area on our own." Since the Kujukuri beaches were the most likely invasion targets, the leaders decided to treat that area as the decisive front, regardless of American actions. Once the landings at Kujukuri were defeated, Japanese forces would turn to deal with the landing forces at Sagami and Kashima.[27]

As soon as an American assault on the Kanto Plain was certain, the 36th Army, the principal maneuver-attack force in the Twelfth Area Army, would move eastward to take up positions along the Chiba-Sakurkura-Narita axis, directly in the rear of the 52d Army, which was assigned to the coastal defense of Kujukuri. An earlier move was prohibited by food shortages in the staging area; to wait until the landings had begun invited destruction by U.S. air attacks. The 36th Army would begin counterattacks "within two to three days after the initial landings by the American forces. . . . The 36th Army was to attack with its main force, without waiting for the deployment of its entire strength, and was to send the units into battle as they arrived." Should the Americans not threaten the adjacent areas of Honshu on the north and south of the Kanto Plain, those area armies were expected to release their forces to the Twelfth. However, these units would only move by night, and they were not expected to reach the battle area for two weeks. By then the decisive battle would almost certainly be over.[28]

Colonel Fuwa was extremely pessimistic about the chances of reinforcement by forces outside the Kanto Plain. In fact, plans called for seven divisions to converge on the Kanto from other areas. When the plan was presented, Colonel Fuwa argued that "it was impossible to have such a great force come together in the Kanto sector from such distant points." Rail movement, he argued, "could not be relied upon due to enemy bombing." Marching overland could require as much as three months, and the logistical problems for such a march would be insurmountable.[29]

While the Japanese planners considered that the Americans might land on Kujukuri, Kashima, and Sagami beaches simultaneously, they considered that possibility remote. A much more likely danger was posed by dual landings on Kujukuri and Sagami. In that case, according to Colonel Fuwa, the Japanese hoped that success on Kujukuri might cause the Americans to change their plans and "divert the troops [scheduled for Sagami] to the Kujukuri . . . front."[30] This bit of wishful thinking indicates either that the Japanese were hoping to be saved by some last minute American change of plans or, more realistically, that they were incapable of defending more than one front.

It appears that the Japanese leaders ultimately had little hope of an effective coordinated defense of the Kanto Plain once Kyushu was lost. Their general plan was to concentrate their main strength, both coastal defense and maneuver-attack units, on the Kujukuri beaches. That area, the most likely American invasion target, would automatically be considered the decisive (main) attack. Should the American landings on Kujukuri be followed by large landings elsewhere, especially at Sagami Bay, the Japanese had little reserve, nor could they disengage and move forces from Kujukuri. Only three coastal defense divisions would defend the Sagami beaches. While these may have presented considerable resistance, once the coastal defenses were broken, there was little behind the beaches to stop the invaders. "Under such circumstances," Colonel Fuwa predicted, "the enemy would have broken through to the outskirts of Tokyo in one move."[31]

ASSESSMENT

Japanese military leaders believed that a combination of rigid beach defense and counterattack would destroy the first wave of the invading forces. This estimate would appear to be optimistic. But short of surrender, such a defense was all that was left to military leaders, and their optimism was born of desperation. Certainly, the kamikazes and the coastal defense forces would have taken a high toll among the assault forces. But the ground defense plan was based on assumptions that almost surely could not be fulfilled. In fact, past experience against the Americans showed as much. Earlier, Japanese commanders had abandoned forward beach defenses because of the devastating effect of naval gunfire and air attack. Early defensive positions in Kyushu were put far back from the beaches for that reason. Higher commanders had to order the positions to be put further forward. That the coastal defense units could have survived the greatest pre-invasion bombardment in history to fight a tenacious, organized beach defense was highly doubtful.

Similarly, that the counterattack divisions could be marched to the battle from 100 to 120 kilometers inland over poor roads and mountain trails in the face of overwhelming enemy air attacks was equally doubtful. Even if these attack units had arrived at the battle, in the interest of time, the Japanese leaders planned to commit them to the counterattack piecemeal. Thus, the very fury and shock that the Japanese counted on would have been dissipated.

Perhaps, the bleakest prospect for the Japanese was the scale of the American landings planned for southern Kyushu. The Americans planned corps-sized (the equivalent of a Japanese army) landings on all three fronts simultaneously. None could be considered the main assault. The Japanese had only one army-sized counterattack force. No doubt, Japanese commanders would have been like a man in the center of a room trying to bar intruders simultaneously from three doors on opposite walls. No matter which intruder he attacked, the other two would overwhelm him.

Some Japanese military leaders boasted that the Americans would be destroyed by the entire nation in arms. It would be impossible to defeat the resistance of the Japanese people. Other leaders admitted that war weariness increased among civilians after the B-29 fire-bombing raids began in March and after the fall of Okinawa in June. Following the war, Japanese military leaders unanimously praised the conduct of the Japanese civilians—their faith in ultimate victory, their support and loyalty to the military, and their willingness to die with the soldiers in the final defense of the homeland. This rhetoric led to the popular belief that the Japanese civilian population was mobilized by the military to fight the Americans with sticks and stones and that the Japanese people, formed into a nation of kamikazes, would have caused large numbers of American casualties.

While the military plans for the final defense of the homeland counted heavily on the continued support of the civilian population, specific and practical measures to mobilize civilians to fight were never undertaken. Planners of the final defense of the homeland wanted three things from Japanese civilians. First, they wanted continued loyalty so that they would have no civil problems in their rear. They wanted civilian help in logistics, military construction, transportation, and supply. Finally, they wanted continued production, both industrial and agricultural. These services would free Japanese soldiers from rear area support and garrison duties for combat duty. Lieutenant General Kawabe Torashiro of the Imperial General Staff explained that "we planned to use a small select number [of civilians] for supporting intelligence and guerrilla operations, but we felt that it would not be practical to use all civilians in combat."[32]

In fact, like most military men in similar situations, Japanese commanders and planners looked on civilians in the battle area more as a handicap than as an asset. According to the commanding general of the 57th Army in southern Kyushu, any attempt to use civilians in combat not only would be "ineffectual" but would also "have disadvantageous effects on the morale of the army" and would hinder, not help, operations. Plans were made to evacuate civilians to rear areas.[33]

As in their military planning, the Japanese faced a dilemma in coping with the evacuation of civilians. Most military leaders agreed that evacuation was the proper military course, but problems frustrated attempts to complete it. The necessary supply and housing facilities would have cut deeply into military stocks and imposed a great burden on an already creaky logistical system. In both Kyushu and Kanto, a dense population lived in the lowland areas near the coast. These areas were the principal objectives of the Americans. These were also areas of heavy food production. Old men, women, and children worked the crops. Moving these people would further reduce the already meager stocks of food, but leaving the civilians in place promised to confuse and complicate military operations. Indeed, according to Lieutenant General Kawabe of the Imperial Headquarters, the army's reluctance to abandon the large civilian populations in the coastal areas was a major reason for adopting a beach defense strategy.[34] As the war ended, Japanese military leaders still had not resolved their dilemma.

Before the war's end, the Japanese army had made only general plans for organizing two types of volunteer units—sector garrison units and volunteer combat units. Garrison units, as their name implied, would primarily be assigned garrison duties, a kind of home guard to relieve regular soldiers for combat assignments. These three-hundred-man units would be commanded by a small cadre of regular officers and would be armed only to the extent that light weapons were available locally. Volunteer units could be organized ad hoc by local commanders. No national plan existed for these units. In fact, the bottom of the homeland manpower pool and equipment reserves had been reached in the third general mobilization in June and July; little more military power could be drawn from militia units. In the opinion of the chief planner of the Second General Army, "Little reliance could have . . . been placed on their [national volunteer corps'] efforts.[35]

Japanese leaders could count on several proven strengths in defending the home islands. They had a homeland army of more than two million men backed by a disciplined populace. Their intelligence estimates were extremely accurate. They predicted the objectives, timing, strength, and scheme of the American assault with great precision. They had a clear terrain advantage. All of the landing beaches in southern Kyushu were backed one to five kilometers inland by continuous lines of bluffs broken only by a few readily discernible and defensible beach exits.

Japanese leaders recognized the formidable nature of the kamikazes and prepared to use them as their chief defense against invasion. The tenacious and deadly qualities of Japanese soldiers fighting from fixed-cave defenses had been proved at Saipan, Iwo Jima, Luzon, and Okinawa. Certainly, the prospects of massed kamikaze attacks and of facing dug-in Japanese in bloody infantry engagements seriously worried U.S. planners.

Yet were the Japanese homeland defenses as formidable as they appeared? Behind the large numbers of planes, the excellent intelligence estimates, and the well-reasoned defense plans were some critical weaknesses. The difficulties in massing kamikazes, the poor quality of homeland defense units, and the difficulty in getting counterattack forces to the battle have already been noted. Some other weaknesses have not. Local communications at division level were by commercial telephone. Below division, messages went by runners or by hand signals. The logistical system, especially in Kyushu, was all but nonexistent. The in-depth planned defense was, in fact, only a tough outer shell. The counterattack forces would not likely make it to the battle on the beaches considering

U.S. air power, the lack of mobility in the homeland army, extremely poor roads, and the mountains that divided northern from southern Kyushu. When the shell of beach defenses was punctured, the battle would be over.

The Japanese problems would have been even greater in the Kanto Plain than in Kyushu. Japan's air forces would have been used up in Kyushu. Because of poor transportation and U.S. air power, the forces could look forward to no reinforcements in the Kanto. They had only enough resources to mount defense of a single beach though the Americans planned two army-sized assaults. The core of their dilemma was unresolved and perhaps unresolvable. In choosing to fight the decisive battle in Kyushu, they would have little left to defend the Kanto Plain.

NOTES

1. Statements of Japanese Officials, Joichiro Sanada, Chief of Staff, Second General Army; Kanetoshi Mashita, staff officer, IGHO. All Japanese Monographs and Statements of Japanese Officials cited in this chapter are housed at Department of Army, Center of Military History, Washington, DC.

2. Report on Operation Olympic and Japanese Countermeasures by British Combined Operations Observers (Pacific), 4 April 1946, CAB 106, No. 97, PRO, Kew, London; Statements of Japanese Officials, Yoshitake Yasumasa, Chief of Staff, 57th Army.

3. Japanese Monograph No. 17, 118, 122–24, 128.

4. Report by British Combined Operations Observers.

5. Ibid.

6. Ibid.

7. Ibid.

8. Ibid.

9. Ibid.

10. Ibid.

11. Ibid.

12. Ibid.

13. Ibid.

14. Ibid.

15. Statements of Japanese Officials, Yoshitake Yasumasa and Haba Yasunobu, operations staff officer, Sixteenth Area Army.

16. Ibid.

17. Statements of Japanese Officials, Yoshitake Yasumasa; Haba Yasunobu; Nishihara Kanji, Commanding General, 57th Army.

18. Japanese Monograph No. 17, 122–24; Statements of Japanese Officials, Nishihara Kanji.

19. Statements of Japanese Officials, Haba Yasunobu; Tabata Ryoichi.

20. Statements of Japanese Officials, Kawabe Torashiro, Deputy Chief of General Staff, IGHO; Miyazaki Shuichi, Chief of Operations, Army Section, IGHQ; Hosoda Hiromu, operations staff officer, IGHQ.

21. Statements of Japanese Officials, Kawabe Torashiro; Amano Masakazu, Chief of Operations Section, IGHQ.

22. Japanese Monograph No. 17, 85; Statements, Fuwa Hiroshi, staff officer, Twelfth Area Army.

23. Statements of Japanese Officials, Fuwa Hiroshi.

24. Japanese Monograph No. 17, 80–82; Statements of Japanese Officials, Iimura Jo, Commanding General, Tokyo Defense Army.

25. Statements of Japanese Officials, Fuwa Hiroshi.

26. Japanese Monograph No. 17, 84–86; Statements of Japanese Officials, Fuwa Hiroshi.

27. Statements of Japanese Officials, Fuwa Hiroshi.

28. Ibid.

29. Ibid.

30. Ibid.

31. Ibid.

32. Statements of Japanese Officials, Kawabe Torashiro.

33. Statements of Japanese Officials, Nishihara Kanji.

34. Statements of Japanese Officials, Kawabe Torashiro.

35. Statements of Japanese Officials, Fuwa Hiroshi; Sanada Joichiro.

Pacific Commands (from *Command Decisions*; Washington, DC: GPO, 1960)

PACIFIC OCEAN AREAS
1 August 1942

——— AREA BOUNDARIES
– – – SUBDIVISION BOUNDARIES

STATUTE MILES ON THE EQUATOR
0   1000   2000

NORTH PACIFIC AREA

CENTRAL PACIFIC AREA

PACIFIC OCEAN AREAS

SOUTH PACIFIC AREA

HAWAIIAN ISLANDS
Midway   Johnston

Palmyra
Fanning
Christmas

Canton

Samoa

Bora Bora

Wake

MARSHALL IS

GILBERT IS   ELLICE IS

FIJI
Viti Levu   Tongatabu

MARIANA IS
Guam

NEW ZEALAND

159°E
SOLOMON IS

Espiritu Santo

New
Caledonia

SOUTHWEST
PACIFIC AREA
AUSTRALIA

159°E

NEW
GUINEA

PHILIPPINE IS

NETHERLANDS INDIES

Formosa

JAPAN

CHINA

U.S.S.R.

CANADA

UNITED
STATES

42°N

42°N

20°N
130°E

8°S
104°E

16°30′S
110°E

0°

0°

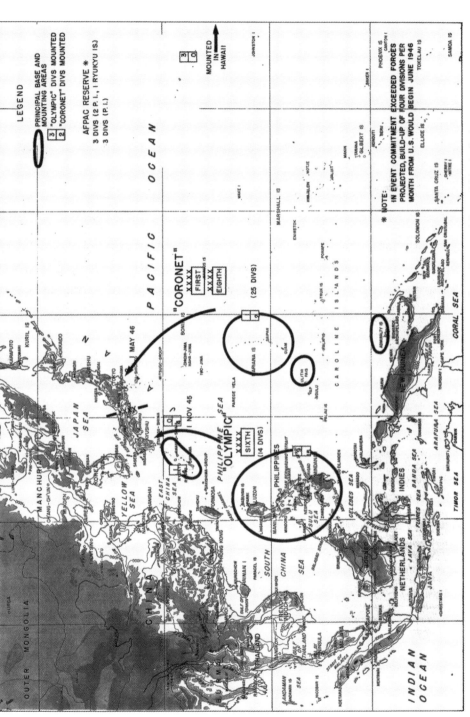

The DOWNFALL Plan for the Invasion of Japan, 28 May 1945 (from *Reports of General MacArthur*)

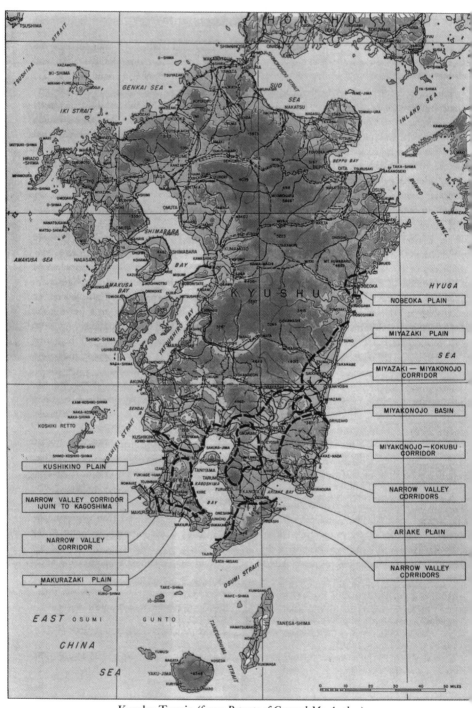

Kyushu Terrain (from *Reports of General MacArthur*)

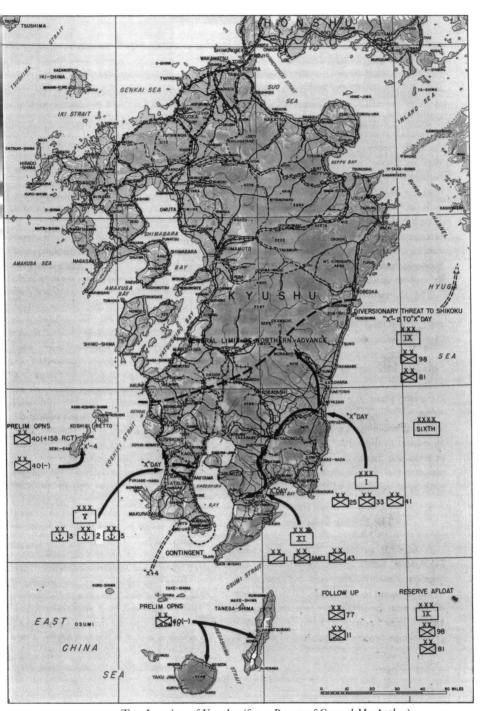

OLYMPIC—The Invasion of Kyushu (from *Reports of General MacArthur*)

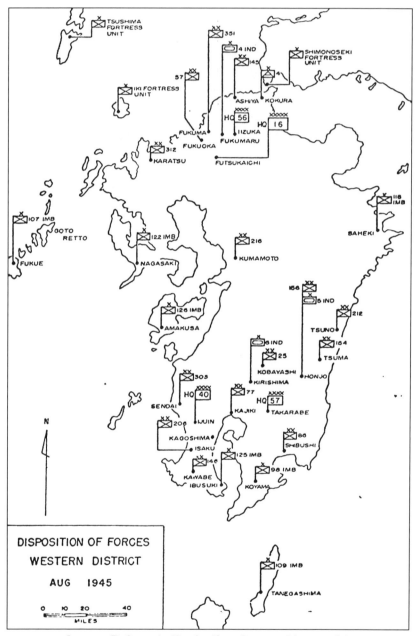

Japanese Defenses in Kyushu (from Japanese Monographs)

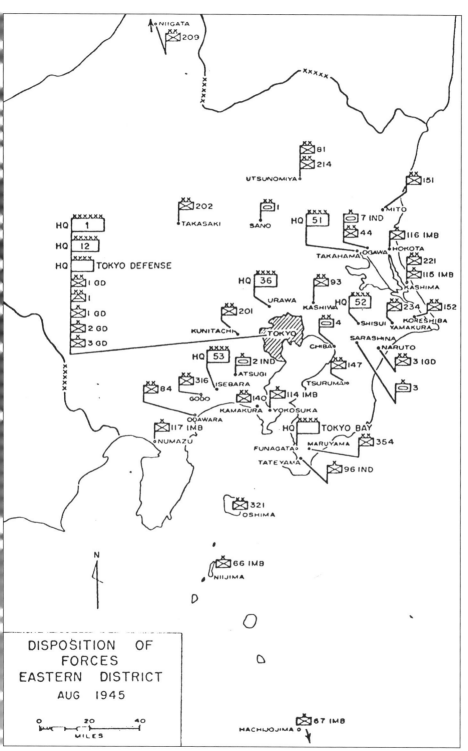

Japanese Defenses in the Kanto Plain (from Japanese Monographs)

Beach Organization for Operation against Kyushu
(from COMPHIBSPAC OP PLAN A11-45, 10 August 1945)

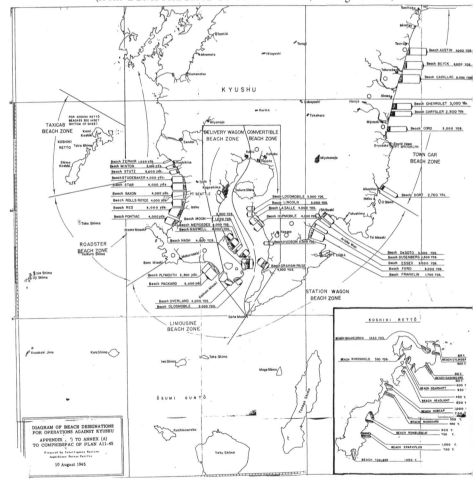

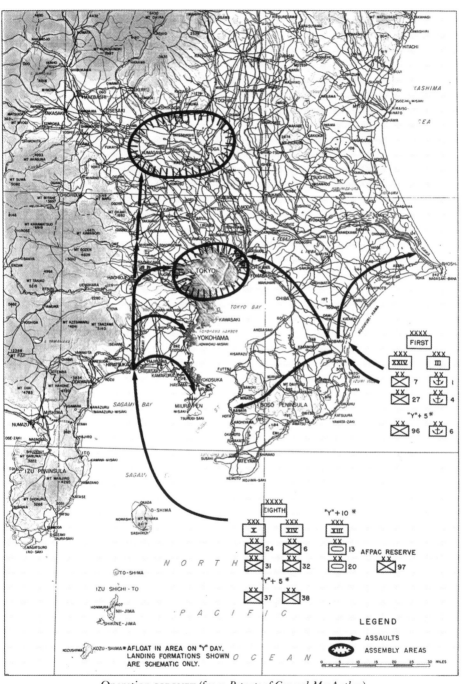

Operation CORONET (from *Reports of General MacArthur*)

Chapter 10

ULTRA and the Invasion

F. W. Winterbotham's *The Ultra Secret*, published in 1974, opened the best kept secret of World War II—that from the early days of the conflict British intelligence was intercepting, decrypting, and routinely distributing to Allied commanders radio messages transmitted by the Wehrmacht and the Luftwaffe. By all accounts this intelligence proved invaluable if not decisive in the war against Germany. Similarly well known is the controversy about the failure of MAGIC, the American code-breaking effort, to decrypt Japanese diplomatic messages that could have revealed the plans for the attack on Pearl Harbor. Less well known is the story of MacArthur's ULTRA—the successful penetration of Japanese army and air force radio messages in the Pacific.[1]

In the spring of 1942 Admiral Nimitz's navy codebreakers worked frantically to crack Japanese naval codes. Their efforts, though not yet complete, were successful enough to allow U.S. carriers to intercept in the Coral Sea and fight off the advance of a Japanese task force on Port Moresby, New Guinea—an offensive that, if successful, could have broken American communications with Australia and prolonged the war for years. These codebreakers' critical intelligence allowed Nimitz to position his carriers at precisely the correct time and place to deal a devastating blow to Admiral Yamamoto's fleet at Midway. Their success is a classic payoff in World War II codebreaking.[2]

Yet as MacArthur's Southwest Pacific Area (SWPA) forces slogged through the fetid terrain of eastern New Guinea in 1942 and 1943, his own codebreakers in "Central Bureau" had just begun their efforts to break Japanese army codes and were meeting with little success. Therefore, in the critical 1942 campaign to protect Port Moresby and in the costly (but eventually successful) campaign in early 1943 to eject the Japanese from their positions around Buna, MacArthur's planners depended heavily on ULTRA intelligence furnished to his staff by U.S. Naval intelligence. But the information came exclusively from decryptions of Japanese navy messages. By the end of 1942, army codebreakers at Arlington Hall in the Virginia suburbs of Washington and at Central Bureau in Australia had only succeeded in reading some addresses of Japanese army messages, and this success had been accomplished with some help from the navy.[3]

During 1943, however, the army codebreakers at Central Bureau and Arlington Hall got lucky. First came the fortuitous capture of the "Japanese Army List," a directory by rank and assignment of forty thousand Japanese officers. Now the codebreakers, by knowing that a particular officer was assigned to a certain unit, could track the location of that unit. This good fortune was quickly followed by breaking the Japanese shipping code. The critical success came in January of 1944 when Australian soldiers near Sio in New Guinea discovered codebooks that belonged to the retreating Japanese 20th Division. Suddenly, after months of effort that had been rewarded only by the decryption of bits and pieces of Japanese Army messages, Central Bureau had hit a bonanza. In March 1944 thirty-six thousand army messages were intercepted and decrypted. ULTRA transformed MacArthur's strategy.[4]

MacArthur's ULTRA was perhaps most valuable for producing accurate estimates of Japanese army and air force orders of battle—the locations, dispositions, and strengths of enemy ground and air units. With only land-based air forces to cover the landings, MacArthur's amphibious leaps had been limited by the range of General George Kenney's fighters, so the army's 1943 drive up the northern coast of New Guinea had proceeded very slowly. But in the central Pacific, Nimitz's carriers gave the navy's amphibious forces far greater range and flexibility. Because of MacArthur's slower progress, SWPA was in danger of becoming secondary to Nimitz's faster moving and more direct central Pacific offensive. ULTRA perhaps saved MacArthur's SWPA offensive. The intelligence informed MacArthur's air commander Kenney where the Japanese air bases were, so that Kenney's airmen could destroy Japanese planes on the ground. The resulting destruction of the Japanese air threat coupled with accurate order of battle information on Japanese ground defenses enabled MacArthur's amphibious forces to bypass strongpoints and strike deeper with greater surprise at weakly held places. Thus, MacArthur's drive on the Philippines gained much greater speed and momentum.[5]

By the spring of 1945 MacArthur's forces were completing the liberation of the Philippines. As he and Nimitz began to plan for OLYMPIC, the interception, decryption, and distribution of ULTRA intelligence had become well organized and organizationally integrated. Nimitz's Joint Intelligence Center, Pacific Ocean Areas (JICPOA) shared information with army intelligence at Arlington Hall and both supplied information to MacArthur's Central Bureau, now staffed by more than four thousand workers.[6] In addition, Special Security Officers had been assigned to all major headquarters to aid in the use and security of ULTRA intelligence. Nonetheless, the system was not problem-free, and the intelligence produced by ULTRA was not without serious gaps. For example, based as it was on radio interceptions, ULTRA could produce highly accurate order of battle information that was extremely valuable to staff planners and to fighting commands. Yet restrictions placed by MacArthur's headquarters on the distribution of ULTRA sometimes narrowed the flow of intelligence to Eighth and Sixth armies. Also, ULTRA could not predict the Japanese strategy that led to a massive Japanese buildup of forces in southern Kyushu during the summer of 1945. ULTRA could, however, track the buildup as it occurred.

The initial intelligence estimate for OLYMPIC was published by Mac-Arthur's G-2, Major General Charles A. Willoughby and his staff on 25 April 1945. The estimate showed only a single Japanese division in southern Kyushu—the 86th Division with a strength of sixteen thousand disposed in and around Miyakonojo. Two infantry replacement regiments numbering thirty-one hundred soldiers each were located in Kagoshima, and a single parachute brigade was located near Miyazaki. Navy ground forces, consisting of special naval landing forces, base defense units, guards, and anti-aircraft artillery units numbered another five thousand. All together, combat troops in southern Kyushu, according to Mac-Arthur's G-2 section, numbered no more than 25,700 troops or the equivalent of 1.5 U.S. divisions. But southern Kyushu housed large army and navy airbase complexes, so the largest troop contingent in southern Kyushu in the spring of 1945 consisted of 45,500 army and navy air forces ground support personnel. Another eight thousand service troops worked in Kagoshima and in Japanese navy installations around Ibusuki near the mouth of Kagoshima Bay.[7]

By November 1945, the target date for OLYMPIC, Willoughby judged that the Japanese were capable of bringing into southern Kyushu another two divisions and a tank regiment, thus raising combat strength to sixty-five thousand. According to the estimate, a single division would defend the Miyazaki-Miyakonojo-Ariake plains on the Osumi Peninsula, and another division would defend the Kushikino-Makurazaki Plain on the Satsuma Peninsula. A third division would be held in reserve near the head of Kagoshima Bay. The estimate realistically concluded that the Japanese navy, except for submarines and suicide boats, would pose little threat to the invasion. After Okinawa, the Japanese air force would attempt to conserve planes for use against the invasion fleet. Even in that event, however, fewer than twenty-five hundred aircraft would rise to attack the invasion fleet. Japanese concentration of air power in southern Kyushu would be further handicapped by the need to hold back reserves to defend the Kanto Plain. Given U.S. carrier strength and plans to begin moving the Fifth Air Force into southern Kyushu directly on the heels of the assault forces, the Japanese air threat would be manageable, predicted the analysts. Finally, once the battle began, U.S. air power and the rugged mountains of central Kyushu would severely limit Japanese ability to move troops from northern Kyushu, southern Honshu, and Shikoku into southern Kyushu.[8]

During the three months following the AFPAC estimate of 25 April, the optimistic predictions presented in that document were overtaken by events, for the Japanese began a surprising and massive concentration of forces in southern Kyushu. ULTRA chronicled the course of that buildup. First, and perhaps most important for the assault forces, ULTRA intercepts of Japanese army messages provided current order of battle information. Codebreakers not only identified units moving into Kyushu from Manchuria, Korea, and other islands in the homeland, but quickly and correctly identified movements of units within southern Kyushu. For example, when the 86th Division moved twenty miles southward from Miyakonojo to Shibushi to better protect Ariake Bay, ULTRA quickly reported the change. Obviously the Japanese had arrived at two strategic conclusions—that the next U.S. assault was aimed at southern Kyushu and that once the battle began, U.S. air power and naval gunfire would make it impossible to move large units. In mid-June ULTRA emphasized that troops were "pouring into this southern bastion of the Empire [Kyushu]." Previously defended by only two "depot" (training) divisions and one fully trained and equipped "field" division (the 86th), by mid-June Kyushu held five divisions, two brigades, and another two divisions not yet identified. Even as this information was being distributed, noted the ULTRA analysts, another division (the 77th) was probably already en route from Hokkaido to Kyushu.[9]

A month later ULTRA provided even more dramatic evidence of a Japanese buildup in Kyushu. The two unidentified divisions from the earlier report were confirmed as the 206th and 212th Divisions, both located in southern Kyushu. Thus, by mid-July the Japanese had expanded their ground forces in southern Kyushu to six divisions, four brigades, and two other unidentified units. Two weeks later another division was located in the south making the total seven divisions. At the same time, ULTRA, which had already identified the 57th Army (equivalent to a U.S. corps) as the major command headquarters for southern Kyushu, picked up the arrival of another army headquarters from Formosa—the 40th. Henceforth, two army headquarters, the 57th in the east and the 40th in the west, would control defense forces in southern Kyushu. Even more threatening, these headquarters appeared to be positioning their subordinate units to defend the three major OLYMPIC assault beaches.[10]

ULTRA also precisely foretold the Japanese strategy for defense of the homeland by listening in on and publishing *verbatim* Japanese General Staff instructions to field commanders: "The air and sea forces must make every effort to annihilate the Allies at sea. If the Allies are so bold as to risk a landing on Japan proper, a full scale offensive will be launched against him with the intention of utterly destroying his forces . . . on the beaches." Units defending the beaches, warned the order, must not "reckon on any continuation of the battle by retreat." These instructions indicated a return to the notably unsuccessful defense strategy used by the Japanese army early in the war—a strategy which led to the destruction of Japanese beach defenses by pre-landing bombardments.[11]

As ULTRA tracked the foreboding buildup of ground forces in southern Kyushu, the intercepts also gave U.S. planners timely and accurate, though perhaps less detailed, information on Japanese air strengths and strategies. ULTRA presented a picture of Japanese air forces that were incapable of seriously interfering with the Allied invasion. Obviously hoping to conserve their inferior air strength for the coming invasion of the homeland, after Okinawa the Japanese launched no kamikazes and refused air combat. In May and June ULTRA counted 6,865 airplanes in Japan; only about one-half were judged fit for combat, and the others were considered useful only as kamikazes. In late June ULTRA also revealed that the Japanese were abandoning airfields in southern Kyushu except for staging bases and removing perhaps 85 percent of the aircrafts to Honshu, Shikoku, and Korea. Some bases like Miyazaki and Shibushi were built so close to the coast that they were vulnerable to naval gunfire. In any case, all were within range of Okinawa-based planes and were vulnerable to carrier strikes. Japanese efforts to disperse and hide their remaining planes not only conceded air superiority to the United States but placed their hidden planes in danger of destruction on the ground. During early July, however, ULTRA uncovered "strong evidence of large scale movement of army suicide aircraft from central Honshu to southern Kyushu." Perhaps as many as two hundred aircraft were involved, and these were judged to be for homeland defense, not for attacks on Okinawa. This new development seemed to promise a gradual abandonment of the dispersal strategy as the invasion approached. If the Japanese continued this forward deployment, the suicide planes would become even more vulnerable to destruction on the ground. On 15 July ULTRA concluded, "Other than for calculated risk of shipping damage from suiciders, the Japanese air force will probably be unable to oppose seriously our landings against any vital area in Japan proper."[12]

The Japanese strategy of conservation through dispersal and conceal-ment could cause "a steady sapping of air strength" prior to the invasion. ULTRA portrayed a Japanese air force where the numbers of aircraft had "ceased to be the measure of the enemy's air capability." Plagued by extreme fuel and spare parts shortages and wracked by continuing U.S. air attacks, ULTRA implied that in the coming invasion the Japanese air threat would prove less than decisive. The picture that emerged from ULTRA was an air force crippled by attrition, shortages, obsolete equip-ment, and inexperienced pilots. A similar picture emerged from the postwar statements of Japanese officials and from the *Strategic Bombing Survey*. Dispersing aircraft in small packets on isolated airstrips presented Japanese air commanders with the added worry of concentrating their air attack forces—both conventional and kamikaze. Radios were in such short supply that few kamikazes received them. The concern about concentrat-ing their kamikazes at the critical moment may have been the reason for the early July movement of some planes back to the airfields in southern Kyushu. Two weeks before the end of the war ULTRA made another estimate of enemy air strength. There were fifty-six hundred conventional combat aircraft in the homeland and twenty-seven hundred planes capable of kamikaze use; photo reconnaissance confirmed these estimates. In this same ULTRA summary, there was a map with base locations, numbers, and types of planes clearly marked.[13]

"The air battle for Japan," concluded the ULTRA analysts, "is being won before reaching its full and inevitable crescendo." Air superiority had already been conceded by the Japanese, and "virtual air supremacy" would soon follow as Japan's remaining planes were destroyed on the ground and the enemy's air effort collapsed completely.[14]

ULTRA revealed a Japanese navy that, except for submarines, suicide craft, and kamikazes, was little threat to the invasion. Air strikes by Halsey's carriers had eliminated almost the last of Japan's surface fleet. By 1 August only a small number of destroyers remained, and they had only enough fuel for a single suicidal foray. ULTRA indicated that of the navy's remaining fifty-two submarines most had abandoned attacks on U.S. ships and were being used as the only remaining means of supplying and maintaining communications with outlying garrisons. Japanese merchant shipping had all but come to a standstill because of U.S. air and submarine attacks and the mining of Japanese ports and channels by B-29s.[15]

Yet ULTRA revealed a growing threat from Japanese suicide boats, midget subs, and kaiten (manned torpedoes). "The Japanese are planning in great detail for the preparation and equipping of surface suicide attack bases," warned an ULTRA summary issued two weeks before the war ended. Japanese naval commanders were selecting and training personnel to carry out "waves edge surprise attacks." Bases were under construction on Shikoku and the east coast of Kyushu, around the Bungo Straits, and on the Kanto coast. ULTRA also revealed plans to send the remaining surface fleet on suicide missions once the invasion began.[16]

The Japanese navy placed suicide attack units to cover the mouths of strategic bays—Tokyo Bay, Ise Bay near Nagoya, Kii Channel near Osaka, and the Bungo Straits. The 5th Suicide Attack Squadron, with headquarters at Ibusuki near the mouth of Kagoshima Bay, was charged with defending the strategic harbors and channels of southern Kyushu. The squadron was composed of the 32d, 33d, and 35th assault units. Each of the units was armed with suicide boats (shinyo), motor torpedo boats, and kaiten. ULTRA showed that elements of the 32d assault unit covered Koshiki Shima, the offshore island that in OLYMPIC would be an objective of the U.S. 40th Infantry Division. Other elements of the 32d were at Kagoshima and Ibusuki. The six kaiten assigned to the 32d were placed at Uchinoura near the mouth of Ariake Bay. The entire 33d Assault Unit—consisting of torpedo boats, suicide boats, and ten kaiten—was deployed on the flanks of Ariake Bay and up the coast at Aburatsu and Miyazaki. The 35th Assault Unit was placed far up the east coast of Kyushu at Hososhima. From these dispositions, it is clear that the Japanese considered U.S. landings at Ariake Bay the gravest threat to southern Kyushu. ULTRA was also able, in some cases, to provide unit locations and even individual boat numbers.[17]

The very rapid and unexpectedly large Japanese buildup of ground forces in southern Kyushu spurred considerable concern both in MacArthur's AFPAC headquarters and in the Pentagon. On 29 July, Willoughby, MacArthur's G-2, published an amendment to his original 25 April intelligence estimate for OLYMPIC. The order of battle information collected from ULTRA differed sharply from earlier predictions, he said, and the continuing Japanese buildup in southern Kyushu threatened to undercut some of the basic assumptions made in the original OLYMPIC studies. Noting that the original intelligence estimate had forecast the possibility of up to ten divisions in all of Kyushu by the target date of 1 November, the 29 July amendment warned that "these divisions have since made their appearance, as predicted, and the end is not in sight." In a matter of weeks the number of Japanese troops in southern Kyushu had grown from 80,000 to 206,000. If not checked, warned MacArthur's G-2, the buildup could endanger the success of OLYMPIC. In the three months since the end of April, seven divisions, two brigades and two tank regiments had entered Kyushu raising the total to eleven divisions, three separate brigades, and three tank regiments. To add to the threat, six of the seven new divisions, one brigade, and two of the tank regiments had been sent to southern Kyushu to cover the most likely U.S. landing beaches. Thus, by the end of July the OLYMPIC assault area was defended by seven divisions, four brigades, and two tank regiments.[18]

The conclusions were inescapable and ominous: (1) the buildup, already "changing the tactical and strategical situation sharply," would continue; (2) the Japanese had determined correctly that the next U.S. objective would be southern Kyushu; (3) the enemy was freely using the coastal roads and railroads to transfer large units from northern Kyushu into the south; (4) the U.S. air forces and the navy had to destroy these routes or the buildup would continue.[19]

In forwarding the new estimate to MacArthur's G-3, Major General Stephen J. Chamberlin, Willoughby warned, "We are engaged in a race against time by which the ratio of attack effort vis-a-vis defense capacity is perilously balanced." He made two recommendations. First, in the OLYMPIC plans, Chamberlin should provide for more rapid reinforcement of the assault elements. Second, the air forces, including the strategic bombers, should immediately turn to destroying the lines of communication linking northern and southern Kyushu. Three days later MacArthur's chief of staff, Lieutenant General Richard K. Sutherland, forwarded instructions to General Kenney. Sutherland instructed that air strikes should "be initiated immediately to isolate southern Kyushu from northern Kyushu and Kyushu from Honshu by . . . a systematic continuous destruction of vital lines of communication in Kyushu" and against units and supplies already in southern Kyushu.[20]

Apparently a copy of Willoughby's 29 July amendment to the AFPAC intelligence estimate quickly reached the Pentagon; a summary of the amendment was soon in the hands of Brigadier General George A. Lincoln, the chief army planner for the Joint Chiefs. Willoughby's revelation of the Japanese buildup in southern Kyushu came as no surprise; the Joint Intelligence Committee was simultaneously reaching similar conclusions. Their report, which summarized Japanese defensive preparations in southern Kyushu, northern Kyushu, Shikoku, and the Kanto Plain, argued that Japanese military leaders had assessed southern Kyushu as the most likely invasion target, followed in order by Shikoku, northern Kyushu, and the Kanto Plain. Moreover, the Pentagon experts concluded that the Japanese, who realized that Allied air power would prevent them from shifting forces after the invasion began, were concentrating their forces "in close proximity to the most threatened points of Allied assault."[21]

The Joint Intelligence report made no recommendations; it simply let the facts speak for themselves. Since early 1945 ground forces in Kyushu had increased from one active and two depot divisions to a strength of eleven active and two depot divisions, from 150,000 army troops to 545,000. In early 1945 75 percent of all ground forces in Kyushu were in the north; now 60 percent were in the south. Similarly, the Japanese had placed the kamikazes within range of the invasion beaches of southern Kyushu. While the Japanese had not ruled out assaults on Shikoku, northern Kyushu, or the Kanto Plain, and those areas had also been strengthened, clearly the Japanese expected the next blow to fall in southern Kyushu.[22]

Using the Joint Intelligence report as justification, the Joint War Plans Committee prepared recommendations for the Joint Staff Planners: "The possible effects on OLYMPIC operations of this build-up and concentration" should cause field commanders to "review their estimates of the situation . . . and prepare plans for operations against . . . alternate objectives." In fact, the Joint Staff Planners had already begun studying alternatives to OLYMPIC.[23]

On 6 August General Handy, Marshall's deputy, warned his chief that the joint planners were worried and that a discussion of the Japanese buildup would likely occur in the next Joint Chiefs' meeting. Any discussion would probably also raise questions about possible alternatives to OLYMPIC. As usual, Marshall sought MacArthur's opinion. On 6 August he sent a personal message to his Pacific commander describing the intelligence reports. Marshall emphasized the large Japanese land and air buildup in Kyushu and southern Honshu and the force reduction in other locations. He also mentioned the possibility of Japanese deception, and Marshall then asked for MacArthur's "personal estimate" of the intelligence information they were receiving and asked if MacArthur had any suggestions for less well-defended alternate invasion sites. Marshall mentioned bypassing southern Kyushu and going directly to the Kanto Plain. He also raised the possibility of going into northern Honshu at Sendai or Ominato.[24]

Marshall's message went out in mid-afternoon. MacArthur replied that same evening. He insisted that the Japanese were no longer any threat in the air; when U.S. ships and planes now approached the shorelines of Japan, the Japanese failed to react. The situation, he pointed out, resembled the one preceding the invasion of Luzon, when estimates erroneously reported concentrated air power there. MacArthur also doubted that the buildup of land forces in southern Kyushu was as great a threat as reported because of the limited ability of the Japanese to move or support troops by rail or sea. His air forces had not yet displaced forward from Luzon to Okinawa. By early September MacArthur anticipated that U.S. air power on Okinawa would grow to two thousand combat planes, and by OLYMPIC would grow to three thousand planes. Coupled with the available B-29s and escorting fighters from the Marianas, the planes would be able to neutralize any existing Japanese air and ground forces.

MacArthur was adamant that OLYMPIC not be postponed or abandoned: "In my opinion, there should not be the slightest thought of changing the OLYMPIC operation. Its fundamental purpose is to obtain air bases under cover of which we can deploy our forces to the northward into the industrial heart of Japan. The plan is sound and will be successful."[25] MacArthur pointed out that if the invasion target were changed to Tokyo, the area was too distant from U.S. heavy air power. If the target were changed to the Ominato area, weather would be a problem. In addition, the area had not been fully studied. If Sendai became the target, U.S. forces could not easily establish bases because of its closeness to the concentration of power in Tokyo. MacArthur concluded that deception was a strong possibility: "Throughout the Southwest Pacific area campaigns, as we have neared an operation intelligence has invariably pointed to greatly increased enemy forces. Without exception, this buildup has been found to be erroneous. In this particular case, the destruction that is going on in Japan would seem to indicate that it is very probable that the enemy is resorting to deception."[26]

Despite MacArthur's suspicions, ULTRA's portrayal of the Japanese buildup in southern Kyushu was amazingly accurate. After the Japanese surrender, under Operation BLACKLIST, elements of the Sixth Army peacefully occupied the area that only weeks before they had been scheduled to invade. The V Amphibious Corps (VAC) was assigned the job of occupying Kyushu. VAC, in turn, assigned the 2d Marine Division and a single battalion of the 32d Infantry Division to southern Kyushu where they took the surrender of Japanese units that had been scheduled to defend the OLYMPIC beaches. The Americans counted 216,627 troops (ten thousand more than estimated by ULTRA) in southern Kyushu organized into two armies—the 40th and the 57th. The 40th, defending the Satsuma Peninsula in the west, commanded three divisions—the 146th, 206th, and 303d—two independent brigades, and various artillery, engineer, and support units. The 57th Army, defending Ariake Bay and Miyazaki, commanded four divisions—the 86th, 154th, 156th, and 212th—two independent brigades, two tank regiments, and various artillery, engineer, and support units. Two additional divisions, the 25th and the 77th, under the command of the Sixteenth Area Army, made up a counterattack force located at the head of Kagoshima Bay. This information largely confirmed ULTRA.[27]

Planners focused primarily on the size of the Japanese buildup in southern Kyushu, a dimension of Japanese defenses that ULTRA was most capable of revealing. But ULTRA also exposed some serious weaknesses that continued to plague Japanese defense of the homeland. Despite their inability to halt the buildup completely, U.S. air and naval bombardments made it difficult for the Japanese to move troops and critical materials like fuel, ammunition, and equipment from northern Kyushu into the south. No doubt as Far East Air Forces, and elements of U.S. Army Strategic Air Forces, Pacific, and Marine air became firmly established in Okinawa, the air bombardment would have become relentless and overwhelming. Food promised also to be a problem for the defenders. The 1945 summer harvest was smaller than usual, and U.S. air power had disrupted distribution. In July ULTRA began to find hints of war weariness and sympathies for peace among the nonmilitary. In July and August Far East Air Forces pilots striking targets in Kyushu reported that some Japanese civilians were waving white flags at their aircraft. There was no evidence, however, that the military leaders had modified their plans for an apocalyptic defense.[28]

ULTRA's ability to reveal the Japanese order of battle and to locate defensive works was not infallible, nor did ULTRA tell all. ULTRA's revelations about the locations of airfields, coastal gun defenses, suicide boat harbors, supply depots, and ground defensive positions could be confirmed and expanded through conventional intelligence, especially photo reconnaissance. Yet other critical information was left hidden. ULTRA could not assess the quality of enemy defenders, their training and equipment, their morale, their state of supply, the readiness of their positions, the quality of their commanders—questions that were as important to the battle as were raw numbers. In these areas, the homeland forces fell short of the standards set by the veteran troops that defended Luzon, Iwo Jima, and Okinawa.

Obviously, the Joint Chiefs had come reluctantly to their decision for invasion, and their reluctance was magnified as the bloody campaign for Okinawa progressed. Their concerns were multiplied yet again by the buildup of forces in southern Kyushu during the last three months of the war—magnified so large that Marshall considered the possibility of abandoning OLYMPIC for a less well-defended site.

So well did Japan's defensive buildup mirror the American invasion plans that some postwar analysts suspected a security breach. But it hardly took special intelligence for Japanese analysts to predict with reasonable accuracy the general target area for the next U.S. assault after Okinawa—southern Kyushu. Terrain analysis could refine the prediction of this large target area to probable specific invasion beaches. Finally, analysis of such constraints as weather and required lead time for planning and gathering forces could produce a reasonably accurate estimate of the time of the assault.

Japanese intelligence experts relied heavily on previous American strategic patterns in finally determining that southern Kyushu was the most probable site for the next U.S. assault. The Americans almost always struck at places with ample space for airbase construction or, preferably, with already established Japanese bases. Southern Kyushu admirably filled that criterion. Good port facilities and anchorages were also important; Ariake and Kagoshima bays filled that requirement. Southern Kyushu could be covered by land-based tactical aircraft from Okinawa; both northern Kyushu and Shikoku were marginal in that respect. So logic and experience pointed to southern Kyushu.[29]

Even a cursory examination of the beaches suitable for large amphibious operations point to three great beaches in southern Kyushu—Fukiagehama, Ariake (modern Shibushi), and Miyazaki. An examination of beach exits and probable critical objectives indicated the probable landing sites with even more precision. Japanese estimates of landing sites were accurate except for Fukiagehama where they predicted landings near Izaku (modern Fukiage) in the center of this thirty-five-mile beach. The actual landings were planned at the extreme northern end near Kushikino. Japanese assumptions for the time of the assault were determined by weather—the typhoon season ends in October. However, the Japanese underestimated the scale of the U.S. assault.

When asked after the war if the Japanese estimates had been based entirely on logic and careful analysis, Major Hori Eizo, the general staff officer credited with the analysis and prediction of U.S. intentions, replied, "It was strategic common sense."[30]

NOTES

1. Edward J. Drea, *MacArthur's Ultra: Codebreaking and the War against Japan, 1942–1945* (Lawrence: Univ. of Kansas Press, 1992) is the definitive work on this subject.

2. For good accounts of the importance of Ultra naval intelligence in the battles of the Coral Sea and Midway see Ronald Lewin, *The American Magic: Codes, Ciphers, and the Defeat of Japan* (New York: Farrar, Strauss, Giroux, 1982).

3. Drea, 37, 57.

4. Drea, 73–77, 92–93.

5. Drea, 96–98.

6. Diane T. Putney, *Ultra and the Army Air Forces in World War II: An Interview with Associate Justice of the U.S. Supreme Court Lewis F. Powell, Jr.* (Washington, DC: Office of Air Force History, 1987), 90.

7. GHQ USAFPAC G-2 Estimate of the Enemy Situation with Respect to an Operation Against Southern Kyushu in November 1945, dated 25 April 1945 in Staff Study OLYMPIC, RG 165, NARA.

8. Ibid.

9. GHQ SWPA ULTRA Intelligence Summary, 15/16 June 1945, RG 457, SRH 203, Part 6, NARA.

10. ULTRA Summary, 15/16 July, 31 July/1 August 1945.

11. ULTRA Summary, 14/15 July 1945.

12. ULTRA Summary, 27/28 June, 14/15 July 1945.

13. ULTRA Summary, 26/27 June, 31 July/1 August, 5/6 August 1945.

14. ULTRA Summary, 15/16 July 1945.

15. ULTRA Summary, 31 July/1 August 1945.

16. ULTRA Summary, 31 July/1 August, 15/16 August 1945.

17. "Suicide Attack Squadron Organization, July 1945," RG 457, SRH 103, NARA.

18. GHQ AFPAC, "Amendment No. 1 to G-2 Estimate of the Enemy Situation with respect to Kyushu, dated 25 April 1945," 29 July 1945, Chamberlin Papers, Box 6, U.S. Army Military History Institute, Carlisle Barracks, PA.

19. Ibid.

20. Ibid.; Memo, Willoughby to G-3, Sub: Destruction of Enemy Lines of Communication and Enemy Forces in Kyushu, 1 August 1945.

21. Memo, n.d., to Chief, S & P Group, Sub: Amendment No. 1 to G-2 Estimate "OLYMPIC," RG 165, ABC 384 Kyushu (4 Jul 44), Sec. 1-F, NARA; JWPC 397 Alternates to "OLYMPIC," 4 August 1945, RG 165, ABC 384 Kyushu (4 Jul 44), Sec. 1-B.

22. JWPC 397 Alternates to "OLYMPIC," 4 August 1945.

23. Ibid.

24. Message, WAR 45369. Marshall to MacArthur, 7 August 45, Nimitz Command Summary, Navy Historical Center, Washington, DC.

25. Message, C 31897, MacArthur to Marshall, 9 August 1945, Nimitz Command Summary, Navy Historical Center, Washington, DC.

26. Ibid.

27. *Reports of General MacArthur*, vol. 1, *MacArthur in Japan, the Occupation, Military Phase* (Washington, DC: GPO, n.d.), 45–46; Drea, 219–21; Report, "Japanese Surrendering to Sixth Army," Sixth Army, File 106–2.5 to 106–2.70,

Box 2446, RG 94, WNRC; Sixth U.S. Army, "Report of the Occupation of Japan," 2 September–30 November 1945, U.S. Army Military History Institute, Carlisle Barracks, PA.

28. Drea, 214; J. V. Crabb, "Fifth Air Force Air War against Japan, September 1942–August 1945," (manuscript, Air Univ. Library, Maxwell Air Force Base, AL, 4 February 1946).

29. For the story of Japanese efforts to predict the invasion, see Alvin D. Coox, "Japanese Military Intelligence in the Pacific: Its Non-Revolutionary Nature," in *The Intelligence Revolution: A Historical Perspective* (Washington, DC: Office of Air Force History, 1991), 197–201.

30. Ibid., 200.

Chapter 11

Planning OLYMPIC

Kyushu, the southernmost island of the Japanese homeland, is 350 miles from Okinawa. It seems to hang from the main island of Honshu like a small deformed hand. Numerous bays and inlets separate the fingers, and the two southern fingers point straight southward toward Okinawa. Between these fingers, large, beautiful Kagoshima Bay forms a natural refuge encircled by two mountainous peninsulas, Osumi on the east and Satsuma on the west. From the outer beaches along these peninsulas narrow avenues lead inland to several small pockets of interior plains and ultimately to the shores of Kagoshima Bay. Kyushu is the Japanese island nearest the Asian mainland, separated from the southern tip of Korea only by the hundred-mile-wide Tsushima Strait. Centuries before the Americans eyed it for their invasion, Kyushu's strategic location made it a target; twice Mongol armies shattered themselves on the shores of Kyushu—in 1274 defeated by the defenders and in 1281 devastated by a typhoon the Japanese called "Kamikaze."

Other than Kyushu, American planners had looked at three options for invasion—the China coast near Shanghai, Korea, and Hokkaido. The first two were rejected because they led to no decisive objective. Hokkaido was an appealing option. Japanese defenses there were weak, and the Allies could achieve surprise. Those advantages, however, were offset by uncertain weather, lack of land-based air coverage for the assault, and distance from the strategically important Kanto Plain. Most important of all, an assault on Hokkaido would have forced both Nimitz and MacArthur off their lines of advance and away from their logistical bases.

As American planners considered the final campaign in the war against Japan, the appeal of Kyushu grew for a number of important reasons. Once a strategy of invasion was agreed on, the strategic location of Kyushu and the island's potential uses appealed equally to the army, navy, and air force. The conquest of Kyushu promised to produce a broad range of military benefits.

First, an assault on Kyushu would unite the hitherto divided pincers of Nimitz's drive across the central Pacific and MacArthur's drive from the southwest onto the Philippines. Uniting these two great offensives would produce naval, air, and ground forces of such awesome size and power that their very existence might persuade the Japanese leaders to end the war. On the diplomatic level, an assault on Kyushu with such overwhelming force might shock the Japanese into accepting unconditional surrender.

On a purely military level, securing southern Kyushu would produce rich dividends. Inherent in the strategy of island-hopping was the operating combat radius of land-based bombers and fighter bombers—a technical limitation that dictated offensive bounds of two hundred to four hundred miles. According to that criterion, Kyushu was logically the next step following Okinawa.

The navy, already prone toward a strategy of blockade, could use bases and harbors on Kyushu to breach the Straits of Tsushima and get surface ships into the Sea of Japan. Some submarines had raided Japanese shipping inside the Sea of Japan by sneaking through the Straits, and aerial mining by the B-29s had been especially effective in cutting Japanese communications with the Asian mainland. Nonetheless, decisively throttling the Japanese home islands required putting surface forces into the Sea of Japan through the Straits of Tsushima. Breaking open the straits would require forward bases for minesweepers, patrol planes, radar, communications, air control, reconnaissance, and resupply. Kyushu and its many offshore islands could provide bases in abundance.

Air planners also saw Kyushu as the next logical step after Okinawa. They could reach strategic targets north to Tokyo with B-29s based in the Marianas. Even the shorter-ranged B-17s and B-24s could reach Tokyo from Okinawa. Yet most of southern Japan was still beyond the reach of Okinawa-based medium bombers and fighter bombers. Moreover, ground and air congestion was an increasing problem on Okinawa. Bases on Kyushu could handle forty additional air groups, almost three thousand planes, and provide space for redeploying air units from Europe. Kyushu-based medium bombers could easily reach Tokyo to cover the next operation, CORONET; fighter-bombers could reach as far north as Osaka. Finally, bases on Kyushu, especially at Kagoshima and Ariake bays, would provide excellent areas for mounting and staging forces for CORONET and for logistical, air, and naval support for that mammoth operation to come in March 1946.

Like the rest of Japan, Kyushu is a mountainous island. Northern Kyushu is separated from the south by a range of central mountains that stretch diagonally across the midsection of the island from southwest to northeast. Ranging in height from three thousand to five thousand feet, they form an effective barrier between northern and southern Kyushu. In 1945 transportation through the mountains was limited to narrow trails that twisted through defiles and winding valleys. Communications between north and south depended entirely upon a single highway and railroad running down each coast.

South of the central mountains, Kyushu is a jumble of beautiful rugged mountains and hills, in many places falling into the edge of the sea along broken, rocky coasts where every inlet hides a fishing village. By Japanese standards the area is rural and sparsely populated. Agriculture and fishing dominate the economy. In winter the farmers hang their vegetables to dry, and fishermen spread their catches in the sun, for the winter climate is cool, bright, and dry.

The southern coast is dominated by two great bays—Kagoshima Wan and Ariake (modern Shibushi) Wan. Three small rolling plains furnish the only level land in the south, and on these the Japanese had built twenty airfields. The Miyazaki Plain stretches for thirty miles immediately inland from the long, straight east coast. Another large level area called the Miyakonojo-Ariake basin stretches for forty miles down the center of the Osumi (southeastern) peninsula. Two smaller level pockets lie on the Satsuma (southwestern) peninsula—the Kushikino and Makurazaki plains, respectively, northwest and southwest of Kagoshima.

The terrain and geography of southern Kyushu held enormous significance for the attackers and the defenders alike. The central mountains made large-scale military communications between north and south all but impossible. For the Japanese the mountains also presented a barrier to military movement, but for the Americans the mountains represented a wall to imprison Japanese ground forces in the north. The coastal railroads passed over many bridges and through numerous tunnels; the highways passed through countless cuts and defiles. American planners thought that these routes were particularly susceptible to interdiction by bombing and by naval gunfire.[1]

If the Americans could cut the coastal routes and move quickly to hold the few narrow mountain passes, they could effectively seal off southern Kyushu from the north and could deny the Japanese movement of large forces from north to south once the battle began. The Japanese would have to fight the battle in static positions with forces deployed in the south and try to guess where the assault would fall.

In fact, guessing the potential landing beaches was not difficult. With only a cursory map examination any competent Japanese staff officer could easily identify four possible landing beaches in southern Kyushu— all backed by the same kind of rugged hills and escarpments that had made cave and bunker defenses so effective for the Japanese and so costly to marines and army infantry at Iwo Jima, Luzon, and Okinawa. An intelligence officer of the Sixth Army concisely analyzed the problems that southern Kyushu's terrain presented for the invasion forces. "The cliff-like terrace fronts, the commanding heights surrounding all lowland areas, and the rugged mountains full of tortuous narrow defiles," he noted, "are ideal for the construction of extensive underground installations." While the broken and fragmented terrain favored Japanese tactics of suicidal cave and bunker defenses, worse still, it tended to neutralize the great American advantages of firepower, air power, and mobility.[2]

If the hills made travel impossible except on the roads, movement was hardly easier in the narrow coastal flats or on the interior plains. Loose volcanic soil hampered cross-country movement. Intensive agricultures, especially rice paddies, were obstacles except during the fall after the paddies had been drained for harvest.[3]

Kyushu was a larger Okinawa, and OLYMPIC was ICEBERG on a grander scale. Operation ICEBERG had been conceived to seize Okinawa and other islands in the Ryukyus and transform them into a giant air and naval base. Operation OLYMPIC, conceived to capture Kyushu, had a similar purpose. In one sense, though, Kyushu would be more immediately valuable than Okinawa. Even as ICEBERG progressed, thousands of engineers had descended on Okinawa to build air strips and port facilities. In Kyushu many of those facilities already existed. The great bay of Kagoshima was a natural anchorage and naval base; so was Ariake Bay on the eastern shore of the Osumi Peninsula. Several airfields around Kanoya on the Osumi Peninsula had long been a hub of Japanese naval aviation. Other bases were located at Miyazaki and on the plains around Miyakonojo. Across the bay, Chiran on the Satsuma peninsula was a center of Japanese army aviation.

Thus the fundamental concept of Operation OLYMPIC was to seize southern Kyushu for its wealth of airfields and bays. As bases were secured, air and naval forces would immediately deploy forward to attack northern Kyushu, Shikoku, and Honshu and to breach the Straits of Tsushima. Kyushu would serve the next operation, CORONET, like Okinawa had served OLYMPIC—as a base area for another leap forward. From bases in Kyushu, land-based air power could expand and extend attacks to every nook and cranny in Japan, and the navy could complete the blockade.

Nine divisions formed into three corps would land simultaneously on three separate beaches, then drive inland to gain the airfields and to encircle Kagoshima Bay. A fourth corps of two divisions would form a floating reserve. The ground forces for OLYMPIC would come from forces already in the Pacific. I Corps would land at Miyazaki, and XI Corps, at Ariake Bay on the eastern side of the Osumi Peninsula. The three Marine

Divisions of V Amphibious Corps would assault the western side of the Satsuma Peninsula near Kushikino. The reserve force, IX Corps, if it had not already been committed elsewhere, would land on the southern tip of the Satsuma Peninsula on X-Day-plus-4.

After securing lodgments, the ground forces would proceed to accomplish three immediate tasks—capture the interior plains on both peninsulas where the Japanese airfields were located, capture the port of Kagoshima and secure the shores and entrance to the bay, and drive northward to the southern edge of the central mountains to seal off southern Kyushu from Japanese forces in northern Kyushu. United States' forces would secure a line diagonally across the island from Tsuno in the east to Sendai in the west, thus isolating and securing the southern one-third of Kyushu.[4]

TWO PACIFIC COMMANDS

On 3 April 1945 two messages went out from the Joint Chiefs to their principal Pacific commanders. Both dealt with the growing awareness that the invasion of Japan now loomed as a real possibility. Time no longer allowed putting off hard decisions. While King and Leahy were not yet wholly convinced of the necessity for invasion, they acknowledged the contingency. To be ready to meet the possibility of invasion, MacArthur and Nimitz had to begin staff work. The joint planners had already drafted an outline plan for OLYMPIC, and the Joint War Plans Committee (JWPC) had sketched a scheme for the assault on southern Kyushu that MacArthur's and Nimitz's staffs would adapt and refine.

One message from the Joint Chiefs ordered MacArthur and Nimitz to begin planning; Nimitz, assisted by his chief planners, Admirals Forrest P. Sherman and Charles "Soc" McMorris, was to concentrate on the "naval and amphibious phases" while MacArthur and his staff were to "make plans and preparations for the campaign in Japan." Each commander was to "cooperate" with the other.[5]

The other message, a command directive sent out by the Joint Chiefs on 3 April, had realigned Pacific forces according to service. All naval forces would be commanded by Nimitz; all army forces (except strategic air forces) would be commanded by MacArthur. Nimitz's titles of commander in chief, Pacific Fleet (CINCPAC) and commander in chief, Pacific Ocean Areas (CINCPOA) already reflected both his naval command and his area command. In addition to his title of supreme commander, Southwest Pacific Area, MacArthur was now designated commander in chief, U.S. Army Forces, Pacific (CINCAFPAC). While the Joint Chiefs wanted the realignment of forces to take place rapidly, they realized that current operations precluded pell mell changes. They left it to MacArthur and Nimitz to work out a timetable for the transition.

The Joint Chiefs themselves would direct Pacific strategy and issue operational directives "assigning missions and fixing command responsibility for specific major operations and campaigns." Normally, the Joint Chiefs emphasized, MacArthur would command land campaigns and Nimitz would direct sea campaigns. Having failed to reach agreement on a supreme commander for the Pacific theater, the Joint Chiefs intended to fill that role themselves.[6]

MacArthur and Nimitz maintained small staffs. Both staffs had long and hard-won experience in planning amphibious operations, and both had developed similar organizations and techniques for planning. In time-honored military fashion, the two commanders preferred that their theater plans state missions, allocate resources, provide for coordination, and set the ground rules under which lower commands would conduct the operation. Detailed planning was left to the lower operational units. Typically too, both MacArthur's and Nimitz's staffs reflected the person-alities and habits of their commanders. Nimitz's staff was affable and informal; MacArthur's was more formal and imperious. His chief of staff, Lieutenant General Richard K. Sutherland, was thought to be especially stiff, arrogant, and abrasive.

The failure of the Joint Chiefs to name a supreme commander for the Pacific and their order that Nimitz draw the plans for the naval and amphibious phases of OLYMPIC, that MacArthur draw those for the land campaign, and that the commanders correlate their separate plans, pre-sented the two commanders with unique and complicated planning prob-lems. Marshall raised the possibility of creating a joint staff to plan the invasion with representatives from both commands. Others suggested locating the headquarters of the two commanders adjacent to one another. But the egos of the commanders and the separate identities of their staffs made these solutions impossible.

MacArthur's views were eventually to win out in establishing the planning process. He was strongly opposed to collocating headquarters or forming a joint staff. MacArthur felt that correlation of the two plans could be done effectively through staff conferences, direct teletypes, and liaison groups.[7]

An initial conference between the staffs of the two Pacific commanders was held in mid-April at Nimitz's forward headquarters on Guam. MacArthur declined to attend and sent a staff delegation headed by Sutherland. The purpose of the conference was two-fold. The recent command directive restructuring the old area command arrangement that had prevailed since 1942 required each commander to relinquish units belonging to the other service. Details of that transfer, especially the logistical complications, had to be sorted out. Simultaneously, the two staffs had to establish machinery for coordinating their respective plans for the invasion.

The three-day conference was not a happy beginning. Nimitz wanted to talk about cooperative planning for the invasion; Sutherland, at his most difficult, pressed for the immediate release by Nimitz of all army units to MacArthur. The Joint Chiefs' directive had not dictated a timetable for the transfer of units or bases. Because of the press of ongoing operations on Luzon and Okinawa, the Joint Chiefs had left the transition to the mutual agreement of the two commanders. Nimitz's Okinawa campaign had only begun two weeks before, and he was reluctant to engage in detailed discussions on the realignment of forces. MacArthur's staff was unprepared to talk about cooperative planning. After three days the conference ended with general and largely self-evident conclusions. Each commander would relinquish forces belonging to the other as soon as practicable and take immediate steps to establish planning machinery for the invasion.[8]

Within hours the news of the first abortive attempt to plan by conference had reached the Pentagon, and almost instantaneously a blistering message from Marshall to MacArthur was drafted by Marshall's staff. After outlining Sutherland's "complete lack of understanding" of the purpose of the conference, the message voiced serious doubts about "the advisability of utilizing Sutherland in further negotiations with the Navy." "Our experience with Sutherland here in the War Department," the message continued, "has been that . . . he appears to be totally lacking in the faculty of dealing with others in negotiations on difficult matters." On a recent trip to Washington, Sutherland had "antagonized almost every official in the War Department with whom he came in contact. . . . Unfortunately, he appears utterly unaware of the effects of his methods." The message concluded with a recommendation that MacArthur remove Sutherland from further negotiations with the navy.[9]

Characteristically, Marshall read and revised the message, then decided not to send it. Instead, he delayed more than two weeks before advising MacArthur to meet personally with Nimitz "rather than depending upon your respective staff officers." "Informal reports that come to me from various sources indicate so much opposition and expression of strong feelings in staff meetings," Marshall warned, that the "situation should be gotten under firm control before great harm is done."[10] MacArthur's reply came immediately. He understood that previous meetings between his staff and Nimitz's had been "entirely amicable." Nonetheless, he had already issued an invitation to meet with Nimitz.[11]

So a personal conference between the two Pacific commanders was arranged. Planning could not proceed at lower levels until the commanders agreed on planning principles and established planning machinery. Equally important was the issuance of common planning guidance for the two commands—responsibilities, command relationships, and logistical and territorial bailiwicks. In short, neither staffs nor subordinate units could proceed with details until the two commanders struck a bargain on who would be responsible for what.

MacArthur pleaded that the press of responsibilities made it impossible for him to leave his headquarters, so on 15 May 1945 Nimitz flew into Manila. In a two-day conference the two commanders agreed on broad divisions of responsibilities. Nimitz would continue developing base facilities in the Ryukyus for the forward redeployment of major elements of the Far East Air Forces that were needed to support OLYMPIC. Command of the amphibious operations was vested in Admiral Richmond K. "Terrible" Turner, the commander of the Amphibious Forces Pacific Fleet (PHIBSPAC). In turn, he would pass command to each successive ground commander "after his arrival and establishment ashore." Marine units would be controlled by MacArthur. Although MacArthur and Nimitz gave little attention to the important subjects of logistics and future planning machinery, their meeting energized their staffs and spawned the first detailed working staff conference between the two commands.[12]

A planning team from MacArthur's headquarters arrived at Guam and set to work on 30 May with their counterparts from Nimitz's staff. This was the first nuts and bolts meeting between the two staffs, and in five days the conferees attacked a myriad of issues. Of paramount importance were their agreements on establishing planning machinery and on the complex and problematic matter of logistics.[13]

The foremost problem in the Pacific was shipping. Vast distances, long turnaround times, the competing demands of other theaters, and huge construction requirements all conspired to produce a perennial shipping shortage. Redeployment, the "roll-up" of rear areas, and preparation for OLYMPIC added to the strain in the spring of 1945. Generally, the conferees agreed that each command would "respectively be responsible for procurement and operation of logistic support shipping" for forces under its control. Control of shipping and port facilities was a more dangerous problem than the scarcity of shipping. Shipping requirements were carefully balanced; tangled control of shipping and congested port facilities could create chaos. Elaborate procedures were worked out between AFPAC and POA for calling ships forward as needed and for eliminating competing claims on port facilities.

The three marine divisions would be mounted and transported to the objective by Nimitz's command. Once ashore, items common to both the army and the marines would be supplied by AFPAC; items peculiar to the navy and the marines would be supplied by Nimitz. Nimitz's command would also support marine corps construction requirements.[14]

The agreement on future planning simply extended the practice of inter-command conferences. The detailed planning for OLYMPIC fell to General Walter Kreuger's Sixth Army staff and Admiral Turner's Amphibious Forces Pacific staff. Turner's PHIBSPAC force would carry the Sixth Army assault forces to their beaches and command them until General Kreuger's headquarters was established on Kyushu. So Admiral Turner sailed to the Philippines, and on June 14 anchored his command ship *Eldorado* in Manila Bay to set up shop near Kreuger's Sixth Army staff.[15] On the same day that Turner arrived in Manila Bay, A number of marine corps officers—specialists in quartermaster, engineering, medical, intelligence, ordnance, transportation, and signal—arrived at Sixth Army Headquarters to establish liaison for V Marine Amphibious Corps.[16]

There, together with Headquarters, Fifth Fleet (the landing force and gunfire support armada) and Far East Air Forces, the four headquarters hammered out detailed plans for OLYMPIC in a series of conferences. The four staffs worked separately, each in its own headquarters; they resolved their differences and coordinated their plans in numerous staff conferences. They worked until the last week of the war. During this period, General Kreuger remembered, the interstaff conferences became "almost continuous." In this way four plans emerged—Sixth Army, Far East Air Forces, Fifth Fleet, and Amphibious Forces Pacific. Similarly, other specialized subjects that would require major annexes to the final plan—deception, communications, logistics—were refined by intercommand conferences.[17]

Once MacArthur and Nimitz had decided not to form a permanent intertheater planning group, the major problem between the two commands became how, in the words of the Joint Chiefs, to "correlate" their plans. Months earlier Marshall in nonspecific context had raised the issue with MacArthur of collocating his headquarters with Nimitz for the invasion of Japan. MacArthur's reply had been negative. Now Admiral King intervened. On 6 June Marshall relayed King's suggestion to MacArthur. It would be wise, King suggested, for MacArthur to move his headquarters to Guam so that he could be in personal touch with Nimitz during the preparations for OLYMPIC. MacArthur fired back, "Please tell Admiral King that I disagree totally with his concept and that a long campaign experience has convinced me that if there is any one feature of a field commander that must be left to his sole judgment it is the location of his command post and the actual disposition of his own person."[18]

Finally, Nimitz, affable and cooperative as ever, tried to prevail on MacArthur to establish his "advance headquarters on Guam well in advance of the coming operation." Nimitz promised that he could furnish sufficient staff space and house MacArthur in "quarters identical with my own." A copy of the letter went to King, who, in turn, sent it to Marshall with the handwritten note, "I am informed by CINCPAC [Nimitz] that reply was in similar vein to CINCAFPAC's [MacArthur's] reply to you re same subject." MacArthur remained impervious.[19]

MacArthur's AFPAC staff study and Nimitz's CINCPAC study were finished by the end of May. These two basic preliminary planning documents for OLYMPIC contained the essential information that lower headquarters would need to draft their operational plans. The studies stated the mission, gave the concept of the operation, provided command relationships and rules for coordination, and listed the forces that would be employed. Detailed operational plans and orders would be left to lower headquarters.

The organization of forces described in the AFPAC and CINCPAC staff studies were mirror images of each other. To carry out the naval and amphibious phases of OLYMPIC, Nimitz designated two fleets—the Third Fleet under Admiral William Halsey and the Fifth Fleet under Admiral Raymond Spruance. Halsey's Third Fleet, heavy with attack carriers, would provide almost two thousand planes to cripple Japanese transport and communications before the invasion and to cover the landings. Spruance's Fifth Fleet would carry the troops to the landing areas and supply the naval gunfire support necessary to get them ashore and keep them there. Under Spruance, Commander Amphibious Forces Pacific Fleet, Admiral Turner would command amphibious operations. Under Turner came the Third, Fifth, and Seventh Amphibious Forces, charged with landing the assault forces respectively at Ariake Bay, Kushikino, and Miyazaki.

MacArthur's counterpart commands for Nimitz's two fleets were General Krueger's Sixth Army and General Kenney's Far East Air Forces. Krueger's Sixth Army would conduct the land campaign in Kyushu; Kenney's FEAF would support OLYMPIC from bases in Okinawa and begin moving air units forward into Kyushu on X-Day-plus-2. Krueger's Sixth Army commanded the assault forces, which were organized into four corps. Each corps was matched to one of Admiral Turner's amphibious forces. I Corps, under Major General Innis P. Swift, would be carried to Miyazaki and put ashore by the Seventh Amphibious Force; Third Amphibious Force would put Lieutenant General Charles P. Hall's XI Corps ashore at Ariake Bay; Fifth Amphibious Force would put Major General Harry Schmidt's V Amphibious Corps of three marine divisions ashore near Kushikino on the Satsuma Peninsula. Major General Charles W. Ryder's IX Corps was matched with the Reserve Amphibious Force. If not needed to reinforce one of the three principal landings, IX Corps was to land on X-Day-plus-4 near the tip of the Satsuma Peninsula.

As these plans were completed, the individual numbered corps and amphibious forces began to draft their plans and orders. These began to be published in the last days of the war. As the war ended, corps staffs were just beginning to schedule OLYMPIC orientations for their respective division staffs.

The outwardly amicable relations between MacArthur and Nimitz, which had been established at the mid-May Manila conference, veiled continued spats and squabbles among their subordinates and suspicions between the two principals. The old army versus navy rivalry that had plagued American conduct of the Pacific war from pre-Pearl Harbor days was far from forgotten.

A primary point of contention was Okinawa. That small island was in Nimitz's domain. MacArthur coveted the island for his Far East Air Forces displacing forward from Luzon and for redeploying air units from Europe. At the end of the May conference, he outlined the agreements in a report to Marshall. His only editorial comment in an otherwise factual list came at the end when he noted for the chief of staff that the agreements did not "represent entirely the views of CINCAFPAC especially with regards [to] methods of control and coordination at Okinawa." Nonetheless, MacArthur seemed to sigh, "They do represent a solution in which it is possible to secure the concurrence of CINCPAC."[20]

The 3 April command directive from the Joint Chiefs had called for the realignment of forces along service lines. Realizing that an immediate wholesale shifting of forces, facilities, and bases at the height of the campaigns for Luzon and Okinawa invited chaos, the Joint Chiefs noted only that the command changes should be made "as expeditiously as possible."[21] This issue had created far more rancor between the two Pacific commands than did planning for OLYMPIC. MacArthur was more eager to gather army forces under his command and to get control of the facilities in Okinawa than Nimitz was to relinquish them. When Sutherland, representing MacArthur in April at the first Guam conference, had demanded immediate release by Nimitz of all army forces, even the Tenth Army on Okinawa (then just beginning the long and bloody conquest of that island), Nimitz had promised only that he would relinquish command of army units as they came out of operations. Immediate and pell mell changes, he argued, would invite disaster.[22]

Both MacArthur's campaign for Luzon and Nimitz's for Okinawa lasted far longer than originally planned. On 14 July, two weeks after the battle for Okinawa ended, MacArthur radioed a message of dissatisfaction to Nimitz. Numerous radiograms, General MacArthur complained, had been exchanged on the subject of realignment of commands since the April command directive, but the results had been "disappointingly meager." It was, he continued, "increasingly embarrassing" for him to plan for the invasion of Japan without knowing the present or future status of army units. Furthermore, MacArthur fumed, he had been forced to "resort to negotiations for each individual unit" with Nimitz. The time had now come, he said, to complete the transition of forces and bases that had been ordered three and one-half months earlier. Four days after MacArthur's blast, the Joint Chiefs told Nimitz to turn over the Tenth Army and its facilities in the Ryukyus to MacArthur. Nimitz would retain naval forces and facilities there.[23]

Command arrangements for the invasion continued to plague the planning. "Unity of command" had been the chief point of contention between the army and the navy in the Pacific since the beginning of the war. The navy interpreted the term to mean generals commanding fleets, specifically supreme command in the Pacific for General MacArthur. The army saw a single commander for the Pacific as essential for effective control of such a huge and complex theater.

The command arrangements for OLYMPIC had been hammered out by the Joint Chiefs in a struggle between Marshall and King. Their compromise, that Nimitz would make plans for and command the naval and amphibious phases of OLYMPIC and that MacArthur would plan and command the land campaign, ensured the development of two plans. In their mid-May meeting in Manila, Nimitz and MacArthur had agreed to write their two plans separately, each clearing the parts that affected the other's forces. The alternative, allowing MacArthur to draft the final plan after receiving Nimitz's naval and amphibious plans, as Nimitz told King, "would carry. . . the *implication* of unity of command."[24] Thus, U.S. forces were headed for Japan with two commanders in chief—one general and one admiral.

PASTEL

As late as 30 July 1945 MacArthur and his AFPAC staff still worried that "despite air and sea blockade operations, Japan will remain capable of restricted movement of major units from the continent."[25] That concern had bothered the planners from the first serious mention of the invasion of Japan; it had also driven the military to seek the intervention of the Soviets to tie down the Japanese forces that were deployed in China and Manchuria. Perhaps deception could help keep Japanese continental forces from reinforcing the homeland.

To keep Japanese ground forces on the continent while OLYMPIC was being launched became a major goal of PASTEL, the deception plan for OLYMPIC.[26] As the invasion neared, it could no longer be hidden from the Japanese, but strategic deception could buy time until it was too late for the Japanese to redeploy from the continent. PASTEL called for measures that would deceive the Imperial General Staff, first as to American strategy and then as to the true invasion site. Uncertainty would force the Japanese to keep their defense forces dispersed and possibly to commit their remaining air and naval units prematurely and piecemeal "prior to our invasion . . . so that they may be destroyed."[27]

Deception planners hoped to convince the Japanese high command that American strategists had rejected a strategy of immediate invasion in favor of a strategy of further encirclement, blockade, and bombardment. According to the story, the Joint Chiefs recognized that immediate invasion would cost many American lives, that the Japanese government might withdraw to the Asiatic mainland to prolong the war indefinitely, and finally that, even if the Japanese islands eventually had to be assaulted, the invasion would be made far easier after a long campaign of blockade and bombing. On the other hand, a strategy of encirclement could be pursued at minimum cost in American lives by building up Chinese forces, by encouraging the Soviets to enter the war, by operating on the China coast, and by building up forces in the Aleutians aimed at the Kuriles and Hokkaido. The plan also called for specific efforts to convince the Japanese that an invasion of Formosa was scheduled for the late summer of 1945, preparatory to seizing bases on the China coast, and that an advance into the Yellow Sea area would come in the winter of 1945–46. So that the Japanese would not be suspicious when these operations failed to materialize, the planners included a warning: deception plans like Formosa and operations against the China coast should provide for cancellation or postponement "in a manner . . . entirely plausible to the Japanese General Staff."[28]

The story was plausible because it rested on partial truth. King had argued vehemently in 1944 for the invasion of Formosa, and the Joint Chiefs had just finished hotly debating the relative merits of invasion versus blockade and bombardment. A plan to gain bases on the China coast in the Shanghai area had been pushed by King throughout the debate as an encirclement alternative to OLYMPIC. Both King's Washington planners and Nimitz's staff had already done considerable planning for this operation, known as LONGTOM. Moreover, some early Pacific plans had focused on the Aleutians and the Kuriles leading to Hokkaido as a less heavily defended approach to Japan. Thus, the Japanese would be encouraged to believe real plans that had been seriously considered before being ultimately rejected in favor of OLYMPIC.

These measures were long-term strategic deception goals that were designed to create a predilection or predisposition in the Imperial General Staff forcing attention away from the home islands and toward the coast of China and the Asiatic mainland. Even if successful, this strategic deception would be overtaken by events as the date for OLYMPIC approached. The joint planners believed that the invasion of Japan would be evident to the Japanese by X-Day-minus-30 and that the general target area for OLYMPIC would be apparent to the enemy by X-Day-minus-10. By then, however, it would already be too late for the Japanese to redeploy large units from northern Japan or from the mainland. The deception problem would be to divert Japanese attention away from the target landing beaches in southern Kyushu.[29]

Thus, the island of Shikoku became the focus for the short-term deception of the Japanese. Again, as in the long-term strategic plan of deception, there was some truth. In fact, the joint planners had looked at Shikoku as a possible invasion site, and the Japanese already believed that Shikoku was a likely invasion target. The island dominated the Inland Sea, it was closer to the Kanto Plain than was Kyushu, and it had good airfield sites and invasion beaches. Yet Shikoku lay beyond the range of Okinawa-based fighters, and it was less desirable for naval bases that could be used to dominate the Sea of Japan and cut Japan's communications with the continent.[30]

Two stories would be fed to the Japanese. First, they would be led to believe that the Okinawa casualties and the logistical and morale problems attending redeployment of forces from Europe had forced postponement of the invasion of Japan to the fall of 1946. In the meantime, U.S. forces would assault the China coast to gain bases for tightening the blockade and intensifying the bombing. Then the story would change. The assault on China's coast would be postponed in favor of an assault on Shikoku.

According to the story, MacArthur and Nimitz, using eight divisions now freed from operations against the China coast, could mount a relatively easy assault against Shikoku, which could provide the airfields necessary for land-based planes to attack Kyushu, Honshu, and Korea.[31]

As deception planning proceeded downward, it became ever more refined and narrowly focused. The joint planners concentrated on more specific strategic stories to be used to deceive the Japanese; MacArthur's AFPAC staff brought deception measures closer to X-Day, created tactical deception measures, and suggested specific means for feeding the story to the Japanese.

The AFPAC plan, PASTEL-TWO, published on 30 July 1945, set fictitious target dates of 1 October and 1 December for the operations on the China coast and for the invasion of Shikoku. The China coast operation would be postponed about 7 September in favor of the invasion of Shikoku. In addition, MacArthur's staff developed specific measures for carrying these strategic deceptions into effect. Obvious beach reconnaissance was ordered in the Chusan area on the China coast; psychological warfare leaflet drops and radio broadcasts were aimed at the area; and air attacks against beach defenses were scheduled. Beginning about 1 September similar activities would be aimed at Shikoku.[32]

Convincing the Japanese of the deception story was to be a delicate, orchestrated affair. Seemingly random bits and pieces of information had to be put forward in so subtle a way that the Japanese would pick them up but would not immediately recognize a pattern. Singly, the bits and pieces of information would seem innocuous. Yet, accumulated and analyzed by the enemy's intelligence experts, the information would point the Japanese toward the desired conclusions—first the China coast, then Shikoku.

Misleading news stories would help tell the story. To underline the importance of the planned leaflet drops and radio broadcasts, stories would be released praising the success of U.S. psychological warfare efforts. Stories noting increased supplies to China and the shipment of Chinese interpreters to the Pacific would be planted to point toward operations on the China coast. To buttress belief in a strategy of encirclement, the Joint Chiefs would be quoted calling for more airbases near Japan before any invasion.[33]

Beginning in late August, news stories would attempt to point the Japanese toward an invasion of Shikoku. Stories would appear hinting that the Joint Chiefs were considering a return to an invasion strategy: redeployment from Europe was going faster than expected; the Soviets were about to enter the war and free the United States from operations on the

Asian mainland; the Japanese people were suffering horribly under the bombs of the B-29s and they were ripe for surrender; and defenses on Shikoku were especially weak.[34]

The planners did not rest with false news stories. Rubber terrain models, first of the Shanghai area and later of Shikoku, were noticeably shipped to the Pacific. Intelligence reports were to be prepared and issued first for Chusan-Shanghai and later for Shikoku. Rumors were intentionally spread among the soldiers of the Sixth Army that their next operation would be in China. The Chinese population in the Philippines was canvassed for people who were familiar with the Shanghai area. Plans were drawn for extensive use of fake radio traffic.[35]

Yet the greatest emphasis in the deception plan went to the probable use of large U.S. airborne forces in the invasion of Japan. Large airborne operations had been used in Europe; every major amphibious operation from Sicily to Normandy to southern France included an airborne force dropping behind the invasion beaches to secure key roads and bridges and to disrupt enemy defenses. MacArthur's staff noted that "our capabilities for large scale airborne operations are known to the Japanese and are probably over-estimated." Making the Japanese believe that major airborne operations were planned would force them to hold defensive forces in the interior away from the invasion beaches. The deception could not endanger actual airborne operations because none were planned.[36]

In late August a dummy airborne corps headquarters would be established at Okinawa to command two divisions. Like the corps, one division would be fictitious; the 11th Airborne Division, the only such unit in the Pacific, would serve as the other. On Okinawa, Far East Air Forces would build twelve dummy gliders per week until one hundred had been constructed. Simultaneously, six real gliders would conduct training flights under enemy observation. Major General Matthew Ridgeway, commander of the U.S. XVIIIth Airborne Corps in Europe, would make a public statement that he expected to "go to the Pacific and help whip the Japs."[37]

News stories would be used to further build up the airborne threat. Stories were planned noting that glider production had increased and that airborne troops were being quickly returned from Europe for retraining. Other stories would intimate that airborne units were training in the northern United States for possible use in Alaska. Large airborne units in Alaska would obviously signal a threat to the lightly defended Kuriles and Hokkaido. Indeed, when the war ended, army war planners in Washington were considering the transfer of airborne units to Alaska in hopes that the Japanese would leave forces in the Kuriles and Hokkaido rather than transferring them to Kyushu.[38]

The airborne threat would also be used for tactical deception. On the night before the scheduled OLYMPIC assault, airborne diversions would be flown to support each of the three landings. Three planes in each assault area would each drop sixty parachute dummies and pyrotechnics. Targets were large Japanese airfields that lay behind the landing beaches. Similar diversions would be launched on the night of X-Day-plus-1 against airfields further inland. The planners hoped to distract and confuse the defenders and force them to hold forces in the interior while the assault forces went ashore.[39]

Except for their worries about large-scale U.S. airborne operations, there is no evidence that after June 1945 the Japanese were deceived by PASTEL. Despite their earlier debate about American intentions to further encircle Japan before invasion, by June they were convinced that Kyushu was the target. The only doubts that remained were whether the United States would invade southern or northern Kyushu. By June even this question had been settled, for the Japanese began pouring everything into southern Kyushu.

NOTES

1. AFPAC Staff Study, "Olympic Operation in Southern Kyushu," 28 May 1945, RG 165, NARA.

2. Headquarters, Sixth Army, G-2 Estimate of the Enemy Situation, Olympic Operation, 1 August 1945, RG 218, WNRC.

3. ETI Study No. 80-5, Terrain and Harbor Study, Kagoshima and Vicinity, Army Forces, Middle Pacific (AFMIDPAC), July 1945, USAMHI.

4. AFPAC Staff Study, "Olympic."

5. Future Operations in the Pacific, WD Ext. 77500, 3 April 45, RG 165, OPD 381 TS, NARA; JWPC 235/3, "Plan for Operation against Kyushu," 4 September 1944, JCS Records (microfilm edition).

6. Command and Operational Directives for the Pacific, 3 April 45, JCS 1259/4, RG 165, ABC 381, Pacific Ocean Area (29 Jan 43, Sec. 3), NARA.

7. John A. Hixson, "Joint and Combined Planning Problems Involved in the Preparation for Operation OLYMPIC," 1 September 1987, (Manuscript in possession of the author), 39.

8. D. Clayton James, *The Years of MacArthur*, vol. 2, *1941–1945* (Boston: Houghton Mifflin, 1975), 726–27.

9. Draft Message, Marshall to MacArthur, 15 April 45, Marshall Papers, Box 75, Folder 2, Marshall Library.

10. Ibid.; Message, Marshall to MacArthur, 4 May 1945, USAFPAC Correspondence, RG 4, MacArthur Archives.

11. Message, MacArthur to Marshall, 5 May 1945, USAFPAC Correspondence, RG 4, MA.

12. Conference of CINCAFPAC and CINCPAC/POA Held at Manila, P.I. on 16 May 1945, in CINCPAC/POA Joint Staff Study—Kyushu Island Operation, 18 June 1945, NHC.

13. Memo for the Record: Arrangements for Preparation, Initiation, and Coordination of Operation OLYMPIC . . . between Staff Conferees of CINCPAC-CINCPOA and CINCAFPAC-SWPA, in CINCPAC/POA Joint Staff Study—Kyushu Island Operation, 18 June 1945, NHC.

14. Ibid.

15. George C. Dyer, *The Amphibians Came to Conquer: The Story of Admiral Richmond Kelly Turner*, vol. 2 (Washington, DC: GPO, 1972), 1108, 1110.

16. Memo from Sixth Army G-4 to Chief of Staff, 15 June 45, RG 338, OLYMPIC Operation Memos, Box 59, File No. 1, Sixth Army G-4 decimal file, WNRC.

17. Walter Krueger, *From Down Under to Nippon* (Washington, DC: Combat Forces Press, 1953), 334.

18. Hixson, 37–38; Admiral King's Correspondence, Series I, Box 5, Jan 45–May 46, NHC.

19. Letter, Nimitz to MacArthur, 1 July 45, Marshall Papers, Box 75, Folder 3, Marshall Library.

20. MacArthur's Report to Marshall on Conference with CINCPOA Relative Control and Coordination of Forces, File No. 704.211–2. n.d., Simpson Historical Center, Maxwell AFB, AL.

21. Command and Operational Directives for the Pacific, 3 April 45, JCS 1259/4.

22. James, 726.

23. Nimitz Command Summary, Book 6, 1 Jan–1 Jul 45, NHC.

24. Message, Nimitz to King, Box 166, O–17, Operations in Southern Kyushu, June–October 45, NHC.

25. AFPAC Staff Study, "Pastel-Two, Cover and Deception, Olympic Operations," 30 July 1945, USMHI.

26. The most complete study of Pastel is Thomas M. Huber, *Pastel: Deception in the Invasion of Japan* (Ft. Leavenworth, KS: Combat Studies Institute, 1988).

27. General Directive for Deception Measures against Japan, 16 June 1945, CCS 284/16/D, RG 165, ABC 381, Japan, 15 April 1943, Sec. 1-B.

28. Ibid.

29. Plan "Pastel," Appendix B to JCS 1410, RG 165, ABC 381, Japan, 15 April 1945, Sec. 5.

30. Ibid.

31. Ibid.

32. AFPAC Staff Study, "Pastel-Two."

33. Ibid.

34. Ibid.

35. Ibid.

36. Ibid.

37. Ibid.

38. Ibid.; Movement of Parachute Troops to Alaska, 6 July 1945, RG 165, OPD 381 TS.

39. AFPAC Staff Study, "Pastel-Two."

Chapter 12

OLYMPIC: The Forces

The combat forces for OLYMPIC were to be drawn from forces already in the Pacific. Except for service units, no redeployment from Europe would be necessary. The scale of OLYMPIC and the size of the invasion force would be unparalleled. Indeed, in the size and scale of the landings, OLYMPIC would dwarf OVERLORD. The assault on Normandy required the simultaneous transport of five divisions over the one-hundred-mile-wide English Channel; OLYMPIC was supposed to land ten divisions simultaneously and a three-division reserve force would be afloat in the target area ready to land if needed. Most of the soldiers and marines would set foot on the beaches of southern Kyushu after sea voyages of several days from the Philippines and the Marianas.

For the first time in the war, all of the resources in the Pacific could be devoted to a single objective. During 1942 and 1943 the Solomons competed with New Guinea. In 1944 Nimitz's Central Pacific operations in the Marshalls and Marianas competed with MacArthur's drive toward the Philippines. In 1945 Iwo Jima and Okinawa competed with Luzon. Now, for OLYMPIC the two offensives would merge and their power would be consolidated.

The naval forces available for OLYMPIC were abundant almost beyond belief—more than 3,000 ships that included 22 battleships, 27 heavy and light aircraft carriers, 36 escort carriers, 50 cruisers, and 458 destroyers and destroyer escorts. Other vessels of all types from attack transports to minesweepers to ocean-going landing craft numbered 2,458—enough to deposit thirteen divisions and one regimental combat team on their beaches in a single sea lift and to support them during the initial phases of the land campaign.[1]

Nimitz designated the Third and Fifth Fleets as the principal naval elements to carry out OLYMPIC. Admiral Halsey would command the Third Fleet and Admiral Spruance would command the Fifth Fleet. The fast carriers and new battleships were concentrated under Halsey. With these forces he was to provide general (strategic) support for OLYMPIC by striking targets along the east coast of Japan from Honshu north to the Kuriles. Spruance's Fifth Fleet would "comprise the amphibious, support, and local covering forces" for the invasion.[2]

Halsey's Third Fleet would consist of the second U.S. carrier task force and the British carrier task force. Task groups 1, 2, and 3 would make up the second task force. Two task groups made up the British task force. Distributed among them were eight attack carriers, four light carriers, seven battleships, fourteen cruisers and forty-five destroyers. The British carrier task force consisted of five carriers and four battleships with attendant cruisers and destroyers. Stripped down to essentials for maximum firepower and speed, Halsey's Third Fleet would travel with a minimum of service support.[3]

The organization for Spruance's Fifth Fleet was far more complex than that of Halsey's, but Spruance had a much more varied and complicated job to do in transporting, landing, and supporting the invasion forces. To provide air cover for the assault, Spruance was assigned the first carrier task force consisting of carrier task groups 4 and 5. These groups were built around seven attack and three light carriers. Escort forces for Spruance's carriers numbered two battleships, eleven cruisers, and thirty destroyers. Just before X-Day, Halsey was to transfer two of his carrier task groups to the Fifth Fleet. Thus, when the landings took place, Spruance would command four of the five U.S. carrier task groups—one for each of the major landing areas. After X-Day, upon Nimitz's direction Spruance was to return the two task groups to Halsey.[4]

Most of the gunfire support ships in the Pacific were assigned to the Fifth Fleet to destroy Japanese defenses and cover the landings—4 battleship divisions, 6 cruiser divisions, and 18 destroyer squadrons. These totaled respectively 13 battleships, 20 cruisers, and 139 destroyers. Close to the beaches, the gunfire of the big ships could be augmented by landing craft (LSTs and LCIs) that had been adapted to fire mortar and rocket barrages. Fleet escort and covering forces comprised 23 destroyer escort divisions containing 167 destroyer escorts and 3 escort carrier divisions with 16 escort carriers. Mines would be cleared by 237 minesweepers. The fleet would be supported and serviced by other specialized vessels from amphibious command ships (AGCs) to net-laying ships (ANs); from rescue tugs (ATRs) to internal-combustion-engine repair ships (ARGs) and distilling ships (AWs).[5]

But the heart and purpose of the Fifth Fleet lay in its TransRons and TransDivs, navy shorthand for Transport Squadrons and Transport Divisions. These were made up of more than four hundred attack transports (APAs), attack cargo ships (AKAs), and high-speed transports (APDs). Together with almost one thousand LSTs and LCIs (sea-going landing craft) these transports would carry the soldiers and marines, their weapons, vehicles, and supplies to the landing beaches.[6]

The element of the Fifth Fleet charged with getting the troops ashore was Amphibious Forces Pacific Fleet commanded by Admiral Turner (COMPHIBSPAC). Irascible and overly certain of his own correctness, "Terrible" Turner found it difficult to get along with soldiers. One army air force commander complained to his superior that he had reached an impasse with his navy counterparts in planning for OLYMPIC, and he blamed his problems on "Admiral Turner and the typical navy mind." Turner, he charged, was ignorant of the capabilities of land-based air power.[7] Nonetheless, Turner could hardly be charged with inexperience; he had been in the business since 1942 when he commanded the amphibious force at Guadalcanal.

Soon after the Joint Chiefs realigned MacArthur's and Nimitz's commands along service lines, they undertook also to realign command of the Army Air Forces in the Pacific. Nimitz had commanded the Seventh Air Force which included land-based army air units operating in his Pacific Ocean area. With no carriers to supply air coverage for his amphibious leaps, MacArthur's land-based army air forces were much larger than Nimitz's. MacArthur's air power was organized under General Kenney's Far East Air Forces, which by 1945 included the Fifth and Thirteenth Air Forces.

Since mid-1944 yet a third semi-autonomous air command had arisen in the Pacific. Always fearful that strategic bombers would be subordinated to the interests of ground commanders (as the very-long-range B-29 offensive promised to become a reality first from bases in China and later from the Marianas) Arnold convinced the other members of the Joint Chiefs that the Twentieth Air Force, the headquarters that directed the B-29s, be retained directly under their control. Thereafter, the Twentieth Air Force took its orders only from the Joint Chiefs, and Arnold, acting as the executive agent of the group, commanded it.

In preparation for the final assault on Japan, however, Arnold wanted an air force counterpart to MacArthur and Nimitz—a general to command all air forces just as MacArthur commanded all army forces and Nimitz commanded all naval forces. He failed to gain the approval of either King, Leahy, or Marshall, and, after some wrangling, Arnold accepted a compromise. General Carl A. Spaatz, commander of U.S. Strategic Air Forces in the European theater, would be brought out to the Pacific to head a new command, U.S. Army Strategic Air Forces in the Pacific (USASTAF). Spaatz would control "all land-based strategic air operations against Japan." He was expected to destroy "Japan's military, industrial, and economic systems."[8]

Not only did MacArthur retain his Far East Air Forces, but the reorganization enlarged the air power under his command. Seventh Air

Force, Nimitz's army air in the central Pacific, was ceded to MacArthur to be integrated into FEAF. Thus, on the eve of the invasion of Japan, Spaatz commanded all strategic air power, Nimitz retained command of all navy air, and MacArthur's FEAF included the Fifth, Seventh, and Thirteenth Air Forces.

General Spaatz, the new USASTAF commander fresh from a similar job in Europe, arrived at Guam on 29 July. The outlines of his new command had only just begun to form when the war ended. Two bomber commands would carry the strategic air war to Japan. The B-29-equipped Twentieth Air Force would continue to operate from the Marianas. Lieutenant General James H. Doolittle would bring his B-17-equipped Eighth Air Force from Europe to be based at Okinawa. Doolittle arrived at Okinawa on 19 July. While the strategic bombers could possibly, in an emergency, be placed under the command of Nimitz or MacArthur to support OLYMPIC directly, they were expected to expand the bombing of Japanese cities and industrial targets.[9]

The burden of tactical air support for OLYMPIC fell upon General Kenny's FEAF, especially the Fifth and Seventh Air Forces, which would be redeployed to Okinawa and other islands in the Ryukyus as soon as bases could be readied. Early plans called for an air garrison in the Ryukyus of fifty-one groups.[10] That number included marine air units and eight B-29 groups redeployed from the Marianas. Later developments scaled down the figure to 48.5 air groups. Yet another reduction of tactical air power came when the number of B-29 groups to be redeployed from the Marianas was increased from eight to twelve. Final FEAF plans called for 1,850 combat aircraft to be in place in the Ryukyus by 15 October— 1,014 fighters, 772 bombers, and 64 air-sea rescue and troop-carrier planes.[11] These figures did not include the planes of the Second Marine Air Wing or the almost two thousand carrier planes of Halsey's and Spruance's fleets that would support the landings.

In 1945 MacArthur's ground combat forces were organized into two field armies—the Sixth and the Eighth. He chose the Sixth Army to conduct the assault on southern Kyushu. Under the name "Alamo Force," the Sixth Army had led MacArthur's drive across New Guinea. Under General Krueger, the Sixth Army had commanded the landing forces at Leyte in October 1944 and at Luzon in January 1945. Before the fight for Leyte was finished, the Sixth Army was relieved by Major General Robert L. Eichelberger's Eighth Army so that Krueger and his staff could ready themselves for the Luzon landings. Similarly, the Sixth Army was relieved on Luzon by the Eighth so that Krueger could begin plans and preparations for OLYMPIC.

Like MacArthur, the commanding general, Sixth Army was an old soldier. Unlike his patrician superior, however, Krueger was neither a West Pointer nor the scion of a military family. He had risen to high command from the enlisted ranks. Over a forty-eight year career, Krueger rose from volunteer private to general in the regular army. Earlier, in 1889 at the age of eight, he had immigrated with his parents to America from Germany. At seventeen he had enlisted in the army to serve in Cuba during the Spanish-American War.

Precise personnel and equipment totals for Krueger's Sixth Army as it readied for OLYMPIC are impossible to determine, for troop lists were under constant revision in the months before the war ended. Nonetheless, the personnel strength for Sixth Army's conduct of OLYMPIC approached six hundred thousand. Of these, about 353,000 were combat soldiers and marines, and approximately 230,000 were service troops and military government personnel.[12]

While the OLYMPIC troop list underwent constant revision, the task list remained remarkably constant. Four corps would control the bulk of Sixth Army's assault forces—three army and one marine. Headquarters, I Corps, scheduled to lead the 25th, 33d, and 41st Infantry Divisions in the assault at Miyazaki, had been with MacArthur since the austere summer of 1942 in Australia. Under Eichelberger, later commanding general of the Eighth Army, I Corps suffered through the bitter and bloody fighting around Buna, New Guinea, in December 1942–January 1943, and participated in the fights for Hollandia and Biak in 1944. The corps, now commanded by Major General Innis P. Swift, assaulted Luzon with Kreuger's Sixth Army on 9 January 1945 and was continually in combat until relieved on 30 June to prepare for OLYMPIC.

I Corps would lead three veteran divisions in the assault at Miyazaki. The 25th Infantry Division, commanded by Major General Charles L. Mullins, had been at Schofield Barracks on Oahu during the attack on Pearl Harbor, had participated in the campaign for Guadalcanal and the Solomons, and had been in combat on Luzon from January to 30 June 1945 with the Sixth Army. Major General Percy W. Clarkson's 33d Infantry Division had arrived in New Guinea in May 1944, and, except for mopping up operations on Morotai, experienced its first combat on Luzon from 9 February to 30 June. The 41st Infantry Division, under Major General Jens A. Doe, had come out to the Pacific in April 1942; entered combat around Buna in January 1943; participated in the fighting around Aitape, New Guinea, and on Biak from April to August 1944; and cleared the island of Palawan in the Philippines. On 11 July 1945 the 41st Division began preparations for Operation OLYMPIC.

XI Corps, directed to lead the landings at Ariake Bay, was formed at Chicago in May 1942 and spent the next two years training troops in the United States. The Corps moved to the Pacific in March 1944 and participated in combat in New Guinea and Leyte, under Major General Charles P. Hall, before fighting in the campaign for Luzon. Upon relief from that campaign, on 1 July 1945, XI Corps was given command of the 1st Cavalry Division, the Americal Division, and the 43d Infantry Division and ordered to prepare the assault on Ariake Bay.

Despite its name and historic mission of patrolling the Mexican border, the "1st Cav" had been transformed into an infantry division and sent to the Pacific in June 1943. From February to May 1944, the division was in combat in the Admiralty Islands. After participation in the campaigns for both Leyte and Luzon, the 1st Cavalry Division was released from combat on 30 June 1945 to begin preparations for OLYMPIC.

The Americal Division had been formed from disparate elements drawn from various parts of the United States in the panicky days of January 1942. Ten days after being organized, the division was en route to Australia. From March to October 1942 it defended New Caledonia and the New Hebrides from possible Japanese invasion. After entering combat on Guadalcanal and Bougainville in the Solomons, the Americal Division participated in combat in the southern Philippines, fighting on Leyte, Samar, Cebu, Bohol, and Negros Oriental. The division was relieved from combat on 20 June 1945 to prepare for OLYMPIC.

The 43d Infantry Division was another early arrival in the Pacific, having come out to New Zealand in October 1942 and served as an occupation force in the southern Solomons from February to June 1943. The division saw combat on New Georgia in 1943 and on New Guinea in 1944. The 43d was in the initial assault at Lingayen Gulf on 9 January 1945 and remained in constant combat until relieved on 20 June 1945 to prepare for the invasion.

Major General Charles W. Ryder's IX Corps had no combat record when assigned the job of leading the Sixth Army Reserve for OLYMPIC. The Corps had been in garrison and training roles in the United States before being ordered to Hawaii in October 1944. There, the IX Corps was given more training responsibilities. It arrived on Leyte on 9 July 1945 to begin preparing corps plans for OLYMPIC.

The 77th Infantry Division, the 81st Infantry Division, and the 98th Infantry Division were assigned to IX Corps. The 77th did not arrive in the Pacific until mid-1944, and went into combat on Guam, followed by commitment to Leyte in November 1944, and finally to Ie Shima and Okinawa April–June 1945. The 81st had engaged in the bitter fight at

Anguar and Peleliu in the Palau Islands in September-October 1944 with the 1st Marine Division. While in reserve on New Caledonia for Operation ICEBERG at Okinawa, the 81st was ordered to Leyte to begin preparations for OLYMPIC. IX Corps' other division, the 98th Infantry Division, had been defending the Hawaiian islands and had not yet seen combat. While still in Hawaii, the division received word in July 1945 that it would participate in the invasion of Kyushu.

Major General Harry Schmidt's V Marine Amphibious Corps was ordered to lead the assault on the west coast of Kyushu. The corps had originally been commanded by Major General Holland "Howling Mad" Smith, but Schmidt had been given command in July 1944, after Smith was made commanding general of the Fleet Marine Force. The V Amphibious corps had fought at Tarawa, Saipan, and Iwo Jima.

Assigned for Operation OLYMPIC were the 2d, 3d, and 5th Marine Divisions. The 2d had fought at Tarawa and Saipan and in the latter battle took 4,488 casualties in fifteen days. The 3d Marine Division had first been in combat at Bougainville in November 1943 before going on to fight at Guam and Iwo Jima. The 5th Marine Division, one of the last two to be formed, made the assault at Iwo Jima and fought through that entire bloody battle.

The 11th Airborne, the only airborne division in the Pacific, was designated Sixth Army's followup force. The division had earlier fought in both the Leyte and Luzon campaigns.

All but one of the army divisions scheduled for OLYMPIC were in the Philippines, six of them on Luzon where they had only recently been released from combat. They were resting, refitting, and retraining. Four more army divisions were in the southern Philippines—two at Cebu and one each at Mindanao and Panay. The 98th Infantry Division was in Hawaii. Two of the corps headquarters, I Corps and XI Corps, were on Luzon. XI Corps was at Tacloban on Leyte. The marines of V Amphibious Corps were scattered. In Hawaii were Corps headquarters and the 5th Marine Division. The other two marine divisions were in the Marianas— the 2d Marine Division at Saipan and the 3d at Guam. Corps headquarters and the 5th Marine Division were scheduled to sail from Hawaii on X-Day-minus-31 to consolidate the corps in the Marianas, where the corps and its divisions would conduct rehearsals.[13]

The task of staging and mounting these troops for the invasion was an immense and complicated undertaking[14]. The overriding principle adopted by the planners put the responsibility for staging and mounting units on the commander who controlled the geographical area where the unit was to be delayed or loaded. Such a policy was essential because of the large numbers and diverse missions of the units involved in OLYMPIC. Staging areas and mounting sites were in the Philippines and the Marianas. The 5th Marine Division would be brought to the Marianas from Hawaii to join the 2d and 3d Marine Divisions, which were already there. The three divisions would be brought together under V Marine Amphibious Corps to conduct rehearsals for their assault on the southwest coast of Kyushu. They would be loaded aboard ships at Guam and Saipan for the week-long trip to their objective. Sixth Army Headquarters and the army divisions of I and XI Corps would stage through the Batangas and Lingayen areas of Luzon. Once aboard the transports, the naval and amphibious phases would begin, so General Kreuger and his Sixth Army would come under naval command.[15]

Air and naval attacks in support of OLYMPIC would already be underway as the assault forces boarded their ships in the harbors of the Philippines and the Marianas. Halsey's Third Fleet with its strike force of three U.S. carrier task groups and two British carrier task groups, a force of twenty-one carriers and ten battleships, with attendant escorts of cruisers and destroyers, would begin raking the Japanese east coast from the Bungo Straits north to the Kurile Islands. Halsey, in general support of the OLYMPIC landings, was to destroy the remainder of the Japanese air force and to isolate the battle area in Kyushu by severing Japanese land and sea communications running south from Honshu and Hokkaido.[16]

Meanwhile, U.S. Strategic Air Forces, consisting of the very heavy B-29s of the Twentieth Air Force in the Marianas and the growing number of B-17s of the Eighth Air Force in the Ryukyus, would continue to pound Japanese strategic targets—aircraft factories, shipyards and port facilities, and Japanese cities. The planes of the FEAF based in the Ryukyus would attack air fields on the China coast, in Korea, and in southern Kyushu, and lines of communications leading into the objective area. As X-Day grew nearer, the FEAF, along with the carrier planes of Spruance's Fifth Fleet, would undertake direct air support of the landings.[17]

Spruance's Fifth Fleet, assigned the mission of carrying the Sixth Army to the assault beaches, getting the forces ashore, and providing direct air and naval gunfire support, was necessarily a large, complex, and diverse force. To provide air support for the fleet and for the landings, Spruance was given ten carriers organized into two carrier task groups. Upon Nimitz's order prior to D-Day, Halsey would pass two of his carrier task groups from Third Fleet to Spruance. Thus, by X-Day, to directly support the landings, Spruance would control four of the seven carrier task groups. In addition, he was assigned sixteen escort carriers. To provide cover for the attack forces and gunfire support for the landings,

Spruance would have 13 old battleships, 20 cruisers, 139 destroyers, 167 destroyer escorts, and attendant minesweeper and anti-submarine warfare groups—altogether an imposing assemblage of nearly eight hundred combat vessels, nearly fifteen hundred transports and amphibious ships, and assorted specialized vessels such as repair ships, tugs, stores ships, and seaplane tenders.[18]

Yet the heart of Fifth Fleet was the amphibious force under Admiral Turner including the fire support groups to conduct the preliminary bombardment, the minesweeper groups, and the attack forces carrying the Sixth Army assault units. Turner's amphibious force, called Task Force 40, included attack forces paralleling the organization of Sixth Army. Third Attack Force would carry General Hall's XI Corps to its assault beaches at the head of Ariake Bay; Fifth Attack Force would transport the marines of General Schmidt's V Amphibious Corps to their landing beaches near Kushikino; and Seventh Attack Force would carry General Swift's I Corps to the Miyazaki beaches. Western Attack Force would transport the 40th Infantry Division and establish it ashore on Koshiki Retto and other offshore islands. Southern Attack Force would carry the 158th Regimental Combat Team for that unit's contingency landings on the northern tip of Tenega Shima. Reserve Attack Force would carry General Ryder's IX Corps to its contingency objectives on the southern tip of the Satsuma Peninsula. Finally, Reinforcement Force would carry the 11th Airborne Division, Sixth Army's reserve.[19]

Until the assault units were established ashore, command rested with the naval commanders—from Nimitz to Spruance to Turner down to the attack force commanders. However, the major ground force commanders traveled with their naval counterparts. Kreuger would embark with Turner in the latter's command ship the *Eldorado;* Hall with Vice Admiral Theodore S. Wilkinson in the *Mt. Olympus;* Schmidt with Vice Admiral Harry W. Hill in the *Auburn;* Swift with Vice Admiral Daniel E. Barbey in the *Ancon.* Each attack force consisted of the transport groups carrying the assault forces and assigned gunfire support, minesweeping, and underwater demolition groups.[20]

Air attacks in support of OLYMPIC would begin about 15 August with the Third Fleet "initiating widespread attacks against Japan to effect maximum attrition of the Japanese Air Force, to interdict lines of communication leading to Kyushu and to destroy enemy naval forces and shipping." The air attacks by Third Fleet were to reach a crescendo during the week of X-Day-minus-14 to X-Day-minus-8. Meanwhile, FEAF in the Ryukyus would concentrate on enemy targets in Kyushu, on the China coast, and on Formosa. Early priority would be given to destroying enemy planes and airbases and to interrupting lines of communications between Honshu and Kyushu, but as X-Day drew nearer, FEAF would begin zeroing in on targets of immediate significance to the landing forces—railroad and highway bridges on both coasts of southern Kyushu, beach defenses, inlets hiding suicide boats, radar facilities, and anti-aircraft batteries.[21]

X-Day-minus-8 was a key date in the schedule of events leading up to the landings. No longer would it be possible to hide the immediate objectives from the enemy. The Fifth Fleet carriers and Task Force 41, the Amphibious Advance Force, made up of the gun ships of the fire support groups, the minesweepers, and the underwater reconnaissance and demolition groups, would come forward into the waters around southern Kyushu to begin their work. Their assigned tasks were to gain air superiority, to bombard the defenses on the landing beaches, and to cover the approach of the attack forces.[22]

The fire support groups were made up of old battleships too slow to accompany the fast carriers of Halsey's Third Fleet, of cruisers and destroyers and landing craft, and of LSTs and LCIs that had been adapted to fire mortar or rocket barrages. A separate fire support group was organized for each of the major attack forces—the Third, Fifth, and Seventh. Clearly, the amphibious planners considered the landings by the Third Attack Force (XI Corps) at Ariake Wan most critical, for the Third Fire Support Group was by far the heaviest of the three—eight battleships, nine cruisers, nineteen destroyers, and fifty-seven rocket-, mortar-, and gun-firing LSTs and LCIs. The Seventh Fire Support Group at Miyazaki was assigned four battleships, thirteen cruisers, seventeen destroyers, and fifty-nine rocket-, and mortar-, and gun-firing landing craft. The Fifth Fire Support Group had only four battleships, ten cruisers, and fourteen destroyers but was given enormous short-range firepower in ninety-eight rocket-, and mortar-, and gun-firing LSTs and LCIs. Fire support groups for the landings on the offshore islands and for the reserve force landings would be temporarily detailed from the three established fire support groups.[23]

The fire support groups would be at their stations on X-Day-minus-8 to protect the minesweepers and the underwater demolition teams from shore fire and to destroy coastal defense guns. They would also bombard airfields within reach of their guns and fire on harbors hiding suicide boats or submarines. The rocket-, mortar-, and gun-firing landing craft would begin trying to isolate the landing beaches by firing barrages at roads and railroads leading to the beaches. Top priority targets for the fire support groups were coastal-defense and anti-aircraft guns, and artillery and anti-tank guns capable of firing on the beaches. Gunners were cautioned that Japanese defenders habitually provided heavy overhead cover and camouflage for their gun positions. Thus, they were instructed to strip the camouflage away with heavy-caliber guns or aerial bombs before firing for destruction.[24]

Minesweeping, underwater reconnaissance, and demolition would begin on X-Day-minus-7 on the offshore islands, on X-Day-minus-5 on the three major invasion beaches, and would continue through X-Day-minus-2. The swimmers of the underwater demolition teams would be the first Americans on the invasion beaches. In fast transports they would be brought to the objectives and at six thousand yards from shore would be put over the side in small boats. Each platoon of twenty-two swimmers would reconnoiter one thousand yards of beach. Some swimmers would swim parallel to shore to get an overall picture of the beach. Meanwhile, other members of the platoon would swim to the water's edge. The teams were to locate and plot minefields and obstacles (both natural and man-made) and plot surf conditions and bottom and beach composition. After completing their reconnaissance, the teams would be picked up by small boats and carried back to their transports. The team members would organize their data as the transports proceeded at high speed to carry the reports to the attack force commanders. Thus, the invasion forces would obtain eyewitness information on the landing beaches that was no more than two days old. Underwater demolition teams would sweep the beaches before X-Day exploding mines and obstacles with delayed charges. On the three main invasion beaches, the reconnaissance teams would begin work on X-day-minus-4 and the demolition teams would begin on X-Day-minus-3.[25]

The advance force—fire support, minesweeping, and underwater demolition groups—called Task Force 41, would be joined on X-Day by the Third, Fifth, and Seventh Attack Forces carrying the troops for the assaults on Ariake Wan, Kushikino, and Miyazaki beaches. For the first time, the entire amphibious force would be together in a single area. United, Turner's command would now become Task Force 40. By that time, American troops would already be ashore on some offshore islands.

NOTES

1. CINCPAC Staff Study "OLYMPIC," 18 June 1945, RG 218, NARA.
2. Ibid.

3. CINCPOA Operation Plan No. 10–45, 8 August 1945; Operations in Southern Kyushu 6/45–10/45, NHC.

4. Ibid.

5. Ibid.

6. Ibid.

7. Memo, F. H. Smith, Jr., Fifth Fighter Command, to Ennis C. Whitehead, Fifth Air Force, 5 August 1945, and Memo, Smith to T. H. Landon, 6 November 1945, File No. 71232245–11, Air Force Historical Center, Maxwell AFB, AL.

8. Wesley F. Craven and James L. Cate, eds., vol. 5 *The Pacific: Matterhorn to Nagasaki*, vol. 5, *June 1944 to August 1945* (Chicago: Univ. of Chicago Press, 1953), 688.

9. Ibid., 688, 700–1.

10. The number of planes in a group varied depending on the type of unit. A fighter group held seventy-five planes, a medium bomber group sixty-four, and a heavy bomber group forty-eight.

11. "Far East Air Force History, 15 June 1944–2 September 1945," 350, U.S. Air Force Historical Center, Bolling Air Force Base, Washington, DC. Hereinafter referred to as FEAF History.

12. Sixth Army Field Order No. 74, Troop List, 28 July 1945, Records of the Strategic Plans Division, Box 187, NHC.

13. CINCPAC Staff Study OLYMPIC; Concentration and Movement Table, 28 July 1945, RG 407, Box 2843, Eighth Army CORONET, Training Requirements, File No. 1, vol. 1, Training Requirements, August 1945, WNRC.

14. Staging is the temporary delay of a unit for training, equipping, etc. at an intermediate place on the way to its final objective. Mounting is loading the unit aboard ships for transportation to the objective.

15. Ibid.

16. CINCPOA Operation Plan No. 10–45.

17. Ibid.

18. Ibid.

19. Amphibious Forces Pacific Fleet Operation Plan No. A11–45, 10 August 1945, NHC.

20. Ibid.

21. Ibid.

22. Ibid.; CINCPAC Staff Study OLYMPIC.

23. Amphibious Forces Pacific Fleet Operation Plan No. A11–45.

24. Ibid.

25. Underwater Demolition Teams Amphibious Forces Pacific Fleet Operation Plan No. 7–45, NHC.

Chapter 13

OLYMPIC: The Assault

In the preliminary phase of OLYMPIC beginning on X-Day-minus-5, the 40th Infantry Division and the 158th Regimental Combat Team (RCT) would land on offshore islands to provide radar facilities, emergency anchorages, and seaplane bases. On X-Day, unless the timing had to be staggered because of bad weather or other unforeseen factors, the three corps would simultaneously assault their respective beaches. I Corps would land in the Miyazaki area and XI Corps at the head of Ariake Wan (both on the east coast of Kyushu), while V Marine Amphibious Corps would land on beaches just south of Kushikino on the west coast. IX Corps, Sixth Army's floating reserve, would be prepared to commit the 98th Division to reinforce any elements of the Sixth Army and to land, if ordered, with or without the 98th, on the south coast of the Satsuma Peninsula east of Makurazaki anytime after X-Day-plus-3. Each corps would establish a beachhead and immediately begin the construction and rehabilitation of roads and airfields. Then each would advance inland to secure more airfields and to open Kagoshima Wan for use by the navy. Finally, all forces would advance to destroy any remaining enemy forces and to secure a defensive line across southern Kyushu from Tsuno on the east coast to Sendai on the west coast. The operation was to be completed in 90 days. For the job, Sixth Army had 582,560 troops, 323,410 of whom were combat soldiers.[1]

The infantrymen of the assault divisions were to assault beaches that were designated with code names fashioned after America's prime obsession—the automobile. The possible landing areas of southern Kyushu were designated "beach zones"—TAXICAB, ROADSTER, LIMOUSINE, STATION WAGON, TOWN CAR, DELIVERY WAGON, and CONVERTIBLE. In turn, each beach zone was subdivided into possible individual landing beaches. Thus, TAXICAB beach zone included ZEPHYR, WINTON, STUTZ, and STUDEBAKER beaches; LIMOUSINE beach zone included PLYMOUTH, PACKARD, and OVERLAND beaches; STATION WAGON beach zone included FRANKLIN, FORD, ESSEX, DUSENBERG, and DE SOTO beaches; and TOWN CAR beach zone included CORD, CHRYSLER, and CHEVROLET beaches. Rather too cutely, the small beaches of the offshore islands, including Koshiki Retto to be assaulted by the 40th Infantry Division, were named for auto parts—BRAKEDRUM, WINDSHIELD, CYLINDER, GEARSHIFT, HUBCAP, RUMBLESEAT,

SPARKPLUG, etc. Subdivisions of individual beaches were designated by colors and numbers—Austin yellow 1, Austin yellow 2, etc.[2]

At first glance, on a map all four of the major landing beaches in southern Kyushu appeared to be ideal for amphibious operations. They were long, open, and inviting. The beaches were relatively flat, fifteen- to thirty-kilometer-long crescents of hard sand. It was behind the beaches that an invader would confront major problems. The invasion beaches at Miyazaki, Ariake Wan, Kaimon Dake, and Kushikino are all backed by rugged, easily defensible hills varying from fifty meters elevation at Miyazaki and Ariake Wan to two hundred meters at Kushikino. These hills are from one to five kilometers behind the beaches and, except for Ariake Wan, run the entire length of the beaches.

Corridors leading away from the beaches into the interior posed yet another problem. Looking at small-scale maps, the observer might easily conclude that open corridors led into the interior plains from the southern ends of both the Miyazaki and Ariake Wan beaches. In fact, when seen from the ground, heights dominated these corridors about ten to fifteen kilometers inland. Rugged, broken hills and terraces were immediately behind both the western Kyushu beaches, those near Kaimon Dake and those near Kushikino.

I Corps drew the task of assaulting the beaches at Miyazaki. Stepping onto the beach at Miyazaki, one sees in the distance twelve-hundred-meter mountains ringing a triangular coastal plain whose broad base is just below Miyazaki and whose apex is up the coast at Tsuno. Proceeding inland about two to three kilometers, however, one encounters a steep fifty-meter bluff rising out of the plain. Here the Japanese placed their strongpoints sited to dominate the exits from the beaches. The corridor that leads away from the southern beaches towards Tano on the western side of the Honjo River was to be used by U.S. forces as an entrance into the Miyakonojo-Kanoya plain. Near Tano, however, an unbroken hill mass three hundred to four hundred meters high blocks the corridor.

The Oyodo River flows down from the mountains and into the sea at Miyazaki, and the mouth of the river divided I Corps' assigned landing beaches. Miyazaki airfield, a prime objective, lay on the beach immediately south of the river's mouth, a geographic fact that would keep I Corps assault forces divided until they drove into the city of Miyazaki and took the bridge across the river. The beaches both north and south of the river's mouth are wide, gently sloping, hard sand—ideal for amphibious landings.

On 4 August I Corps published a tentative field order for the assault on Miyazaki. The plan called for landing the 25th Infantry Division on CORD

Beach south of the river's mouth and the 33d Infantry Division on CHRYSLER Beach immediately north of the river's mouth. In floating reserve, the 41st Infantry Division was to be prepared for three contingencies—to reinforce either assault division, to follow up the 25th Division on X-Day-plus-2, or finally, to make an assault landing on CHEVROLET Beach immediately north of CHRYSLER Beach to extend the corps beachhead northward.[3]

Both divisions were to land with two regimental combat teams abreast. The 25th Division would capture Miyazaki airfield, and then attack southward to "seize a position which will deny the enemy small arms fire and observed artillery fire on CORD Beach and will block enemy advance from the south." Upon completing that job, the 25th would attack west down the corridor that ran towards Tano and through the mountains towards Miyakonojo. There, if possible, the 25th would meet elements of the XI Corps driving north towards Miyakonojo from its beachhead at Ariake Wan.[4]

After getting ashore at CHRYSLER Beach, the 33d Division was to capture Miyazaki, seize the main coastal highway and bridge at Miyazaki and then establish contact with the 25th Division to the south. The 33d then would drive west to expand the corps beachhead and north up the coast to Hirose to block enemy troops coming from that direction.[5]

Corps planners noted several critical objectives that had to be taken early. Among the most critical were the Miyazaki airfield, the coastal highway, and its highway bridge across the Oyodo River. Without the highway and bridge the corps would have no means of north-south communications. Planners also considered it critical that the enemy be driven from the bluff or "terrace" that blocked the beaches two to three kilometers inland, especially a one-hundred-meter hill north of Miyazaki that provided enemy observation over all of Miyazaki and CHRYSLER Beach and another hill south of CORD Beach that could enfilade the entire 25th Division assault.[6]

I Corps would advance inland to secure a beachhead inside a general line from Sadohara in the north through Honjo and Takaoka to Aoi Dake in the south. Even as the divisions drove inland, on their heels would come the engineers and service troops of Army Service Command, Olympic, Base 3, to begin repairing and constructing airfields, bases, roads, and storage facilities.[7]

Ariake (Shibushi) Wan lies only thirty-two air miles southwest of Miyazaki. Yet the two assault areas are as isolated from one another as if they were hundreds of miles apart. Separated by rough, forested hills and mountains, some almost one thousand meters high, only a single provincial road wound down the rugged, rocky cliffs of the east coast. Although Sixth Army designated none of the corps' landings as the main attack, certainly the XI Corps landings at Ariake Wan were critical to the overall success of the invasion.

Ariake Wan is a cul-de-sac flanked on the east and west by three hundred to four hundred meter heights. The fifteen-kilometer-long beach at the head of the bay is inviting, and the small port of Shibushi at the eastern end makes the area even more attractive for amphibious operations. Rapid movement inland would place the invaders on the Miyako-nojo-Kanoya Plain, a feature of great strategic importance for its many airbases and for its access to the head of Kagoshima Bay.

The bay and the beach, however, provided good defensive sites. Heavy guns could be placed on both flanks of the bay, and the heights on both flanks provided complete observation of the bay and the beaches. Heavy guns on the small island of Biro Shima, five miles offshore and smack in the middle of the bay, could fire on the invasion fleet and on any of the beaches. The eastern half of the beaches is backed by continuous twenty-five to fifty meter bluffs ranging behind the beaches five hundred meters on the extreme east to one kilometer in the west. These bluffs are cut in several places by narrow stream valleys that form exits through the hills. Here the Japanese positioned strongpoints sited for all-around defense with tunnel networks under the hills. From these positions, some of which were manned by two battalions of the Japanese 86th Division, the defenders could dominate both the beaches to the front and the stream valleys on the sides. Heavy 150mm guns could fire from cave openings in the hillsides onto the beaches or the stream valleys. At the western end of the beaches the Kushira River plain makes the terrain substantially more open than that behind the eastern half. The main route to Kanoya runs through this open country. Fifteen kilometers into the interior, however, the route crosses fifty-meter hills. Here the Japanese had disposed the 188th Infantry Regiment to block mobile forces moving from the beaches into the interior.

Perhaps because of the critical nature of the Ariake Wan assault, the job was given to Lieutenant General Hall's XI Corps. Hall was given three veteran divisions and one separate regimental combat team to assault this key objective—the 1st Cavalry Division, the Americal Division, the 43d Infantry Division, and 112th RCT.

On 6 July 1945 XI Corps Chief of Staff Brigadier General John A. Elmore called all of his staff officers to a meeting to begin preliminary planning for the assault on Ariake Bay. Logistics was the greatest concern. In addition to landing the divisions and their equipment, thirty-five thousand tons of cargo had to be landed across the beaches from X-Day to X-Day-plus-4. Beach congestion was inevitable. The beaches could accommodate sixty LSTs at one time—ten per mile. General Elmore noted that if necessary they could be placed "gunwale to gunwale." The allocation of space in the beachhead for dumps, bases, headquarters areas, etc., required detailed planning and close coordination with Army Service Command, Olympic (ASCOM "O"), whose units would come close on the heels of the combat units to begin construction and repair of the bases that would receive the air units of Far Eastern Air Forces (FEAF). General Elmore closed the conference with the admonition that a field order and an administrative order "should be blocked out at the earliest possible time," although, he concluded, "some things cannot be done until more definite information becomes available."[8]

Three days later General Elmore called the commanders and staffs of the 1st Cavalry, 43d Infantry Division, and 112th RCT to meet with XI Corps staff. The Americal staff, far away at Cebu in the southern Philippines, did not attend. That division received its orientation on 13 July when General Elmore and his G-2, G-3, and G-4 flew down from Luzon. Although he could not yet give a detailed scheme of maneuver, Elmore said, "We do not have everything we want," yet "this time we are definitely out of the 'shoestring' department." In addition to the three divisions and the 112th RCT, he continued, XI Corps would be assigned four additional battalions of artillery, one battalion of anti-aircraft artillery, two tank battalions, two amphibious tractor battalions, one tank destroyer battalion, and two amphibious tank companies. The tank destroyer battalion would be equipped with 90mm rather than the usual 75mm guns. In addition, six of the corps' 155mm-gun battalions would be self-propelled. All these mobile, powerful direct-fire weapons would be attached to the divisions "as caves, tunnels, and other fortifications are encountered." All this additional armament, Elmore said, means that "the XI corps is the heaviest corps going in," and, he wryly noted, "We are duly honored."[9]

Final XI Corps' plans for the assault on Ariake Bay were never issued. Tentative plans made in early July indicated a traditional "two up and one back" assault. The 1st Cavalry on the left and the 43d division on the right would land abreast at the head of Ariake Wan. The role of the 112th RCT remained tentative when the war ended. The unit could have been attached to one of the assault divisions or held in corps reserve to be committed later on either flank of the corps. The Americal Division would be in floating reserve and scheduled to cross the beaches anytime after X-Day-plus-2. The 43d Division, landing on DUSENBERG and DE soto beaches would capture Shibushi airfield and the port of Shibushi. Then the division would drive northward up the corridor towards Miyakonojo and eventual linkup with the 25th Division (I Corps) driving westward from Miyazaki. Meanwhile, the 1st Cavalry Division landing on FORD Beach would drive straight ahead westward through a natural corridor toward Kanoya and the western shore of Kagoshima Bay. The end of phase I would find XI Corps units advanced to the Aoki-Iwagawa-Takakuma-Kanoya line.[10]

Such a lodgment by XI Corps would gain great prizes—port facilities and a sheltered anchorage in Ariake Bay, the great Japanese Navy airbases near Kanoya and others near Miyakonojo, and the interior plains around Kanoya and Miyakonojo, where even more airfields could be built. Japanese strategists were quite correct in seeing the assault on Ariake Wan as the most dangerous threat to southern Kyushu.

Stretching in a thirty-kilometer crescent along the western side of the Satsuma Peninsula, Fukiagehama is the most beautiful of all the proposed invasion beaches. Perhaps because of its beauty, it presented the greatest terrain problems for the invasion forces. The beach itself is firm white sand backed within fifteen feet of the water's edge by ten-foot-high dunes of loose sand. Immediately behind the dunes is a dense band of scrub pine. Next comes a narrow solidly agricultural one- to five-kilometer plain backed by high hills. Ten kilometers into the interior, these hills give way to small three hundred to six hundred meter mountains packed very closely. These small mountains resemble parts of eastern Belgium, the Dalmatian coast of Yugoslavia, or central Italy. The mountains are cut by three very narrow corridors that lead across the peninsula toward Kagoshima Bay. The southern corridor follows the Kaseda-Kawanabe-Chiran axis. The central corridor is the shortest, leading directly from Fukiage to Taniyama. The northern corridor travels southeastward from Kushikino to Kagoshima. In fact, these corridors are so narrow and winding that they could hardly be called corridors at all. The shortest route is only twenty kilometers, but small numbers of Japanese could have contested every inch.

The northern five kilometers of Fukiagehama is cut off from the long southern beach by twenty-meter cliffs. Between these cliffs and the city of Kushikino lie two confined beaches, each only two thousand yards wide. These beaches, code named STUTZ and WINTON, were the landing beaches of the V Marine Amphibious Corps (VMAC). After assaulting their narrow landing beaches, Major General Harry Schmidt's marines faced rugged, mountainous terrain cut by only a few winding, narrow, constricted avenues of advance.

The mission of the VMAC was to land in the Kushikino area, secure a beachhead to include Sendai, and block the advance of enemy forces coming down the west coast. Then, upon order, the marines would drive inland across the peninsula to secure the Kagoshima-Kawakimicho-Ichi-ino-Sendai line. Corps planners decided to land the 2d and 3d Marine Divisions abreast—the 2d across STUTZ Beach on the right and the 3d across WINTON Beach on the left. Both divisions would conduct the assault with two RCTs abreast. The 5th Marine Division would be in floating reserve prepared to reinforce either of the assault divisions over STUTZ or WINTON beaches or make a separate assault on ZEPHYR Beach to the north or STAR Beach to the south.[11]

After crossing STUTZ Beach, the 2d Marine Division would drive southeast to block enemy reinforcements that might attack the corps' right flank. In doing so, the division would also be securing the entrance to the narrow, winding corridor that ran southeastward across the peninsula to Kagoshima, the route the division would have to take to capture Kago-shima. Meanwhile, the 3d Marine Division would turn northward towards Sendai to block enemy forces coming down the coast from the north. All divisions would then advance to secure the Kagoshima-Sendai line.[12]

The marines faced perhaps the most difficult task in the invasion. Landing on narrow beaches backed by dunes, they faced an immediate river crossing of the Ozato Gawa, which ran parallel to the beach five hundred yards inland. One kilometer behind the river rose six-hundred-foot hills that provided observation of the entire beach. The roads running inland crossed rice paddies that, according to one VMAC planner, would "not take much heavy traffic before [the marines] simply squash down into the paddy." It would have been, he concluded, "an unpleasant landing at best."[13]

Major General Ryder's IX Corps, without any previous combat experi-ence, had to prepare for a myriad of contingencies. Designated as Sixth Army floating reserve, the corps would serve as a diversionary threat to Shikoku from X-Day-minus-2 to X-Day. The 98th Infantry Division was ordered to be ready, if necessary, to reinforce any of the Sixth Army beaches after X-Day-plus-3. Likewise, the 77th Infantry Division follow up might be called upon by X-Day-plus-5. With or without the 98th Division, IX Corps was to prepare for contingency landings on the southwestern tip of Kyushu anytime after X-Day-plus-3. The IX Corps beaches lay immediately west of the entrance to Kagoshima Bay.[14]

The IX Corps' beaches stretch westward from the foot of Kaimon Dake, an almost perfectly formed three-thousand-foot volcanic cone. While the beach is about ten kilometers long, only the eastern seven kilometers are useful for amphibious landings. The western end is backed by broken and rocky cliffs coming down to the beach. The usable beach is hard, black sand. A low ridge immediately backs the beach. Behind the ridge are low hills set in extremely irregular patterns—a jumble of broken, randomly placed hillocks, many with terraced sides. The maze-like, small compartments thus created are composed of rice paddies. Rolling country opens behind the western end of the beach running northward toward the large Japanese Army airfield at Chiran. Unfortunately, the beach directly in front of this corridor is rocky and broken—unsuited for amphibious landings.

The two landing beaches selected for IX Corps were PACKARD Beach, five thousand yards to the right, and PLYMOUTH Beach, twenty-five hundred yards on the left. The 98th Division, unless previously committed elsewhere, would land on the corps' left at PLYMOUTH Beach, drive north to seize Byu airfield, and, on order, continue attacking northward to seize the large Japanese Army airfield at Chiran. The 81st Infantry Division would land on PACKARD Beach adjacent to Kaimon Dake. Then the division would drive straight across to Kagoshima Bay and clear the tip of the peninsula. Reconstruction of airfields and construction of naval facilities near the mouth of the bay would begin immediately.[15]

The 40th Infantry Division, beefed up from its normal complement of fourteen thousand to more than twenty thousand, drew the mission of being the first into battle in Operation OLYMPIC. The division's task was to seize several offshore islands south and west of Kyushu to obtain radar sites, emergency anchorages, and seaplane bases. On X-Day-minus-5 elements of the 40th Division would assault Kuchinoyerabu Shima, Kuro Shima, Kusakaki Shima, and Uji Gunto. On X-Day-minus-4 the remaining elements of the division would land in both the north and south of Koshiki Retto, a large island group thirty miles directly west of the VMAC beaches. Similarly, the 158th Regimental Combat Team "afloat in the Okinawa area" on or after X-Day-minus-5 would be prepared upon order to land on the northern coast of Tanega Shima. This operation would be contingent upon the strength of Japanese air and naval defenses in the Osumi straits, the narrow channel between the Osumi peninsula and Tanega Shima through which the amphibious forces supporting and carrying both I Corps and XI Corps would have to pass.[16]

The 11th Airborne Division, Sixth Army Reserve, would be mounted in the Philippines on turnaround shipping and would be available for commitment on X-Day-plus-22. The divisions of the AFPAC reserve, to be committed only on order of General MacArthur, were designated on 3 August. The 7th Infantry Division on Okinawa would be ready on 10

November and the 6th and 96th Infantry Divisions, in Luzon and Mindoro respectively, would be ready by 20 November.[17]

General Kreuger's Sixth Army Headquarters, aboard the command ship the *Eldorado*, would accompany XI Corps to Ariake Wan. After the corps headquarters had moved ashore, General Kreuger would establish a temporary headquarters in the center of the beach near Hishida. As the corps pressed inland, Sixth Army headquarters would displace forward to Matsuyama and then to the Miyakonojo area. Finally, a permanent headquarters would be established at Kokubu, near the head of Kagoshima Wan.[18]

POSTWAR ASSESSMENTS

During the first months of the occupation, both VMAC and IX Corps observers went to southern Kyushu, studied the terrain and the Japanese defenses, and projected the course of the battle if Operation OLYMPIC had been launched. The observers from both corps saw the rugged terrain of southern Kyushu as the chief Japanese defense advantage and conversely the greatest American problem. Rough hills behind the beaches with narrow corridors leading into the interior gave little room for maneuver and neutralized the great American superiority in mobility as the U.S. troops drove inland. Yet both reports also concluded that the Japanese defense plans would have been far from complete by the time of the invasion, that Japanese communications, supplies, and transportation were woefully inadequate; and that Japanese plans for a rigid beach defense coupled with counterattacks by interior reserves were impossible to execute.[19]

Except for the graveled national highways that ran down both coasts, roads on southern Kyushu were unimproved and incapable of bearing heavy military traffic. Many bridges were built of logs and lashed together with ropes. While the railroads were better developed than the roads, the routes ran through many tunnels and defiles and could easily be closed or disrupted by air attack. Japanese military communications depended heavily on commercial telephones and at lower levels on a few obsolete radios and field telephones linked together with unburied wire. Required stocks of ammunition and other supplies had not been accumulated. According to the VMAC observers, preliminary air attacks and naval bombardment would have so damaged the railroads, communications, and supply dumps that they would have been practically useless. For the same reason, their postwar study concluded, the Japanese would have found it impossible, as required in their plans, to move units from northern Kyushu into the south or to march counterattack forces from the interior to the beaches.[20]

With the massing of ships in forward areas and increasing tempo of air and naval bombardment, U.S. forces could not expect to hide their intentions past X-Day-minus-10. The 40th Division and 158th RCT landings on offshore islands beginning on X-Day-minus-5 would provide certain evidence of the American objectives in southern Kyushu. The offshore islands that were the 40th Division objectives were defended only by a few outpost units and almost certainly would have fallen easily. However, the 158th RCT faced a more difficult and probably costly task in the assault on Tanega Shima. That island was defended by more than six thousand first-quality Japanese troops.[21]

Japanese defenses relied heavily on coastal defense guns in fixed fortifications to protect harbor entrances, ports, and strategic narrows. Upon opening fire on the invasion fleet, these guns would almost certainly have been destroyed by naval gunfire. In fact, the locations of these guns were already well known to U.S. planners. The observers surmised that getting ashore, at least for I Corps at Miyazaki and XI Corps at Ariake Wan, would have been much easier than pushing inland through the rugged country and narrow corridors of the interior.[22]

The coastal plain around Miyazaki would have made a beach defense by the Japanese extremely difficult. The weight of the I Corps landings and the intensity of U.S. air attacks and naval bombardment would have carried the beaches. Considering the importance that the Japanese placed on Miyazaki, they undoubtedly would have attempted to commit forces from central Kyushu and to move south the 212th, a coastal defense division located up the coast. These units, if they made it to the battle at all in the face of air and naval attacks, would certainly have arrived piecemeal and late. I Corps, however, would have been faced with heavy fighting as they moved inland and encountered the Japanese defenses placed on the inland ridges.[23]

The high hills flanking Ariake Wan posed problems for the XI Corps assault. Furthermore, gun positions on the small offshore island of Biro Jima in the middle of the bay dominated the approaches and the beaches at the head of the bay. Air attacks and naval gunfire would have to destroy these gun positions before the assault. Yet once ashore, the divisions of XI Corps faced more open country than did I Corps at Miyazaki. A wide corridor led from the south end of the beaches directly west across the peninsula to Kanoya. Another led north toward Miyakonojo. This same open country, however, would have allowed the Japanese to more easily move reserves toward Ariake Wan. United States' air attacks and a rapid advance by XI Corps could have held the Japanese reserves north of Miyakonojo. Moreover, the open country inland from Ariake Wan allowed the Americans to employ their vastly superior mobility and firepower.[24]

No doubt the marines of VMAC drew the toughest assignment in Operation OLYMPIC. Both terrain and Japanese defenses posed formidable obstacles. Immediately behind the landing beaches ran a low ridge that would provide some defilade for the defenders. Behind the ridge lay a band of flatland covered with rice paddies "dominated by mountains and wooded commanding ground" that "provided innumerable advantageous sites for observation, the emplacement of weapons, and for cover and concealment." After getting off the beaches, the marines faced even more daunting tasks. The 3d Marine Division had to swing left and force open the corridor to Sendai—a route "narrow and difficult and dominated by mountainous, forbidding terrain." The 2d Marine Division was to swing southeastward and get on the winding road to Kagoshima, a road also dominated along its entire course by high ground on both sides.[25]

Yet each assault division of VMAC would face only a Japanese battalion defending each landing beach. Japanese intelligence analysts had predicted the U.S. landings would come farther south on the more open beaches of Fukiagehama, and they had deployed their larger units there. Thus, as the 2d Division moved across the peninsula towards Kagoshima, the division would have faced great pressure on its right flank from the 206th and 146th Japanese Divisions, especially if it became apparent that they were in danger of being cut off in the southern tip of the peninsula. Movement down the coast of the 303d Division to counter the advance of the 3d Marine Division on Sendai would have been difficult. At best, the units of the division would have arrived piecemeal.[26]

The broken terrain, lack of mobility, and U.S. air attacks would probably have made any concentrated defense impossible in the VMAC area, and the Japanese could have been defeated in detail. Nonetheless, the Japanese had "the advantage of the choice of sites for defensive weapons and troop dispositions." Since the terrain allowed no maneuver room for either the attackers or the defenders, the marines would have had to fight the Japanese where they found them. "Fighting . . . would have been desperate due to the number of defenders that would have been cut off," the observers predicted. Sixth Army's northward move to the Tsuno-Sendai line would "by virtue of terrain alone have been slow and difficult."[27]

The IX Corps observers who examined that corps' objectives on the southern tip of the Satsuma Peninsula also found difficult terrain and local road problems. Yet when the war ended, they found that Japanese defensive preparations there had hardly begun. None of the units that were supposed to man the positions were in place at the war's end, and none were supposed to arrive before 1 October. Among the units scheduled to be deployed there, equipment shortages were acute and the quality of training was poor. The units had made no plans for erecting obstacles or laying minefields. No defense in depth was contemplated. The 146th Division, the principal coastal defense unit in the IX Corps area, had been able to give rifles to only 10 percent of the men. In any case, ammunition supplies were limited. The 40th Japanese Army, responsible for defense in the VMAC and IX Corps areas, had only 186 trucks, 46 armored cars, and 64 other vehicles. Half were inoperable from lack of maintenance, and the remainder could hardly be used because of inadequate fuel supplies.[28]

Terrain in the IX Corps area favored the Japanese defenders, but the observers found that the Japanese had done little to capitalize on this advantage. While the landing beaches could be enfiladed from the right by guns emplaced on three-thousand-foot Kaimon Dake and from the left by guns placed on a rocky peninsula, the Japanese had made no efforts to prepare gun positions on these strategic flanks. Nor had they prepared defensive positions on the rugged ridges that dominated the many lowland compartments immediately behind the beaches.[29]

In fact, the IX Corps observers saw the terrain and poor road net in the area as their chief obstacles. The hard, black volcanic sand beaches would allow "dry" landings, but the beach was backed by a continuous, tree-covered bluff twenty to forty feet high. The only beach exits were narrow foot paths. "It would have required a major engineer effort to cut through the bluff and gain egress from the beaches," the IX Corps observers noted. Even then, the assault divisions faced "an intricate pattern of terraces" interspersed with "deep gullies, finger ridges, foothills, and congested villages." Such "natural defensive works" required "little more than occupation by troops and emplacement of weapons to make the area a fortress." There were no two-way roads in the area; the narrow, soft-surfaced roads and the many rickety bridges would not have borne military traffic after the first rain.[30]

In this terrain maze IX Corps had to establish a beachhead and then launch attacks in two directions—one division towards the great Japanese Army airfield at Chiran ten miles to the north and another turning west across the foot of the peninsula to the eastern shore of Kagoshima Wan. Despite the great problems posed by the terrain, concluded the observers, the extreme weakness of Japanese defenses made it possible for IX Corps to fulfill its mission.

That overwhelming U.S. air, naval, and ground power would have prevailed, as it had at Iwo Jima, Luzon, and Okinawa, can hardly be doubted. Japanese defenders were formidable in numbers, but their defenses were incomplete, new recruits were largely untrained, and their beach defenses were a thin shell. Southern Kyushu's rough terrain and primitive roads would have slowed U.S. progress and caused the operation to fall behind schedule. But poor roads and lack of mobility would perhaps have handicapped the Japanese defenders even more. Units not in place on the beaches on X-Day would not get to the battle.

BASE CONSTRUCTION

Flying from Okinawa, fighters and medium bombers, the workhorses for support of ground operations, could reach any place on Kyushu. Flying from bases on southern Kyushu, long-range fighters and medium bombers could reach all of the Kanto Plain. Therein lay the chief reason for the invasion of southern Kyushu and for the massive construction program that was to follow. Southern Kyushu was to become a giant air, naval, and ground base for finishing the war against Japan. From its many air bases, planes could attack most targets in Japan. Ground and naval forces could stage through the bases for Operation CORONET, and from bases in southern Kyushu, the navy could breach the straits of Tsushima and complete the blockade of Japan.

The base-building effort would be immense and would require tens of thousands of engineer troops. A brigade of combat engineers would accompany each assault corps onto the landing beaches. Immediately behind the combat forces, even as the fighting continued, the first construction battalions would arrive. The base-building effort in southern Kyushu would be the greatest yet in the Pacific, a theater that had already required enormous construction and service commitments because of the scattered nature of objectives and the lack of infrastructure. In the Sixth Army troop list, engineers numbered 117,570 (21 percent of Sixth Army's strength). That number included neither navy construction units nor other service units.[31]

While all of the combat troops in OLYMPIC would come from the forces already in the Pacific, a large number of engineer and service units would be redeployed from Europe. Redeployment would bring to the Pacific many construction units, medical and quartermaster units, and port companies. The Sixth Army troop list indicates that fully 50 percent of service units would be obtained from redeployment. Most of the redeployed units were scheduled to arrive in the Philippines and stage through

Luzon. Others would be obtained from the roll-up of rear areas in New Caledonia, the Solomons, and New Guinea. Still others would come from the United States.[32]

Planners envisioned three giant base complexes capable of supporting 720,000 troops and airfields that could handle 2,800 aircraft. Sixth Army was charged with beginning construction of the bases immediately after taking the area. On X-Day-plus-30 Sixth Army would turn over the construction effort to ASCOM "O." CINCPAC was to plan naval facilities. Each base would include camps to house troops, hospitals, shops, covered storage, and bulk petroleum storage. Considerable effort also would be made to build and repair roads and railroads serving the bases. Airfield construction and repair would also begin immediately with priority given to all-weather runway construction and command and control buildings. Hardstands for the aircraft would be built later.[33]

Three base commands would be responsible for all construction and logistic support for all forces in the area. These commands would receive, store, and issue all supplies for units in their areas. Resupply for OLYMPIC units would come directly from the United States. Ships would be prepacked on the west coast of the United States. Each ship would be loaded with standard quantities of commonly used supplies—rations, clothing, medical supplies, etc. Other ships would be prepacked with bulk items—ammunition, petroleum, and construction materials. These preloaded resupply ships would begin leaving the United States at intervals weeks before X-Day. They would be held at western Pacific harbors like Okinawa before being sent forward to the assault beaches as required. Base commands would also be responsible for short-term hospitalization of casualties after X-Day-plus-15. By X-Day-plus-90 the base commands would have enough hospitals to care for all casualties except those requiring more than thirty days hospitalization.[34]

The largest of the base commands, Base 1 in the Kagoshima area, would be built to house four hundred thousand troops. This base would serve all facilities in the Satsuma Peninsula, including the VMAC area. Facilities to store 245,000 barrels of fuel would be built at four installations. Port facilities, especially at Kagoshima, would be built to simultaneously dock fourteen lighter craft, four small ships, and ten liberty ships. Pipelines to get fuel forward to the combat units and to serve airfields in the southern tip of the peninsula would be laid from Kushikino to Sendai, and Kagoshima to Kajiki. The engineers would build nine hundred thousand square feet of covered shop space, 1.8 million square feet of covered storage, and by X-Day-plus-135 would have built hospitals totaling 13,250 beds.[35]

Base 2, to house 185,000 troops, would be built in the Shibushi-Kanoya-Miyakonojo area. To serve the many airfields planned for this area, bulk petroleum storage for 497,000 barrels would be built, and pipelines would run from the main terminal at Shibushi westward to Kushira, Kanoya, and Takasu, and northward to Iwagawa and Miyakonojo. Dock facilities in Ariake Wan were limited, but once Kagoshima Bay was opened, ships could also dock across the peninsula at Takasu near Kanoya. The plan called for 1.25 million square feet of covered storage and shop space and, by X-Day-plus-135, 15,500 hospital beds. Moreover, forty-five thousand square feet of headquarters office space had to be provided in the Shibushi area to receive one thousand personnel of MacArthur's forward headquarters. The presence of this headquarters in the Base 2 area would also require the construction of twenty-five buildings to house signal and other communications facilities.[36]

Because there was no port or sheltered anchorage at Miyazaki, Base 3 was planned to be the smallest of the three base areas in southern Kyushu. It would accommodate only 135,000 troops, bulk fuel storage of only 121,000 barrels, 4,500 hospital beds, and only 150,000 square feet of covered shop and storage space.[37]

Nimitz also planned to build a number of naval installations in southern Kyushu. The largest was planned for Takasu on the eastern shore of Kagoshima Bay adjacent to Kanoya airfield. At Takasu the navy would construct an artificial harbor with piers to handle ten attack transports and one tanker simultaneously. In addition, the base would be capable of repairing small boats and landing craft and would have storage facilities for fuel and naval ammunition. Covered storage of one million square feet would provide supplies for servicing the fleet. Nearby, the navy would adapt one of the airfields at Kanoya to receive planes of the Naval Air Transport Service. Smaller and more specialized naval facilities were planned at Uchinoura, a small bay on the southern flank of Ariake Wan, at the mouth of the Manose Gawa near the southern end of Fukiagehama, and at Yamagawa at the mouth of Kagoshima Bay. Uchinoura would serve naval forces operating near Ariake Wan, the facilities at Manose Gawa would allow tankers to discharge fuel for nearby marine air bases, and Yamagawa would be developed as a PT-boat base. All of these naval installations were to be operational by X-Day-plus-120.[38]

The massive construction effort and the great demand for engineer units put strains on the planners. Because of the poor roads and difficult terrain in southern Kyushu, Sixth Army foresaw huge, unprecedented requirements for engineers to support combat operations. When that demand was combined with the engineering resources that were required in the base-building effort, even with redeployment there were not enough engineers to go around.

Sixth Army Engineer Brigadier General S. D. Sturgis, Jr., was especially concerned that the construction program outlined for the first sixty days of OLYMPIC was far too ambitious. "Even without any fighting," he warned his superiors, the program could not be met. In his opinion, the number of engineer units would have to be doubled to meet the program. FEAF also complained that the number of engineer construction units allocated to airfield construction was inadequate to allow the air buildup called for in the OLYMPIC plans. General Kenney "urgently recommended that additional engineer effort . . . be allocated to Air Force projects." AFPAC promptly denied his request citing the "anticipated critical shortage" of both engineer units and construction materials in the OLYMPIC objective area. Acceding to the request, argued Brigadier General D. R. Hutchinson of MacArthur's air staff, could be done only "by retarding some other project in the air program."[39]

A running debate occurred in June and July between the Sixth Army staff and MacArthur's staff over the allocation of engineer units. The Sixth Army staff wanted to retain some engineer construction units for use in combat operations while the AFPAC staff wanted to use them for base development. The initial OLYMPIC troop list assigned two heavy construction engineer groups and several construction battalions for use in building roads and bridges along the army's lines of communication. AFPAC suggested that on X-Day-plus-30 these units should revert to ASCOM "O" to be used in base construction. Sixth Army engineer Sturgis and his assistant, Colonel John C. B. Elliott, argued that it was "inconceivable that an army commander would be denied these units on a major operation." They also threatened to urge General Kreuger to go directly to General MacArthur. If Sixth Army failed to get enough engineer support, they emphasized, "the ground forces will suffer materially."[40]

Two weeks later the issue remained unresolved, and General Kreuger wrote General MacArthur. The Luzon campaign, Kreuger argued, had proved the desirability of attaching heavy construction groups to field armies. OLYMPIC, he predicted, would require much greater heavy construction support for tactical operations than any previous operation. The issue remained unresolved as the war ended. The argument, nonetheless, underlined a central problem that had plagued the Pacific war from the beginning—the necessity for building huge bases with limited resources.[41]

But to get bases to move the air power of FEAF forward from the Philippines and Okinawa was the chief reason for OLYMPIC. Both the Japanese navy and army had established air bases in southern Kyushu, and these bases became key objectives for the assault. FEAF, consisting of the Fifth, Seventh, and Thirteenth Air Forces, augmented by the First Marine Air Wing in support of VMAC, was responsible for the direct air support of OLYMPIC. Based in the Philippines, FEAF could not cover Kyushu, and even before Nimitz's Tenth Army began its assault on Okinawa, General Kenney and his staff began to study the prospect of moving forward into new bases on Okinawa and neighboring islands in the Ryukyus. In June AFPAC and CINCPAC reached agreement. Even as the agreement was being struck, a mammoth base construction effort was underway in the Ryukyus.[42]

The air planners found Okinawa and the other nearby islands in the Ryukyus ideal for an air buildup. They planned bases on Okinawa and on the small offshore islands of Ie Shima and Kikai Jima. Groups from the Fifth and Thirteenth Air Forces would be located on Okinawa, Seventh Air Force groups would move to Ie Shima, and the First Marine Air Wing would move to Kikai Jima. Plans called for an air garrison in the Ryukyus of 48.5 groups by 1 November, the target date for OLYMPIC. The units of FEAF began moving forward from their Philippine bases in July, the beginning of a buildup that was expected to rise by 15 October to 1,850 planes, not including the planes of the First Marine Air Wing, nor twelve groups of B-29s of the Twentieth Air Force.[43]

Despite the rural, agrarian, and somewhat isolated character of southern Kyushu, the Japanese had developed twenty airfields in the area. Southern Kyushu guarded the Strait of Tsushima, the southern entrance into the Sea of Japan. Air bases in southern Kyushu also guarded Japanese shipping lanes to the south. The Japanese had a single base near Kagoshima and two others near the head of Kagoshima Bay. Another base was located at Miyazaki. Two bases, Tojimbara (near Kaseda) and Chiran (a large army air base), were located near the southern tip of the Satsuma Peninsula, and, as the war ended, the Japanese were at work on a third base in that area at Byu near Matsunaga. The largest complex of Japanese air bases was spread through the corridors of the Osumi Peninsula from the head of Ariake Wan across the peninsula to Kanoya and north of Ariake Wan around Miyakonojo. American planners wanted to make use of these same locations to base the huge air garrison that would begin to arrive within days after the first amphibious landings.[44]

The OLYMPIC air plan called for the first air units to arrive at Miyazaki and Shibushi on X-Day-plus-2; and the first to arrive across Kagoshima Bay at Chiran would arrive on X-Day-plus-7. The first air units into the area would be command, communications, air control, and other service elements. Planes and pilots would begin arriving on X-Day-plus-4. To ensure air superiority and to support the ground operations, fighters would arrive first; the medium and heavy bomber groups would come later. Sixty days after the assault, 40.5 air groups totaling 2,794 airplanes were to be in place. As the land-based planes arrived in the OLYMPIC area, they would begin to replace the carrier-based planes in protecting the beachheads and supporting the advance of Sixth Army.[45]

The OLYMPIC planners laid out three air complexes in southern Kyushu—each located in one of the base areas. The Miyazaki area would base 7.5 groups of the Fifth Air Force on two seven-thousand-foot runways. The largest air base complex in southern Kyushu would be developed in the Shibushi-Kanoya-Miyakonojo area. Air bases would be located at Shibushi, Kushira, Kanoya, Iwakawa, and Miyakonojo to accommodate 24.75 groups from the Fifth, Seventh, and Thirteenth Air Forces. An advance headquarters of FEAF would be established at Kanoya. Across Kagoshima Bay, near the tip of the Satsuma Peninsula, the old Japanese air fields at Chiran and Byu would be rebuilt by navy construction battalions to house 5.75 groups of the First Marine Air Wing and one group of navy search planes.[46]

NOTES

1. Sixth Army Field Order No. 74, Troop List, 28 July 1945, Records of the Strategic Plans Division, Box 187, NHC.
2. Amphibious Forces Pacific Fleet Operations Plan No. A11–45, 10 August 1945, NHC.
3. I Corps Field Order, 4 August 1945, RG 94, Box 3089, File 201–3.9, WNRC.
4. Ibid.
5. Ibid.
6. Ibid.
7. Ibid.
8. XI Corps Staff Conferences on OLYMPIC, 6, 9 July 1945, RG 94, Box 4159, File 2.11–0.5, WNRC.
9. Ibid.
10. Sixth Army Field Order No. 74; XI Corps Tentative Plan for AAA Employment for Operation OLYMPIC, 8 July 1945, RG 338, Box 17, Operations Reports and Related Records, 1944–46, WNRC.
11. Amphibious Corps Operation Plan No. 1–45, 6 August 1945, USMC Geographic File, Japan, Box 52, WNRC.
12. Ibid.

13. Brigadier General Samuel G. Taxis, USMC (ret.), Oral History interview, 1988, USMC Historical Center, Washington, DC.

14. IX Corps Field Order No. 1, Operation OLYMPIC, 12 August 1945, RG 94, Box 4105, File 209–3.9, WNRC.

15. Ibid.

16. Sixth Army Field Order No. 74.

17. Ibid.; AFPAC Operations Instructions No. 1/9, 3 August 1945, RG 338, Box 193, Sixth Army Engineer Section, Plans and Operations, 1943–1945, WNRC.

18. Sixth Army Field Order No. 74; Memos, Chief of Staff, Sixth Army to Sixth Army Engineer, 17 and 22 July 1945, RG 338, Box 191, File 4, Sixth Army Plans and Operations, 1943–1945, WNRC.

19. V Marine Amphibious Corps Operations Report, Occupation of Japan, Appendix 3 to Annex C, 30 November 1945, Marine Historical Center, Washington, DC; IX Corps Report of Reconnaissance and Survey of Japanese Dispositions, Southern Kyushu (Operation OLYMPIC-MAJESTIC), 15 December 1945, RG 94, Box 4104, File 209–2.0, WNRC.

20. V Marine Amphibious Corps Operations Report.

21. Ibid.

22. Ibid.

23. Ibid.

24. Ibid.

25. Ibid.

26. Ibid.

27. Ibid.

28. IX Corps Report of Reconnaissance.

29. Ibid.

30. Ibid.

31. Karl C. Dod, *Corps of Engineers: The War Against Japan* (Washington, DC: GPO, 1966), 676.

32. Troop List of Service Troops to Stage through Luzon, 19 July 1945, RG 338, Box 59, Sixth Army G-4 Decimal File, 1943–1946, File 4, WNRC.

33. Engineer Annex to USAFPAC Operations Instructions No. 1, 20 June 1945, RG 338, Box 193, Sixth Army Engineer Section Plans and Operations, 1943–1945, WNRC.

34. Basic Logistic Plan, OLYMPIC, in Fifth Air Force Logistical Plan for Operation OLYMPIC, U.S. Air Force Historical Center, Bolling Air Force Base, Washington, DC.

35. Engineer Annex to USAFPAC Operations Instructions No. 1.

36. Ibid.

37. Ibid.

38. CINCPAC Operations Plan OLYMPIC, USMC Geographic File, Japan, Box 50, Folder B1–1, WNRC.

39. Memo, Sixth Army Engineer to Chief of Staff, 3 June 1945, RG 338, Box

59, Sixth Army G-4 Decimal File, 1943–1946; Letters, Allied Air Forces to CINCAFPAC, 3 August 1945, and CINCAFPAC to CGFEAF, RG 338, Box 191, File No. 5, Sixth Army Engineer Section Plans and Operations, 1943–1945, WNRC.

40. Memo, Colonel Elliot to General Kreuger, 28 June 1945, Sub: Command Request for Construction Groups and Construction Battalions for Olympic, RG 338, Box 196, Sixth Army Engineer Section Plans and Operations, 1943–1945, WNRC.

41. Letter, Kreuger to MacArthur, 10 July 1945, RG 338, Box 196, Sixth Army Engineer Section Plans and Operations, 1943–1945, WNRC.

42. FEAF History, 338–40, U.S. Air Force Historical Center, Bolling Air Force Base, Washington, DC.

43. Ibid., 344–47, 350, 353–54.

44. CINCPAC Operations Plan OLYMPIC.

45. FEAF History, 370; Fifth Air Force Tentative Shipping List No. 2 for OLYMPIC Air Garrisons, 30 June 1945, RG 338, Box 195; CINCPAC Staff Study OLYMPIC, 18 June 1945, NHC.

46. Fifth Air Force Tentative Shipping List No. 2; FEAF History, 370–71.

Chapter 14

Operation CORONET

The Kanto Plain is the largest level area in Japan, measuring seventy miles from north to south and ninety miles from east to west. Mountains, rising in some places to six thousand feet, ring the plain on the north and the west. The Kanto was the emotional soul of modern, post-Meiji Japan. In addition, it contained the economic and political heart of the empire. Fifty percent of Japanese war industry was located there, and almost eighteen million people lived there in 1945—nearly one-fourth of all Japanese. The key to the plain was Tokyo Bay. On the south this great bay opens into the Pacific Ocean through Uraga Strait, a narrow, ten-mile-wide mouth formed by two hilly and rugged peninsulas—the Boso on the east and the smaller Miura peninsula on the west. Along the northern and western shores of Tokyo Bay lie the large industrial and port cities of Tokyo, Kawasaki, and Yokohama. Inside Uraga Strait just south of Yokohama was the large Japanese naval base at Yokosuka.

Facing the Pacific fifty to seventy-five miles east of Tokyo, two beaches were suitable for amphibious landings by U.S. forces. Kashima and Kujukuri are long, open arcs of flat sand with broad shallow slopes, but are distant from the critical objectives of Tokyo and Uraga Strait. More strategically located just east of Uraga Strait and directly south of Tokyo lies Sagami Beach, a gray volcanic sand beach at the head of Sagami Wan.

Kashima, the northernmost of the two Pacific beaches, is backed by a major river and other water barriers to military movement; forces landing there would face long drives toward Tokyo and southwestward towards the western shore of the Boso Peninsula. Kujukuri Beach is closer to the critical Boso Peninsula.

Kujukuri Beach from Choshi (Inubo Point) on the east to Ichinomiya in the west is approximately fifty kilometers long. Like Omaha Beach at Normandy, it is a compartment with high steep bluffs that come down to the water's edge on either end. The ground is perfectly flat for about seven kilometers inland. At that point a steep line of bluffs rises abruptly, not unlike Omaha Beach but much further from the sea. On that line of bluffs, the Japanese placed their main defenses.

The hills rise to fifty meters and form an almost uninterrupted wall from Ichinomiya to Choshi. At several points this wall is cut by narrow valleys with roads leading towards Tokyo. At these points the Japanese had placed their strong points—battalion and company-sized positions on high ground with anti-tank guns sited to fire on the roads. All around the base of the hills, the Japanese had dug tunnels, many passing all the way through the hills. Firing positions on the front of the hills could be served through tunnels from the reverse slopes. At intervals the Japanese had dug rooms off the tunnels for barracks, command posts, storage, etc. Many had wells inside to supply fresh water.

Near Togane, where the main road to Tokyo at this time passed through the hills, the Japanese placed an entire regimental system of strong points. At the lower end of Kujukuri Beach in the bluffs near Ichinomiya, the Japanese dug tunnels in solid rock to serve heavy gun positions that could fire straight up the beach for several thousand yards. These positions would have been practically impervious to naval gunfire and aerial bombing.

Sagami Beach today is built up with industry and commercial establishments; in 1945 it was less so. The beach is good firm sand unbacked by troublesome dunes. The usable beach is about fourteen kilometers in length. In the western section is the Sagami River valley—a flat, now industrialized, but then agricultural plain that runs north like a highway into western Tokyo. For thirty kilometers inland this valley provides a natural corridor suitable for high speed, mobile forces. Thirty kilometers into the interior the corridor is obstructed by high ground rising above 150 meters. On the eastern end of Sagami Beach about two to three kilometers from the beach, a thirty-meter-high ridge protrudes westward about seven kilometers blocking movement into the interior.

Sagami Beach was the Achilles heel of the Kanto Plain defenses. Kujukuri Beach was ideal for amphibious landings, but the landing forces would have faced several handicaps there: bluffs blocked movement into the interior five to seven kilometers behind the beaches; Japanese cave defenses were well developed; Kujukuri lacked a good port; and the terrain favored Japanese counterattacks. But at Sagami the counterattack would have already been spent because the Japanese planned to consider landings at Kujukuri the main attack. The terrain at Sagami favored U.S. mobility and armor. The more compact and level geography at Sagami would have facilitated U.S. air power and naval gunfire.

On the Kanto Plain, American leaders sought to "inflict a decisive defeat upon the Japanese Army in the heart of the Empire," or failing that, to gain positions from which Allied forces could continue the conquest of Japan. But the plans for CORONET were still only a broad outline when the war ended. On the same day of Japan's surrender, MacArthur's AFPAC Headquarters published the first draft of the still incomplete CORONET staff study "as a matter of interest only and for the completion of files of all concerned."[1]

EARLY PLANNING

In mid-1943, when U.S. forces were still thousands of miles from Japan, planners recognized the importance of the Kanto Plain in any invasion of the Japanese home islands. Yet they also foresaw a long struggle to gain bases for a bombing campaign against Japanese industry and the necessity for destroying the Japanese navy, and they understood the importance of having a solid base in either Kyushu or Hokkaido from which to launch the final assault on the Kanto. These early studies were necessarily undetailed and lacked specifics; they even contained a tone of equivocation about the necessity for invasion.[2]

Initial planning for operation CORONET began in Washington during the summer of 1944 by the Joint War Plans Committee. The Joint Chiefs intended to present their British counterparts with a new invasion strategy at the OCTAGON Conference at Quebec in September of 1944. The earliest plans for CORONET outlined an ambitious scheme for an invasion by three armies comprising twenty-five divisions. "A" Army Group Headquarters, undoubtedly Bradley's 12th Army Group from Europe since no such organization existed in the Pacific, would command the invasion. On Y-Day "B" Army would land on Kashima Beach opposite Mito, and led by an armored corps, drive across the northern Kanto plain to seal off the northern entrances into the plain. Simultaneously, "C" Army would land on Kujukuri Beach, seize Choshi, and drive across the Boso Peninsula to clear the eastern shore of Tokyo Bay. On Y-Day-plus-30 "D" Army would land on Sagami Beach, seal off the passes through the mountains to the west, and seize the Miura Peninsula and Yokosuka naval base. After achieving these objectives, the three armies would simultaneously launch a final assault on Tokyo.[3]

During the summer of 1945, in both Washington and Manila, the plans for CORONET were refined. Early in May the joint planners in the Pentagon issued a revised version of their earlier outline plans. Recognizing the problems of redeploying combat forces from Europe, the planners now scaled down the size of CORONET. Now the planners suggested, two armies, not three, would suffice, and assaults should occur only on Kujukuri and Sagami beaches. The earlier plans' call for an invasion force of twenty-five divisions was reduced to twenty-three divisions—twenty in the assault and immediate followup and three in reserve. Infantry divisions would number eighteen and armored divisions, five. The landings on Kujukuri were designated as secondary; the Sagami force would mount the main attack. No mention was made of an army group headquarters to command the two armies conducting the invasion.[4]

On D-Day one army would land on Kujukuri with a corps of three infantry divisions at Katakai and a corps of two infantry divisions at Ioka just west of Choshi. The Katakai force would drive directly across the Boso Peninsula to clear the eastern shore of Tokyo Bay. After seizing the port of Choshi, the Choshi force would align on the right flank of the Katakai force for the drive across the Boso Peninsula. By D-Day-plus-35 nine divisions, including two armored divisions, would be ashore.[5]

On D-Day-plus-10 the Sagami force would begin putting forces ashore in the Oiso-Katase area of Sagami Beach. Presumably, the planners reasoned that by then the Japanese would have already committed all their reserves and major counterattack forces to the east against the landings at Kujukuri Beach. To draw the Japanese even further out into right field, the plans called for convoys carrying two divisions of the Sagami force to conduct a demonstration off Kashima Beach on D-Day-plus-7 and D-Day-plus-8. These divisions would then proceed to their landings at Sagami Beach on D-Day-plus-14. Thus, the main attack, totaling eight infantry and three armored divisions by D-Day-plus-30, could drive with great force and speed straight north into western Tokyo after taking the Miura Peninsula, Yokosuka, and Yokohama.[6]

As the joint planners refined their outline plan, MacArthur's planners were also busily engaged in putting together their strategic plan for DOWNFALL; the first edition was published only three weeks after the release of the revised outline plan from the joint planners in Washington. CORONET, as outlined in DOWNFALL, differed considerably from the joint planners' outline plan. DOWNFALL retained the earlier three-army, twenty-five-division plan. Eighth Army and Tenth Army would lead the assault with a combined force of fourteen divisions. First Army Headquarters, redeployed from Europe, would lead followup forces of ten divisions. A single airborne division in Kyushu, presumably the 11th, would serve as AFPAC reserve. MacArthur's plan also provided no army group head-quarters to command the operation.[7]

Even as this new planning progressed, however, some questioned the adequacy of air support based in Kyushu. Only long-range fighters could reach the Kanto Plain from bases in Kyushu, and unless closer airstrips were found, air support for the assault would depend heavily on carrier-based planes. The Joint War Plans Committee was asked to study the feasibility of small landings to gain air bases closer to the Kanto Plain. In early June the planners' report was ready. They had studied the area around Sendai in northern Honshu, sites on Shikoku, the Hamamatsu coastal lowlands between Tokyo and Nagoya, and the Izu Islands, an island chain south of Tokyo Bay. In the end, however, they rejected them all, judging the possible costs of these assaults to be disproportionate to the advantages gained. The Japanese, they predicted, would react violently to these intermediate assaults, producing high American losses for relatively slight gains; some of these assaults would require such large forces that the launching of CORONET might be delayed. Finally, the planners concluded, "Kyushu-based and carrier-based fighters, properly coordinated, should be capable of furnishing adequate fighter support for CORONET."[8]

With these outline plans in hand, AFPAC set about producing a full staff study for CORONET. When the war ended, MacArthur's planners were just finishing the first draft, and it was published in an incomplete form. Like all military plans, no doubt the CORONET plans would have been altered in many details before the invasion. Units would have been substituted, missions changed, phase lines adjusted, and thousands of other modifications would have been made. Yet, by the time the war ended, the units had been chosen, the scheme laid out, and the Japanese reaction assessed.

FINAL PLANNING

The CORONET assault would be done by two field armies—the First, redeployed from Europe, and the Eighth. For reasons that are not apparent in the records, the Tenth Army, formed for the conquest of Okinawa, was dropped from the troop list. Eighth Army had been the second field army activated in MacArthur's Southwest Pacific Area. Formed in the United States in June 1944, Eighth Army Headquarters moved out to the Pacific in September, where General Eichelberger, who had been with MacArthur since the dark days of 1942, was given command of the newly arrived army headquarters. Eighth Army spent the remaining months of the war mopping up after Sixth Army at Leyte and Luzon and conducting countless small amphibious operations to liberate the central and southern Philippines. First Army had fought across Europe from Normandy to VE-Day under General Omar Bradley and later under General Courtney Hodges. First Army's command and staff experience in handling large mechanized forces on the large European land mass, an experience not shared by any army headquarters in the Pacific, may have convinced planners to put First Army in the CORONET assault. No army group headquarters would command the two armies.

Instead, an advance echelon of MacArthur's AFPAC would command the campaign in the Kanto Plain.[9]

For the assault, First Army would command two veteran corps—the XXIV Corps, made up of the 7th, 27th, and 96th Infantry Divisions, and the III Amphibious Corps, composed of the 1st, 4th, and 6th Marine Divisions. Although not constituted until March 1944, Lieutenant General John R. Hodge's XXIV Corps had fought through two tough Pacific campaigns, landing at Leyte in October 1944 and at the Hagashi beaches in Okinawa in April 1945. All three of the divisions assigned to XXIV corps for CORONET had participated in both the campaigns for Leyte and Okinawa.

Of the Marine Corps' six divisions in 1945, three were scheduled to participate in OLYMPIC. The other three—the 1st, 4th, and 6th—commanded by III Amphibious Corps, were to participate in CORONET. III Amphibious Corps had landed at Guam in July 1944 while the V Marine Amphibious Corps (VMAC) had landed at Saipan and Tinian. The III Corps also commanded the bloody assault on Peleliu and with the XXIV Army Corps led the assault on Okinawa. In CORONET III Corps would command the most senior marine division, the 1st, and Marine Corps' newest, the 6th. The 1st had won battle honors in the toughest campaigns from Guadalcanal to Peleliu to Okinawa. The 6th had been formed just before Okinawa, and that campaign accounted for its only battle experience. The III Corp's other marine division, the 4th, had last fought at Iwo Jima where in twelve days, from 19 February to 3 March, the division had lost half its men.

Eighth Army commanded three corps—the X, the XIV, and the XIII. X Corps had been constituted in the United States in May 1942 and had gone to New Guinea in July 1944. The corps fought through the Leyte campaign. Of the three infantry divisions assigned to X Corps, the 37th had the most extensive combat experience, having fought on New Georgia, Bougainville, and in the assault and campaign for Luzon. The 24th Infantry Division had fought at Hollandia, New Guinea, and Leyte. From January 1945 to the end of the war, the division had been engaged in clearing the southern Philippines. The 31st Infantry Division trained in the United States from the time it was federalized in November 1940 to its movement to New Guinea in 1944 for more training. The division entered combat at Morotai and in April and May 1945 helped clear Mindanao.

XIV Corps commanded the 6th, 32d, and 38th Infantry divisions. XIV Corps had been sent to the Pacific in January 1943 to command the forces at Guadalcanal after the marines were augmented by two army divisions.

The corps later commanded forces at New Georgia and Bougainville. It led the assault at Lingayen Gulf under the Sixth Army on 9 January 1945, and was engaged in the campaign for Luzon until August 1945. Three veteran divisions were assigned to XIV Corps for Operation CORONET. The 6th Infantry Division was a regular army unit that had entered combat at Wakde Island in 1944 and had participated in the assault at Lingayen and the subsequent Luzon campaign. The division had served mostly under XIV Corps. The 32d Infantry Division was the most veteran division in MacArthur's command, having been sent out to Australia in May 1942. The division was in the bitter fight for Buna from November 1942 to January 1943 and participated in the 1944 campaign across northern New Guinea. The division was in both the Leyte and Luzon campaigns. The 37th Infantry Division, a National Guard division like the 32d, had seen combat at New Georgia and Bougainville before participating in the assault at Lingayen.

XIII Corps, along with its two divisions, the 13th and 20th Armored Divisions, were the only redeployed units scheduled for the CORONET assault. The XIII Corps had experience leading armored forces in Europe, a skill lacking among corps' headquarters in the Pacific since no armored divisions had been deployed there. The 13th and 20th Armored Divisions had entered combat in Europe during the last days of the war and had suffered few casualties.

Each field army was scheduled to receive an additional corps of three infantry divisions on Y-Day-plus-30. When the CORONET staff study was published, the corps' headquarters were still unnamed, but undoubtedly they would have been redeployed from Europe. The six divisions assigned to these corps were all to be redeployed from Europe. First Army's "B" Corps would command the 5th, 44th, and 86th divisions; Eighth Army's "D" Corps would command the 4th, 8th, and 87th.

Likewise, with the single exception of the 11th Airborne Division, all AFPAC reserves for the invasion would be constituted from redeployed units. The 97th Infantry Division, scheduled to be in floating reserve on Y-Day, had entered combat late in the European war. "C" Corps, AFPAC reserve, contained three veteran European divisions—the 2d, 28th, and 35th. "E" Corps, AFPAC's strategic reserve, consisted of the 91st, which had fought in Italy, and the 95th and 104th, veteran European divisions.

While the plans failed to identify the corps and corps commanders that would command these redeployed divisions, Marshall emphasized to his assistant, General Hull, chief of OPD, that he did not wish to get MacArthur's personal approval before redeploying corps commanders to the Pacific. Instead, he wanted to select those who were acknowledged as the best from the European theater and send them out. If MacArthur had specific objections, Marshall said, he could make them known at that time. Marshall suggested

III Corps under Major General James A. Van Fleet
V Corps under Major General C. R. Huebner
VII Corps under Lieutenant General J. Lawton Collins
XIII Corps under Major General Alvan C. Gillem
XVIII Corps under Major General M. B. Ridgeway.[10]

Planning papers for the naval and amphibious phases of CORONET had not yet been drafted when the war ended. Yet it is clear from the AFPAC staff study that CINCPAC's role in the invasion and the relationships between Nimitz's and MacArthur's staffs would have been very similar to those for OLYMPIC. CINCPAC would make the plans for the naval and amphibious phases while AFPAC would make the plans for the land campaign. The same arrangements were made for passing command from the amphibious forces commander to the ground commanders as they were established ashore. The naval and air bombardment of the objective areas would begin on Y-Day-minus-15 with naval gunfire, and carrier- and land-based planes concentrating on targets in the objective area.[11]

On Y-Day the two field armies would make simultaneous assaults. Although a preponderance of force was allocated to Eighth Army, neither attack was designated the main assault. First Army would land elements of the XXIV and the III Amphibious Corps near the center of the southern half of Kujukuri Beach. The 7th and 27th Infantry Divisions and the 1st and 4th Marine Divisions would establish a beachhead. On Y-Day-plus-5 the 96th Infantry Division and the 6th Marine Division would come ashore.[12]

First Army would face three major tasks after securing a beachhead. Initially, forces would be turned west and south across the Boso Peninsula to clear the defenses guarding Tokyo Bay. Forces would also turn north up Kujukuri Beach towards Choshi to secure that small port. From the First Army landing beaches an open corridor leads northwestward directly towards Tokyo. The corridor is bounded on the south by Chiba and the northern shore of Tokyo Bay and on the north by Imba-Numa and Tega-Numa, large lakes just south of the principal river in the Kanto, the Tone-Gawa. Between Chiba and Imba-Numa the corridor narrows to a width of only ten miles. First Army was charged with driving through the corridor and seizing Tokyo.[13]

Eighth Army would assault the beaches at the head of Sagami Bay on

Y-Day with elements of the X Corps (24th and 31st Infantry Divisions) and XIV Corps (6th and 32d Infantry Divisions). After securing a beachhead, these forces would attack eastward to clear the Miura Peninsula and capture the naval base at Yokosuka. On Y-Day-plus-10 the XIII Armored Corps would come ashore. The 13th and 20th Armored Divisions would drive straight north up the Sagami River valley and establish positions north of Tokyo from Kamagaya to Koga to disrupt the Japanese rear and block reinforcements from the north. Then XIII Corps was to be prepared to turn its tanks southward on Tokyo if necessary. Meanwhile, other elements of Eighth Army would seize Yokohama and assist First Army in taking Tokyo.[14]

The same kind of massive base development that had been planned for Kyushu following OLYMPIC was also planned for CORONET. Construction would start on extensive air, naval, and logistical bases immediately following the assaults in both the Kujukuri and Sagami areas. From these bases almost every place of importance could be brought under air attack, or, if necessary, amphibious assault. The naval base at Yokosuka would provide a base to tighten the naval blockade. Harbor facilities would be needed early, and the planners all emphasized the early necessity for clearing the shores of Tokyo Bay to get port facilities. The small port of Choshi at the northern end of Kujukuri Beach was made an early objective for First Army, but its capacity was far too small to supply the army. Until the Uraga Straits could be breached, all support for the ground forces would have to come in over the beaches, an especially dangerous procedure at Kujukuri, where Pacific storms could interrupt supplies at any time.

In general, however, those planning the logistics foresaw no great problems in supporting the operation. Although the planners worried about the restricted size of Sagami and the possibility of storms interrupting the supplies to First Army across Kujukuri, they believed that in good weather each army could be supported across the beaches. As in OLYMPIC, much of the supply would come from ships loaded with standard packaged loads. Road nets in both areas were adequate to get supplies forward, and the early capture of Yokohama would give more than ample port capacity for the Sagami beachhead. The largest problem was fuel. CORONET would require 22 million barrels (924 million gallons) of fuel in the first thirty days. Such consumption would have necessitated using all tankers then under American control.[15]

But the planners wanted insurance against Pacific storms. Taking a note from the famous "Mulberries," the manmade harbors built for the Normandy invasion, naval experts planned an artificial harbor for Kujukuri to be placed either at Katakai or Ioka to handle lighters and Liberty Ships. Beginning on X-Day-plus-2, a two-mile-long breakwater would be constructed more than a mile from the beach with oblique breakwaters made of sunken vessels, wrecked tanks, and other heavy debris extending to the beach at either end. Ships would enter through six-hundred-foot-wide side openings. Pontoon causeways would lead to the beach from Liberty Ship berths along the breakwater, and LST wharves and lighter piers would be constructed on the beach. All was scheduled to be ready by X-Day-plus-12.[16]

In both the Kujukuri and Sagami areas, as in Kyushu, plans called for building large bases, including troop camps, storage and communications facilities, and detention camps for Japanese POWs and civilians. Hospitals alone in the two base areas would provide care for 42,750 casualties. Another forty-five thousand beds would be available in the western and central Pacific areas.[17]

Again similar to plans for Kyushu after OLYMPIC, the repair of Japanese airfields and the construction of new ones would proceed as soon as the ground forces moved inland, so that land-based air groups could be brought in at the earliest practicable moment. By X-Day-plus-15 nine groups would already be in place; by X-Day-plus-30 more than thirty groups would be deployed in the Kanto Plain. As in Kyushu, maximum use would be made of already existing Japanese airfields. Airfields to be constructed or improved in the Sagami area would be located at Atsugi, Fuchu, Hara-Machida, Kawagoe, and Odawara. Those in the Kujukuri area would be located at Choshi, Hikata, Katori, Kioroshi, Miyakawa, Mobara, Narita, and Naruto. These land-based planes would release the carriers and be in position to carry the air war throughout Honshu and Hokkaido. They would also be well placed to support further amphibious landings in central and northern Japan should the Japanese not surrender after the occupation of the Kanto Plain.[18]

Planners could not hope to hide the objectives and intentions of CORONET completely, so in developing a plan of deception, the experts set out to deceive the Japanese about the timing of CORONET and the specific landing places. And by threats to other areas of Japan, even after CORONET began, they hoped to frighten the Japanese into keeping their forces scattered—to prevent Japanese forces from concentrating in the Kanto Plain.[19]

The story to be fed to the Japanese would cause them to misread American strategic intentions. Good deception is based on real alternatives, and the Joint Chiefs had vigorously debated the question of invasion versus blockade and bombing. Now the Japanese were to be led to believe that the Joint Chiefs had opted for the latter. Even after Kyushu, the story would go, the United States would need more bases to encircle Honshu and wear down Japan's military strength through tight blockade and heavy bombing before delivering the knockout blow on the Kanto Plain. In fact, the false story had some truth in it. The deception story would emphasize that reequipping, retraining, and redeploying troops from Europe were essential to CORONET, but would indicate that these steps could not be completed until 1947. Thus, the interim period would be used to seize more bases in addition to Kyushu, bases from which the blockade would be tightened and the bombing intensified.[20]

Three objectives, which in reality had been debated as alternatives to Kyushu, would continue to be emphasized to the Japanese—the Pusan area of Korea, Shikoku, and Hokkaido. Even after Y-Day, planners hoped that threats to these areas as additional objectives could force the Japanese to keep their forces in place far from the Kanto Plain. All three of these fictional objectives had been part of an overall plan of strategic deception for the last stages of the war against Japan. Finally, assaults on Korea and Shikoku, launched from new U.S. bases in Kyushu would seem to be natural followups to OLYMPIC.[21]

At the time of OLYMPIC, planners would begin to emphasize the threat to Korea and time their deception so that the Japanese would believe an assault on the Pusan area of Korea would come about Y-Day-plus-60. Successfully executed, the threat to Korea could prevent the Japanese from bringing troops from the mainland to Honshu even after CORONET began. The threat to Shikoku, begun before OLYMPIC, would be continued to convince the Japanese that Shikoku was the next objective after Kyushu—that landings there would be only the first step in obtaining a chain of bases leading to the Kanto Plain. While the threat could not be maintained after Y-Day, planners hoped that it would convince the Japanese to shift forces to Shikoku before CORONET. Finally, the fiction of a buildup in the Aleutians would be continued and would intensify Japanese fears. Because the Japanese already feared that the USSR would enter the war, the Japanese would be convinced of a threat to the Kuriles and Hokkaido. Planners believed that this threat could tie down Japanese forces in that area until perhaps Y-Day-plus-90.[22]

Japanese intelligence specialists would be encouraged to believe the threats to Korea, Shikoku, and Hokkaido by a variety of means. Leaks to American newspapers, which U.S. intelligence analysts assumed their Japanese counterparts read avidly, would publicize requests for Korean experts and interpreters. Rumors would be planted among CORONET followup troops that they were headed for Korea or Shikoku. Planes would drop leaflets alerting Korean guerrillas or warning Japanese civilians to avoid certain areas in Shikoku or Hokkaido. Agents would plant false documents; for example, the U.S. commanding general's headquarters in China would release a fictional campaign plan for Korea. False radio traffic would be broadcast among fictional U.S. units, and in the case of Hokkaido, message traffic would be carried on in a code that was known to be compromised. Dummy bases would be built in the Aleutians to house fictional divisions, and dye markers would be dropped off Hokkaido beaches. Rubber boats and other underwater demolition equipment would be put ashore in all three areas by submarines. Obvious photo reconnaissance and air attacks would be carried out against all three areas.[23]

While the efforts to direct Japanese attention to Korea and Hokkaido would continue even after CORONET began, the planners also developed an immediate "Tactical Deception Plan" to mislead the Japanese once the time and place of CORONET could no longer be hidden. While three major beach areas—Sagami, Kujukuri, and Kashima—were vulnerable to assault, landings would be made only on Sagami and Kujukuri. So that the Japanese leaders would have to cope with the possibilities of landings at all three beaches and scatter their forces accordingly, part of the Sagami followup force would threaten landings at Kashima between Y-Day and Y-Day-plus-9. Hoping to make the Japanese believe that CORONET was only part of a grand design to land at several places from Tokyo Bay northward, on Y-Day-plus-9 the forces demonstrating off Kashima together with empty transports from the Kujukuri landings would proceed northward and simulate pre-assault operations off Sendai, two hundred miles up the Pacific coast of Honshu from Choshi.[24]

These demonstrations would be preceded by heavy air strikes of intensity similar to those at the real invasion beaches. Other pre-assault activities would also be faked—underwater demolition would be simulated by air dropping delayed explosives and abandoning rubber boats on the beaches. Minesweepers would begin work, and smoke, pyrotechnics, and radio traffic would point towards an assault. On Y-Day-plus-7 bombardment of beach defenses would begin with the same intensity as at Kujukuri and Sagami. All this elaborate deception was designed to convince the Japanese that an assault on Kashima would occur about Y-Day-plus-9 and on Sendai about Y-Day-plus-10.[25]

Both the strategic and tactical deception plans for CORONET were elaborate and expensive. No doubt the Japanese would have been confused about the grand design of American plans. But by the end of the war, for the Japanese to know the grand design was less important than to fight the immediate battle. With extremely limited and dwindling resources and with little strategic mobility, the Japanese had to treat the present battle as the last one. Like the Americans, they saw the Kanto Plain as crucial to the empire and thus decisive. Other areas would have to fend for themselves. The great fear upon which American deception was based—that the Japanese would move forces into the Kanto Plain—was perhaps less important than the Americans thought. American air power and the lack of Japanese mobility would have seen to that.

Intelligence analysts for the Joint Chiefs began in July to assess the Japanese military's ability to defend the Kanto Plain. Their conclusions were far different from the oft-repeated postwar predictions of suicidal Japanese defenders exacting an unacceptably high cost. While the analysts recognized the last-ditch mentality of Japan's military leaders and understood that CORONET would be no walkover, they assessed Japan's defenses as considerably less formidable than was commonly known.

Japanese air power, particularly the use of massed kamikazes, was a major concern for the planners of OLYMPIC. That prospect was less worrisome to the analysts looking toward CORONET. While the Japanese never made a clear choice on whether to fight the decisive battle in Kyushu or in the Kanto Plain, their rapid buildup of both air and ground forces in southern Kyushu during the last month of the war indicated that, in fact, they would fight the battle in southern Kyushu and worry about the Kanto later. American intelligence experts believed that remaining Japanese air and naval power, both conventional and suicide units, would be largely used up in OLYMPIC. Thus, they estimated, no more than two thousand aircraft would be available to oppose CORONET. With a serviceability rate of only 20 percent, the Japanese could launch no more than one hundred sorties per day before being destroyed entirely in four days. The Japanese navy would be even weaker, limited to suicide sorties by boats, midget submarines, kaitens, and a few remaining destroyers.[26]

To the experts, Japanese ground forces represented the chief threat to CORONET, yet even here, they saw the threat as less than formidable. Approximately thirty-four regular divisions and twelve depot divisions would be available for defense of the home islands. After the United States secured southern Kyushu, the Japanese would be unable to reinforce from the continent, and ten divisions would be immobilized in northern Kyushu by the American lodgment in the south. On Y-Day the Japanese would have nine regular divisions and three depot divisions deployed in the Kanto Plain under command of the Twelfth Area Army. Three were deployed to defend the Kashima-Kujukuri beaches, two to defend Sagami Beach, and four were held in reserve north of Tokyo. While they could reinforce the Kanto Plain from other areas of Japan in the weeks before Y-Day, once CORONET began, Allied air power and the vulnerability of the roads and railroads leading into the plain would greatly reduce the Japanese ability to move troops. The analysts concluded that peak defensive strength would never exceed twelve to fourteen divisions.[27]

POST-CORONET OPERATIONS

By the end of the war, American planners had given little thought to developing a strategy for operations after CORONET should that invasion fail to produce unconditional surrender. In preparing their chiefs for the Potsdam Conference, the Joint Staff Planners on their own initiative presented recommendations to the Joint Chiefs. First, they advised that the Joint Chiefs should avoid discussion of post-Kanto operations with the British and Soviets. Then, in a brief paper, the planners outlined "the trend of thought on the planning level in respect to operations following the invasion of Honshu." Their suggestions were general and unspecific: to expand the aerial bombardment and tighten the naval blockade from bases in the Kanto Plain and Kyushu; to invade into the interior from these bases; and to launch additional amphibious operations that would seize other critical areas. There is little evidence that the Joint Chiefs gave much thought to the matter or that the joint planners studied the problem in much detail. Ideas on how to force the surrender of the almost two million Japanese soldiers on the Asian mainland were not developed beyond the decision to depend on the Soviets to deal with the Japanese forces in China, Manchuria, and Korea and on the British to mount offensives in Southeast Asia. No suggestions emerged, however, to commit large U.S. combat forces to the Asian mainland. The possibility that U.S. forces might be required to carve out enclaves on the east China coast to supply Chiang's Nationalist army remained open. Certainly a substantial strategy would have developed and detailed studies and plans would have been written had the war lasted longer, for a few outline plans were already beginning to appear in the summer of 1945.[28]

In May 1945 the Joint Intelligence Committee, in response to a request from the Joint War Plans Committee, prepared a study on Japan's military, economic, and political capabilities to continue the war after the occupation of the Kanto Plain. In examining the overall military situation, the experts all but wrote off the Japanese navy and air force. The planners concluded that by mid-1946 the Japanese navy would be "practically impotent and incapable of effective defense," except for a few submarines, some isolated cruisers and destroyers in hiding, and small numbers of suicide boats. Similarly, Japanese air power would have been "almost completely annihilated," its few remaining formations "widely dispersed and thoroughly disorganized." The few hundred remaining aircraft, the experts concluded, could pose only isolated guerrilla threats.[29]

After CORONET, Japanese ground forces, though weak and too isolated to be mutually supporting, would remain Japan's most formidable military arm. The planners reckoned that north of Indochina and excluding by-passed garrisons in the Pacific, the Japanese Army still contained fifty-four to fifty-nine divisions (1.9 to 2.15 million men). Thirty-three of these divisions (1.2 million men) were deployed in China, Manchuria, and Korea. By mid-1946 U.S. air and naval power would be able to prevent the movement of most forces from the continent to the home islands. Another five divisions (170,000 men) would be isolated on Formosa. Troops in the home islands by mid-1946 "would not exceed the equivalent of about fifteen divisions (500,000 men)." Two of these divisions would be deployed in the far north on Sakhalin and in the Kuriles and another eight to ten divisions would be held in place in Kyushu following OLYMPIC. The remaining three to five divisions would be guarding the mountain passes leading out of the Kanto Plain. Perhaps ten more "depot divisions"— unorganized, poorly equipped, and largely untrained—would be scattered through the remainder of the home islands.[30]

Analysts estimated that located in the Kanto Plain were 22 percent of Japan's armaments industry and 65 percent of the electronics industry. The intelligence specialists predicted that by mid-1946 the production of heavy armaments would be reduced to a fraction of 1945 levels. Still, by cannibalizing unserviceable equipment and dispersing production, the Japanese would still be able to produce significant quantities of light weapons. Perhaps most important, the increasingly effective Allied air and sea blockade by early 1946 would have almost completely shut down the importation of raw materials. Consequently, the Japanese would be forced to draw down stockpiles to keep industry operating. Yet, the Japanese would find it increasingly difficult to move the remaining stocks of raw materials within the country. Industrial and raw materials produc-tion in Korea, Manchuria, and north China would be less affected, and barring entrance into the war of the USSR, Japanese forces on the continent would be able to sustain themselves for some time.[31]

This continental base, however, would prove no use to the homeland forces, for by June 1946 the analysts predicted that the blockade of the Tsushima Straits and the Sea of Japan would be 75 to 90 percent effective, while the blockade of the north China coast would be almost complete. Communications within Japan would be increasingly difficult after the establishment of Allied air power in the Kanto Plain. Japan's roads had been inadequate even in peacetime, and the railroads were especially vulnerable to air attack. With Allied air power established in both Kyushu and the Kanto Plain, the Japanese could scarcely depend, as in the past, on small vessels plying coastal shipping routes.[32]

Food supplies would become critical in the large urban areas. While northern Honshu and Hokkaido normally produced food surpluses, difficult communications would keep the surplus from being moved to the food-deficit areas in central and southern Honshu and northern Kyushu—especially the cities of Osaka, Kobe, Nagoya, and Kyoto. On the continent food would be in excess of Japanese needs, but getting the surplus across the Sea of Japan to the home islands would have been difficult.[33]

After Iwo Jima and Okinawa, many experts predicted that Japan's diehard military elite would exert an iron control over the Japanese people and lead them into a fanatical and suicidal defense of the homeland. But the military analysts doubted this scenario. While they recognized that "some extremists might . . . prefer to go down fighting," they felt that all Japanese would see "the inevitability of defeat" and react with "extreme depression and resignation to fate." The events following Japan's surrender proved this assessment to be accurate. Even if the diehards succeeded in dominating the government, the administrative machinery would break down and cripple the government's ability to control the populace. Should the diehards remove the government to the continent and attempt to continue the fight from there, the Japanese people would feel deserted and "might well accept an alternative regime set up by dissident factions or Allied military authority." Even on the continent, the Japanese could expect to control only those areas occupied by Japanese troops.[34]

The Joint Chiefs never set a firm course for post-CORONET military operations; they hoped that the Japanese would surrender after OLYMPIC and that CORONET would be unnecessary. Certainly, they hoped also that some explanation of the doctrine of unconditional surrender would convince the Japanese leaders to end the war short of complete destruction, and they worked to get such an amelioration of unconditional surrender. Also, the Joint Chiefs placed no faith in the atomic bomb. Planning for the defeat of Japan proceeded without consideration of the bomb's power. Indeed, the effects, even the feasibility of the bomb, were unknown before 16 July 1945.

In fact, ten days after the first atomic bomb test, the joint war planners circulated a preliminary paper on post-CORONET operations. The plan emphasized intensifying the blockade and widening the campaign of aerial bombing from the new bases in Kyushu and the Kanto Plain. The planners also called for more amphibious assaults on key strategic areas in the home islands.

These new landings, coupled with overland attacks from the OLYMPIC and CORONET lodgments, would seal the Japanese defeat.[35]

The planners targeted five key areas for possible assault and occupation following CORONET. These were the Shimonoseki Straits area of northern Kyushu; the urban-industrial complex of Osaka-Kobe-Kyoto on the inland sea; Nagoya; the Hakodate-Aomori area on the Tsugaru Straits separating Northern Honshu from Hokkaido; and the Sapporo Plain on Hokkaido. The landings would require five divisions for the assault on the Sapporo Plain and nine divisions for the assault on northern Kyushu. For the other landings, the planners projected eight divisions each. While the planners set a target date of 1 July 1946 for the first of these operations, too many factors were still unknown for them to recommend which area should be the first target. Instead, they listed contingencies that would guide the selection of targets. The most important was the level of Japanese defenses. If the Japanese retained large forces in northern Kyushu after both OLYMPIC and CORONET, then the choice might fall on weakly defended northern targets in Hokkaido. If the Japanese stripped the defenses in the Nagoya-Osaka area, then the choice might fall on that strategically important coast. If the USSR had entered the war and needed large quantities of American supplies, then either the Shimonoseki Straits operation or the Hokkaido operation might be necessary to open a sea route to Soviet Siberia. In short, the planners found it too early even to make a tentative judgment on the first post-CORONET operation.[36]

The Shimonoseki Straits and northern Kyushu formed one of the most strategic areas in Japan, a large industrial complex that spread north from Fukuoka to Moji on the southern shores of the straits. A tunnel under the straits provided communications between Kyushu and Honshu. The Shimonoseki Straits connected Tsushima Straits and the Sea of Japan with the Inland Sea. In the outline plan for northern Kyushu, the main assault would come in the Fukuoka area. After gaining a beachhead, the forces would drive northward to seize the industrial complex of Yawata, Kokura, and Moji, and to gain control of the Shimonoseki Straits.[37]

In 1945 Osaka was Japan's second largest city; Nagoya was the third largest. Both were important ports and industrial centers. Consequently, after Kyushu and the Kanto Plain they were strategically the most important areas in Japan, and they would be heavily defended. Other than Northern Kyushu, the most difficult assaults would be at Osaka and at Nagoya. Osaka lies at the head of the narrow Kii Channel, the eastern entrance to the Inland Sea. Nagoya lies at the head of Ise Bay, with a geography faintly resembling that of Tokyo Bay. After examining the narrow channel and the terrain around Osaka, the planners rejected a direct assault on Osaka and decided instead that the best approach was to take Nagoya and then advance the short distance overland into the Osaka-Kobe-Kyoto complex.[38]

The geographic problems presented in taking Nagoya were not unlike those presented by the Kanto Plain, and the solution offered by the planners was similar to CORONET. The entrance to Ise Bay was as narrow as the entrance to Tokyo Bay. The outline plan called for four divisions to seize the three peninsulas forming the entrance to the bay. After securing the bay entrance, two divisions would progress up the western side of the bay in a series of amphibious bounds, a third division would sweep the eastern shore, and a fourth division would land on D-Day-plus-5 at the tip of Chita Peninsula and drive north toward Nagoya.[39]

After taking Nagoya, these forces would be augmented for the drive into the Osaka-Kobe-Kyoto area. Only a narrow mountain pass at Sekigahara separated Nagoya from Kyoto in the lowlands around Biwa Ko. Thus, forces could advance from Nagoya through the back door to the Osaka-Kobe-Kyoto area, a much easier and less costly procedure than an amphibious assault on Osaka.[40]

An amphibious assault on Hokkaido would present the Allies with a relatively undefended area. The planners predicted that only one regular division would be on Hokkaido and another on northern Honshu. Landings in the Hakodate-Aomori area would secure a major naval anchorage in Matsu Wan, an airfield site, a major port at Hakodate, and passage through Tsugaru Straits into the Sea of Japan. To secure these objectives, however, would require a complex operation involving fourteen separate landings.[41]

Far simpler was a plan to occupy the Sapporo Plain on Hokkaido—a large, level area that could provide airfield sites from which Allied planes could control the Tsugaru Straits to the south and La Perouse Straits to the north. Moreover, the assault would require only five divisions landing on open, lightly defended beaches very near their objectives.[42]

While CORONET was a far larger operation than OLYMPIC, it possibly would have proved less costly. The Japanese would have expended their remaining air power in Kyushu, the more open terrain of the Kanto Plain would have favored U.S. mobility, and U.S. combat power strengthened by redeployment would have been simply overwhelming.

NOTES

1. Outline Plan for the Invasion of the Kanto Plain, RG 218,CCS Honshu (7–19–44), NARA; AFPAC Staff Study CORONET, 15 August 1945, RG 165, NARA.

2. Appreciation and Plan for the Defeat of Japan, JWPC 46/5, 9 July 1943, RG 218, NARA.

3. Eighth Army, CORONET Operation, G-3 Plans (Invasion of Japan), May–June 1945, RG 407, Box 2836, WNRC.

4. Outline Plan for the Invasion of Japan, Honshu (7–19–44), RG 218, CCS 381, NARA.

5. Ibid.

6. Ibid.

7. AFPAC, DOWNFALL, Strategic Plans for Operations in the Japanese Archipelago, 28 May 1945, RG 165, OPD 350.05, NARA.

8. Operations Preceding CORONET, JWPC 359/1, RG 218, NARA.

9. AFPAC Staff Study CORONET.

10. Memo, Marshall to Hull, 28 May 1945, Verifax 1193, Item 2288, and Message, Hull to MacArthur, 29 May 1945, Verifax 1193, Item 2799, Marshall Library.

11. AFPAC Staff Study CORONET.

12. Ibid.

13. Ibid.

14. Ibid.

15. Logistical Plan for the Invasion of the Kanto Plain, JLPC 47/10, 8 May 1945, RG 218, NARA.

16. AFPAC Staff Study CORONET.

17. Ibid.

18. Ibid.

19. Staff Study of Cover and Deception Objectives for CORONET, JWPC 190/16, 26 July 1945, RG 218, NARA.

20. Ibid.

21. Ibid.

22. Ibid.

23. Ibid.

24. Ibid.

25. Ibid.

26. Defensive Preparations in Japan, 2 August 1945, JIC 311; Japanese Reaction to an Assault on the Kanto Plain (Tokyo) of Honshu, JIC 218/9, 10 July 1945, RG 218, NARA.

27. Ibid.

28. Operations Following Invasion of Kanto Plain (Broad Plans), JCS 1417, 10 July 1945, in CCS 381 POA (4–21–45), RG 218, NARA.

29. Operations Following Kanto Plain, JIC 286, 14 May 1945, in CCS 381 POA (4–21–45), RG 218, NARA.

30. Ibid.

31. Ibid.

32. Ibid.

33. Ibid.

34. Ibid.

35. Operations in Japan Following CORONET, JWPC 333/1, 26 July 1945, Records of the Joint Chiefs of Staff (microfilm edition).

36. Ibid.

37. Ibid.

38. Ibid.

39. Ibid.

40. Ibid.

41. Ibid.

42. Ibid.

Chapter 15

Allied Participation

Early in the war against Japan, Soviet participation had been considered highly desirable if not essential. And despite the Soviet-Japanese neutrality pact of April 1941, considerable effort had gone into ensuring that the Soviets would eventually declare war on Japan, preferably before OLYMPIC. Yet the participation of the air and ground forces of the other Allies in the final assault—Britain, Australia, Canada, and France—did not come under serious consideration until very late in the war—so late that it would have been possible only to include them in CORONET. Unlike Soviet participation, the involvement of the other Allies in CORONET was viewed by U.S. military leaders with considerable ambivalence.

THE SOVIETS

In the darkest days of early 1942, General Marshall thought it wise to encourage Soviet-Japanese hostilities. It was immediately apparent, however, that because of their desperate struggle against Hitler in the west, the Soviets would seek to avoid conflict with Japan.[1] As the war progressed and as U.S. forces compressed the Japanese Pacific empire, the desire to get the Soviets into the Pacific war assumed even greater urgency. The Soviets could furnish two vital services: they could contain the vaunted Kwantung Army in Manchuria and furnish Siberian bases from which American heavy bombers could reach the industrial cities of Japan. By early 1945 the latter goal faded. Bases had been acquired in the Marianas, and it was increasingly evident that the Soviet leaders had no intention of allowing American bombers to operate from Siberia. Yet the prospect of invasion not only remained but, in the last months of 1944, loomed ever more probable. The consequent need to neutralize the dangerous Kwantung Army and prevent the Japanese from removing its million men to the mainland made Soviet participation seem even more vital.[2]

To deal with the Soviets on military matters, the Joint Chiefs chose Brigadier General John R. Deane. In September 1943 General Deane had just completed a year in Washington as secretary to the combined chiefs of staff. A non-West Pointer, Deane had risen through the ranks of the U.S. Army after enlisting as a private during World War I. When he flew to Moscow in October 1943 as the American military observer at the foreign minister's conference, he was already under orders from Marshall to remain in the USSR capital to organize a new American military mission. Up until then, Soviet-American military relations had been carried on by a military attache and a lend-lease representative.

Deane's mission eventually numbered 135 people from both the army and the navy. Deane, although responsible to Ambassador Averell Harriman, reported directly to the Joint Chiefs, and he was invited to all of the major wartime conferences. His job was to coordinate all Soviet-American military affairs. It fell to him to deal with the Soviets on the military details of their entry into the war against Japan.[3]

At the top of the Deane agenda during 1943 and 1944 was the matter of obtaining U.S. Army Air Force bases in the western USSR. The aim was to begin a campaign of shuttle bombing of Germany—take off from bases in England or Italy, bomb the targets, fly on to bases in the Soviet Union, rest, refuel, rearm, and bomb targets on the return to the home bases. Deane noted that although shuttle bombing bases in the USSR would enhance the efficiency of the Eighth Air Force, the "ultimate objective was Soviet-American collaboration in the war against Japan." He wrote, "[Shuttle] bombing bases in western Russia would be a proving ground for the vast American air operations which were visualized later to take place from Siberia. Every difficulty that could be overcome in the European operations would mean time saved in hastening the final pay-off in the Japanese war."[4]

General Deane described the roles to be filled by the USSR once that country had entered the war against Japan. "We thought," he wrote after the war, "the Red Army would launch an offensive against the Japanese in Manchuria and Korea designed to eliminate the Kwantung Army." The other benefit would be the establishment of air bases "in the Maritime Provinces [eastern Siberia] from which to bomb the Japanese islands and soften them for the final American invasion." Early in the war the prospect of defeating Japan without the help of the USSR was especially fearsome for the American military. It could be assumed that the largely self-sufficient Japanese forces on the Asian mainland would continue to fight even if the homeland fell, and planners were wary about committing American forces to mainland Asia. Before the assaults on the Marianas and Okinawa were even conceived, airbases in Siberia seemed a prerequisite for a strategy of bombardment.[5]

American military leaders had long feared the Japanese forces on the Asian mainland. The cream of the Japanese army was deployed there, and the vaunted Kwantung Army defending Manchuria was considered a special threat. In 1941 that army was the elite unit of the Japanese ground forces. Throughout the war, the Soviets maintained thirty divisions on the Manchurian border to counter the Kwantung Army despite the Japanese-Soviet neutrality pact signed in 1941 and the dire need for forces to defend western Russia against Hitler's armies.[6]

In the summer of 1945 the Kwantung Army comprised 713,000 men grouped into twenty-four infantry divisions and eleven separate brigades. In Korea, the Kuriles, and Sakhalin were another 280,000 men formed into ten infantry divisions and three separate brigades. Non-Japanese auxiliary troops furnished another 214,000 soldiers—a total force of 1.2 million men—the equivalent of more than fifty divisions.[7] In sheer numbers this was a formidable array. The possibility that it would be withdrawn in the last stages of the war for a suicidal stand in the homeland was even more intimidating.

Soviet leaders gave verbal commitments as early as 1943 that their forces would enter the war against Japan. General Deane, Secretary of State Cordell Hull, and Ambassador Averell Harriman all were told in separate instances by Stalin and his advisers that the USSR would enter the war against Japan after the defeat of Germany. At the Teheran Conference in November 1943, in a plenary meeting attended by Roosevelt, Churchill, and the combined chiefs of staff, Stalin promised that his Siberian forces would be reinforced after the defeat of Germany, and "then by our common front we shall win."[8]

These statements by the Soviet leaders no doubt relieved the anxieties of the American leaders, but for the next year, despite repeated efforts by allied leaders, the Soviets resisted all attempts to translate their general promises into concrete, detailed plans. Among the members of the Joint Chiefs, General Hap Arnold was the most interested in immediate Soviet cooperation. The very-long-range B-29 bombers were being readied for deployment by early 1944, but the airmen lacked bases within range of Japan's industrial heart. From bases near Vladivostok, the B-29s could reach almost all important industrial targets in the Japanese home islands.

The questions on the minds of the joint planners were large and fundamental. When would the Soviets be able to take the offensive against the Kwantung? Would the Soviets allow American bomber bases in Kamchatka and in Siberia? Could the Soviets help cut Japan's communications across the Sea of Japan? Would American supplies need to be stockpiled for Soviet use in an offensive against the Kwantung Army? Would the U.S. Navy need to breach the Japanese-held Kuriles and open a north Pacific supply route to Siberia? The major operations would require long lead time and might require a reallocation of resources and revisions in strategy. Hence, for the planners, Soviet promises were useless without specific coordination; the planners wanted requirements, timetables, intelligence, and specific commitments.[9]

In October 1944 Churchill and his foreign secretary Anthony Eden went to Moscow to meet with Stalin. General Deane and Ambassador Harriman used the occasion to brief Stalin on Allied plans in the Pacific and to ask in return for some specifics from the Soviet leader. Obliging, Stalin said that the Soviets presently had thirty divisions in the Far East and would need twice that number to begin offensive operations against the Japanese. Such a buildup would require at least three months after the end of the war against Germany. The United States could count on strategic bomber bases in Kamchatka and north of Vladivostok and could send a survey team to inspect base sites. Finally, the Trans-Siberian Railroad would be completely occupied in transporting Soviet armies from the west, so the United States would need to ship more than a million tons of cargo across the Pacific and stockpile it for the Soviet offensive. The Soviet leader concluded by promising that his military staff would meet with General Deane to work out details.[10]

No such meetings followed, and Deane's frustration mounted. Deane had received countless general assurances of cooperation and friendship from the Soviets, but almost never did they meet with him to discuss details or to provide answers to specific American questions. Deane wrote Marshall in frustration that the Soviets were unsurpassed at expressions of friendship and at making sweet toasts of friendship at banquets. Yet "after the banquets we send the Soviets another thousand airplanes, and they approve a visa that has been hanging fire for months. We then scratch our heads to see what other gifts we can send, and they scratch theirs to see what else they can ask for." He lamented the lack of constructive and specific contact: "In our dealings with the Soviet authorities, the U.S. Military Mission has made every approach that has been made. Our files are bulging with letters to the Soviets and devoid of letters from them." Marshall forwarded the letter to Secretary of War Stimson who, in turn, forwarded it to the president.[11]

A similar tone of realism crept into JCS 1176, a major study of Soviet participation in the war against Japan presented to the Joint Chiefs by its staff on 23 November 1944. That paper recognized that Soviet participation was desirable but not so essential as to draw resources from the main U.S. efforts in the southwest and central Pacific. The authors of the study also recognized that only one major factor would dictate decisions—the interests of the USSR. Most crucial to the United States was the timing of Soviet entry. If the Soviets attacked too soon, the Japanese might be able to launch a counteroffensive, cut the Trans-Siberian Railroad, and effectively isolate the Soviet armies in eastern Siberia. American resources might be required to bail them out—to the detriment of the invasion of Japan. According to the planners, "The Russian offensive into Manchuria . . . should be launched at least three months prior to our invasion of Kyushu." Such timing, reasoned the planners, would ensure the "maximum commitment of Kwantung Army troops at the time of our landings." A Soviet offensive that came simultaneously or after the invasion would allow the Japanese to withdraw forces from the mainland to defend the home islands. The planners recognized, however, that the interests of the Soviets would be better served "if they attack after our initial lodgement . . . and Japanese forces in Manchuria have begun to move to reinforce Japan."[12]

In the first weeks of 1945, as the Yalta Conference approached, the Joint Chiefs still lacked specific Soviet answers to essential American questions. Would the Soviets require a north Pacific supply route once hostilities with Japan began? Would they agree to American airbases in Siberia and Kamchatka? Could Americans be assured that "combined planning in Moscow" would be "vigorously pursued"? Other specific questions dealt with stockpiling supplies, the Soviet clearance of La Perouse Strait, and the Soviet conquest of southern Sakhalin.[13]

A few days before they left for the combined staff conferences at Malta that preceded Yalta, the Joint Chiefs sent the president a memorandum for his guidance in the forthcoming discussions. Early entry of the Soviets into the war against Japan "consistent with her ability to engage in offensive operations" was necessary, they told the president. The Soviets should be encouraged toward three objectives: to defeat the Kwantung Army, to collaborate with American forces in air operations against Japan, and to help cut Japanese lines of communication with the Asian mainland.

The memo then listed several major questions, which so far the Soviets had left unanswered. Heading the list was the date of Soviet entry. Knowing the date for the beginning of Soviet operations was extremely important for planning American operations, the Joint Chiefs emphasized. Ideally, the Joint Chiefs wanted the Soviets to begin offensives against the Kwantung Army several weeks before American landings on Kyushu. Such a schedule would make it impossible for the Japanese to redeploy the Kwantung Army to the homeland before the American invasion.

The Soviets had failed to furnish information for planners to determine whether it would be necessary to open a sea route through the Kuriles once Soviet-Japanese hostilities began. Two critical unknowns remained: what supplies from America would the Soviets need that could not be brought over the Trans-Siberian Railroad and would the Soviets allow

America to establish airbases in Siberia? Until these questions were answered, the necessity for opening a sea route to the Siberian ports could not be judged.

The Joint Chiefs could now foresee the end of the war in Europe, and the need to redeploy air forces was imminent. Suitable areas within B-17 and B-24 range of Japan were extremely limited. American airmen wanted bases in eastern Siberia, and they recommended that Roosevelt press for Soviet agreement. Other subjects were specific—American help to the Soviets in defending Kamchatka, Soviet use of American bases in the Aleutians, and the installation of American weather stations on Soviet territory. Finally, the Joint Chiefs once more raised a subject that had plagued them and Deane throughout the war—the frustrations of American-Soviet military coordination. "The working efficiency of U.S. and USSR collaboration to date has been low," the Joint Chiefs complained. General agreements were easy to get from the Soviets, they noted, but Soviet "administrative delays" and "reluctance . . . to exchange . . . information" hampered efforts to carry these general agreements into effect. A special planning mission under Brigadier General Frank N. Roberts was already in Moscow to begin detailed planning with their Soviet counterparts. Thus far, the Joint Chiefs noted pointedly, no meetings had been scheduled by the Soviets.[14]

At Yalta the answers were prompt and unequivocal. The Soviet military leaders insisted that they had not changed the general plans they had outlined for Churchill, Harriman, and Deane at the October conference in Moscow. Approximately thirty divisions would begin redeployment to Siberia in early 1945, and the Manchurian offensive would begin about three months after the defeat of Germany. All the other questions posed by the Joint Chiefs—American airbases in Siberia, stockpiling supplies, and opening a supply route across the north Pacific—were answered in the affirmative.[15]

In October 1944 at a followup meeting to the Churchill conference, Stalin had given Ambassador Harriman and General Deane the Soviet requirements for stockpiling before the offensive began. The requirements included more than 200,000 tons of gasoline and collapsible tanks, 180,000 tons of food, 500 amphibious jeeps, 1,000 amphibious tractors, 30,000 trucks, 400 C-47s, 100 C-54s, 20,000 tons of miscellaneous signal and engineer equipment, 10 frigates, 20 corvettes, 2 minelayers, 30 minesweepers, and 50 submarine chasers. Stalin was very concerned about secrecy. According to Deane, the Soviet leader feared a preemptive strike by the Japanese should they suspect the coming Soviet offensive. Such a strike could cripple the entire effort by cutting the Trans-Siberian Railroad and taking Vladivostok.[16]

From the Yalta Conference, the Joint Chiefs sent staff officers out to the Pacific to brief the major commanders there on the results of the conference. Brigadier General George A. Lincoln, chief of the Strategy and Policy Group of the Operations Division, met with MacArthur on 25 February 1945 and recorded the commander's views on Soviet entry into the war. In a message to Marshall, Lincoln stressed that "General MacArthur considers it essential that maximum number of Jap[anese] divisions be engaged and pinned down on Asiatic mainland, before United States forces strike Japan proper." Only a few days earlier another visitor from the Army staff in Washington had recorded a similar report. Colonel Paul L. Freeman spent an hour and a half with MacArthur on 13 February and reported that MacArthur was "apprehensive as to the possibility of the movement of the bulk of the Manchurian army and other Japanese forces from China to the defense of the homeland. . . . He emphatically stated that we must not invade Japan proper unless the Russian army is previously committed to action in Manchuria."[17]

Between the Yalta Conference in February and the Potsdam Conference in July, the Joint Chiefs' thoughts regarding the participation of the Soviet Union in the war against Japan changed considerably. Despite the forthright answers that the Soviet leaders gave at Yalta, especially their promise for close cooperation and planning, nothing much happened. American planners who had been sent to Moscow to begin working with the Soviets got little cooperation. The Soviets had also promised that American teams would be allowed to survey airbase sites in Siberia. The teams sat in Fairbanks, Alaska, for three weeks in March and April waiting for Soviet visas that never came. In fact, the agreement to base B-29s in Siberia was rapidly losing importance. Air force studies indicated that the problems and costs of such a plan, especially supply and logistics across the northern Pacific, were far out of proportion to the small benefits to be gained. This conclusion was made even firmer when the Joint Chiefs concluded that Soviet success in Manchuria would not require the opening of a supply route through the Kurile Islands by the U.S. Navy. Thus, in April 1945 the Joint Chiefs in rapid succession canceled the plan to put B-29s on Siberian bases, instructed General Deane to limit any attempts to put more American personnel into the USSR, and put the plans to open a northern Pacific supply route in abeyance. Obviously, the Washington planners no longer considered Soviet intervention essential. Oddly, the increasing realization among the planners that the invasion of the home islands might be unavoidable to bring about unconditional surrender buttressed the conclusion that Soviet participation might be superfluous. Japan's navy was gone; her merchant fleet sunk or paralyzed by mines. The now-weakened Kwantung Army no longer appeared to threaten the invasion. In any event, planners estimated that the Japanese could bring no more than one division per month from the mainland to the home islands. Soviet entry into the war against Japan to contain the Kwantung Army, the planners now concluded, was "no longer necessary to make invasion feasible."[18]

When the Joint Chiefs met with Truman on 18 June 1945 to discuss OLYMPIC, the president also wanted to talk about the entry of the USSR into the war against Japan. Admiral King told the president bluntly that the Soviets were "not indispensable" and that while their participation might be desirable, the final defeat of Japan could be accomplished without them. The Joint Chiefs no longer saw the Soviet contribution as neutralizing the Kwantung Army, but as a general "clean-up of the Asian mainland."[19]

Just before the Joint Chiefs were scheduled to leave for the Potsdam Conference in Berlin, the joint planning staff handed them a report on Soviet entrance into the war against Japan. "The defeat of the Japanese Army in north China including Manchuria would be a valuable contribution to the early and economical termination of the war," they advised. But, they concluded, "We believe that we can defeat the Japanese in the main islands regardless of Russian entry, because of our estimated ability to restrict movement of Japanese reinforcements from Asia."[20]

The Kwantung Army was strong in numbers, but by 1945 it was weak in quality. Almost all the best units had been withdrawn to Japan and the Pacific and replaced with poorly trained reservists and recent draftees. All but five of the infantry divisions had been formed in 1945. All units were short of critical equipment—especially tanks and anti-tank guns—and many weapons were obsolete. So weak were their forces in Manchuria by 1945 that the Japanese commanders had to abandon their traditional offensive strategy and replace it with a defensive plan.[21]

The declining military necessity to have the Soviets deal with the Kwantung Army was reflected in the American positions at Potsdam in late July. Many historians, by pinpointing increasing confidence that the atomic bomb would end the war, have oversimplified the reason for the hardened American attitudes toward the Soviets. A more complete explanation would attribute a large share of the cause to *military* reasons. Soviet entry was no longer needed to assure the success of OLYMPIC. Nonetheless, a Soviet declaration of war against Japan might provide the shock that would bring the Japanese leaders to accept unconditional surrender, and

Soviet participation would preclude the necessity for landing American forces on mainland Asia.[22]

BRITAIN, AUSTRALIA, CANADA, AND FRANCE

At the OCTAGON Conference at Quebec in September 1944, Churchill had suggested to Roosevelt that a British Pacific Fleet should join the U.S. Pacific Fleet for the final campaigns against Japan. Roosevelt immediately accepted. Like most seemingly straightforward high-level decisions between the two great Allied powers, there was considerably more behind this simple agreement than appeared on the surface.

Unlike the European and Mediterranean theaters, the war in the Pacific was an American affair. Australians and New Zealanders fought alongside the Americans in MacArthur's Southwest Pacific Area (SWPA), but MacArthur hardly treated them as equal partners. While the British had heavy commitments in Burma and India against the Japanese, they had no presence in the Pacific until the arrival of the Pacific Fleet in early 1945. No Allied command was formed after the dissolution of ABDA command in the disastrous days of early 1942. Scenting victory in 1944–45, American planners and commanders were not altogether enthusiastic about letting Allied forces in on the kill. Churchill himself had come around to offering British forces only after long prodding from his own chiefs of staff. The prime minister preferred instead to use British naval power in the Indian Ocean and Southeast Asia to help recover Britain's lost colonies. Finally, Admiral King, an anglophobe, was opposed to the Royal Navy's participation in the Pacific. He noted that British equipment, ammunition, and tactics were different from American standards and that British fleets were not equipped, as were the American, to stay at sea far from their bases for long periods. The British Fleet, he warned, would become an added logistical burden on American resources.[23]

Despite King's misgivings, Churchill's offer was accepted with the proviso that the British would provide their own logistical train. At the peak of its power, the British Pacific Fleet comprised five fleet carriers, four light carriers, seven escort carriers, four battleships, eight light cruisers, twenty-eight destroyers, thirty-three destroyer escorts, three minelayers, and twenty-two submarines—far the largest single force put to sea by the British during the war. The British Pacific Fleet participated in the assault on Okinawa, and in July and August 1945, while assigned to Halsey's Third Fleet, helped rake the coasts of Honshu and Hokkaido. When the war ended, the British Pacific Fleet was scheduled to participate in OLYMPIC. Yet some of King's fears were borne out by events. The ships of the British Pacific Fleet proved short-ranged and required frequent refueling. Weak fleet support frequently kept ships in port, and much of the British equipment, especially aircraft, was below American standards.[24]

Yet the precedent was set for Allied participation in the final defeat of Japan. For political and diplomatic reasons further offers of support had to be made by the Allies, and for reasons other than military necessity, these offers had to be accepted by the United States. Britain, France, and Canada wanted to maintain postwar presences in the Pacific, and Australia, as long a participant in the war against the Japanese as the United States, wanted in on the finish. America's political leaders, despite some hesitancy by their military advisors, could hardly refuse such offers of help. They could not afford to risk the criticism that they had allowed the Allies to stand idly by while American soldiers and sailors bore the full cost of defeating Japan. But the integration of Allied contingents into the invasion forces, although acceptable to the U.S. military in principle, posed complex problems that had not been resolved at war's end.

Very-long-range B-29s of the U.S. Twentieth Air Force had been carrying the strategic air war to the cities of Japan from bases in the Marianas since November 1944. By war's end, shorter-ranged B-17s and B-24s, redeployed from Europe, were beginning to fill up new bases on Okinawa. Britain also wanted a presence in the air war against Japan by sending Lancaster bombers to participate in the strategic bombing. Adapted for air refueling, these planes could reach out fifteen hundred miles, a combat radius comparable to American B-29s. At the same OCTAGON Conference in September 1944, where Churchill offered Roosevelt the British Pacific Fleet, the British air staff offered 40 squadrons of Lancasters, 640 heavy bombers—320 equipped for bombing and 320 equipped as tankers for aerial refueling. The U.S. Joint Chiefs accepted the offer but made no commitments on the size of the force nor on the location of bases.[25]

Reflecting Admiral King's reluctance to use the British Pacific Fleet, U.S. Air Chief Arnold hesitated to accept large British strategic bombing contingents. Redeploying units from Europe would give the United States ample bombing capacity and would strain the available space on Okinawa, and the shortage of engineers would make it impossible to build bases for the British. Nonetheless, like King, Arnold had to yield. In May 1945 the Joint Chiefs accepted ten squadrons of British Lancasters to be based on Okinawa, *provided* that the British built their own bases with their own engineers and furnished their own service troops. The first British convoy of engineers and equipment sailed for Okinawa in late June. A second convoy was set to sail as the war ended.[26]

The contribution of British air and naval forces had been settled by the end of the war, yet the use of Allied ground forces in the invasion of Japan, while approved in principle, was still considerably unsettled in detail. Neither U.S. combat forces redeployed from Europe nor Allied ground forces were on the OLYMPIC troop list. CORONET, however, was a different story.

American planners took no note of the possibility that Allied ground troops might participate in the invasion of the Kanto Plain. The published plans indicated that assault, followup, and reserve units would all come from U.S. forces. As the CORONET plans were being refined during the summer of 1945, all the major Allied countries offered ground forces, and a debate developed at the highest levels of command over the size, mission, equipment, and support of these contingents.

The British, Canadians, Australians, and French all desired to field ground forces in CORONET. American leaders could hardly refuse, but military planners foresaw problems in compatibility of equipment, in supply, and in differing tactical doctrine. In all cases where Allied components were offered, American commanders insisted that they had to be integrated into larger U.S. commands. Furthermore, General Mac-Arthur insisted that Allied units be issued U.S. equipment and that they not require special items or separate channels of supply.

Canada was the first Allied nation to receive a definite commitment to participate in CORONET. General Marshall was sent a request for Canadian participation in September 1944, but the Joint Chiefs did not reach agreement on the training, supply, and employment of this force until May of 1945. A Canadian division, organized like similar American units, using American equipment, trained in the United States, and supplied through American channels, would be employed as a followup unit in the invasion of the Kanto Plain, not in the main assault.[27]

When presented with a similar proposal by MacArthur, Australian Commander in Chief General Thomas A. Blamey objected and requested a special line of communications for his Australian troops. MacArthur noted that a shortage of shipping made that impossible, and there the question of a separate Australian force rested until the end of the war.[28]

British authorities knew generally of the American scheme to invade southern Kyushu in the fall and the Kanto Plain in the spring, but they were ignorant of the details of OLYMPIC until 12 June 1945, when a member of the British air staff in Washington sent a sketchy outline of the landing scheme.[29]

With only air and naval units scheduled for OLYMPIC, the British wanted ground forces in CORONET principally for political reasons—to show the Americans that they were willing to pull their share of the load and to reestablish British prestige in Asia. They wanted a large independent force of five divisions.[30]

At the Potsdam Conference in July 1945, the British chiefs of staff proposed a force of three to five divisions consisting of components from Britain, Australia, New Zealand, and India, and, perhaps, the Canadian division already accepted by U.S. planners. The British gave assurances that these forces would be transported in British ships and "provided with the necessary assault lift." The force, they promised, could be supported by the British fleet and fifteen squadrons of British tactical aircraft.[31]

The British proposal was passed to MacArthur for his comment with the advice that the acceptance of British forces would undoubtedly meet with wide public approval by lessening the need for U.S. troops. MacArthur's reaction was immediate and negative. The difference in organization, composition, equipment, training, and doctrine, he argued, would complicate command and logistics. These incompatibilities might adversely affect combat effectiveness. The use of British troops in the assault with a separate line of communications should be discouraged, he wrote. Instead, MacArthur suggested, the British should think of a single corps of only three divisions—one British, one Canadian, and one Australian—all furnished with U.S. equipment, trained in amphibious warfare, and supplied through the U.S. logistical system. This corps, he concluded, could be used as the AFPAC reserve afloat. Three weeks later the British accepted MacArthur's specifications.[32]

Even earlier than the British, the French had expressed a desire to send troops to the Pacific, but they had received little encouragement from the Joint Chiefs. In May 1945 French Foreign Minister Georges Bidault personally approached President Truman. For CORONET he offered two French colonial divisions, several squadrons of planes, and supporting troops all organized along U.S. lines. Truman agreed "in principle" to the French request but indicated to Bidault that the final decision on the use of the French contingent would be MacArthur's. As in the case of the British offer, an immediate message was sent to MacArthur asking his views.[33]

MacArthur replied the next day. He would be glad, he said, to have the French ground forces provided that they were employed in the followup echelons and not in the initial assault. It was essential, he continued, that "the assault elements be completely homogeneous." However, he flatly refused the French air elements. Limited airspace in the objective area and the need for extremely close teamwork among various air elements made the introduction of non-U.S. air units too hazardous.[34] The French ambassador soon raised the issue with Assistant Secretary of War John J. McCloy, for on 14 June McCloy asked Marshall for a report. Both MacArthur and the Joint Chiefs wanted to use the French divisions, Marshall reported, but when, where, and in what capacity was still not settled. He reported MacArthur's views that French air should not be accepted and that French ground forces should not be in the CORONET assault. Meanwhile, Marshall told McCloy, he had sought the advice of General Eisenhower, who had much experience dealing with the French. Eisenhower, he said, had recommended that "a detailed written agreement on the governmental level covering all major aspects of employment of French forces under U.S. command" be negotiated with the French. Marshall ended with a promise to advise McCloy and the French as soon as studies covering the use of French forces were completed. In mid-July, the French offer was accepted by the Joint Chiefs "in principle," provided that the French divisions were completely under U.S. command and equipped and trained to U.S. standards.[35]

Clearly, American political and military leaders were obliged to accept Allied offers of support in the last campaigns against Japan. The American public, already war weary and shocked at the casualties of the last Pacific campaigns, could hardly be expected to forego Allied aid. Morale demanded it as well. For American soldiers, the use of one Allied soldier freed one GI to go home.

Yet just as clearly, U.S. military leaders, for honest reasons, viewed the use of allied units in the invasion of Japan with considerable ambivalence. There were rational military reasons for restricting the use of Allied forces. CORONET was narrowly within the limits of U.S. logistical capabilities. Complicating the system or adding requirements threatened logistical integrity. Much of the early supply for CORONET was to be by prepackaged ships direct from the West Coast of the United States. Special requirements for Allied forces would complicate this system. Space for the deployment of more units in the objective area was limited. Thousands of details from communications nets to fire control and air control had to mesh, and the addition of forces who were unfamiliar with these complexities and who spoke a different language could tear the carefully woven web. Since 1942 both Nimitz's and MacArthur's staffs and the headquarters of lower units had developed the planning and conduct of amphibious operations to a high art. But it was an arcane and complicated art learned largely through experience. To introduce commanders, staffs, and units unfamiliar with this art could create command and staff confusion and special logistical demands in an already precariously balanced operation. Base facilities were also extremely scarce, as were engineers who were needed to build them. While these were legitimate concerns, chauvinism no doubt also played a role in MacArthur's reluctance to accept Allied ground units.

Should CORONET have failed to bring surrender, Allied units almost certainly would have been used in post-CORONET operations. But even before the end of the war, the use of Allied units in the initial stages of CORONET had been all but ruled out.

NOTES

1. Grace P. Hayes, *The History of the Joint Chiefs of Staff in World War II: The War against Japan* (Annapolis: Naval Institute Press, 1982), 131, 668.

2. Ibid., 668.

3. John R. Deane's postwar memoir, *The Strange Alliance: The Story of Our Efforts at Wartime Co-operation with Russia* (New York: Viking Press, 1946) is a literate, informal, and entertaining chronicle of his often frustrating mission.

4. Ibid., 107

5. Ibid., 224–25.

6. David M. Glantz, *August Storm: The Soviet 1945 Strategic Offensive in Manchuria*, Leavenworth Papers No. 7 (Ft. Leavenworth, KS: Combat Studies Institute, 1983), 25.

7. Ibid., 29.

8. *The Entry of the Soviet Union into the War Against Japan: Military Plans, 1941–45* (Washington, DC: Department of Defense, 1955), 22; *FRUS: Conferences at Cairo and Teheran, 1943* (Washington, DC: GPO, 1961), 500.

9. Hayes, 669–70.

10. Ibid., 671.

11. *FRUS: Conferences at Malta and Yalta* (Washington, DC: GPO, 1955), 447–48.

12. *The Entry of the Soviet Union*, 40–41.

13. *FRUS: Conferences at Malta and Yalta*, 762–63.

14. Ibid., 396–400.

15. Ibid., 834–39.

16. Ibid., 371–74.

17. *The Entry of the Soviet Union*, 51.

18. Ibid.; Deane, 254, 264–65.

19. *The Entry of the Soviet Union*, 78, 85.

20. Report by the Joint Staff Planners, Details of the Campaign against Japan, JCS 1388/4, 11 July 1945, in CCS 381, Japan (6–14–45), RG 218, NARA.

21. Glantz, 33–34.

22. Deane, 267.

23. H. P. Willmott, "Just Being There: An Examination of the Record, Problems, and Achievement of the British Pacific Fleet in the Course of Its Operations in the Indian and Pacific Oceans between November 1944 and September 1945," (Manuscript in possession of the author).

24. Ibid.

25. AFPAC Intelligence, "Final Phase: Plans and Operations to 15 August 1945," in Studies in the History of General Douglas MacArthur's Command in the Pacific, RG 4, Folder 5, p. 71, part 4, MacArthur Archives; Flight Refueling of Lancasters, AIR 8/814 and VLR Bombing of Japan—British Participation (Tiger Force), AIR 8/1284, PRO, Kew, London; British Participation in VLR Bombing of Japan, 18 September 1944, Records of the Joint Chiefs of Staff, CCS 691.

26. John A. Hixson, "Joint and Combined Planning Problems Involved in the Preparation for Operation OLYMPIC," 1 September 1987, manuscript in possession of the author, 52; British Participation in VLR Bombing, 10 May 1945, JCS 1120/1; for a complete history of British planning for the deployment of Tiger Force, see AIR 8/1284–1289, PRO.

27. Hixson, 57–58; Message W73669, Marshall to MacArthur, 28 April 1945, USAFPAC Correspondence WD, RG 4, MacArthur Archives.

28. Hixson, 56–57.

29. Memo, Brigadier Haydon to British War Office, 12 June 1945, WO 106/3463; British Participation in the War Against Japan, DEFE 2/1313B, PRO.

30. British Participation in Operation CORONET, DEFE 2/165, PRO.

31. Hixson, 52–53; Memo, Sub: British Participation in the Invasion of Japan, 7 July 1945, RG 165, OPD 336.2 TS, NARA; *FRUS: Conference at Berlin, 1945*, vol. 1 (Washington, DC: GPO, 1960), 936–37.

32. British Participation in Invasion, OPD 336.2 TS; Hixson, 54; British Participation in CORONET; *FRUS: Conference at Berlin*, vol. 2, 1336–7.

33. Message W10226, Marshall to MacArthur, 2 June 1945, USAFTAC Correspondence WD, RG 4, Folder 4, MA.

34. Message, MacArthur to Marshall, 2 June 1945, USAFTAC Correspondence WD, RG 4, Folder 4, MA.

35. Memo, Marshall to McCloy, Sub: Status of Two Far Eastern Divisions, 22 June 1945, George C. Marshall Papers, Box 76, Folder 76, Marshall Library; Memo for the Record, "Employment of French Corps," 30 July 1945, RG 165, OPD 336.2 TS.

Chapter 16

The Atomic Bomb and the Invasion

In the summer of 1945 events threatened to overwhelm newly installed President Harry Truman. Were it not for his chief civilian and military advisers whom he inherited from his predecessor, no doubt the several critical issues demanding resolution would have driven the president to despair. These issues, held mostly in the background until the defeat of Germany, all concerned the Pacific war, and all, more or less, revolved around the question: how can Japan be forced to unconditional surrender? The war against Germany had held these issues at bay, and in fact, nobody had yet found any clear resolutions. With Germany's defeat in early May, these critical issues pressed in on the inexperienced president and his more experienced advisers.

Several important threads were being spun out, and before Japan would surrender, they somehow had to be tied together—hardly an easy job since Truman's principal advisers were not all of one mind on how to end the Pacific war. Dominating all considerations was the obstacle of unconditional surrender. Clearly, by any rational measure the Japanese were already defeated in May 1945. The Imperial navy had been sunk. The sea lanes over which passed the oil and raw materials from the Indies were cut. Allied aircraft could attack the home islands unopposed. The Japanese homeland was only a step away from complete blockade. Yet the Japanese military persisted with hopeless and suicidal defenses at Iwo Jima and Okinawa and planned a similar defense for the homeland. Was there any "political solution" acceptable to the Japanese yet commensurate with unconditional surrender? After long and tedious debate the Joint Chiefs had chosen a military strategy of prolonged bombing and blockade followed by invasion of the homeland. Would the costs of invasion be too high? Was there another way? A strategy of invasion presupposed entry of the USSR into the war against Japan. Yet Soviet participation was not an unmixed blessing. What postwar demands would the Soviets make? Would their assistance be worth granting their demands? Already Soviet actions in eastern Europe promised similar postwar problems in the Far East. Finally, of course, there was the atomic bomb. By May 1945 much was known: a bomb would be ready for testing in July and others would be ready for use in August. The power of the bomb was, however, unknown. Estimates of explosive power ranged from the equivalent of seven hundred to fifteen thousand one-ton conventional bombs.[1] Could the bomb alone force unconditional surrender, or would invasion still be required?

Few of Truman's advisers could see all of these issues with all their permutations. Acting Secretary of State Joseph Grew understood the intimidating nature of unconditional surrender, and he favored a softening of the policy. Yet he knew nothing of the bomb. Admiral Leahy knew of the bomb but was convinced that it would never work. No civilians outside the War and Navy Departments were familiar with the details of the invasion plans. By July James F. Byrnes, a Truman confidant and later secretary of state, was able to take a broad view of the issues affecting Japan's surrender, but he had come to his key role so late that his knowledge was somewhat shallow. Secretary of Navy Forrestal knew of all the issues, but his knowledge of the bomb was not deep. Only two men, both old soldiers, could see the whole picture. Both Secretary of War Stimson and Army Chief of Staff Marshall had served throughout the war, and they had intimate knowledge of the bomb, the invasion plans, and the issues and problems surrounding the entry of the Soviets into the war against Japan. Marshall, the architect of the Allied Overlord strategy in Europe, was more than any other the proponent of the invasion of Japan, and Secretary Stimson had shepherded "S-1," the atomic bomb, to completion. The ideas of these two men dominated the debate over how to end the Pacific war.

One of the great historiographical arguments of modern America concerns generally the defeat of Japan and specifically the use of the atomic bombs. A great number of books and articles have been published on the subject, especially in the 1960s and 1970s. Perhaps the most extreme position in this debate was taken by Gar Alperovitz in his book *Atomic Diplomacy: Hiroshima and Potsdam.* He argued that the bombs were dropped on Japan to make the Soviets more amenable in the postwar world; that the bomb's use "did not derive from overriding military considerations" but from diplomatic calculations; that all members of the Joint Chiefs were already convinced that Japan would have surrendered without the bomb and without invasion; that Japanese leaders were desperately trying to surrender, but "after Alamogordo neither Truman nor his senior advisers were interested in exploring Japanese surrender"; and that, finally, Truman's views of the bomb represented a break with Roosevelt's more benevolent and urbane views.[2]

Other historians have taken a more moderate view. Historians like Martin J. Sherwin, Barton Bernstein, and Thomas T. Hammond admitted that Truman and his advisers were certainly influenced by the impression the bomb would make on the Soviets, but, they argued, Truman and his advisers would have been derelict and incompetent *not* to understand that the bomb would be a powerful lesson to the Soviets. It does not follow, however, that the bombs were used for that purpose. Furthermore, these historians argue that Truman, as he did in other respects, followed Roosevelt's precedents and policies.[3]

Whatever their positions in this debate, historians have reached a rough consensus on the bomb and the surrender of Japan. Certainly, it is clear that the policy of unconditional surrender limited both military and diplomatic options. All now concede that the growing schism between the United States and the USSR influenced American views on how to end the Pacific war, especially on the entry of the Soviets. Most, though not all, agree that the decision to use the bomb was inherent in its development. Historians, however, disagree over the need for using the bomb and the degree to which U.S.-USSR relations influenced the decision to drop the bomb on Japan. Some historians even question that the prospect of a bloody invasion drove American leaders to employ the bomb.

The views of the historians who engage in these sometimes tedious arguments frequently drift away from the objective evidence into a high degree of speculation; sometimes even their facts are wrong. More important, however, their arguments are off target and peculiarly one dimensional. These are diplomatic historians writing about diplomatic issues, and their arguments usually turn to the single issue of the bomb. The military dimension is left out of their equations. The military problems, options, and dangers that faced decision makers in the summer of 1945 are hardly to be found in their work. Yet in July and August Truman and his advisers faced an immediate problem: because Japanese military leaders were apparently determined to continue a hopeless and suicidal struggle, the United States had to somehow force the Japanese leaders to surrender unconditionally without unacceptably high American casualties.

More than any other individual, it was Secretary Stimson, seventy-seven years old and so ailing that he had to ration his strength, who saw how to settle the disparate and tangled issues affecting the end of the Pacific war. The death of Roosevelt and the accession of the inexperienced Truman to the presidency created Stimson's opportunity. Roosevelt had gone his own way on atomic policy, bringing few advisers into his counsel. Stimson's crucial role in the use of the atomic bombs against Japan began with Truman's accession.[4] The policies and actions that brought a Japanese surrender without an apocalyptic battle in the homeland are Stimson's legacy.

Secretary Stimson brought his long experience in high office to his self-appointed mission of ending the Japanese war without an invasion. He had served as secretary of war under President William Howard Taft a full generation before. President Calvin Coolidge had made him governor general of the Philippines. He had been Herbert Hoover's secretary of state. In 1940, as Franklin Roosevelt faced the oncoming war and planned his precedent-breaking third term, he was determined to gain bipartisan support by choosing Republicans to head both services. As secretary of the navy, he chose Frank Knox, Alf Landon's vice-presidential running mate in 1936. To head the War Department, he selected Henry Stimson.

Five years later, when Truman, called away from a late afternoon drink in Speaker Sam Rayburn's office, assumed the presidency in the White House cabinet room on the evening of 12 April, the end of the war in Europe was only weeks away. Even then the members of the Joint Chiefs were in hot debate hammering out their military strategy for Japan's final defeat. Operation ICEBERG, the invasion of Okinawa, had begun twelve days earlier on 1 April. The landings were all but unopposed, but as Truman swore his oath, the Marines and soldiers of Tenth Army were encountering the dug-in cave defenses manned by the one hundred thousand Japanese of General Ushijima's 32d Army—the beginning of the battle that, for the numbers involved, was the bloodiest of the war. The campaign for Okinawa, which proceeded through the first three months of Truman's presidency and coincided with the debates on how to defeat Japan, surely weighed heavily. As he approved the Joint Chiefs' plans for OLYMPIC on 18 June, the president remarked that he did not want another Okinawa "from one end of Japan to the other."[5]

Stimson also feared that an invasion of the homeland would repeat the experiences of Iwo Jima and Okinawa on a grand scale, and he so informed President Truman two weeks before Potsdam. Stimson had toured Japan before the war and now remembered his impressions. The terrain in Kyushu, he recalled, was unfavorable for maneuver and "susceptible to a last ditch defense such as has been made on Iwo Jima and Okinawa." The struggle, he feared, would be "long, costly, and arduous." If possible, he informed the president, some other way to force the surrender must be found.[6]

Stimson had been thinking for some time about ways of ending the war with Japan. As the Joint Chiefs concentrated on finding a military strategy for bringing Japan to unconditional surrender, Stimson worked on a political-diplomatic strategy that he hoped would end the war short of invasion, and not only save American lives but save the Japanese people from a hopeless and cataclysmic struggle imposed by die-hard militarists.

Stimson believed that militarily the Japanese were already defeated, though still capable of bleeding their enemies in hopeless stands like Okinawa. Stimson also had some sympathy and admiration for the Japanese people and Japan's accomplishments, and he feared that an invasion of the homeland would drive the Japanese people more tightly into the arms of the militarists. He came to believe that a series of severe shocks, delivered in rapid succession, might force the Japanese to their senses. These shocks had to come quickly before the date of OLYMPIC.[7]

Stimson approved of the plans to invade Japan but recognized the invasion as only a contingency if all else failed. The day following the 18 June White House meeting at which Truman put his approval on the plans for OLYMPIC, Stimson confided his thoughts to his diary. "The Chiefs of Staff had taken their position [for OLYMPIC] at the [White House] meeting on Monday," he wrote, "and Forrestal and I have agreed to it as far as the purely military side of it goes." But, he continued, "There was a pretty strong feeling that it would be deplorable if we have to go through the military program with all its stubborn fighting to a finish." It was necessary to plan for the invasion, he recognized, but "some way should be found of inducing Japan to yield without a fight to the finish."[8]

Stimson's surrender program consisted of three progressive actions. First, Japan should be given a stern warning by the Allied leaders emphasizing the overwhelming destructive power that would be brought to bear and outlining the already stated Allied war aims—to demilitarize Japan, to punish war criminals, and to strip Japan of its conquests. But, Stimson suggested, the warning should also reassure the Japanese that the nation would not be destroyed and, moreover, that the imperial system could be continued. Second, he saw the entry of the USSR into the war as providing a profound shock to the Japanese. Third, Stimson counted on the atomic bomb. These measures would be delivered in quick succession, still leaving time if they failed to carry through the invasion on 1 November 1945.[9]

Stimson—with his colleagues, Acting Secretary of State Joseph Grew and Secretary of Navy James Forrestal—had long advocated modifying unconditional surrender to encourage the Japanese to negotiate. The three cabinet members also had the support of the Joint Chiefs, though these military men saw unconditional surrender as a political policy and there-fore hesitated to declare openly against it. At Potsdam the Joint Chiefs argued that for military reasons alone the emperor's position should be protected. If unconditional surrender meant the elimination of the impe-rial institution, they warned, the Japanese would fight to the bitter end. At a Potsdam meeting on 17 July 1945, the Joint Chiefs examined, purely in military terms, the problem of retaining the emperor; Marshall, who believed that retention was a military necessity, asked that the members draft a memorandum to the president recommending that the Allies "do nothing to indicate that the emperor might be removed from office upon unconditional surrender." The emperor's status was no small matter. He could be necessary, Marshall said, to ensure the surrender of millions of Japanese troops deployed in Asia and the Pacific.[10] The Japanese army in China numbered more than a million men and was still capable of offensive operations. Another million Japanese soldiers remained in Manchuria, Korea, and Formosa. Yet another million troops remained in Southeast Asia, the East Indies, and on by-passed islands in the Pacific. An army of two million was poised to defend the home islands.[11] The Joint Chiefs advised Truman that "from a strictly military point of view the Joint Chiefs of Staff consider it inadvisable to make any statement or take any action at the present time that would make it difficult or impossible to utilize the authority of the emperor to direct a surrender of the Japanese forces in the outlying areas as well as in Japan proper."[12]

When the Allied leaders at Potsdam issued a final ultimatum to the Japanese, it did not explicitly express the position of the Joint Chiefs concerning the emperor. Neither did the ultimatum call for elimination of the emperor. In fact, the Potsdam declaration did not mention the emperor; instead, it emphasized the elimination of Japan's "militarists." The term *unconditional surrender* appeared only once and then only at the end of the document, attached to a qualifying prepositional phrase, "unconditional surrender of all the Japanese armed forces."[13]

The entry of the USSR into the war against Japan had, of course, been looked on earlier as a military necessity to deal with Japanese forces in Manchuria and Korea. Stimson was adamant that U.S. forces should not be committed to combat on the Asian mainland. Now, in the summer of 1945, as the bomb became nearer a certainty and as the naval blockade and aerial mining campaign promised to isolate the home islands from the continent, others began to question the necessity for Soviet entry. Marshall, however, pointed out to Stimson the shock value of Soviet entry. It might, Marshall pointed out, prove to be the decisive blow to force a Japanese surrender. Stimson immediately agreed. Thus, as Admiral King and Secretary of State Byrnes pointed out in June and July, Soviet entry was no longer militarily necessary. Stimson and Marshall believed, however, that it could prove to be a heavy psychological blow to Japan's political and military leadership.[14]

Some historians have argued that after the 16 July 1945 test of the bomb, American leaders saw immediately that the Soviets were no longer needed. This exaggerated belief does not take into account the military problems of defeating Japan. Certainly, Soviet entry was no longer crucial to hold the Kwantung Army in place. Yet even in July 1945 there was no guarantee that a surrender of the Japanese government would be honored by the 2.6 million troops in Korea, Manchuria, and China. At Potsdam, after the news of the test arrived, Truman asked Stimson for Marshall's estimate of the need for Soviet entry. Uncharacteristically, Marshall equivocated. The objective of keeping the Kwantung Army in place had already been accomplished by the Soviet buildup on the Manchurian frontier, he told Stimson. Nonetheless, Marshall refused to say that the Soviets were no longer needed. As Stimson recorded, "Of course Marshall could not answer directly or explicitly." Stimson then interpreted Marshall's remarks to indicate that since the bomb was a success, the Soviets were no longer needed, and he so informed the president.[15]

Far from indicating a clear and abrupt change in Anglo-American policy, the overall conclusions about the bomb, the invasion, the entry of the Soviets, and the Japanese surrender that came from the Potsdam Conference were ambiguous and uncertain; there was no sudden realization that the bomb had changed everything. High hopes but no major policy change arose from the successful test of the bomb. The Combined Chiefs reaffirmed the necessity for invading the home islands, and the Allied leaders' warning to Tokyo omitted any mention of the bomb. Stimson also failed to convince the president to add even oblique assurances that the Emperor's position would be protected. As for Soviet entry, Truman maintained that he went to Potsdam to get the Soviets into the war against Japan, and long after the war he continued to maintain that position.[16]

The success and unexpected power of the test bomb had changed pre-Potsdam calculations about forcing Japan to unconditional surrender— but not as much as some have claimed.[17] Stimson's warning could now be backed by concrete and dramatic action. Soviet entry was less necessary. Perhaps the invasion would not be necessary. But other questions remained. The Japanese had already endured four months of conventional incendiary bombing without yielding. Would a Soviet declaration of war coupled with atomic bombings produce surrender? If the Japanese refused to surrender, the invasion would still have to proceed. Even faced with the bomb, the Japanese might not yield.

Little systematic thought or analysis had been given to the relationship between the bomb and the invasion. Because the development of the bomb was charged to the U.S. Army Corps of Engineers and the "Manhattan Engineer District" was created to direct the project, the commander of the district, Major General (later Lieutenant General) Leslie R. Groves, reported to Army Chief of Staff George Marshall, who in turn was directly responsible to Secretary of War Stimson. After Roosevelt's death Stimson and his chief aides—Harvey Bundy, George Harrison, and John J. McCloy—along with Marshall were the most knowledgeable officials in government on the progress of building a bomb. It was Stimson who briefed Truman on the project soon after his inauguration.[18]

The development of the atomic bomb depended on the production of fissionable uranium (U-235) and plutonium (U-239) at Oak Ridge, Tennessee, and Hanford, Washington. The production of sufficient fissionable material was only the beginning; somehow the material had to be detonated—that is, fission had to be initiated. Building a workable bomb was the job of scientists and engineers at Los Alamos, New Mexico. Planned and built in 1942 and 1943, these secret facilities were working furiously by 1944. At the end of 1944 Groves was able to give Stimson a tentative schedule for the first bombs. A plutonium bomb would be ready for testing in July, and a uranium bomb would be available for use against Japan by August. Scientists were so certain of the success of the uranium bomb that no test was considered necessary.[19] By early April 1945, just before Roosevelt's death, Stimson was convinced "that success is 99% assured." Clearly in April and May, as his subordinate Marshall argued relentlessly for a strategy of invasion, Stimson's mind was turning more and more to the bomb. On 10 May Stimson talked to Marshall and voiced hope that any invasion could be put off "until after we had tried S-1" (the atomic bomb). Five days later he confided to his diary that while Marshall and his colleagues should proceed with invasion plans, "Fortunately the actual invasion will not take place until my secret is out." Before the invasion, the "two great uncertainties" of the war against Japan would be resolved—the entry of the USSR Union and the bomb. Though left unsaid, he obviously hoped these "two great uncertainties" would settle the matter short of invasion. By May Stimson clearly thought of the atomic bomb as perhaps the most important of the plans to shock Japanese leaders into a quick surrender.[20]

Yet Stimson thought of the bomb as a military weapon only in the broadest sense. It was to be mainly a political weapon delivering a doomsday message to Japanese leaders. The military planners of the invasion of Japan took no note of the bomb in their plans. The outline plans for OLYMPIC and CORONET were drawn in mid-1944 by the joint planners in the Pentagon, who knew nothing of the bomb nor took any account of it in their work. Neither MacArthur nor Nimitz, the two Pacific commanders charged with the final planning and conduct of the invasion, knew of the bomb. MacArthur only learned of the bomb in late July when Brigadier General Thomas Farrell, Groves's deputy, was sent out to the Philippines to inform him. Nimitz learned of the bomb in February 1945 after King sent a messenger to brief him. When the young officer told Nimitz that a bomb would be ready by August, Nimitz remarked that August was "a long time from now, and in the meantime I have a war to fight." However, Nimitz was far more impressed with the bomb's promise in late July when Captain William S. Parsons, the bomb commander for the Hiroshima mission, arrived at Guam and showed film of the Alamogordo test.[21]

Most decisions about using the first bombs were in the hands of the Interim Committee, the creation of Henry Stimson. At the same time that he had briefed newly inaugurated President Truman on the Manhattan Project, Stimson had suggested that the president appoint a committee to make recommendations about the bomb and to study the problem of postwar international atomic controls. The president approved the idea within a week, and Stimson submitted a list of recommended members. Stimson himself would chair the committee, and the members, chosen by Stimson with advice from his assistants George Harrison and Harvey Bundy, were three scientists—Vannevar Bush, James B. Conant, and Karl T. Compton—and two government officials—Under Secretary of the Navy Ralph A. Bard and Assistant Secretary of State William L. Clayton. Also included as the personal representative of the president was James F. Byrnes, former senator from South Carolina, recently resigned chief of the Office of War Mobilization, and soon to be secretary of state. None was a military man, although Marshall and Groves met frequently with the committee. None except Stimson had knowledge of both the bomb and the invasion plans.[22]

The committee met on several occasions between mid-May and mid-June. At no time was the use of the bomb seriously debated; the only question was how to use it and against what kind of target. The committee decided against a demonstration of the bomb in some remote area and against giving a specific warning to the Japanese. The bomb would be used without warning on a war plant surrounded by workers' houses. Most of the committee's time, however, went to discussions of the possible postwar spread of atomic weapons and postwar controls of atomic energy. At no time did the committee discuss the invasion of Japan or the bomb's possible role in preventing the invasion.[23]

Marshall's enthusiasm for the bomb's potential to end the Japanese war quickly was not so great as Stimson's. If the strategic use of the bomb failed to end the war, Marshall considered using atomic bombs in the invasion. Marshall remained unconvinced, even as the Interim Committee met, that naval blockade, conventional bombing, or even the atomic bomb could force the Japanese to unconditional surrender. If all else failed and the invasion had to proceed, the bomb would be a devastating weapon in the pre-invasion bombardment. Marshall did not see the invasion and the bomb as representing two discrete alternatives, and like most army officers he refused to see the bomb as only a strategic weapon—a grander version of strategic bombing. Instead, he saw the bomb as another in a package of progressive shocks along with Soviet entry, blockade, conventional strategic bombing, and, if necessary, invasion to force the Japanese to surrender.[24]

"There were supposed to be nine more bombs . . . and they would be largely in time for the first landing on the southern tip of Japan," Marshall told his biographer Forrest Pogue in 1957. There had been studies done at Alamogordo, he continued, and "it was decided then that the casualties from the actual fighting would be very much greater than might occur from the aftereffects of the bomb action." Three bombs were planned for each of the Corps landing areas in OLYMPIC. One or two would be dropped on each beach during the pre-invasion bombardment. The others would be reserved for defensive positions further inland or for counterattack forces attempting to move to the beachhead. Marshall told a similar story to John P. Sutherland in 1958 with the understanding that it not be published until after his death. "In the original plans for the invasion of Japan," he told Sutherland, "we wanted nine atomic bombs for three attacks." Two bombs, he said, were to be used "for each attacking army [corps?], or six in all, in the initial attack." The remaining three bombs would have been used "against Japanese reserves which we were sure would pour into the areas."[25]

In both these interviews Marshall may have been remembering informal conversations that took place in May, June, and early July of 1945 at the highest levels in the Pentagon. Besides, plans had already been made to use the next bombs on strategic targets. Yet there is some evidence that in the last days of the war Marshall was thinking of reserving future bombs for OLYMPIC in case the Japanese refused to surrender. On 13 August, Marshall's assistant, Lieutenant General John E. Hull, called Colonel L. E. Seeman, one of Groves' assistants, about future bomb production. Hull explained that Marshall wanted to know the production schedule "so we can determine how to use them." Hull related that Marshall was considering whether to drop the bombs "as originally planned [on cities]" or "in direct support of major operations [OLYMPIC]." Seven bombs would be ready by 31 October, said Seeman. He cautioned, however, that the bombs were not "pinpoint" weapons and might endanger nearby U.S. troops. Hull replied that the bombs might be used against communications centers and troop concentrations "a couple or three days" before the landings. "Nearer the tactical use than the other?" Seeman asked. "That's what it amounts to," replied Hull. Clearly, had the war not ended when it did, Marshall would have considered using atomic bombs to support OLYMPIC.[26]

Marshall's incipient planning to use atomic bombs to support the OLYMPIC assault points to the military problem of achieving unconditional surrender at a tolerable cost in a reasonable length of time. Certainly U.S. leaders were conscious of the bomb's collateral effects on the postwar conduct of the USSR, but the core problem in the late summer of 1945 was not the postwar conduct of the Soviets but the political-military problem of ending the war with Japan. And the hard kernel of that core was a military dilemma—defeating Japan's military, which still had five million men under arms, without large casualties and without abandoning unconditional surrender.

The large casualty figures for the invasion of Japan, cited by Truman, Stimson, and Churchill in their postwar writings, were without basis in contemporary planning. Nonetheless, military and political leaders were very concerned about high casualties. The bomb, whether used strategically or tactically, promised to keep U.S. casualties at an acceptable level. The bombs also would shock Japanese leaders, and combined with other demonstrations of the hopelessness of continued resistance, might tip the balance toward surrender. Military and political leaders, certainly not Marshall or Stimson, did not see the bomb as a discrete and cataclysmic weapon. Instead, the bomb was another powerful component in a crescendo of force that also included a Soviet declaration of war, imminent invasion, and the inevitability of destruction and strangulation through bombing and blockade.

NOTES

1. Leslie R. Groves, *Now It Can Be Told: The Story of the Manhattan Project* (New York: Harper and Brothers, 1962), 269.

2. Gar Alperovitz, *Atomic Diplomacy: Hiroshima and Potsdam* (New York: Simon and Schuster, 1965), 237, 239.

3. See Martin J. Sherwin, *A World Destroyed: The Atomic Bomb and the Grand Alliance* (New York: Alfred A. Knopf, 1975); Barton Bernstein, *The Atomic Bomb:*

The Critical Issues (Boston: Little Brown, 1976); Thomas T. Hammond, "Atomic Diplomacy Revisited," *Orbis*, 19 (Winter 1976): 1403–28.

4. Sherwin, 87–88 and note, 109–111, 115.

5. *FRUS: Conference at Berlin, 1945*, vol. 1 (Washington, DC: GPO, 1960), 909.

6. Henry Lewis Stimson Diaries, vol. 52, 5 (2 July 1945), microfilm edition, reel 9, Manuscripts and Archives, Yale Univ. Library, New Haven, CN.

7. Ibid., 5–10; Richard G. Hewlett and Oscar E. Anderson, Jr., *A History of the United States Atomic Energy Commission: The New World, 1939–1946* (University Park: The Pennsylvania Univ. Press, 1962), 361.

8. Stimson Diaries (microfilm edition), vol. 51, 183 (19 June 1945).

9. Ibid., vol. 51, 183 (19 June 45); Ibid., vol. 52, 5–10 (2 July 45); Hewlett and Anderson, 361–65.

10. *FRUS: Conference at Berlin*, vol. 2, 39–40.

11. *Reports of MacArthur*, vol. 1, *The Campaigns of MacArthur in the Pacific* (Washington, DC: GPO, 1966), 460.

12. *FRUS: Conference at Berlin*, vol. 2, 1269.

13. Ibid., 1474–76.

14. Stimson Diaries, vol. 51, 183 (19 June 45); *FRUS: Conference at Berlin*, vol. 1, 905.

15. Stimson Diaries, vol. 52, 35–36 (23 July 45).

16. Hewlett and Anderson, 292–94. For the ambiguous and unclear nature of the products of Potsdam, see Barton Bernstein, "Roosevelt, Truman, and the Atomic Bomb: A Reinterpretation," *Political Science Quarterly* 90 (Spring 1975).

17. Early predictions by Groves to Marshall in late 1944 indicated that only two bombs would be available in 1945, the first with explosive power equal to five hundred tons of TNT and the second equal to one thousand tons. As late as May 1945 scientists predicted that the test bomb would have explosive power of no more than five thousand tons of TNT. The actual test bomb produced an explosion equal to twenty thousand tons of TNT. See Groves, 269; Ferenc M. Szasz, *The Day the Sun Rose Twice: The Story of the Trinity Site Nuclear Explosion, July 16, 1945* (Albuquerque: Univ. of New Mexico Press, 1984), 117; Herbert Feis, *Churchill, Roosevelt, Stalin: The War They Fought and the Peace They Sought* (Princeton: Princeton Univ. Press, 1957), 501–2.

18. Stimson Diaries, vol. 51, 70–72 (25 April 45); Sherwin, 162–63.

19. Groves, 288.

20. Sherwin, 133, 140; Stimson Diaries, vol. 51, 117, 129 (10 and 15 May 45).

21. Walter S. Schoenberger, *Decision of Destiny* (Athens: Ohio Univ. Press, 1969), 42–43; D. Clayton James, *The Years of MacArthur*, vol. 2, *1941–1945* (Boston: Houghton Mifflin, 1972), 775–76; E. B. Potter, *Nimitz* (Annapolis: Naval Institute Press, 1976), 381–82, 384.

22. Stimson Diaries, vol. 51, 70–72 (25 April 45); Hewlett and Anderson, 344–45.

23. Hewlett and Anderson, 353–61; Notes of Interim Committee Meeting, 31

May and 1 June 1945, Yale-Atomic Weapons File, Truman Library, Independence, MO.

24. Leon V. Sigal, *Fighting to the Finish: The Politics of War Termination in the United States and Japan, 1945* (Ithaca: Cornell Univ. Press, 1988), 137, 209, 214.

25. George C. Marshall Interviews and Reminiscences for Forrest C. Pogue: Transcripts and Notes, 1956–57, Tape 14M, 390, George C. Marshall Research Foundation, 1986, Marshall Library, Lexington, VA; John P. Sutherland, "The Story General Marshall Told Me," *U.S. News and World Report*, November 2, 1959, 53. Marshall was remembering incorrectly for Sutherland. His reference to three attacking armies is puzzling, for Olympic was to be conducted by three corps under Sixth Army. In the same interview he remarks that Bradley would have commanded one of the three armies. Marshall had suggested Bradley for command of one of the armies scheduled to conduct Coronet, but when the war ended, no appointment had been made.

26. Marc Gallicchio, "After Nagasaki, General Marshall's Plan for Tactical Nuclear Weapons in Japan," *Prologue* 23 (Winter 1991): 396–404.

Conclusion

During the summer of 1945 the U.S. government received numerous indications that a peace group was forming in Japan. MAGIC, the interception and decryption of Japanese diplomatic messages, revealed a debate inside the Japanese government about seeking an end to the war without accepting unconditional surrender.[1] Allen Dulles, the Office of Strategic Services (OSS) representative in Europe, maintained contact with the Japanese legation at Berne, Switzerland, through Per Jacobsson, economic adviser to the Bank of International Settlements in Basel. The Japanese made it plain that unconditional surrender and the postwar status of the emperor were the principal obstacles to peace. Other contacts with the Japanese confirmed the importance of allowing the Japanese to keep the emperor. In Portugal the OSS was told by an agent that a member of the Japanese legation, Masutaro Inone, reported Japanese willingness to end the war if the home islands could be preserved and the term "unconditional surrender" dropped. The OSS demanded proof that Inone spoke for the Japanese government and informed him that the United States would discuss only unconditional surrender. Another OSS contact indicated that the Japanese government would make peace if allowed to keep the emperor and to continue obtaining food from Korea. These contacts, however, were undertaken by Japanese army and navy officers on their own initiatives. The Japanese officers routinely reported their contacts with the OSS to their navy superiors in Tokyo but received no encouragement. All this information was routinely forwarded to President Truman and officials in Washington, who correctly assessed these contacts as neither authorized nor sanctioned by the Japanese government.[2]

Meanwhile, the Japanese government hoped to obtain an end to the war through Soviet mediation. At the request of the Japanese government, former premier Hirota Koki, onetime ambassador to the Soviet government, met on two occasions in June and July with the Soviet ambassador to Japan, Jacob Malik, attempting to offer concessions in Asia for Soviet cooperation. Hirota received little encouragement, and several more attempts to meet with Malik were rebuffed. Foreign Minister Togo Shigenori, with the approval of the emperor, then appointed Prince Konoye Fumimaro as special envoy to Moscow with instructions, also approved by the emperor, to seek the good offices of the Soviets in ending the war.

When the Soviets refused to allow Konoye into the country, the Japanese ambassador, Sato Naotake, was instructed to approach them with an offer to end the war on any terms short of unconditional surrender. The Soviets delayed, and the Japanese were too late. Soviet leaders had already left for Potsdam, and the Red Army was already massing on the Manchurian border readying for war. Sato finally received his audience with Soviet Foreign Minister Molotov on 7 August. The old Bolshevik opened the meeting by reading the Soviet declaration of war against Japan.[3]

The Hiroshima bomb had fallen the day before the Soviet declaration of war, and the Nagasaki bomb was being readied for delivery the next day. To all Japanese leaders except the die-hard militarists, even the forlorn hope of avoiding unconditional surrender was now gone. The Potsdam declaration of 26 July had warned the Japanese that they faced "utter devastation of the Japanese homeland" unless Japan "ceases to resist." But, the Allies emphasized, the Japanese people would not be "enslaved as a race or destroyed as a nation." Nowhere, however, did the Potsdam Conference address the critical issue of the status of the emperor. The Potsdam declaration, earlier rejected by the Japanese because it failed to guarantee the emperor's position, now had to be accepted. In both Tokyo and Washington, the days from 10 to 15 August were frenetic. At Manila and Guam MacArthur's and Nimitz's staffs already were shifting their attentions from Operation OLYMPIC to BLACKLIST and CAMPUS, their respective plans for the occupation of Japan. In the process of coordinating the two plans, MacArthur's staff notified Nimitz's representatives that "any landing whatsoever by naval or marine elements prior to CIN-CAFPAC's personal landing is emphatically unacceptable to him."[4]

Events in Tokyo had reached a crisis on 9 August. The cataclysmic shocks of the Hiroshima bomb, the Soviet entry, the Nagasaki bomb, and the promise of more bombs forced a cabinet crisis in Japan and allowed the peace party to come into the open despite the desire of the military leaders to continue the fight. Prime Minister Suzuki Kantaro and the civilian ministers wanted to accept the Potsdam declaration if the emperor's position could be assured. The army wanted to argue for other conditions—no occupation, self-disarmament, and Japanese trials of war criminals. The cabinet was deadlocked and sought counsel from the emperor. The members reconvened just before midnight in the emperor's bomb shelter. Foreign Minister Togo stated the peace party's view, and General Anami Korechika gave the argument of the die-hard militarists. At that point the emperor, in an unprecedented direct intervention, stated that the war must be stopped. Suzuki and Togo had cut the ground from under the militarists by arguing that the Potsdam declaration should be accepted "with the understanding that the said declaration does not comprise any demand which prejudices the prerogatives of His Majesty as a Sovereign Ruler." The message accepting the Potsdam declaration with that proviso went out at seven A.M. through Switzerland and Sweden.[5]

Secretary Stimson had been arguing vigorously and unsuccessfully for weeks that a specific guarantee of the emperor's status should be included in the Potsdam declaration. Now, as he prepared to leave on holiday, word of the Japanese acceptance arrived. "That busted our holiday," and referring to the lingering question of the emperor, he lamented, "It is curious that this was the very single point that I feared would make trouble." According to Stimson, President Truman and Secretary of State Byrnes had struck out the explicit guarantee of the emperor's position contained in the first Potsdam draft, preferring instead to handle the matter in secret negotiations that were sure to follow.[6]

On 10 August in Washington, a series of tense meetings attended by Truman, Byrnes, Stimson, Forrestal, and Leahy began to debate a reply. To specifically guarantee the status of the emperor, argued Byrnes, would contravene the policy of unconditional surrender and make it difficult to get British and Soviet agreement. In earlier debates on the same subject Byrnes had also pointed out the dangers of domestic political reaction. Stimson and Leahy argued that only the emperor had the stature to enforce a surrender on the nation and, in particular, on the Japanese Army. Forrestal took a middle ground, suggesting that the reply could be worded in such a way as to reassure the Japanese that the imperial system would not be destroyed without explicitly guaranteeing the emperor's status. Truman instructed Byrnes to draft a reply embodying Forrestal's ideas. Byrnes's aide, Benjamin Cohen, set to work on the reply. Finessing the question of the emperor, the reply stated that "the authority of the emperor and the Japanese government . . . shall be subject to the supreme commander of the Allied Powers." The implication was clear; after the surrender there would be an emperor.[7]

Though other formalities remained and the surrender was not signed until 2 September, the Pacific war was over. The architect of that surrender, without the necessity for invasion, was Henry Stimson, whose program had succeeded. Considering the continuing high casualties of the incendiary raids, the imminent sealing of the naval blockade, the growing food shortages in the cities, and the promise of high Japanese casualties in the invasion, it can be argued that the early end of the war saved far more Japanese lives than American.

As the war came to an end, the debates about how it ended were about to begin. First came the official postwar studies and the memoirists. Navy advocates claimed that Japan, a maritime nation, had been defeated by the destruction of her navy and the subsequent blockade. In 1949 Hanson W. Baldwin, a naval academy graduate and former naval officer, published a thin volume called *Great Mistakes of the War*. In the course of arguing that Roosevelt gave too much to the Soviets in return for their agreement to participate in the war against Japan, Baldwin charged that there was no need to give the Soviets anything. "At the time of Yalta [February 1945] Japan was already beaten," he asserted, "not by the atomic bomb, which had not yet been perfected, not by conventional bombing, then just starting, but by attrition and blockade." American military leaders, he charged, were blinded to Japan's plight by fanatical Japanese resistance and by fear that the Kwantung Army would come home from Manchuria to defend the homeland—an army that according to Baldwin was a mere skeleton of "green conscripts and second rate troops." While the Japanese could still mount fanatical defenses in specific areas, they were strategically defenseless. Their navy was gone. The lines of communication with the empire were severed. There was little fuel for industry or planes. Blockade, Baldwin says, not only *could have* defeated Japan but clearly did so.[8]

After the war most of the major decision makers made their views plain. Admiral Leahy, who, as chairman of the Joint Chiefs had questioned the need to invade Japan, continued his opposition after the war. Leahy blamed the army for forcing the invasion plans. "The JCS did authorize the preparation of plans for an invasion," he remembered, "but the invasion itself was never approved." (In fact, the invasion of southern Kyushu was ordered by the Joint Chiefs on 25 May 1945 to be done on 1 November 1945.) "The Army," he continued, "did not understand that the Navy, with some Army air assistance, already had defeated Japan." A tight blockade, Leahy emphasized, would have caused Japan to "fall by its own weight."[9]

King believed that planning the invasion had been necessary, but he saw it only as contingency planning. Plans did not mean invasion. In fact, King was convinced that naval blockade and air bombardment would defeat Japan before an invasion could be launched. Even if Kyushu were invaded, King saw the assault as primarily necessary to gain more naval and air bases to tighten the blockade and intensify the bombing.[10]

The postwar debate among memoirists over blockade versus invasion was not altogether an army versus navy argument. At least one prominent admiral favored invasion, and one important general argued that Japan could have been brought to surrender through blockade alone. Admiral

Halsey stated bluntly, "The strategy of gradual encirclement and strangulation . . . I considered a waste of time."[11] General Wedemeyer, a top
planner on the army staff before going to China in 1944 to become chief
of staff to Chiang-Kai-Shek, thought that "it was a mistake ever to visualize
a landing in force against the Japanese main islands. . . . The Japanese
lived by the sea, and once their navy, shipping, and air force were
destroyed, it was certain that they could be starved into surrender."[12]

The advocates of sea power found ready allies among the advocates of
strategic bombing. Despite their title "Army Air Forces," air power
advocates had gained considerable autonomy during World War II; the
most independent of all airmen were the proponents of strategic bombing.
They had long seen massive strategic bombing, coupled with naval
blockade, as the way to defeat Japan.

After the war the airmen could rightly claim a major share of the credit
for Japan's defeat, and, indeed, they claimed a large share. Headquarters,
Army Air Forces (AAF), in 1946 published a thin paperback book entitled
Mission Accomplished. The book used dozens of interviews with former
Japanese officials to convince readers that strategic bombing had won the
war against Japan. The *Strategic Bombing Survey*, written ostensibly to
evaluate the effectiveness of strategic bombing, also pressed the air force's
claim to credit for winning the war against Japan. The commission was
named by Stimson under a 1944 directive from Roosevelt, but, in fact,
the commissioners were chosen and the study was sponsored from within
the AAF.[13] While most commission members approached their duties with
objectivity, leaders of the AAF certainly hoped that the study would
show the war-winning value of strategic bombing and help their drive for
an independent air force.

Whatever its purposes, the *Strategic Bombing Survey* opened with the
statement that "Japan's acceptance of defeat without invasion, while still
possessed of 2½ million combat equipped troops and 9,000 kamikaze
airplanes in the home islands, reveals how persuasively the consequences
of our operations were translated into political results." At the end of the
study, after paying courtesies to the efforts of the other services, the
commission concluded that airpower was "the major factor which determined the timing of Japan's surrender and obviated any need for invasion." In the commission's opinion, "Certainly before 31 December 1945
and in all probability before 1 November 1945, Japan would have surrendered even if the atomic bombs had not been dropped, even if Russia had
not entered the war, and even if no invasion had been planned or
contemplated."[14]

The debate about which service could claim the most credit for winning the war against Japan soon gave way to a growing debate among historians reexamining the defeat of Japan and the role of the atomic bombs. As an explanation and justification for the use of the atomic bombs against Hiroshima and Nagasaki, Truman's and Stimson's arguments that the decision was made solely to save huge numbers of American casualties stood unquestioned for two decades following the end of the Pacific war. But in the 1960s academic historians began to question those assumptions proposing that the bomb may have been used for other reasons. Some charged that the decision was made to intimidate the Soviets; others claimed that the decision was racist; still others claimed that the bombs were unnecessary—that Japan was trying desperately to surrender as the bombs were dropped. History is not so neat as some historians would have it. Single theses flowing from arranged rows of facts and arguments cannot explain the use of the bombs and the end of the Pacific war. In the spring and summer of 1945 many currents were flowing simultaneously, and some were contradictory; others became dead ends; still others were overtaken by events before maturing. Any explanation for the end of the war with Japan should acknowledge that it defies attempts to impose order and simplicity almost two generations later. Any grand thesis attempting to explain the end of the Japanese war is by its nature oversimplified.

It is clear, however, that unconditional surrender prolonged the Pacific war and drove both belligerents to last-ditch military strategies. Designed as a political statement that German and Japanese militarism would be eradicated, the possible effects of unconditional surrender on military strategy were not adequately examined by American civilian leaders. More than any other factor, unconditional surrender drove the Joint Chiefs reluctantly toward a strategy of invasion as the only means of forcing an end to the Pacific war within a reasonable time. Also, it is inarguable that the policy similarly restricted Japanese options in the summer of 1945 and strengthened the calls of the military hardliners for an apocalyptic defense of the homeland. Surely other factors encouraged invasion over prolonged blockade and bombing—speed and the massive Allied military force available by June 1945—but it was unconditional surrender that drove the war to extremes of violence in 1945 and made the atomic bomb seem almost a benign alternative to an invasion.

The policy of unconditional surrender was amazingly inflexible as Stimson, Grew, and Forrestal found when they tried to get it ameliorated during the spring and summer of 1945. Roosevelt had proved adamant in rebuffing any attempt to soften or even to explain the policy. Truman, with far less proprietary interest in the policy than Roosevelt, was nonetheless reluctant to abandon it. He no doubt feared hostile public and congressional reaction to any softening of the policy.

In choosing a strategy of invasion over blockade and bombing, the Joint Chiefs felt acutely the press of time. At the QUADRANT Conference in August 1943, Roosevelt, Churchill, and the combined chiefs had all agreed that "operations should be framed to force the defeat of Japan as soon as possible after the defeat of Germany." The defeat of Japan, they concluded, should be accomplished within twelve months of the defeat of Germany. All hoped that blockade and bombing would produce unconditional surrender, but some planners, especially the army, doubted it. Furthermore, long lead times for planning, for logistical and troop buildup, and for redeployment dictated that invasion planning had to begin early. Invasion planning could not be deferred to await the outcome of a prolonged campaign of blockade and bombing. Arnold and King, who concurred in the necessity to begin planning, looked on invasion as a contingency. In July 1945 at the Potsdam Conference, less than four months before OLYMPIC was scheduled to begin, General Arnold confidently assured his colleagues that the B-29s would break Japanese will by October.[15]

The problems associated with the redeployment of forces from Europe to the Pacific after the defeat of Germany also pushed the Joint Chiefs towards a strategy that promised to end the war quickly. Morale, both overseas and on the homefront, threatened to erode under a long, slow strategy of defeat by blockade and bombing. While no ground combat units were scheduled for OLYMPIC or for the assault echelons of CORONET, European veterans did not know this, and morale in units scheduled for redeployment was precarious. Similarly, on the homefront the will to sustain a long siege of Japan was questionable, especially after the high casualties at Iwo Jima and Okinawa.

Unlike many postwar historians, the Joint Chiefs never regarded the options of invasion, blockade, and bombing as discrete and mutually exclusive choices. Certainly, naval officers emphasized blockade and air officers advocated strategic bombing, but both of these strategies would require bases on the Asian mainland or in Japan that would have to be gained by amphibious assault. Clearly, officers from the different services looked at the problem of how to defeat Japan through the lenses of their separate services. Yet the argument among the Joint Chiefs over invasion versus blockade and bombing was one of emphasis, not exclusion. With or without the invasion, blockade and bombing would go on. Finally, the very existence of the huge Allied naval, air, and ground forces being focused on Japan by the summer of 1945 argued for invasion.

The decision to invade the home islands was made soon after Iwo Jima, the most costly amphibious assault of the war, and in the midst of the two largest and most costly campaigns of the Pacific war—Luzon and Okinawa. United States' casualties and the hopeless, suicidal, and seemingly fanatical nature of the Japanese defenders shook military and civilian leaders. So did Ketsu-Go and the raising in Japan of a new homeland army of two million men. So did the revelations of ULTRA showing a massive buildup of forces in southern Kyushu during the summer of 1945. The concerns of the Joint Chiefs and their civilian superiors are reflected in such suggestions as the tactical use of gas or the use of atomic bombs to support the OLYMPIC assault.

That Japanese homeland defenses were, in fact, of questionable quality was a conclusion that conservative military planners in 1945 could ill afford to draw, for they were planning the invasion in the shadows of Iwo Jima and Okinawa. If the kamikazes would have proved less threatening than the planners believed, the suicide pilots nonetheless symbolized to Americans a fanaticism that was both frightening and infuriating. That the homeland army was poorly trained and equipped—with uncertain communications, transportation, and supply—was less important to the planners than the huge buildup of forces in southern Kyushu reported by ULTRA in the summer of 1945. After OLYMPIC the Japanese would have had little left to defend against CORONET—small comfort in the summer of 1945 to American leaders faced with immediate military problems.

Yet now, from the vantage point of fifty years, it is apparent that the homeland army was largely untrained, ill-equipped, and pitifully supplied. Its most potent weapon, the kamikazes, had to be scattered into Korea and southern Honshu to escape U.S. air attacks. When they concentrated for attack of the OLYMPIC forces, the kamikazes could be destroyed on the ground. On the ground, the Japanese strategists staked everything on a forward defense of the beaches coupled with counterattack forces held in the interior. But even when the war ended, the beach defenses were incomplete and many were unmanned. Minefields had been planned, but most fields remained unlaid because of shortages of mines. The Japanese ground forces lacked strategic and tactical mobility because of gasoline and vehicle shortages and poor roads. Once Far East Air Forces were fully deployed to Okinawa, U.S. air attacks would have restricted strategic movement almost completely, and tactical movement would have been limited to infiltration of individuals and small units. Because of U.S. air superiority and Japanese shortages in transportation and supplies, the ground forces could not be resupplied after the battle began. Units had to stockpile supplies before the battle. In short, the main Japanese advantage lay in numbers. The U.S. advantages lay in complete air and naval superiority and unprecedented and overwhelming combat power—power so great that Japanese military leaders themselves admitted the invasion would be irresistible. They only hoped to gain an amelioration of unconditional surrender by inflicting large losses on the Americans.

Eight months after Japan's surrender intelligence officers on the army general staff completed a "what if" study of the invasion of Japan. Their charge was to study the course of events in the war "on the assumption that the U.S. did not use, and had not the capability of using, atomic bombs in the war against Japan." They looked at three major contingencies had the war not ended in August 1945—the effects of the great typhoon of October 1945 on the preparations for OLYMPIC, the course of surrender psychology in the Japanese government and military, and the results in the event OLYMPIC had been launched.[16]

On 9 October 1945 a vicious typhoon with winds near 140 miles per hour swept over Okinawa before veering northeastward to strike Japan near Osaka. Had the war not ended in August, the harbors and airfields of Okinawa would have been packed with ships, planes, and supplies being gathered for OLYMPIC. Yet the analysts concluded that OLYMPIC would not have been derailed by the typhoon. An attrition factor for amphibious craft had already been built into the OLYMPIC plans, and although 1 November was X-Day for planning purposes, no final determination of X-Day had been made. All major ground units for OLYMPIC were to be mounted in the Philippines and the Marianas and would have been unaffected by the typhoon. Airplane losses on Okinawa would have been more serious, but, the analysts predicted, repair to buildings and communications could be done locally, and airplanes that were beyond repair could be quickly replaced from the Philippines. The most serious losses would have been to "slow-tow" vessels—freighters, gasoline, and supply barges—that had been assembled in Okinawa. These losses, coupled with the destruction of supplies stacked in the open, would have been serious enough to delay OLYMPIC by thirty to forty-five days.[17]

After evaluating the effects of the October typhoon on the preparations for OLYMPIC, the analysts turned to the invasion itself. They were convinced that, even without the atomic bombs, OLYMPIC would never have been launched. Japanese leaders, they noted, had been seeking peace through Soviet mediation since June 1945. They concluded that the failure of these efforts and the sudden Soviet declaration of war on 9 August would have been sufficient, even without the atomic bombs, to end the war. However, in the unlikely event that the Japanese continued in the war even after the entry of the USSR, and OLYMPIC had been launched, "The island of Kyushu would have been occupied in not over two months at a cost of 75,000 to 100,000 casualties." In that case, concluded the analysts, the war would have ended no later than 15 February 1946, and CORONET would not have been necessary.[18]

This author's study of the record leads to similar conclusions. The OLYMPIC timetable allotted four months for securing the southern one-third of Kyushu and building bases. Japanese resistance, rough terrain, poor roads, and a chronic shortage of engineers and other service troops almost certainly would have prolonged that process. However, given the Japanese strategy of forward defense adopted in Ketsu-Go, the poor quality of the homeland army, and the unreadiness of Japanese defenses, it is difficult to see how the Japanese defenders could have stopped the U.S. onslaught. Similarly, to achieve the level of destruction promised by the kamikazes, the Japanese needed to mass their planes near their targets. The Japanese had virtually conceded air superiority to the Americans, so when massed, their planes would be vulnerable to destruction on the ground.

United States' forces were as strong as the Japanese were weak. OLYMPIC was to be by far the largest amphibious operation of the war. The American array was imposing—650,000 troops, almost 2,500 ships, 5,000 planes—all backed by an abundance of resources and a logistical system unmatched in history. Unlike Luzon and Okinawa, the Japanese planned their defenses far forward, literally under the guns of this massive force. Wherever possible, U.S. doctrine emphasized the massive use of firepower to minimize American casualties. By American standards, casualties in OLYMPIC were likely to be high but tolerable—sixty thousand to seventy-five thousand with the dead numbering fifteen thousand to twenty thousand—somewhere in the range of Okinawa or Normandy. Japanese casualties would have been incalculable, perhaps 250,000 in the OLYMPIC area alone. In addition, continued firebombing, with the force now augmented with the bombers of the redeployed Eighth Air Force, would have incinerated thousands more in Japanese cities.

The postwar analysts were certainly correct in their estimate that CORONET would not have been necessary. While Imperial General Headquarters had not formally chosen to fight the climactic battle in southern Kyushu, their deployments indicated that they planned to stake all in defending against OLYMPIC. Little would have been left to defend the Kanto Plain against CORONET, and the Japanese would have chosen surrender. However, had CORONET been launched, it would have been far easier and less costly than the assault on Kyushu. Carrying on the war after the

Occupation of the Kanto Plain was apparently never seriously considered by Japanese planners, and postwar statements by Japanese leaders indicate that no plans existed for prolonged guerilla warfare. Finally, what of the atomic bombs and the invasion? The connections between the use of the bomb and the decision to invade Japan are neither direct nor close. United States' military leaders had little role in decisions about the use of the atomic bombs. Nor did U.S. military leaders rely on the bomb as a decisive instrument of war. The bomb was not a military weapon in the sense that it lessened Japan's ability to defend the homeland; it was a psychological weapon aimed at Japan's military leaders. The bomb's use was foreshadowed by Iwo Jima, Luzon, and Okinawa. Those who still search for an explanation of why the atomic bombs were used against an already defeated Japan need look no further than the conflict between America's rigorous insistence on unconditional surrender and the irrational, suicidal, and hopeless nature of Japan's last defenses.

NOTES

1. Ronald Lewin, *The American Magic: Codes, Ciphers, and the Defeat of Japan* (New York: Farrar, Strauss, Giroux, 1982), 280–85.

2. File "OSS Memoranda for President Truman, February–September 1945," Truman Library; Robert J. C. Butow, *Japan's Decision to Surrender* (Stanford: Stanford Univ. Press, 1954), 103–11.

3. Butow, 90–92, 117–18, 121–23, 124–28, 153.

4. Commander, Seventh Fleet to CINCPAC/POA, Box 166, 0–17, Operations in Southern Kyushu "OLYMPIC" 6/45–10/45, NHC.

5. Richard G. Hewlett and Oscar E. Anderson, Jr., *A History of the United States Atomic Energy Commission: The New World, 1939–1946* (University Park: The Pennsylvania Univ. Press, 1962), 403–5; Butow, 178, 244.

6. Henry Lewis Stimson Diaries, vol. 52, 72 (10 August 45), microfilm edition, reel 9, Manuscripts and Archives, Yale Univ. Library, New Haven, CN.

7. Hewlett and Anderson, 404–5; Leon V. Sigal, *Fighting to the Finish: The Politics of War Termination in the United States and Japan, 1945* (Ithaca: Cornell Univ. Press, 1988), 250–51; Butow, 245.

8. Hanson W. Baldwin, *Great Mistakes of the War* (New York: Harper and Brothers, 1949), 79–83.

9. William D. Leahy, *I Was There* (New York: McGraw-Hill, 1950), 259.

10. Thomas B. Buell, *Master of Sea Power: A Biography of Admiral Ernest J. King* (Boston: Little, Brown and Company, 1980), 490–91; Ernest J. King and Walter M. Whitehall, *Fleet Admiral King: A Naval Record* (New York: W. W. Norton, 1952), 598.

11. William F. Halsey and Joseph Bryan, *Admiral Halsey's Story* (New York: McGraw-Hill, 1947), 250.

12. Albert C. Wedemeyer, *Wedemeyer Reports* (New York: Henry Holt, 1958), 428.

13. David MacIsaac, *Strategic Bombing in World War II: The Story of the United States Strategic Bombing Survey* (New York: Garland Publishing, 1976), 22.

14. *USSBS*, no. 2, "Japan's Struggle to End the War," 1, 13.

15. Ray S. Cline, *Washington Command Post: The Operations Division* (Washington, DC: GPO, 1951), 336–40, 346.

16. Memorandum, Col. R. F. Innis, Chief Intelligence Group, to Chief, Strategic Policy Section, Strategy and Policy Group, OPD, Sub: Use of Atomic Bomb on Japan, 30 April 46, in OPD (ABC) 471–6 Atom (17 Aug 45), Sec. 7, in folder 6, Atomic Bomb (xerox 1482/196), National Archives Project, Marshall Library, Lexington, VA.

17. Ibid.

18. Ibid.

Bibliography

ARCHIVAL SOURCES

Records and documents concerning the proposed invasion of Japan can be found in a number of important archives and libraries. The most extensive holdings are in the National Archives in Washington, DC. Those used most extensively for this study were the Records of the Combined and Joint Chiefs of Staff (JCS) and the Records of the Operations Division (OPD) of the War Department. ULTRA material cited in this study can also be found in the National Archives. Naval and Marine Corps records concerning the invasion can be found at the Navy and Marine Corps Historical Centers at the Washington Navy Yard, Washington, DC.

Records of major Pacific commands can be found at the Washington National Records Center, Suitland, MD. The records of MacArthur's headquarters, Southwest Pacific Area, and Army Forces Pacific, are kept there, as are the records of Sixth and Eighth Armies and the records of some corps headquarters.

The Records Branch of the Center of Military History in the Department of the Army, Washington, DC, possesses originals of the Japanese Monographs and Statements of Japanese Officials. Both collections were compiled during the occupation of Japan, by former Japanese officers and government officials at the direction of General MacArthur's Far East Command. These furnished much of the source material for the chapters on Japanese defenses. The U.S. Air Force Historical Center at Bolling Air Force Base, Washington, DC, and the Historical Records Agency at Maxwell Air Force Base, Montgomery, AL, have basic documents on the invasion of Japan as well as oral histories and histories of air force units. The U.S. Army Military History Institute at Carlisle Barracks, PA, has an extensive oral history collection and histories of army units.

Important original materials, including valuable collections of correspondence, are held by the George C. Marshall Library, Lexington, VA, and the MacArthur Archives, Norfolk, VA. Some materials, especially on Allied participation in the invasion of Japan, are available at the Public Record Office, Kew, London.

Abbreviations that are used in the notes for these repositories are:

AFHC   Air Force Historical Center, Bolling AFB, Washington, DC
CMH   Center of Military History, Washington, DC
HRC   Historical Records Center, Maxwell AFB, AL
MA   MacArthur Archives, Norfolk, VA
MHC   Marine Historical Center, Washington, DC
MHI   Military History Institute, Carlisle Barracks, PA
ML   Marshall Library, Lexington, VA
NARA   National Archives, Washington, DC
NHC   Navy Historical Center, Washington, DC

PRO   Public Record Office, Kew, London
WNRC   Washington National Records Center, Suitland, MD

SELECTED OTHER SOURCES

Adams, Henry H. *Witness to Power: The Life of Fleet Admiral William D. Leahy.* Annapolis: Naval Institute Press, 1985.
Alperovitz, Gar. *Atomic Diplomacy: Hiroshima and Potsdam.* New York: Simon and Schuster, 1965.
Appleman, Roy E., James M. Burns, Russell A. Gugeler, and John Stevens. *Okinawa: The Last Battle.* Washington, DC: GPO, 1948.
Armstrong, Anne. *Unconditional Surrender: The Impact of the Casablanca Policy upon World War II.* New Brunswick, NJ: Rutgers Univ. Press, 1961.
Arnold, Henry H. *Global Mission.* New York: Harper & Brothers, 1949.
Army Battle Casualties and Nonbattle Deaths in World War II, Final Report. Department of the Army, 1953.
Baldwin, Hanson W. *Great Mistakes of the War.* New York: Harper & Brothers, 1949.
Bartley, Whitman S. *Iwo Jima: Amphibious Epic.* Washington, DC: GPO, 1954.
Bauer, K. Jack, and Alan C. [Alvin D.] Coox. "Olympic *vs.* Ketsu-Go." *Marine Corps Gazette* 49 (August 1965): 32–44.
Bernstein, Barton J. *The Atomic Bomb: The Critical Issues.* Boston: Little, Brown, 1976.
———. "The Birth of the U.S. Biological Warfare Program." *Scientific American* 256 (June 1987): 116–21.
———. "Roosevelt, Truman, and the Atomic Bomb: A Reinterpretation." *Political Science Quarterly* 90 (Spring 1975): 23–69.
Birdsell, Dale. *The Chemical Warfare Service: Chemicals in Combat.* Washington, DC: GPO, 1966.
Briggs, Richard A. *Black Hawks over the Danube: The History of the 86th Infantry Division in World War II.* West Point, KY: Richard A. Briggs, 1953.
Brophy, Leo R., and George J. B. Fisher. *The Chemical Warfare Service: Organizing for War.* Washington, DC: GPO, 1959.
Brown, Frederic J. *Chemical Warfare: A Study in Restraints.* Princeton: Princeton Univ. Press, 1968.
Buell, Thomas B. *Master of Sea Power: A Biography of Admiral Ernest J. King.* Boston: Little, Brown, 1980.
Butow, Robert J. C. *Japan's Decision to Surrender.* Stanford: Stanford Univ. Press, 1954.
Cline, Ray S. *Washington Command Post: The Operations Division.* Washington, DC: GPO, 1951.
Coakley, Robert W., and Richard M. Leighton. *Global Logistics and Strategy, 1943–1945.* Washington, DC: GPO, 1968.
Cochrane, Rexmond C. "History of the Chemical Warfare Service in the United

States." Manuscript, Office of the Chief, Chemical Corps, 1947.

Crabb, J. V. "Fifth Air Force Air War against Japan, September 1942–August 1945." Manuscript, Air University Library, Maxwell Air Force Base, AL, 4 February 1946.

Craven, Wesley F., and James L. Cate, eds. *The Army Air Forces in World War II*. Vol. 1, *Plans and Early Operations, January 1939 to August 1942*. Chicago: Univ. of Chicago Press, 1948.

————. *The Army Air Forces in World War II*. Vol. 3, *Europe: Argument to V-E Day, January 1944 to May 1945*. Chicago: Univ. of Chicago Press, 1951.

————. *The Army Air Forces in World War II*. Vol. 5, *The Pacific: Matterhorn to Nagasaki, June 1944 to August 1945*. Chicago: Univ. of Chicago Press, 1953.

————. *The Army Air Forces in World War II*. Vol. 6, *Men and Planes*. Chicago: Univ. of Chicago Press, 1955.

Coox, Alvin D. "Japanese Military Intelligence in the Pacific Theater: Its Non-Revolutionary Nature." In *The Intelligence Revolution: A Historical Perspective*. Washington, DC: Office of Air Force History, 1991.

Deane, John R. *The Strange Alliance: The Story of Our Efforts at Wartime Co-operation with Russia*. New York: Viking Press, 1946.

Detwiler, Donald S., and Charles B. Burdick. *War in Asia and the Pacific, 1937–1949*. Vol. 12. New York: Garland Publishing, 1980.

Drea, Edward J. *MacArthur's Ultra: Codebreaking and the War against Japan, 1942–1945*. Lawrence: Univ. of Kansas Press, 1992.

Dod, Karl C. *Corps of Engineers: The War against Japan*. Washington, DC: GPO, 1966.

Dyer, George C. *The Amphibians Came to Conquer: The Story of Admiral Richmond Kelly Turner*. Vol. 2. Washington, DC: GPO, 1972.

The Entry of the Soviet Union into the War against Japan: Military Plans, 1941–45. Washington, DC: Department of Defense, 1955.

"Far East Air Force History, 15 June 1944–2 September 1945." Air Force Historical Center, Bolling Air Force Base, Washington, DC. Manuscript.

Feis, Herbert. *Churchill, Roosevelt, Stalin: The War They Fought and the Peace They Sought*. Princeton: Princeton Univ. Press, 1957.

The Fifth Infantry Division in the ETO. 1945. Center of Military History Library. Photocopy.

Gallicchio, Marc. "After Nagasaki, General Marshall's Plan for Tactical Nuclear Weapons in Japan." *Prologue* 23 (Winter 1991): 396–404.

Glantz, David M. *August Storm: The Soviet 1945 Strategic Offensive in Manchuria*. Ft. Leavenworth, KS: Combat Studies Institute, 1983.

Groves, Leslie R. *Now It Can Be Told: The Story of the Manhattan Project*. New York: Harper & Brothers, 1962.

Halsey, William F., and Joseph Bryan. *Admiral Halsey's Story*. New York: McGraw-Hill, 1947.

Hammond, Thomas T. "Atomic Diplomacy Revisited." *Orbis* 19 (Winter 1976): 1403–1428.

Hansell, Haywood S., Jr. *Strategic Air War against Japan*. Washington, DC: GPO, 1980.

Hayes, Grace P. *The History of the Joint Chiefs of Staff in World War II: The War against Japan*. Annapolis: Naval Institute Press, 1982.

Hester, Mildred V. "Redeployment." Occupation Forces in Europe Series, 1945–1946. Manuscript, Office of the Chief Historian, European Command, U.S. Army Center of Military History.

Hewlett, Richard G., and Oscar E. Anderson, Jr. *A History of the United States Atomic Energy Commission: The New World, 1939–1946*. University Park: The Pennsylvania Univ. Press, 1962.

Hixson, John A. "Joint and Combined Planning Problems Involved in the Preparation for Operation OLYMPIC." 1 September 1987. Manuscript in possession of the author.

Huber, Thomas M. *Pastel: Deception in the Invasion of Japan*. Ft. Leavenworth, KS: Combat Studies Institute, 1988.

Ismay, General Lord. *The Memoirs of General Lord Ismay*. New York: Viking Press, 1960.

James, D. Clayton. *The Years of MacArthur*. Vol. 1, *1880–1941*. Boston: Houghton Mifflin, 1972.

———. *The Years of MacArthur*. Vol. 2, *1941–1945*. Boston: Houghton Mifflin, 1975.

Keisuke, Matsumoto. "Japanese Preparations to Conduct a Decisive Battle in Kyushu." U.S. Army–JGSDF Military History Exchange, Carlisle Barracks, PA, 26 October 1987.

Kimball, Warren F., ed. *Churchill and Roosevelt: The Complete Correspondence*. Vol. 3. Princeton: Princeton Univ. Press, 1984.

King, Ernest J., and Walter M. Whitehall. *Fleet Admiral King: A Naval Record*. New York: W. W. Norton, 1952.

Krueger, Walter. *From Down Under to Nippon*. Washington, DC: Combat Forces Press, 1953.

Leahy, William D. *I Was There*. New York: McGraw-Hill, 1950.

Lewin, Ronald. *The American Magic: Codes, Ciphers, and the Defeat of Japan*. New York: Farrar, Strauss, Giroux, 1982.

Love, Robert W., Jr., ed. *The Chiefs of Naval Operations*. Annapolis: Naval Institute Press, 1980.

MacIsaac, David. *Strategic Bombing in World War II: The Story of the United States Strategic Bombing Survey*. New York: Garland Publishing, 1976.

Matloff, Maurice. *Strategic Planning for Coalition Warfare, 1943–1944*. Washington, DC: GPO, 1959.

Matloff, Maurice, and Edwin M. Snell. *Strategic Planning for Coalition Warfare, 1941–1942*. Washington, DC: GPO, 1953.

McFarland, Stephen L. "Preparing for What Never Came: Chemical and Biological Warfare in World War II." *Defense Analysis* 2 (1986): 107–21.

Miles, Rufus E., Jr. "Hiroshima: The Strange Myth of Half a Million American

Lives Saved." *International Security* 10 (Fall 1985): 121–40.

Miller, Edward S. *War Plan Orange.* Annapolis: Naval Institute Press, 1991.

Millett, John D. *The Organization and Role of the Army Service Forces.* Washington, DC: GPO, 1954.

Morgan, Henry G. "Planning the Defeat of Japan: A Study of Total War Strategy." Manuscript, U.S. Army Center of Military History, 1961.

Morison, Samuel Eliot. *History of United States Naval Operations in World War II.* Vol. 7, *Aleutians, Gilberts, and Marshalls, June 1942–1944.* Boston: Little, Brown, 1964.

Moseley, Leonard. *Marshall: Hero for Our Times.* New York: Hearst Books, 1982.

Palmer, Robert R., Bell I. Wiley, and William R. Keast. *The Procurement and Training of Ground Combat Troops.* Washington, DC: GPO, 1948.

Pogue, Forrest C. *George C. Marshall: Education of a General.* New York: Viking Press, 1963.

Potter, E. B. *Nimitz.* Annapolis: Naval Institute Press, 1976.

Powell, John W. "A Hidden Chapter in History." *The Bulletin of Atomic Scientists* 37 (October 1981): 43–52.

Putney, Diane T. *Ultra and the Army Air Forces in World War II: An Interview with Associate Justice of the U.S. Supreme Court Lewis F. Powell, Jr.* Washington, DC: Office of Air Force History, 1987.

Reports of General MacArthur. Vol. 1, *The Campaigns of MacArthur in the Pacific.* Washington, DC: GPO, 1966.

Reports of General MacArthur. Vol. 1, supplement, *MacArthur in Japan: The Occupation, Military Phase.* Washington, DC: GPO, 1966.

Saunders, Chauncey E. "Redeployment and Demobilization." USAF Historical Study no. 77. USAF Historical Division, 1953. Air Force Historical Center, Bolling Air Force Base, Washington, DC.

Schoenberger, Walter S. *Decision of Destiny.* Athens: Ohio Univ. Press, 1969.

Sherry, Michael S. *The Rise of American Air Power: The Creation of Armageddon.* New Haven: Yale Univ. Press, 1987.

Sherwin, Martin J. *A World Destroyed: The Atomic Bomb and the Grand Alliance.* New York: Alfred A. Knopf, 1975.

Sigal, Leon V. *Fighting to the Finish: The Politics of War Termination in the United States and Japan, 1945.* Ithaca: Cornell Univ. Press, 1988.

Smith, Robert Ross. "Luzon versus Formosa." In *Command Decisions.* Washington, DC: GPO, 1960.

Smith, Robert R. *United States Army in World War II: The War in the Pacific: Triumph in the Phillipines.* Washington, DC: GPO, 1963.

Sparrow, John C. *History of Personnel Demobilization in the United States Army.* DA Pamphlet 20–210. Department of the Army, July 1952.

Stimson, Henry L. "The Decision to Use the Atomic Bomb." *Harper's* 194 (February 1947): 97–107.

Henry Louis Stimson Diaries. Microfilm edition. Manuscripts and Archives, Yale University Library, New Haven, CN.

Sutherland, John P. "The Story General Marshall Told Me." *U.S. News and World Report*, 2 November 1959, 50–56.

Szasz, Ferenc M. *The Day the Sun Rose Twice: The Story of the Trinity Site Nuclear Explosion, July 16, 1945*. Albuquerque: Univ. of New Mexico Press, 1984.

Truman, Harry. *Memoirs*. Vol. 1, *Year of Decision*. Garden City, NY: Doubleday, 1955.

United States Department of State. *Foreign Relations of the United States: Conference at Berlin, 1945*. 2 vols. Washington, DC: GPO, 1960.

———. *Foreign Relations of the United States: Conferences at Cairo and Teheran, 1943*. Washington, DC: GPO, 1961.

———. *Foreign Relations of the United States: Conferences at Malta and Yalta*. Washington, DC: GPO, 1955.

———. *Foreign Relations of the United States: Conferences at Washington, 1941–1942, and Casablanca, 1943*. Washington, DC: GPO, 1968.

———. *Foreign Relations of the United States: Conferences at Washington and Quebec, 1943*. Washington, DC: GPO, 1970.

United States Strategic Bombing Survey: Pacific War. Nos. 62 and 63. Washington, DC: Military Analysis Division, 1947.

Villa, Brian L. "The U.S. Army, Unconditional Surrender, and the Postdsam Proclamation." *Journal of American History* 63 (June 1976): 66–92.

The War Reports of General of the Army George C. Marshall, General of the Army H. H. Arnold, and Fleet Admiral Ernest J. King. Philadelphia: J. B. Lippincott, 1947.

Wedemeyer, Albert C. *Wedemeyer Reports*. New York: Henry Holt, 1958.

Weigley, Russell F. *The American Way of War: A History of United States Strategy and Policy*. Bloomington: Indiana Univ. Press, 1977.

Wiley, Bell I. *Redeployment Training*. Army Ground Forces Study No. 38. Washington, DC: Historical Section, AGF, 1946.

Willmott, H. P. "Just Being There: An Examination of the Record, Problems, and Achievement of the British Pacific Fleet in the Course of Its Operations in the Indian and Pacific Oceans between November 1944 and September 1945." Manuscript in possession of the author.

Index

ABDA (American, British, Dutch, Australian), 12–13
Aburatsu, 140
Aerial mining, 49–50
AFPAC, 194–95, 206
Alamo Force, 170
Alamogordo, 235
Aleutians, 160, 209, 224
Allies, 219–32
Alperovitz, Gar, 235
Amano Masakazu, 125
Amphibious Forces Pacific Fleet, 156–57, 169
Amphibious operations, 1
Anami Korechika, 248
Ancon, 175
APHRODITE, 90
ARCADIA Conference, 11–12
Ariake (Shibushi) Bay: defense of, 120, 140, 143; in OLYMPIC, 4, 103–104, 122–23, 145, 149, 151, 179–82, 188. *See also* Japanese homeland defenses; Ketsu-Go
Arlington Hall, 134–35
Armies, Air General, Japanese: 1st Air Army, 107; 2d Air Army, 107; 5th Air Army, 107; 6th Air Army, 107, 119, 122
Armies, Area, Japanese: Fifth Area Army, 107; Eleventh Area Army, 107; Twelfth Area Army, 107, 124, 127, 211; Thirteenth Area Army, 107; Fourteenth Area Army, 102; Fifteenth Area Army, 107; Sixteenth Area Army, 107, 118–20, 122, 124, 144; Seventeenth Area Army, 107
Armies, General, Japanese: First General Army, 107, 127; Second General Army, 107, 125–26;

32d Army, 102, 237; 36th Army, 118, 123, 125–28; 40th Army, 119–23, 137; 53d Army, 125–26; 56th Army, 123; 57th Army, 119, 121–23, 137, 143; Tokyo Defense Army, 126
Armies, U. S. Army: First Army, 67, 203–207; Sixth Army, 71, 136, 143, 156–57, 163, 170–71, 174–75, 179, 187, 189, 192–94, 203; Eighth Army, 67, 136, 170, 202–206; Tenth Army, 75, 159, 202–203, 237
Army Service Command, Olympic (ASCOM "O"), 181, 183, 192, 194
Army, U. S.: and early Pacific strategy, 34; views on central Pacific offensive, 35
Army Air Corps, U. S., 45
Army Air Forces, U. S., 90, 251; Fifth Air Force, 137, 169–70, 196; Seventh Air Force, 169–70, 196; Eighth Air Force, 170, 174, 220; Thirteenth Air Force, 169–70, 196; Twentieth Air Force, 169–70, 174; Far East Air Forces (FEAF), 144, 155–58, 169–70, 174–75, 183, 194–96, 254; and gas warfare, 97; U. S. Army Strategic Air Forces, Pacific (USASTAF), 144, 169
Arnold, Henry H. (Hap), 26–28, 94; and aerial mining campaign, 49; and Billy Mitchell, 26–27; on British bombers, 228–29; and German rockets, 91; and JB-2, 92; on JCS, 12; and OLYMPIC, 169; and redeployment, 69; and USSR, 221; and strategic bombing, 27–28, 50
Atomic bomb, 93, 96, 214, 234–44, 257

France, 230–31
Freeman, Paul L., 225
Fukiagehama, 145, 189
Fukuoka, 215
Fuwa Hiroshi, 127–28

gas warfare, 84, 92–97; caves and
  bunkers, 94–95; agents, 94
germ warfare, 84
Gillem, Alvan C., 206
Granite Peak, Utah, 84
Grew, Joseph C., 41, 54, 78, 235,
  238, 252
Groups, U. S. Army Air Forces:
  487th Heavy Bombardment, 71;
  319th Medium Bombardment, 71.
  See also Army Air Forces, U. S.
Groves, Leslie R., 241–42
Guadalcanal, 1, 33
Guam, 159

Hall, Charles P., 158, 172, 175, 182
Halsey, William, 157, 16, 174, 251
Hamamatsu, 203
Hammond, Thomas T., 235
Handy, Thomas T., 142; and early
  study, 36; on invasion casualties,
  78; on LONGTOM, 52
Hansell, Haywood: and aerial mining
  campaign, 49; and precision bomb-
  ing, 48
Harbin, Manchuria, 84
Harriman, Averell, 220–22
Harrison, George, 241
Hart, Thomas C., 33
Hill, Harry W., 175
Hiroshima, 252
Hirota Koki, 247
Hodge, John R., 204
Hodges, Courtney, 203
Hokkaido, 148, 160–64, 209, 216
Hokodate-Aomori, 215
Hollandia, 171
Hood, Reuben C., 92

Hoover, Herbert, 77
Hopkins, Harry, 25
Hori Eizo, 145
Horn Island, Mississippi, 84
Hornet, 100
Huebner, C. R., 206
Hull, Cordell, 221
Hull, John E.: and atomic bomb,
  243–44; on biological warfare, 85;
  and chemical warfare, 87; on
  invasion, 58, 205
Hutchinson, D. R., 194

Ibusuki, 140
ICEBERG, 151, 237
Ichinomiya, 199–200
Iimura Jo, 126
Imba-Numa, 206
Imperial General Headquarters, 107,
  124. See also Japanese Homeland
  Defenses
Inland Sea, 215
Interim Committee, 242
Invasion of Japan, 50–58; and atomic
  bomb, 6; and casualties, 6; costs of,
  6; Japanese intelligence on, 102–
  104. See also CORONET; DOWNFALL;
  OLYMPIC
Ioka, 202, 208
Ise Bay, 215–16
Ishii Shiro: and biological warfare, 84
Ismay, Hastings, 21
Iwakawa, 196
Iwo Jima, 150, 253–54, 257; defenses
  on, 88, 96, 234; as USAAF base, 47
Izu Islands, 203

Jacobsson, Per, 247
James, D. Clayton, 30
Japan: and food supplies after CORO-
  NET, 214; and gas warfare, 97;
  industrial capacity after CORONET,
  213; political weakness after CORO-
  NET, 214; strength of army, 213,